P9-DMF-374

THE NATIONAL TRUST

A BOOK OF GARDENING

THE NATIONAL TRUST
A BOOK OF GARDENING

A PRACTICAL GUIDE BY

PENELOPE HOBHOUSE

Little, Brown and Company
Boston Toronto

For John, who works with me at Tintinhull

Foreword copyright © 1986 by John Sales
Text copyright © 1986 by Penelope Hobhouse

ALL RIGHTS RESERVED. NO PART OF THIS BOOK MAY BE REPRODUCED IN ANY FORM OR BY ANY ELECTRONIC OR MECHANICAL MEANS INCLUDING INFORMATION STORAGE AND RETRIEVAL SYSTEMS WITHOUT PERMISSION IN WRITING FROM THE PUBLISHERS, EXCEPT BY A REVIEWER WHO MAY QUOTE BRIEF PASSAGES IN A REVIEW.

LIBRARY OF CONGRESS CATALOG CARD NO. 86-80077

FIRST AMERICAN EDITION

Illustration credits and copyright acknowledgements appear on page 256

Edited by Penny David
Editorial Consultant: Russell Ash
Designed by Craig Dodd
Artwork by John Woodcock
PRINTED IN ITALY

Photographic captions

Page 1: A wall border at Snowshill Manor

Frontispiece: A door leading into the enclosed gardens at Barrington Court, where planting is in the style of Gertrude Jekyll.

Page 6: At Hidcote hedges and clipped topiary establish a firm garden structure inside which hardy plants grow in box-edged beds.

CONTENTS

Preface

This book is a practical guide to gardening in National Trust properties. It is not intended to be descriptive of the gardens themselves: the Trust's own guidebooks fulfil this function, as does Mr Graham Stuart Thomas's *Gardens of the National Trust*. Instead it explains how the actual gardening is done, with reference to a particular planting theme or garden feature which is only a part of a larger garden. Usually planting plans appropriate to the historical context and the soil, climate and aspect of a garden are prepared by one of the Trust's Gardens Advisers. These plans are then interpreted and realized by the gardeners in charge on the spot. This book, by presenting some of these plans in detail and by drawing on the individual gardener's experience, is intended to bridge a gap between the theory of garden design and its appropriate and practical use.

The arrangement of the book is intended to help readers draw on National Trust gardening policy and adapt detailed planting plans to areas in their own gardens. As in all gardening practice there are guidelines rather than hard and fast rules; textbook instructions are interpreted by individual gardeners in the most practical way for the particular garden, bearing in mind the amount of labour available for maintenance through the year, and many other factors. The first chapter relates to the structural framework of gardens and includes features such as hedges, topiary and formal planting patterns, all readily adaptable for use in any garden. Further chapters discuss garden features such as the border, the rose garden, the herb garden, the use of water, ferneries and rockeries, which may be situated inside this frame. Less structured garden styles such as the informal woodland, meadow gardening and low-maintenance techniques precede a final chapter on the practical aspects of grass care, machinery and specific soil treatments.

In many places in the book a Head Gardener has contributed the details of complete planting and maintenance programmes for a garden area. During my visits I have spent many hours learning from the 'man on the spot'. My own practical gardening knowledge has been much extended – and I hope that the reader will benefit from that aspect of my writing as well as from the gardeners' own contributions. (Quotations from the gardeners themselves are indicated in the text by a pair of National Trust symbols.) I could not have written this book without the help and stimulation of these dedicated gardeners. This is an opportunity not only to thank them for giving me this help, but, on behalf of the whole visiting public, to express our appreciation of the beauty of the Trust gardens and of the high standards with which they are maintained. As a Gardening Tenant of the National Trust myself, I feel I shall be inspired to garden better as a result of the experience I have gained while writing the book.

I also wish to thank the four Gardens Advisers who look after all the National Trust properties – Mr John Sales, Mr James Marshall, Mr Anthony Lord and Mr Michael Calnan – for their help and encouragement. Each of them has provided an essential element of the book, contributing specialist skills and knowledge that I lack. I am particularly grateful to Mr Lord for checking plant names.

The book would be nothing without the beautiful photographs, many of them specially commissioned. Gardening photography not only demands technical skills but, especially in a wet summer such as 1985, requires perseverance and patience to achieve such perfection.

I am most grateful to Colin Webb at Pavilion Books for allowing me to plan and execute this book. Russell Ash and Penny David have supervised the manuscript; without the former I would have lacked essential encouragement at early stages of planning and writing, without the latter I could not have achieved the organization of so much detailed information. An author becomes dependent on skilled editors and I have been fortunate. Thanks are due, too, to Craig Dodd, for his design skill in organizing the book's visual material.

Many others have helped me during the last year. Besides contributing to the book, gardeners and Gardens Advisers have been frequently consulted on a personal level. Lyn Sales gave up many hours to coordinating plans and illustrations.

The National Trust sets a standard in garden design and maintenance, which we sometimes take for granted. I hope this book shows my appreciation of all who have contributed or do contribute to this achievement.

PENELOPE HOBHOUSE

Foreword

Garden visiting is one of the most popular summer pastimes in Britain and reflects our abiding love of gardens and our almost obsessive interest in gardening, which has been gathering strength for at least three hundred years. In variety, quality and quantity Britain's gardens are unrivalled in the world and the many visitors from abroad testify to their unique attraction. This practice of visiting gardens is a great stimulus to creativity and improvement. Rarely does a keen gardener return without an idea, or even a plant, with which to improve his own garden. The unique purpose of this book is to facilitate this process by interpreting features and techniques found in the many gardens owned by the National Trust.

Never before has one organization owned so many gardens of such historic and horticultural significance, and which exhibit such enormous diversity. The Trust's gardens advisory staff visit about 110 gardens regularly, as well as another 90 or so properties from time to time, where there is some form of garden or landscape planting. These properties vary from tiny town gardens like Carlyle's House in Chelsea to large and complex historic gardens like the 31.5 hectares (78 acres) at Mount Stewart in Co. Down or the 72.8 hectares (180 acres) at Cliveden, Bucks. They cover the whole range of soil, site, climate and habitat found in these islands and contain, taken together, the world's greatest collection of cultivated plants, trees and shrubs. It is axiomatic that almost every garden style developed over the past 300 years or more can be discovered somewhere in the Trust, but much more significant is the impact of the individuals and the families that were the gardens' former owners. A great garden may be the distinctive product, like any other work of art, of a genius (or more often two individuals working together) – as are Hidcote and Sissinghurst; or it may have been created like Powis and Blickling from the 'bones' of an original layout by successive generations of owners over two or three hundred years, each adding their own contribution, in response to the fashion of the day, their interests and their means. Because of the unique stability that has existed in Britain for three centuries, this latter quality, by which the garden shows evidence of continuous cultivation and an evolutionary quality in its style and planting, does not exist elsewhere in the world and is particularly precious.

In these respects historic gardens have much in common with historic houses, they can be pure examples of a style or a palimpsest, reflecting the history of the house and the fortunes and tastes of its owners through the years. But gardens have another dimension, they are constantly changing. Only the artefacts in them remain comparatively unchanged unless deliberately altered or allowed to fall into disrepair. Plants, whether small and herbaceous or large and woody, are constantly growing, developing and decaying and this is what gardeners enjoy: pitting their wits against the uncertainties of plant growth and climate and exploiting to the fullest extent the limitations imposed by soil and site. A garden is more of a process than an object and for its long-term conservation a distinct and consistent policy is needed to direct inevitable change in a way that preserves the unique character of the garden. A valid policy can only be arrived at through a thorough knowledge of the garden, its history and its former owners, its circumstances and its plants.

It is one thing to make a garden to be enjoyed in one's own lifetime and quite another to anticipate change and to provide for its continuous conservation, which is the purpose of the National Trust. Not only does it demand a policy, both for the general approach to its style and character and for the details of its planting or upkeep, but it also requires a consistency of purpose that goes beyond individual Head Gardeners and tenants. Of course the effect of the person directly in charge always shows through and a positive approach is vital if a garden is to remain fresh and interesting. The Trust does not aim to stifle this livening influence provided that it can be accommodated within the policy, the tradition and, not least, the budget for that particular garden. Even the great artist-plantsmen of this century such as Lawrence Johnston and Vita Sackville-West were always experimenting and making changes, and it is necessary for the well-being of their gardens that each part should be reworked within the character and the colour scheme originally intended.

Rarely is it possible or even advisable to revert totally and exactly to an original scheme, even if the details are precisely known, which is not often the case. Historic gardens need constantly to be reinterpreted in response to changed circumstances, physical and financial. Gardens continue to exist only if the quantity and the quality of the upkeep is sufficient. Many Trust gardens are being run with as few as ten per cent of their original labour force, a discrepancy that requires considerable ingenuity to overcome. Without eliminating all inessentials and using every modern aid and technique to the maximum it would be impossible. But if the Trust's objects are to be met such methods have to be directed constantly towards the retention or the restoration of the special character of the garden; the temptation to make changes merely for convenience and economy must be resisted.

The advent of visitors in large numbers is a fundamental change. Paradoxically, the problem of minimizing their impact, while protecting the garden's design and as far as possible its character as a private garden, often make it necessary to make changes. These may be aimed for example at improving circulation and spreading people out so as to avoid the appearance of overcrowding.

Clearly, then, Penelope Hobhouse has had plenty of scope from which to draw examples of designs and techniques capable of being adapted for private gardens of a different scale. While obviously avoiding the grandest schemes, she has chosen widely and wisely, covering most aspects of gardening out of doors and 'within the ha-ha'. In anything to do with the Trust it is difficult to generalize; colour schemes that might be considered vulgar in a garden influenced by Gertrude Jekyll could be just right in a Victorian scheme; techniques and planting for the rock garden at Rowallane are unlikely to suit the gigantic layout at Cragside. Penelope Hobhouse has avoided this trap very sensibly by using specific cases and inviting Head Gardeners to comment on them. By quoting some of the Trust's most skilled gardeners she has brought forth a wealth of valuable practical experience for others to share. These contributions are invariably authoritative, searching and direct, and particularly valuable when dealing with aspects of management, which is of course the key to successful garden conservation. A well-researched policy, consistently and sensitively applied, is essential. But in the absence of a resident expert tenant, it falls largely on the Head Gardener and his staff to provide the thoughtful, observant and energetic upkeep that distinguishes a true garden from an institutional open space.

Guided above all by its elected and voluntary national and regional committees and more directly by its expert Gardens Panel, the Trust's gardens are managed regionally and advised nationally. In some cases the Trust is able to benefit from the presence of a resident expert donor or tenant, but in three-quarters of its gardens it relies mainly on its permanent staff. The Head Gardener or Gardener-in-Charge is accountable for the day-to-day management of the garden, and property management is the responsibility of the Land Agent, who is in turn responsible to the Regional Director. Detailed advice on all aspects of conservation and upkeep is given by one of four national Gardens Advisers who visits regularly. These three – gardener, manager and adviser – discuss priorities and agree a programme of work, which is set out in some detail in the Gardens Adviser's subsequent report. With consistent aims, this continuity can achieve a great deal, little by little over the years, despite limited resources. Where there is no donor or tenant the Regional Historic Buildings Representative provides historic research and aesthetic sensitivity. From time to time help from a variety of experts inside and outside the Trust is sought, but no garden has ever been run successfully by a committee. Courageous and decisive management is essential for the long-term conservation of gardens and for their restoration.

As tenant Penelope Hobhouse has been part of this process at Tintinhull, where she has used her skill and artistry to great effect in the conservation of Mrs Reiss' little masterpiece. In looking beyond she has cast her discerning eye on some of the greatest gardens ever made. Her commentary reveals a vast range of design ideas and a wealth of practical tips from which any garden owner can select and adapt.

JOHN SALES
NATIONAL TRUST GARDENS ADVISER

I
THE GARDEN FRAMEWORK

Structural Planting

Using plants or objects to suggest to the eye a division, as well as using an actual physical barrier such as a wall, fence or the continuous planting of a hedge, is an effective way of establishing the architectural structure of a garden design. Upright shapes in lines or geometrical arrangements will emphasize a ground pattern and give a third dimension to the two-dimensional garden plan. As well as being architectural features, these divisions provide seclusion, shade and an opportunity to display plants in various different ways.

The diverse subjects that constitute a garden's structure will overlap and interrelate as topics of discussion, just as the physical elements overlap and work together in the garden. Here, for convenience, they are grouped as a series of broad themes. Perhaps the most functional barriers and divisions, walls and walled enclosures, are one special case, to be considered separately later on; and hedges – barriers of living plants – are another. The training or pleaching of rows of trees to make avenues, alleys and so on, and constructions such as pergolas, form a different sort of three-dimensional element in the garden. When the effect of some of these techniques is not so much to form physical garden divisions as to become pattern and ornament for its own sake, it becomes the subject of the discussion 'Planting in Patterns'.

Among the growing structural elements in the garden framework are hedges. Like walls and fences, they can mark a continuous boundary around the garden perimeter, or can divide up the space within the garden into a series of compartments. An inner hedge that appears to be a division might act as a screen, either hiding some unsightly object or area, or by first concealing a landscape view or garden feature from the visitor, introducing it as a surprise later.

An avenue is not necessarily the great landscape feature that the word is inclined to evoke. In design terms it is a series of ornamental objects – not always trees or even plants – placed at regular intervals on either side of a directional path. Size and actual spacing distances will determine the effect of linear perspective: occasionally, to increase or diminish the apparent distance, the elements are deliberately set nearer or farther apart. The scale can be proportionate to the situation. The dictionary defines an avenue as a passage or path of entrance or exit, particularly the chief approach to a country house, usually bordered by trees – hence any broad roadway marked by objects at regular intervals. It is a dramatic device using rhythmic repetition in perspective to enhance the grandeur of the approach, or to pace the view towards a focal point.

Pleached trees suggest a continuous row and garden division but usually allow a clear view below boskage. In the Middle Ages pleaching was used as a device to create shady and secluded garden walks before it became a useful feature of garden design. By regularly cutting back new growth of specially trained trees, dense young foliage makes a solid impenetrable shape, at a deliberately chosen height. An alley is usually of pleached trees trained to meet overhead and quite distinct from the French *allée*, which is a ride or walk cut through massed trees where the sides are clipped up to a considerable height. An alley (or tunnel) is very similar to a pergola, where a double row of strong supports with cross bars provides a frame for climbing plants which are carefully trained and tied to it.

Treillage or trellis work, where a patterned open frame of light wood gives the appearance of a substantial division, is another structural device, and provides a frame on which to grow ornamental plants as well as being highly decorative in itself.

Many National Trust gardens contain some or all of these architectural features. Some of them will have been introduced by previous owners for comfort and use and to display plants as well as because they were fashionable at the time the garden was being made; others will have been devised as design techniques to emphasize dimension and define space. In some properties where the Trust has developed or restored a garden style appropriate to the date or historical connections of the house, new features have been introduced much more recently.

Hedges

Hedges, which are a continuous line of planting, can make solid boundaries to protect the garden area from outsiders, and give a feeling of security to the garden owner who wishes to stress his separateness from the outside world. Equally, hedges of different heights partition the garden into inner compartments which can contain separate seasonal or planting themes.

The very first paradise gardens created by the Persians in the Middle East needed barriers to keep out wild animals (and even human enemies), and the earliest English gardens were safely within the confines of castle keep or monastery walls. By Tudor times brightly painted palisades defined garden areas, but dwarf hedging plants – already used for making intricate knot patterns – were increasingly employed to divide gardens into separate areas. All through the seventeenth century and in the early years of the eighteenth, fashionable garden designs were based on the ideal of the Italian Renaissance gardens, where a series of outside 'rooms' were linked together and to the house by pathways and terraces, and by steps between different levels. Hedging plants and walls built of local brick and stone were used to make these barriers, materials for building varying greatly in different regions.

The history of gardening shows how the development of design depends as much on the availability of plants and a knowledge of how to grow them as on the quirks of fashionable thought or philosophy. It is worth remembering that in these early gardens the cost of labour was negligible, local stone and brick was cheap, but nurseries to supply suitable hedging plants, in sufficient quantity, were few and far between. Today, on the other hand, the cost of good masonry barriers is almost totally prohibitive, and even the National Trust, intent on an accurate historical reconstruction, can seldom do more than mend existing walls. Fortunately they can make the best use of local skilled craftsmen and masons, and do even, as at KINGSTON LACY, reopen stone quarries long deemed uneconomical to work.

Many Trust properties have houses and gardens which date from Tudor or Restoration times, when garden areas were separated from the countryside and divided up by walls and hedges; the latter of plants such as yew (*Taxus baccata*), holly (*Ilex aquifolium*), hornbeam (*Carpinus betulus*) and beech (*Fagus sylvatica*). For more rustic barriers the common 'quick' (*Crataegus monogyna*) was often planted, although native common privet (*Ligustrum vulgare*), box (*Buxus sempervirens*) from chalky uplands, hornbeam and common holly proved effective when locally available. Genera were frequently mixed, as in the recently replanted hedges at IGHTHAM MOTE and LITTLE MORETON HALL. Beech has become more popular in the last hundred years, its pleasant habit of retaining buff-coloured leaves all through the winter making it an attractive alternative to other deciduous hedge plants. The purple-leaved beech,

Top: Immaculate box hedging contains the beds of old shrub roses in the walled garden at Mottisfont Abbey in Hampshire.

Above: At Blickling Hall in Norfolk a line of tightly clipped yew in front of oriental plane trees demonstrates contrast of form and texture.

Page 11: The pergola at Mount Stewart (in Northern Ireland) firmly defines the area of the sunken garden as well as becoming a frame for climbing plants.

today usually *Fagus sylvatica* 'Riversii' (introduced in the late eighteenth century) or one of its variants, is sometimes used for hedging, often mixed with the ordinary green-leaved species to produce a tapestry effect. Incidentally, Lady Stamford's rose garden at DUNHAM MASSEY was originally surrounded by a hedge of purple beech kept clipped to 1.5–1.8 m (5–6 ft), admitting plenty of sun and air. Today the neglected beech plants have grown to trees 9 m (30 ft) tall, completely altering the character of the site by turning it into shady woodland instead of airy, open sunlit garden.

In his discourse *Sylva* (1662), John Evelyn did much to popularize the ordinary English yew as a plant for inner hedges (where its poisonous qualities would be harmless to stock): 'I do name them for hedges, preferable for beauty and a stiff defence, to any plant I have ever seen and may . . . without vanity be said to have been the first who brought it in to fashion.' Many of the places where Evelyn's advice was taken were typical of the seventeenth-century gardens which are now in the care of the Trust, for example WESTBURY COURT.

Often all barriers and divisions made by walls or plants were swept away in the second half of the eighteenth century, when landscape parks came up to the windows of the great house, and the only dividing line allowed was the 'invisible' ha-ha. The Trust has recently 'restored' landscape gardens, allowing the eye once again to travel uninterruptedly across parkland and to distant views. At both KILLERTON and SALTRAM in the 1960s the Trust removed hedges which obscured the view and built ha-has, but by far the longest and finest, complete with stone facing, has been built at FLORENCE COURT between the Pleasure Ground and the Park. With modern earth-moving machinery the cost of excavation is relatively low, although building the retaining wall is expensive in materials and labour.

Opposite: Garden compartments are divided by low neatly clipped hedges at Ascott in Buckinghamshire. Horizontal and vertical lines give structure to a garden and the surfaces of yew and mown lawn reflect contrasting light and shadow.

To most of us increasingly used to a mainly urban landscape this extension of outlook seems even more important today than it must have been to the casual visitor in the eighteenth century. The initial expense is fully compensated for by the relative cheapness of subsequent upkeep, and the advantages of a ha-ha are not to be disregarded even by the private owner, for a site in unspoilt countryside.

By the twentieth century, when the National Trust started to acquire or receive properties, many of the landscape parks attached to classical eighteenth-century houses had already had some form of more intimate gardening style incorporated into their designs. Earlier Elizabethan or Jacobean houses retained the vestiges of their contemporary layout, or in Edwardian times had had their gardens reconstructed into a series of compartments, sometimes closely related to the seventeenth-century style. Even Victorian gardens, although not always strictly compartmental, often had areas of the so-called Italianate or 'Dutch' style: for example, ICKWORTH and ASCOTT respectively, where evergreen hedges and topiary helped frame elaborate parterres. The Trust has been able to restore gardens to the original plan when it is considered appropriate.

Edwardian gardens, despite William Robinson's influence on planting, remained firmly structured. (The more naturalistic woodland and 'wild' garden of the period is discussed in Chapter 4.) In the main, garden architecture led by Blomfield, Lutyens (inspired by Gertrude Jekyll and often with her practical help), Sedding and Peto stressed the importance of strong directional lines and vertical and horizontal surfaces. Lutyens was responsible for the fortress-like hedges at CASTLE DROGO, Sedding worked at ASCOTT and Peto designed the hedge-lined water garden that drops down to the lake at BUSCOT PARK. Hedges or walled enclosures were arranged in geometric patterns around a house, and this rigid framework provided the perfect foil for the more flowing plant shapes which furnished the area. Stone, patterned brick or just grass linked the separate areas so that the garden was united as an integral whole, and was not just a collection of disparate parts and themes. Essentially this seems a garden 'fashion' eminently suitable for large or small gardens, a firm architectural structure providing the setting and frame for more free-flowing and informal planting. It is as adaptable for a large country garden as it is for subdividing the elongated town plot.

Two of the most important National Trust gardens, HIDCOTE and SISSINGHURST CASTLE, depend for their effects on hedges which partition the garden areas. Both gardens were made in this century and represent the epitome of this style. A strong rigid framework provides the perfect foil and background for the massed colours and fluid shapes of cottage-type planting. Inside each garden division plants are tightly packed to perform at their best in a particular season, or arranged in definite colour schemes or planting themes. Hedges are in yew, hornbeam, box and holly, all giving different 'green' effects as their individual leaves and habits of growth reflect light in different ways. Further interest is given by the shapes and angles at which the hedge sides and tops are cut. TINTINHULL HOUSE, a much smaller third garden owned by the Trust, has a similar design, the system of axial paths and hedged and walled enclosures making the two-acre garden seem much larger than it is.

At Ickworth in Suffolk green rides are edged with clipped hedges to emphasize perspective.

Hedges in design terms provide not only straight lines to contrast with the more billowing shapes of other plants, as at ICKWORTH. Sometimes hedges of different plant materials are seen by the observer as horizontal bands of contrasting foliage and texture. A tall hedge in the distance will tower above a nearer lower planting. At LYTES CARY a row of pleached lime outside the garden backs the long inner boundary hedge of privet, revealing interesting variation in leaf 'greens' as well as varying density and habit of growth. At Tintinhull the low hedge of *Lonicera nitida* makes a line of dense twiggy growth in quite a different green to the dark yew hedge silhouetted against the light behind it. Elsewhere, glossy bright green box contrasts with the dull heavy yew foliage in a similar way.

When hedges divide up the available space in a garden into a series of inner compartments, they make the whole area seem larger than the sum of its parts. Furthermore, each line of hedging provides shelter and an attractive background for other planting. Straight horizontal lines, trimmed to a regular height, and vertical or sloping 'battered' sides all provide the contrast with curving and billowing plant shapes which makes a garden stimulating. As Ruskin said, 'Straight lines are the best foil to the grace of natural curves in plant and flower.' Among the taller-growing evergreens which make satisfactory hedging plants are the traditional English yew (*Taxus baccata*), holly (usually common for cheapness, but sometimes cultivars of *Ilex* × *altaclerensis* or *I. aquifolium*) and various narrow-leaved conifers. The evergreen oak (*Quercus ilex*) is suitable only for mild areas.

Lower-growing plants such as the dwarf form of box (*Buxus sempervirens* 'Suffruticosa'), santolina, rosemary and lavender can be clipped into neat little hedges. These will divide areas visually into further subcompartments and can be used for making patterns such as knots. Other plants with a more casual form of growth including shrub roses, potentillas and non-woody perennials such as catmint make a less strictly geometrical delineation.

Whether for boundary or inner division, the plant chosen must be 'right' for the type and period of house and garden. Its ultimate height and shape, how its top and sides are contoured, and its leaf colour and texture, will determine the character of the space enclosed. Darker leaves make a space seem smaller and the walls of hedges close in, while pale foliage increases dimensions and gives a feeling of freedom. A hedge of dark yew is sombre all the year, although young growth in early summer contributes interwoven leaves of a paler colour, and provides perhaps the best of all backgrounds to flowering plants through the seasons. Hornbeam and beech leaves change from fresh light airy green to a heavier mature texture in late summer and the dead leaves in winter have a warm rusty-buff colouring.

In a modern garden creating barriers with green and living plants is usually a much cheaper option than introducing any form of masonry, although they are more expensive to maintain. When making a choice of available plants it is worth considering various factors. Firstly, which plants will make the most beautiful feature in the particular garden, and which will thrive on the site? Which plants will need the most care in planting and subsequent maintenance? Which will grow most rapidly and therefore will most quickly establish the 'pattern' of the garden, providing the vital framework in which all other planting is best displayed? There are pitfalls here for the unwary. Hedges which grow quickest have to be clipped most often. *Lonicera nitida*, introduced from western China only at the beginning of this century (1908), has a dense twiggy habit and small evergreen leaves, and responds well to cutting back. Popular after its introduction for speed and density of growth, easily reproduced by the nursery trade, hardy, vigorous, and pleasant to look at, yet it has disadvantages. It is rather greedy and takes much goodness out of the soil, to the disadvantage of neighbouring plants. It needs cutting back at least four or five times annually. Its density makes it particularly vulnerable to collapse from heavy snowfalls. At TINTINHULL, a low lonicera hedge divides the kitchen garden from the garden proper. Placed on a low raised wall, with narrow beds on either side, its prominence demands a high standard of upkeep, and the need for frequent trimming upsets the garden routine. The garden at Tintinhull was made in the 1930s and 1940s, and in this historical context the lonicera is retained.

Creating a new hedge successfully requires good preparation and the correct choice of young plants. Hedges consist of a row of identical plants. Where uniformity is the aim, as with avenues and topiary, take cuttings from one clone, since seedlings have a considerable variation in colour and form. Because they are planted unnaturally close, these living plants need special care. The soil should be well dug to a depth of at least two spits. If the subsoil is of poor quality, break it up with a pickaxe. Preparing the soil to a considerable depth encourages roots to delve deep rather than to straggle laterally searching for moisture or food. A layer of organic manure is then placed in the trench and covered with soil. Today most evergreens such as yew, holly and *Quercus ilex* are container-grown and can be planted in March or April; deciduous hedging plants of beech and hornbeam usually come bare-rooted and should be planted in autumn, to get well established before the following growing season. In Trust gardens hedges are planted to last for the foreseeable future and it is more important to choose the best subject for the long term than to aim simply for quick effects. It seems generally accepted now that single-line planting at an appropriate distance for the type of plant is better than 'staggered' rows, previously favoured for making thick and solid hedge bottoms. Frequent trimming of the sides during the first few years ensures bushy uniform growth. And cutting fiercely where growth is thinnest (against natural instinct) immediately stimulates growing points.

Yew hedges at Montacute House in Somerset have, over centuries, developed strange undulating surface shapes which give interesting textural contrast but are difficult to clip.

In Trust properties only recently acquired it is found that many of the old hedges have grown both too high and too wide through years of comparative neglect. This was especially true when labour was scarce during the 1939–45 war. In fact hedges fifty years old or so, even if well maintained, will also tend to grow beyond the proportions which are convenient. The private owner acquiring an old property may find himself faced with similar problems, even if on a smaller scale.

At MOUNT STEWART Lady Londonderry used the Monterey cypress (*Cupressus macrocarpa*) to make inner garden compartments in the 1920s. High hedges and a pergola surrounded a sunken garden, and to the west of the house a Spanish-style garden was lined with the macrocarpa, in which arcaded windows were cut, very similar to the arcades of Italian cypress (*Cupressus sempervirens*) which frame the view of the city of Florence from the terraces of Villa Gamberaia. By the late 1960s the macrocarpa, attractive with its fine textured foliage of bright green, had become bare and woody at the base and a series of bad winters had cut it back, even in this very sheltered Irish garden. The Trust has now replaced it with the darker green Leyland cypress (× *Cupressocyparis leylandii*), which is reliably hardy and quick-growing. In other parts of the garden the macrocarpa has been replaced with yew. Low hedging of coloured foliage – berberis, thuja and rue – is used at Mount Stewart to enclose flower beds in patterned colours. Their coordinated colour schemes and maintenance are described more fully by Mr Nigel Marshall in Chapter 2.

At POWIS CASTLE, SISSINGHURST CASTLE, LYTES CARY and more recently at CHARTWELL, DUNHAM MASSEY and KINGSTON LACY, overgrown yew has been treated severely. At first the top and one side is pruned right back to the main stem; within a season or two, as these make new healthy young shoots, the second side is trimmed back. Liberal mulching with organic manure or compost plus feeding with slow-acting artificial fertilizers promotes and maintains growth. At HARDWICK HALL both the yew and hornbeam alleys which meet at a *rond-point* have had similar and successful treatment. Beech responds more slowly but has been successfully reduced at ANGLESEY ABBEY, where the hedges are a special feature.

Often the problem with an old yew hedge is an outward-curving bow from the base upwards, instead of sides sloping slightly inwards on a 'batter' from a wider base, which allows maximum light to reach the lower part. A good shapely 2.4 m (8 ft) hedge may have a 1.5 m (5 ft) spread at the base (preferably less) and slope gradually inwards towards the top so that all the surfaces get plenty of light. With very old and misshapen yew it is not possible to use half measures. All branches have to be 'stumped' right back, ideally back to the main stem: simply cutting back into bare wood will not induce rejuvenation. The ideal time to do this is late winter or early spring, but in many gardens it is done in late autumn when there is relatively less pressure of work. Trees and bushes are mulched with well-rotted organic matter (compost or manure) or fed with a balanced general fertilizer with trace elements, such as Vitax Q4, as growth begins in the spring. If the sun is very strong in April and May the new fuzzy growth may even be scorched when it is at its most vulnerable.

Apart from the famous topiary yews planted at the end of the seventeenth century, many of the yew hedges at POWIS CASTLE were first planted by the wife of the Fourth Earl in the years just before the outbreak of the First World War. Now almost 80 years old, the planting suffered from two wartime periods of neglect and by the time the Trust acquired the property in 1952 it found many of the formal hedges, so important in outlining the structure of the garden, had grown to widths of over 2.4 m (8 ft), and had lost their 'batter'. The Head Gardener, Mr Jimmie Hancock, described the process of improving the overgrown hedges as well as the routine maintenance. One side of yew is cut back right to the main trunk, and the tops are cut down to the required height. Yew starts to sprout and make fuzzy growth in the following spring and summer. After three years of regeneration the other side is cut, the whole operation taking almost eight years before hedges are neat and trim again. Feeding of any high-nitrogen fertilizer is maintained over this period. In one place at Powis where the hedge had been cut down to 1.2 m (4 ft) some years ago to save work, each plant was cut back to ground level, and is now growing on to the required height to match another hedge with which it forms a green alley.

Opposite top: A yew hedge at Powis Castle in Wales has been 'stumped' back to the main trunk. This sort of drastic treatment is necessary when, over years, hedges have grown too wide.

Opposite below: The box hedging at Powis is cut in June and July when the young growth is still soft. Strings are used to ensure even clipping.

This sort of treatment seems drastic but results are worthwhile. Now at Powis, using machines with reciprocating double-action blades, annual clipping begins for both the yew hedges and the topiary shapes in the third or fourth week in August and continues until the third week in October. Men working an eight-hour day at this gruelling work need the lightest practical machine. For clipping the very high yew a petrol-driven engine would be too heavy to use each day for several weeks at a time.

The great informal yews where the contoured shapes which have evolved over almost three hundred years are carefully and smoothly followed, are started in September and take six weeks to complete. Now very tall, in places to 9 m (30 ft) but on steep terraces needing a ladder to 14 m (45 ft), the work has to be carefully planned and safety systems coordinated. For ordinary hedging scaffolding is used, but when doing these strange-shaped giants the ladders are tied to the yew, and men even walk carefully across the thick top surface. As branches of yew die back (often due to 'ringing' of bark by mice or squirrels, or by some taut wire overlooked during the years) new moulded shapes emerge.

The box hedges at Powis, both the dwarf edging box, *Buxus sempervirens* 'Suffruticosa', and the taller *B. sempervirens*, are cut earlier, in June or July, when young growth is still soft. This prevents aphids which attack soft shoots from doing damage and allows clipping time to be staggered throughout the summer months. The lower box plants which edge the long terrace borders and the flower beds in the old orchards below are cut in June, the taller hedges in early July. The latter suffer in places from being shaded by overhanging trees, which leads to die-back and bare woody growth. In the winding path lined with tall box which descends to the formal

garden below the terraces, growth is weak and bare at the base, where there is minimal light.

Box is slow-growing, especially in such shady situations, and its tailored shapes are very vulnerable to damage. Heavy snow or any sort of abuse can make unsightly holes which takes years to recover. At PACKWOOD HOUSE the boxwood on the spiral path was completely replanted in 1975. Butcher's broom (*Ruscus aculeatus*) was placed at the base of the inner edge of the well-trodden path, creating a protective barrier prickly enough to discourage children from falling against the hedge in play and causing damage. It is possible in favoured situations to restore straggly and woody dwarf box by the drastic method of cutting it back to ground level, but certainly there is a greater risk with box than with yew. It is a technique which **Mr Ted Bullock**, the Head Gardener, has used with success at FELBRIGG HALL. There, half a mile of low box hedging has to be cut with a sloping batter. By cutting in this way not only do the plants do well, remaining thick and bushy right to the ground, but the sloping sides reveal colour and texture as light is reflected at different angles. Mr Bullock writes:

❧ At Felbrigg the boxwood hedging in the walled garden is over half a mile in length. It is 38 cm (15 in) high and 20 cm (8 in) across the top with sloping sides making a wide base. Cut in August, the top is trimmed with a petrol-driven hedge cutter (a Japanese T.A.S. or Shingh) and the sloping sides are cut with hand shears. On straight sections strings and rods are used to obtain a good level; curved sections are done by eye. We usually trim our box hedging once a year only. Box does benefit from an application of Vitax Q4 fertilizer applied in the spring.

We have successfully renovated old leggy box by cutting back to 10 cm (4 in) in March, and giving a feed of fertilizer when there are signs of regrowth. ❧

Incidentally, Ted Bullock finds that box hedging is easier to cut when wet, and even uses a watering can to moisten the leaves and stems in the section ahead of him as he works.

Opposite: Half a mile of boxwood hedging is used to edge the borders in the walled garden at Felbrigg Hall in Norfolk. The elegant grass *Stipa gigantea* contrasts with the formal box.

Avenues

Avenues are usually of live growing trees, shrubs or plants, and this is the sense in which Evelyn used the term in the seventeenth century. In garden design an avenue can equally be composed of a row of stakes or a series of ornamental statues or, on a smaller scale, of flowerpots. In the past, the grand avenues of country houses linked the house, garden and landscape. Trees lining the approach road, rather than striding through the countryside, framed the house itself at the end of a vista, the narrowing perspective making it appear far away.

Such grand design features may seem to have little relevance to the more modest gardener today, but in any layout the same principles are involved: the eye needs direction; diminishing height in perspective adjusts scale, and space is divided to create compartments and define perimeters. The eye picks up rhythms established by anything in a simple repeating pattern, just as even a single pair of similar plants or architectural features will make the eye concentrate on what they frame.

The essence of an avenue is its even and regular appearance. It is important for its ultimate success to ensure that plants grow at a similar rate. The trees or plants placed at regular intervals must have enough light and space to thrive. Obviously the distance apart will vary with each tree type, and depends greatly on whether the trees are of fastigiate habit or have broad spreading heads. A double row of trees, too, must be adequately spaced out. The choice of young plants is important. Seedlings vary enormously in characteristics and while this can create an attractive and even desirable tapestry effect in hedging, it can spoil the symmetry which is so important in a classic avenue. For the best results, choose young plants propagated vegetatively from one clone, or grafted on to a stock plant characterized by uniform habit and growth, to ensure complete regularity in the future. A subtle exception to this rule is at WIMPOLE, where six clones of hybrid lime from the park have been mixed along the double avenue to give a degree of diversity and to simulate the variation that exists in many ancient avenues.

In many great Trust parks variations in conditions such as aspect, shelter, sun or shade, and soil moisture will lead to some difference in performance and growth rate between trees at one end of an avenue and those at the other. At BUSCOT PARK willow, poplar and lime avenues radiate from the plateau on which the house itself stands, diving down into the depths of damp frost-filled valleys and rising steeply again to the heights of windswept hills. It is impossible to ensure uniform growth in such circumstances: the undulating nature of the English countryside has always made it difficult to copy the French style of the seventeenth century. Whereas avenues in France were often cut through blocks of natural forest and were planned to give a feeling of distance as well as being aligned on some focal point (an effect that the Trust has consciously aimed at north of the house at DUNHAM MASSEY), trees in England had to be planted in open countryside and were exposed to variations of weather and conditions. For this as well as other reasons, many avenues planted in the second half of the seventeenth and beginning of the eighteenth centuries were swept away in the landscape movement. In fact, although avenues are traditionally reputed to be of great age, there are few complete avenues in existence which date from more than two hundred years ago. Among the exceptions are the oldest of the sweet chestnuts (*Castanea sativa*) at CROFT CASTLE, the common limes (*Tilia × europaea*) at CHARLECOTE PARK and the sycamore (*Acer pseudoplatanus*) and beech (*Fagus sylvatica*) at LANHYDROCK. Among others which escaped the change in style of the eighteenth century are the lime avenues of CLIVEDEN, DUNHAM MASSEY and KINGSTON LACY, and the original approach avenue of beech at TATTON PARK.

At Buscot Park in Oxfordshire avenues radiate from the house to march through the landscape in French style. In the undulating terrain it is sometimes difficult to get uniform growth.

Just as plants chosen for any part of a garden will depend on their ready availability through the nursery trade, so the actual trees used for avenue planting were apt to change as new types were introduced from abroad or as nurseries such as those in Holland in the seventeenth century discovered how uniform was the growth of the common lime, itself a sterile hybrid, but very easily propagated from basal shoots. Today this characteristic makes it less desirable. When in 1963 at SIZERGH CASTLE it was decided to plant a lime avenue leading to a memorial seat, the small-growing *Tilia × euchlora*, with an elegant arching habit and shining dark green leaves, was chosen rather than either *Tilia × europaea* or *T. platyphyllos*, both of which are susceptible to attacks from aphids causing honeydew, which is a nuisance as it is dropped in the summer. Sadly, however, after twenty years the young *T. × euchlora* specimens at Sizergh have become diseased with lime-flux bacteria. The entire avenue is to be replaced by *Sorbus aucuparia* 'Beissneri', an unusual mountain ash with a decorative orange-brown stem and autumn colouring. Its fruits are very freely carried.

Native beech, oaks and chestnut grow easily from seed, but produce variable plants. At CHARLECOTE the west avenue of elms, killed by Dutch elm disease since 1970, has been replaced by Turkey oaks (*Quercus cerris*), which thrive on the poor dry Warwickshire soil. The Church avenue, which runs at an oblique angle to the avenue of oaks, is of the disease-resistant clone of the Huntingdon elm (*Ulmus × vegeta* 'Commelin') with slightly narrower habit and narrower leaves than the type. At HIDCOTE the approach avenue of Huntingdon elm, also dead from the disease, has been replaced with alternating hornbeam (*Carpinus betulus*) and Turkey oak. In the long term either the hornbeam or the oak will be removed.

Among the most spectacular avenues planted in this century is that of the quadruple rows of alternating horse chestnut (*Aesculus hippocastanum*) and London plane (*Platanus × acerifolia*) at ANGLESEY ABBEY planted by Lord Fairhaven in limy Cambridgeshire soil in the thirties. In this case the young London planes unexpectedly began to break up in the wind and were renewed. Now the chestnuts are being thinned. Very much in the French grand style of the seventeenth century, the avenues at Anglesey run along almost level ground, and visual effects are increased by cutting grass at different heights, allowing the horizontal surfaces to further emphasize the direction and scope of the broad-headed tree shapes.

New narrow avenues of *Tilia cordata*, the small-leaved lime, were planted in triple rows at DUNHAM MASSEY in 1983, each tree closely spaced at 3 m (10 ft). Limes often grow upwards too fast for stability; complete and immediate trimming back of side shoots encourages a young plant to grow tall and thin, lacking wind resistance. Instead, 'feathering' promotes a gradual thickening and swelling of the trunk. On one-year-old trees which have been newly planted, side shoots or 'feathers' are allowed to develop to encourage the sap to spread horizontally; these side shoots are later trimmed back flush with the main stem. This process is repeated until the young trees have established a sturdy trunk.

Where avenues are in pasture or deer park, elaborate tree guards have to be built and maintained, and the National Trust has developed its own designs, which are functional as well as elegant. One guard is composed of pressure-treated softwood rails and 2.4 m (8 ft) strong posts. The Trust, with plenty of commercial woodland, can make such guards very cheaply. Lines of barbed wire, or even sheep netting to 90 cm (3 ft) from ground level, can reinforce effectiveness. Where the newly planted trees do not have to be stock-proof, spiral-shaped plastic guards are usually effective against rabbits and partially effective against squirrels. Although 'maidens' (young trees the first year after budding or grafting, where no attempt has yet been made to clean the stem) are much cheaper to buy, to stake and maintain, most private owners will plant trees, even in avenue quantities, as standards (having a clean stem to 1.65 m or 5 ft 6 in) or half-standard (stem 1.35 m or 4 ft 6 in) and will prepare the site and soil as in planting any garden tree. In windy sites avenue trees may need careful staking, but the Trust has no fixed policy about whether to use one or two stakes. If two stakes are employed, neither touches the tree stem, which is linked to them by a cross-bar support. More usually one strong stake is quite sufficient. A rigid plastic tie providing a buffer between the stake and the stem can be expanded as the girth of the tree stem increases. An important principle is that staking should be the minimum practicable to prevent the tree from rocking or blowing over, and ties placed as low as possible to encourage the tree to thicken naturally.

Throughout Trust properties many different trees and shrubs are used to create avenue effects, from the grand parkland features discussed above to the rather surprising avenues of palm (*Trachycarpus fortunei*) at SHEFFIELD PARK and in the almost tropical garden at OVERBECKS. In the walled garden at ACORN BANK, orchard planting is divided by a grass path lined with a yew hedge cut to a level of 1.2–1.5 m (4–5 ft), on the outside of which young trees of *Prunus cerasus* 'Rhexii' make an evenly spaced avenue, stressing the line and direction of the yew. This cherry with attractive double white flowers has been grown in England since the sixteenth century, and is an appropriate choice where a more recent exotic would be out of place, linking the two parts of this domestic orchard of mixed pears, apples, medlars and mulberries. On the grand scale at MONTACUTE

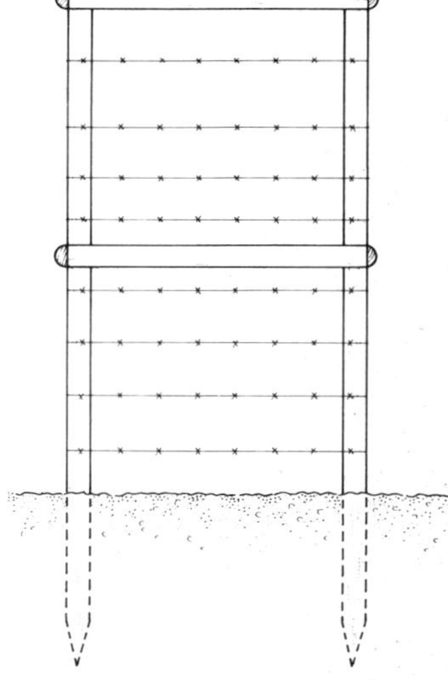

All newly planted parkland trees need stockproof protection for at least twenty years. Designs vary and are often a combination of wood and galvanized barbed wire.

Avenues are not always grand. At Tintinhull House in Somerset spaced domes of clipped box lead the eye down the long axial path.

HOUSE, the west front of the Elizabethan house looks down a wide sweep of grass edged by an avenue of sentinel Irish yews (*Taxus baccata* 'Fastigiata') backed with mixed planting of limes, beeches and wellingtonias (*Sequoiadendron giganteum*) and a recently planted outer avenue of limes behind.

On a much more intimate scale at nearby TINTINHULL HOUSE, a double line of box (*Buxus sempervirens*) edges the axial path which takes the eye to the bottom of the garden. The formal symmetry requires that each dome should have just the same curved pudding shape, and those near to the greedy roots of an overhanging holm oak (*Quercus ilex*) need extra watering and feeding in dry spells. Box, like yew, needs clipping only once a year when it is mature or has reached the desired height and width, but can be made grow more quickly when young by more frequent cuts, which are combined with extra feeding. The Tintinhull domes are given a slow-acting fertilizer at the end of the winter; additional dried organic fertilizer is applied to the roots when the soil is moist at any time during the growing season. Feature plants such as this can seldom be fed with heavy mulches of organic manure, as birds scratch and scatter the loose substance over edge and lawn. At WIGHTWICK MANOR clipped yew 'thimbles' have flat heads and line a central pathway from the house, framing the view of a paddock beyond. Planted in the early years of this century, they mark the period when Thomas Mawson gave advice here, although much of the earlier yew hedging and topiary were planned by Alfred Parsons some years before. Round the base of the yew shapes the grass is tightly mown, while panels of longer-textured turf fill in at the sides of the lawn.

At HIDCOTE, in the pillar garden, where 22 tall yews dominate a mixed border of peonies, fuchsias and roses, an avenue effect is created by the regular spacing between the meticulously sculptured yews. Here an annual cut keeps the yews in shape and feeding is part of the maintenance programme for the whole double border area. In the same garden is another sort of avenue. A double line of hornbeam (*Carpinus betulus*), fourteen trees on each side, in two rows of seven, are grown with trunks bare to 1.8 m (6 ft). The sides and tops are clipped to make growth which is not only rectangular in form, but dense and very green in summer (matted and twiggy in winter). To step inside the ranks of trees and look upward is like being in a tree room, with walls and ceiling.

Many other Trust gardens have avenues as fea-

The pleached hornbeams at Hidcote Manor in Gloucestershire are like clipped hedges on stilts.

tures inside quite small garden enclosures. At PENRHYN CASTLE, where the soil is acid, an avenue of elegant pinnate-leaved *Eucryphia glutinosa* lines the central path below the top terrace in the walled garden. The regular almost pyramidal habit of these deciduous eucryphias makes them an excellent choice to define a pathway, and the creamy-white flowers which are carried so freely on the upright branches in July and August are an extra bonus. The leaves colour a rich red before falling in autumn. At ERDDIG Portugal laurel (*Prunus lusitanica*) bushes appear to be planted in ornamental Versailles wooden containers, and line a gravel pathway stretching out to the south of the house, between rows of pleached lime. In fact the laurel is planted directly in the ground to save watering, and the wooden surrounds are 'dummies' and give protection in winter.

Pleaching, Arbours and Tree Tunnels

The pleaching of living trees and bushes into what is now often called an aerial hedge is a device usually used to delineate inner garden compartments, but may also be used to provide additional height at the boundaries of town gardens. The technique makes a valuable architectural feature which becomes an important part of the whole garden design. Because pleaching, or 'plashing' as it is sometimes called, is a very old gardening practice, the National Trust often finds that its function in defining separate garden areas, as at ERDDIG, is appropriate when recreating gardens around houses which date back to the sixteenth and seventeenth centuries, as well as in those Edwardian-style gardens which based their design on this earlier fashion. The technique can equally be used to make shady tunnel walks where living plants arch overhead, or to form the corner or central arbour or bower (there is one covered with elm at SHUGBOROUGH) which protects and shades a sitting place. Sometimes the Trust has taken over properties where pleached trees are already a feature. The famous hornbeams at HIDCOTE, perhaps the first to be known as 'houses on stilts', and the pleached lime walk at MOTTISFONT ABBEY, are examples. Such features have to be maintained and often in due course completely renewed and replanted.

Pleaching, from the French *plessier* meaning to plait or intertwine, seems to have been a known garden practice all through the Middle Ages, and was probably less common in England than in Europe, where the hot summers made shady walks even more desirable. However, pleaching is first recorded in England as early as 1324, when workmen were paid a penny for every two perches completed – a perch being the equivalent of about five and a half yards. There has occasionally been some confusion between the terms 'plashing' and 'pleaching', the former possibly applying to the process of cutting and laying a farm hedge (which will often have been of quickthorn). The use of plashing to make a perimeter hedge dense and stock-proof is described in the Oxford dictionary with a reference to 1563: 'Cutting young trees half a sunder and bowying downe theyr toppes to the grounde, and *plasshying* the boughes that growe thicke oute of the sydes wyth bushes and thornes betwene them, they brought to passe that their hedges were as good a defence to them as a wal.' Pleaching, on the other hand, has over the years come to mean *overhead* work.

Young flat-headed trees are planted at regular intervals, in a line, each one tied to a post at least 3 m (10 ft) high. Horizontal wires about 30 cm (12 in) apart are stretched tight between the posts; the young side branches are trained on them and pruned hard annually. All growth that points in the wrong direction is removed. Usually the sides of leafy growth, above the stems or trunks – which are bare to 60–90 cm (2–3 ft) or more – are kept formally clipped. On a grand scale such as at ERDDIG, once the trees have grown tall, special equipment is necessary for the annual pruning. Platforms on high trestles, or even on wheeled trolleys as in France, lighten the work.

When plant material such as hornbeam (*Carpinus betulus*) is treated in this way, its thick twiggy growth makes it possible to produce the dense effect of solid rectangular shapes sitting atop the bare trunks, as in the Stilt Gardens at HIDCOTE. Lime trees, too, and in particular *Tilia platyphyllos*, are frequently used for pleaching. Their fresh pale green leaves flutter slightly in the breeze, giving a sense of movement and freedom in the garden that is not present when dense small-leaved plants are used for barriers. Pleaching has the practical advantage of acting as a wind-filter where a solid hedge can cause turbulence as great as that around masonry walls. *Tilia × euchlora*, planted in 1975 when the formal early-eighteenth-century garden at ERDDIG was carefully restored by the Trust, will eventually grow to give the effect of aerial hedges. Facing each other across the central walk south of the house, two double rows of pleached limes will partly conceal the pyramid-shaped fruit trees.

Pleaching can play a number of roles in garden design. The walk of pleached limes designed by Geoffrey Jellicoe at MOTTISFONT in 1936 has more the effect of an avenue than of a barrier, closing and concentrating the view and leading the eye to a stone urn placed centrally on a plinth. The lime walk is effective in spring with its underplanting of glory of the snow (*Chionodoxa luciliae*) happily established in the short turf: pleached trees and shrubs that lose their foliage make ideal frames for spring gardens as well as becoming comfortable shady places in the hot summer months. At LYTES CARY the fresh green leaves of the short avenue of pleached limes that borders the approach to the house offers an attractive tonal and textural contrast with the dark solid shapes of clipped yew near by.

Perhaps the best-known pleached lime walk is at SISSINGHURST CASTLE. Its history carries a relevant warning to gardeners keen to reproduce similar features elsewhere. Vita Sackville-West (Mrs Harold Nicolson) originally planted the common lime (*Tilia × europaea*). This produced its vigorous suckering basal shoots, spoiling the purity of design and disguising the clean straight trunks, so carefully underplanted with a riot of many-coloured spring bulbs. It was also prone to aphids, which deposit a soot-like film of honeydew on plant leaves underneath the trees. In 1976, ten years after the property was given to the Trust, it was decided to replace these unsatisfactory trees with the non-suckering lime, *Tilia × platyphyllos*. (This 'clean' hybrid lime, incidentally, has flowers narcotic to bees: do not plant it near a swimming pool or even a small children's playground.) At the same time the central pathway was repaved. Now each spring sheets of blue *Anemone apennina*, forget-me-nots, scillas, grape hyacinths, small daffodils, fritillaries and erythroniums carpet the ground while the lime branches are still bare.

Pollarding is just another form of pleaching, where rounded heads are produced on tall trunks. It was originally adopted as a method of protecting young growth on trees which would be coppiced annually, to keep the heads just out of reach of livestock, but is now used ornamentally and, in hot countries, to create shade. A row of pollarded willows or, on a larger scale, plane trees can be an attractive garden feature with their mop growth. At BLICKLING HALL high limes on either side of the south approach to the house are pollarded every three years. At ICKWORTH the holm oaks in the formal garden are regularly pollarded to keep them in scale.

Above: At Erddig in Clwyd double avenues of pleached limes enclose newly planted orchards.

Bateman's

Kipling's alley of pears is an architectural feature in the garden at Bateman's. Small plants thrive under the light shade of the pear foliage and later-flowering clematis twine through the framework.

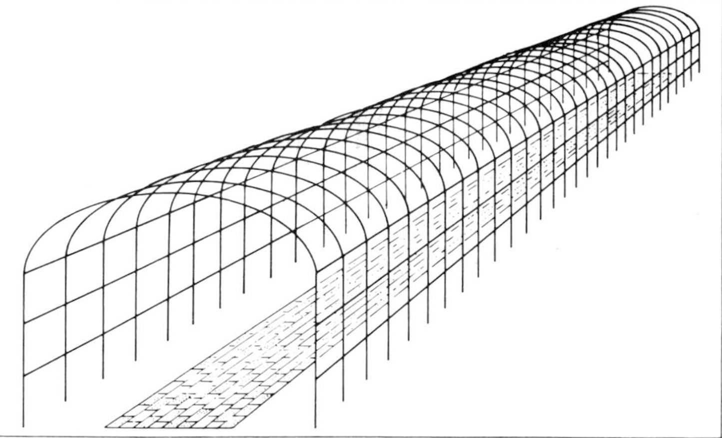

A further form of pleaching is that used for making tree arbours or tunnels, sometimes called 'alleys' (not to be confused with the French term *allée*). Strictly speaking, alleys are pathways lined with high enclosing hedges as in the wilderness at HAM HOUSE or as defined in yew at LYTES CARY. Arbours, on the other hand, are made by training supple young shoots from two rows of trees planted perhaps 2.4 m (8 ft) apart. These are bent over metal or plastic-coated hoops to form a covered walk, at least 2.1 m (7 ft) high in the centre. Originally a rough framework of laths would have been used, and this framework developed into the more elegant trellis work seen in French Renaissance gardens. Sometimes the shoots overhead are grafted together where they meet: 'Overhead the branches joined one another and their foliage intermingled; nature itself seemed a work of art.'

At BATEMAN's Rudyard Kipling designed a spacious pear alley shortly after his move there in 1902. Spring flowers grow at the base of the pear trees, which themselves make a froth of white blossom in May. Clematis planted outside the pears twine among the branches to give a summer display. At the end of the alley a wide seat is welcoming. **Mr Alan Champion**, the Gardener-in-Charge at Bateman's, writes about the maintenance of the alley:

The pear trees, which are a mixture of 'Conference', 'Doyenné du Comice' and 'Winter Nelis', are pruned in winter. All unwanted lateral growth is cut back to three or four buds: some are needed to train to replace dead branches. All dead wood is removed. It is usual with pears to summer-prune as well, but this is impractical here because of the clematis, honeysuckle and *Cobaea scandens* which help clothe the arch in summer. To prevent excessive growth the tree trunks have been given two opposing cuts like two horseshoes one above the other about 5–7 cm (2–3 in) apart. This slows down the whole growth of the tree, but the trees here are for decoration rather than fruit. This is a task which should only be undertaken by an experienced person; if incorrectly carried out the tree will die. The cuts slowly heal themselves and need to be cleaned out every two or three years. After cutting the wounds are painted with Arbrex as a cosmetic.

After the pear trees are pruned, the honeysuckle (*Lonicera etrusca*) which is trained over the seat at one end of the arch is cut back to a framework. Then the clematis are pruned back to ground level, leaving some stems to lengthen the flowering season the following year. These will be removed completely the next pruning season and others left in their place.

The beds beneath the pear arch are weeded, edged and mulched. The clematis are given fertilizer and a sprinkling of lime. Most of the plants are shade-loving ground-cover plants which need little maintenance. The main clumps of plants are kept together, but any odd plants which come up unexpectedly are normally left to help cover the beds and give a natural look. As things die back in the autumn the foliage is tidied, ending with the vincas which are cut back at Christmas.

Plants under the Pear Arch at Bateman's

Ajuga pyramidalis
A. reptans multicolor
Allium moly
Anemone coronaria
Astilbes
Bergenias
Bluebells
Brunnera macrophylla
Camassia leichtlinii
Convallaria majalis 'Fortin's Giant'
Epimedium × versicolor
Ferns
Galanthus nivalis
Geranium endressii
G. macrorrhizum
Helleborus corsicus
H. foetidus
Hostas
Hyacinths
Lamium maculatum
L.m. aureum
L. 'Beacon Silver'
Leucojum aestivum 'Gravetye'
Lilium candidum
Liriope muscari
Narcissus
Pachyphragma macrophyllum
Pachysandra terminalis
Polygonatum × hybridum
Primroses
Pulmonaria officinalis
Saxifraga fortunei
Symphytum grandiflorum
Tiarella cordifolia
Vinca minor
Viola cornuta alba
V. labradorica purpurea
V. odorata sulfurea

Clematis alternating with pear trees

C. 'Alice Fisk'
C. 'Barbara Jackman'
C. 'Gipsy Queen'
C. 'Huldine'
C. 'Jackmanii Rubra'
C. 'Jackmanii Superba'
C. 'Lady Betty Balfour'
C. 'Madame Baron Veillard'
C. 'Miss Bateman'
C. viticella

At BENINGBROUGH HALL old pear espalier trees have been adapted to make attractive arches in the walled garden which has now been grassed over. Originally lining the central path, in traditional kitchen-garden fashion, the espalier trees seemed to have no function once paths and beds had disappeared. Long new shoots, instead of being cut off, have been trained across hoops to meet the shoots of espaliers on the opposite side. These archways make a feature down the middle of the garden.

Apple trees can also be trained to arch overhead, but the harder wood curves less elegantly, and the visual effect is harsher and stiffer. To plant up a new pear arch use two-year-old bushes already trained as cordons and give plenty of support, tying in loose shoots tightly and continually. For good crops of fruit as well as the ornamental effect, careful systematic pruning is necessary, cutting the previous year's growth back to a hand's breadth, to leave six or eight buds at the most as the fruiting spurs of the future.

The *berceau*, a form of trellis work covering a walk, makes a support for greenery and was a feature of early French and Dutch gardens, the forerunner of the more substantial pergola. Trellis work or *treillage* gives the appearance of a more solid architectural feature, yet is made in light, relatively flimsy batons in either square or diamond patterns. Its versatility makes it useful as a tool in garden design, where tricks with false perspective can control garden dimensions and narrowing bars of trellis work give the effects of distance or frame a fictitious distant path. In mediaeval gardens even the great bindweed (*Calystegia sepium*), known as poor man's rope, and with handsome bell-shaped flowers, was sometimes used for ornamental display on trellis. Today this most invasive deep-rooting weed is seldom allowed a place of importance; indeed, no well-maintained Trust garden allows it to flourish. More usually, fruiting vines combined use with beauty, just as today at FELBRIGG HALL grapevines are trained on timber pyramids, giving a strong architectural flavour to the garden and reminiscent of a French potager.

Bowers and arbours are places for sitting in for rest or contemplation. They can be angular, like sentry boxes of woodwork or trellis, or smoothly curved frames on which plants can twine. At WESTBURY COURT in the walled garden where shrub roses mingle with seventeenth-century herbs (or at least plants known in English gardens by 1700), corner hooped arbours very much like those at the Château de Villandry on the Loire, but on an appropriately smaller scale, provide the structure on which climbing roses flourish. Other shady arbours can be of one tree or climbing plant only. The oriental plane tree (*Platanus orientalis*) can be trained or Boston ivy (*Parthenocissus tricuspidata* 'Veitchii'), often wrongly known as Virginia creeper (actually *P. quinquefolia*), will provide cool shade through the hottest months and make a crimson umbrella in late summer.

Top: At Moseley Old Hall in Staffordshire, where planting is seventeenth-century in style, the design of the wooden arbour is taken from Thomas Hill's *A Gardener's Labyrinth* (1577).

Above: The lattice-work arbour at Tatton Park in Cheshire has a French flavour and is pure decoration.

Opposite: Simple trellis work divides garden areas at Lamb House in East Sussex, and provides a frame for climbing roses.

At MOSELEY OLD HALL a wooden arbour leads to a shady hornbeam tunnel across a corner. The decorative arbour, its pattern taken from Thomas Hill's *A Gardener's Labyrinth* (1577) is the frame on which climbers known at the period have been encouraged to twine. The dark-leaved claret vine, *Vitis vinifera* 'Purpurea' is interlaced with the fragrant virgin's bower (*Clematis flammula*) and purple virgin's bower (*C. viticella*), both European natives. Under the arbour and edging the walk are hedges of old English lavender (*Lavandula angustifolia*) with grey-blue leaves and dense spikes of blue. The visitor then emerges to a pathway lined with nut trees which leads on to a simple orchard of quince, mulberry and medlar, all fruit trees grown in the seventeenth century.

A tree tunnel or shady arbour at LYTES CARY conceals a pathway linking separate garden areas and the leafy greenness prepares the eye for appreciating more colourful garden flowers beyond. Although the garden at Lytes Cary is Edwardian, it is laid out as a series of formal garden rooms and yew alleys which might well have been its pattern in the sixteenth century, when it was lived in by Sir Henry Lyte (1529–1607). He was the author of *A niewe Herball or Historie of Plants* (first published in 1578 and basically a translation of De l'Ecluse's French edition of Dodoens' *Cruydeboeck*). Appearing before Gerard's *Herbal* of 1597, and well before Parkinson's *Paradisi in Sole Paradisus Terrestris* (1629), his book described plants only for their medicinal qualities.

A hornbeam tunnel leads to an inner secret garden at Lytes Cary in Somerset.

At a focal point where a south vista from the house meets a terraced yew alley at a central stone-edged pool, the hornbeam tunnel leads on to a secret garden in the shape of an ellipse. The tunnel is 21 m (70 ft) long and 2 m (6 ft) across, with the hornbeams (*Carpinus betulus*) planted at a spacing of about a yard. The hornbeam is trained to meet overhead and needs careful pruning and tying once a year. Beyond the tunnel a lawn and statues of Flora and Diana are surrounded by a ring of *Weigela florida* 'Variegata', underplanted with the spreading *Euphorbia amygdaloides robbiae*, an almost evergreen spurge from Asia Minor with lime-green flowers, which rapidly colonizes the ground in sun or shade.

It is perhaps hard to draw a clear distinction between tunnels and pergolas, which have a formal framework of brick, stone or wooden uprights, with cross-bars in lighter wood. Once clothed in climbing plants a pergola performs many of the same functions as a tunnel, linking areas of the garden and creating shady and secret retreats, as well as providing a frame for a wide range of plants. The framework creates a three-dimensional garden feature and the straight lines contrast firmly with flowing plant shapes. It is possible to intertwine many natural climbers, extending the season for both flower and foliage interest, and at the feet of the upright supports more flower-bed space allows low-growing shrubs and herbaceous plants to line a central pathway.

These open-air retreats, which become leafy enclosures in the summer, can be beautiful in the early season with cascades of hanging flower. At NYMANS a wisteria drapes its 60 cm (2 ft) long pale violet racemes on a giant pergola, and the clambers upwards into old holly and other trees at the side. *Wisteria floribunda multijuga* was grown here from the first seeds introduced to England from Japan. It is a spectacular sight in early May, and later provides a dark shady summer walk, while large clustered roses give scent and colour at the end of June. Along the lower edge of the pergola a massed line of *Hydrangea arborescens* with greenish-white globular flowers is spectacular in August and later through the winter months as even the dying flower-heads are decorative. Forms of *Iris sibirica* are planted in strong clumps to flower earlier, and under the pergola walk alchemilla and herbaceous geraniums flower in the light shade. A raised walk runs under the pergola, which borders the roadside. From the main garden glimpses of the woodland garden to the south are obtained through the pergola's framework.

The structure originally built in 1903 with sandstone piers and a larchwood overhead frame was later altered. The piers were found to be too far apart. Now strong larch poles alternate with the stone piers and make the tying in of plants more manageable. A lighter weight of larch poles is used overhead. Larch, oak or chestnut timbers will all last for as long as 20 years before they have to be renewed.

One of the most spectacular and showy pergolas is that at MOUNT STEWART in Co Down, where the winter climate compares favourably with gardens in Cornwall although it is on the same latitude as Glasgow. A very humid atmosphere and comparatively little frost permit plants such as mutisias and the scented almost evergreen Himalayan rose, *Rosa gigantea*, with wide yellowish-white single flowers followed by red autumn fruits, and a very vigorous habit, to flourish and twine overhead. Not only tender plants are grown, however, and *Lonicera etrusca* and lavender-mauve *Solanum crispum* 'Glasnevin' extend the blue and yellow theme of planting in the beds below. Although many of the plants that flourish in a favourable site like Mount Stewart are of doubtful hardiness it is, in fact, well worth while attempting to grow them in the average garden. Provided that they are well protected from harsh winds and low temperatures during their early years while they become established, many such plants can prove surprisingly tough.

At Mount Stewart the pergola on a raised terrace closes in the three sides of the sunk garden, west of the house. It is now sheltered by a tall hedge of the Leyland cypress (× *Cupressocyparis leylandii*). Below the frame, shrubs and perennials scramble in shade and sun, taking advantage of the well-drained soil.

The pergola pillars are made of sandstone, known locally as Scrabo, the name of the hill above Newtownards from where it comes. Each 45 cm (18 in) square pillar is placed about 6 m (20 ft) apart, and the overhead frame is of Douglas fir (*Pseudotsuga menziesii*), which proves hard-wearing and durable. It was last renewed in 1965.

In shade to the south the scarlet-flowered *Mitraria coccinea*, honeysuckle and small-flowered clematis species on the pillars are mixed with roses. On the sunnier sides the rare *Mutisia decurrens*, callistemon, *Jovellana violacea*, the tender Australasian *Hakea sericea* with white flowers and awl-shaped leaves and little violas grow beneath the pergola where the roses 'Easlea's Golden Rambler', 'Climbing Lady Hillingdon' and 'Rêve d'Or' make a lot of growth. Recent severe winters have killed the rare *Dendromecon rigida* from California, which is so difficult to propagate, with its narrow hard glaucous leaves and poppy-like buttercup-yellow flowers, but *Lardizabala biternata* from Chile, a twining evergreen with chocolate-purple flowers still survives. Mr Nigel Marshall, the Head Gardener, feels that the tender dendromecon would do better against a warm wall, and is not really suited to an open pergola.

A large plant of the Chinese gooseberry (*Actinidia chinensis*), which bears fruit at Mount Stewart, scrambles over the pergola frame. Vines, the more delicate *Billardiera longiflora* from Tasmania with greenish-cream bell-flowers, *Clematis* 'Etoile

At Nymans in West Sussex the wisteria pergola is a feature at the edge of the garden.

Violette', *C.* × *durandii* and the yellow rose 'Lawrence Johnston' named for the maker of the gardens at Hidcote (perhaps in its colour patterns a model for some of Lady Londonderry's schemes at Mount Stewart) all grow luxuriantly. Under the pergola flourish shade-loving *Waldsteinia ternata*, moon trefoil (*Medicago arborea*) with clusters of yellow peaflowers through the summer, and the little *Felicia pappei*, and there are large plants of *Ceanothus rigidus* 'Autumnal Blue' and *Chaenomeles speciosa* 'Falconnet Charlet' with double pink flowers which appear before the leaves in spring. Clumps of *Calceolaria integrifolia* and orange-flowered *Alstroemeria aurantiaca* match the planting of yellow and orange in the sunken garden below.

Steps lined with *Erica lusitanica* lead down to this lower garden, where Gertrude Jekyll made designs for the planting. These beds reflect the same attention to colour detail as in the Italian garden to the south of the house, and are linked deliberately with the flower colour on the pergola above. With house and pergola on three sides, the sense of enclosure is very strong. On the house terrace formal clipped bays are interrupted by beds of the apricot-flowered bush rose 'Mrs Oakley Fisher' underplanted with bronze-leaved *Crocosmia* × *crocosmiiflora* 'Solfatare' with apricot-yellow flowers on 60 cm (2 ft) stems and pale blue *Salvia patens* 'Cambridge Blue', a subtle colour-scheme which might be copied, even if, in less favoured gardens, other plants had to be used.

At BODNANT steps descend below the lily terrace and lead to curving walls over which light wooden pergola frames are covered with climbing roses, mauve-flowered *Solanum crispum* 'Glasnevin', the spring-flowering evergreen *Clematis armandii*, and the Chilean coral plant, *Berberidopsis corallina*. Tied back against the walls and given shelter by the pergola and the twining overhead plants are wall shrubs such as ceanothus, leptospermum, tree heaths, *Drimys winteri*, the tender *Photinia glomerata* with almost translucent young growth, and *Rhododendron edgeworthii*. In summer white libertia (*Libertia formosa*) and in September dark pink Japanese anemones make a flowery underplanting, and blue campanulas seed in the dry wall.

Perhaps most famous of all at Bodnant is the spectacular laburnum walk in June. Planted already at the end of the nineteenth century by the present Lord Aberconway's great-grandfather, the tunnel curves gently and is formed by training pleached laburnums over metal hoops held on a rigid frame. The original bushes will have been the common European laburnum (*Laburnum anagyroides*), but over the years these have been replaced with the newer 1928 hybrid cultivar *L.* × *watereri* 'Vossii' with longer, very free-flowering racemes. The bushes are trained and pruned in the same way as is described for pleached lime trees.

At GREYS COURT plants of the giant Japanese wisteria (*Wisteria floribunda*) cover an area between two walled gardens, and gnarled trunks, of considerable age, have to be supported by strong wooden props. Large wisterias can seldom be pruned twice a year as recommended, with a quick tidy in summer immediately after flowering followed by heavy pruning in winter before the sap rises again for a new season. Like so many plants it is in the first few years that particular care has to be taken; as wisteria matures, it continues to perform well with little attention and still flowers profusely if given only the winter cut-back. Under this wisteria in almost total shade the blue-flowered *Buglossoides purpurocaerulea* thrives and gives interest in summer, making a weed-suppressing mass.

Above: The laburnums at Bodnant in North Wales are trained on metal hoops to make a covered walk.

Opposite: The curving trellis-work pergola on the lower terraces at Bodnant makes a frame for climbing roses. In the beds below, grassy-leaved libertia flourish in half-shade.

Planting in Patterns

The idea of pattern takes the controlling element – the shaping of trees and hedging plants – a stage further; instead of using plants structurally, as barriers, planting is for decoration and artifice. While topiary may vertically emphasize the structure of a lay-out, its clipped shape is pure ornament. In the horizontal plane, knots and parterres use dwarf hedging as outlines for garden conceits. When the neat clipped lines contain freer plant forms, the decorative effect is richer; when colour is also present, the patterns become luxury items – jewelled embroideries.

Such patterns are quite deliberately contrived, emphasizing rather than modifying the artifice of gardening. They become the central and dominant feature and need to be framed accordingly by cool green lawn and simple lines of hedging. These geometric designs, often elaborate and grandiose on a large scale, can be effectively modified for a small area; in fact are more suitable than 'naturalistic' curves in confined spaces.

Topiary

The cutting of trees and shrubs to ornament the garden has been practised since Roman times. In Pliny's garden, box was clipped into innumerable shapes, some even as letters spelling out the name of the gardener or his master. Originally the word 'topiary' came from the Latin *topiarius*, correctly translated as the person tending the garden, but it quickly assumed a more specific definition, until *ars topiaria* implied a degree of skill in shaping living plants. The art of topiary was revived in Renaissance Italy, when humanist writers and architects looked to classical sources for inspiration. First described in the Rucellai garden at Villa Quaracchi in Florence, shapes were varied and eclectic: 'spheres, porticoes, temples, vases, urns, apes, donkeys, oxen, a bear, giants, men, women, warriors, a harpy, philosophers, popes and cardinals'. The fashion for topiary spread from Italy through France and Holland to reach England by the seventeenth century.

These clipped shapes become important in garden design whether taking the place of statues, or emphasizing a focal point, or simply contrasting with freer plant growth. For topiary, plants should be slow-growing, of dense habit and amenable to regular cutting. Evergreens such as box, yew and holly (although the latter is less satisfactorily close-growing) are most often used. Forms of phillyrea also respond well, and both *Phillyrea latifolia* and *P. angustifolia* were much used in English seventeenth-century gardens, and are now coming back into fashion. At WESTBURY COURT phillyreas are used as clipped specimens in the Trust's recent restoration of the garden to its original appearance dating back to the end of the seventeenth century. Juniper (the common native *Juniperus communis*) is also practical for topiary; seldom used today, it did feature in English Restoration gardens. Portugal laurel (*Prunus lusitanica*) can be clipped into regular geometric shapes, but like beech or hornbeam does not grow densely enough to make elaborate topiary specimens. At ERDDIG a wide path is edged with mushrooms of Portugal laurel clipped into neat pyramids. The more tender bay (*Laurus nobilis*) and holm oak (*Quercus ilex*) also make attractive textured shapes, but cannot be clipped into the more complicated structures.

Fashions come and go, and even in 1625, when the craze for topiary shapes had still a hundred years of popularity to run, Francis Bacon, writing *Of Gardens*, is scornful: '. . . images cut out in juniper or other garden stuff be for children'. By 1712 Joseph Addison writes in *The Spectator*, objecting to the fashion ('We see the marks of the Scissors on every bush'), while Alexander Pope in the following year in *The Guardian* invents a 'Catalogue of Greens' to be used by an aspiring gardener: '. . . A pair of Giants, stunted, to be sold cheap . . . A Queen Elizabeth in Phylyraea, a little inclining to the Green Sickness, but full of growth.' In the grander gardens, topiary ceased to be popular, and gardens became landscape parks. Even hedges enclosing separate garden areas were swept away to allow fields with grazing cattle and sheep to sweep up to the mansion windows.

By the middle of the nineteenth century, Charles Barry and W. A. Nesfield were again designing gardens in Italianate style where domes or cylinders of green or golden yew or variegated hollies defined garden patterns. At BLICKLING HALL Nesfield designed the parterre on the east terrace, and strangely shaped dense yew blocks known as the 'grand pianos' still sit on the lawn today. At the corners of the square beds, redesigned for herbaceous planting

Yews at Packwood House in Warwickshire are tapered to make conical shapes.

by Mrs Norah Lindsay in the 1930s, yews are sentinel acorns.

Although most of the tall tapering yews were planted only in the 1850s, the yew garden at PACKWOOD HOUSE represents the topiary style of the Restoration. To today's eyes successful topiary effects depend not only on the outline and solidity of the shape, but also on the textural contrasts and on the incidence of light falling on horizontal, vertical and curved surfaces. In the area where the tall yew shapes and yew arbour dominate the upper garden at Packwood, the lawn is edged with old box bushes, interesting in the variability of surface colour and the shape of the box leaves. Although remaining botanically identifiable as *Buxus sempervirens*, individual box plants can vary greatly from one another and show a wide range of different colours and textures.

Above: Yews are clipped into massive shapes at Blickling Hall in Norfolk. Originally planted by W. A. Nesfield in the nineteenth century, these dense masses are known as the 'grand pianos', and give architectural interest.

Opposite: Yew can be trained to any shape, but the more intricate models are moulded round metal or willow-work frames and take some years to mature. At Nymans (top) a giant bird rests by the ruined house. At Cliveden (middle) topiary spirals and a peacock are as important as statuary. At Hidcote Manor (bottom) the peacocks have recently been rejuvenated, the yew cut back tightly to the main branches.

Box shares this characteristic with yew. The side hedges and cross hedge just below the Mount with its spiralling path of box, has a tapestry pattern in different green tones. Grown thick and bulky with age, it makes great mounded waves, almost as interesting as the soaring yew shapes. The Trust are replanting a considerable number of the box bushes, as with age and clipping it is almost impossible to keep the base from getting bare and woody.

Yew hedges and yew specimens for topiary cutting or for more bulky shapes may be grown from seed, and plants are then selected for their suitably dense habit of growth, but for the best results the plants used should be vegetatively produced from the same sturdy clone. In fact, a batch of yew plants bought in from a nursery may be very variable; worse, plants taken as cuttings from side shoots will fail to make leaders, but will put on considerable horizontal growth. Seedling yews also vary in density of growing habit and in leaf colours. For both topiary and hedges a dense habit will permit much more tailored effects; in a hedge colour variation is often attractive, but in shaped topiary conformity of colour and texture is usually desirable.

At both PACKWOOD and NYMANS die-back to a few inches became noticeable and unsightly in 1985. It was discovered that the tortrix moth (*Ditula angurosina*) was laying eggs in the yew hedges: the hatched caterpillars hibernated through the winter, and then 'barked' the ends of the young shoots in spring. The caterpillar is about 1 cm (½ in) long, greenish-greyish in colour, and affects malus, pyrus and prunus as well as yew. An insecticide containing permethrin, to which caterpillars and aphids do not build up a resistance, is effective. Bats, which have now become rare, are thought in the past to have been the natural predator of the tortrix moth.

At Packwood many of the tall yews dating back to the 1840s were actually beginning to die by the 1970s. This was due not to old age, but to a combination of factors: the heavy, sticky clay soil caused waterlogging and surface rooting; there was competition (from grass) for water in a series of dry seasons, and increased numbers of visitors caused compaction. The situation is now being relieved by drainage, particularly surface drainage; by top dressing with sharp sand; by frequent spiking and by replanting on slight mounds. The yews were also cut back drastically to the bare stem, and are rejuvenating successfully.

At POWIS CASTLE Mr Jimmie Hancock, the Head Gardener, finds that die-back in yew branches halfway up a hedge or in a cut topiary shape is often caused by the nibbling of squirrels or even mice, which 'bark' a stem completely round. These stems have to be cut out, and it is several years before the surface returns to one smooth plane. The strange mounded 'waves' in very old yew such as that at Powis and MONTACUTE HOUSE may originally derive from a cause such as this, and make it difficult to clip them evenly.

The Irish yews (*Taxus baccata* 'Fastigiata') that make such satisfactory free-standing specimens, and in paired alignment make superb avenues, all derive from the yew discovered in 1780 at Florence Court in Northern Ireland. They must all be vegetatively produced from cuttings. The branches grow upwards almost vertically. Interestingly, Mr Alan Mitchell has remarked that the most fastigiate forms from Ireland grow less tall and narrow the farther east in Great Britain they are planted. At FELBRIGG HALL in Norfolk, for example, their habit is markedly dumpier and less soaring.

The best way to shape the trees is to clip or prune the outside annually, as is done at ERDDIG, MONTACUTE, ROWALLANE and SNOWSHILL. A traditional

At Nymans yew topiary shaped as crowns marks four corners and frames an Italian fountain. Clipped shapes emphasize formality and contrast with natural plant outlines. Near the house elegant clipped pyramids rest on firm hedging. Vertical, horizontal and sloping sides reflect light at different angles.

practice has been to use wires to hold the branches in place and maintain a good shape, but this is not recommended: it creates work, and causes damage to stems. Unfortunately once begun it has to be continued, and any necessary cutting out of dead wood has to be done by pulling down the outer branches, as is the practice with Italian cypresses. Clipped Irish yews make a vertical pattern on the banks round the edge of the sunken north garden at MONTACUTE HOUSE. **Mr Graham Kendall**, the Head Gardener, describes how their shape is maintained by careful clipping:

❧ A large number of Irish yews were planted in the Montacute garden in the middle of the nineteenth century. Although some have since been removed, we still have 96 specimens of up to 4.8 m (16 ft). They are a dominant feature of the garden.

The smooth dense growth of English yew makes it ideal for use as a hedging or topiary plant. It can be cut tightly using mechanized clippers. The looser Irish yew, with its tiered springy growth and radially arranged leaves, is most successfully treated as a lightly trimmed specimen often seen, as at Montacute, in a sentinel role.

Irish yew pruning at Montacute is done annually, by hand, using secateurs. We usually start in September. The bottom of the tree is pruned first, working round the base removing the paler green fingers of new growth to restrict overall girth. Where shoots have become crowded, the weakest or untidiest stems are cut back to older wood and care is taken to produce a good overall shape.

When the bottom is finished, wooden ladders with boards tied across the top to distribute weight are leant against the tree. We use wooden ladders because they are warmer than aluminium and because the greater weight helps them to rest better in the top of the tree. Pruning is continued in the same way, except for the top which is cut into a tight crown using shears.

The shape, conical with a domed top, is held in place by wires 75 cm (2 ft 6 in) apart. These can be tightened, loosened or replaced as is necessary. Occasionally, wires are removed altogether, to allow the cutting out of dead wood from the inside.

One tree takes a minimum of two man-hours for just the basic pruning, and with the large number of trees involved, it is a task which is on the fringe of acceptability. However, the quality of result justifies the many hours of work, and it would be sad to see such detailed attention abandoned. ❧

At Ham House the knot garden to the east of the house has been reconstructed to a plan of 1670. Box-edged beds, their corners accentuated by pyramid box bushes, are arranged in a series of diagonals, each bed massed with silvery cotton lavender.

Many topiary gardens disappeared in the landscape movement, and the Trust now often reintroduces some appropriate form of clipped ornament when restoring a garden attached to a seventeenth-century house. In the front entrance garden at MOSELEY OLD HALL, where the surrounding border is composed of plants known in the seventeenth century, the central grass panels flanking the path to the front door are decorated in period style with finials and corkscrew spirals of Box.

Other Trust gardens have old and intricate topiary. The complete restoration of misshapen peacocks or even of more simple cones, spheres and finials is difficult, as few evergreens will 'break' from dead wood, but need the slow process of 'stumping' back to a main stem or trunk. Many Victorian gardens which have passed into Trust ownership still have evidence of topiary which can be reshaped, however overgrown. The great domes of golden yew on the terraces to the east of the house

In the Pillar Garden at Hidcote Manor the square base of each tapered yew is almost hidden by flowing plant shapes.

at SHUGBOROUGH were nursed back to shape but did not need completely 'stumping' back as has been necessary where neglect has been more severe over a long period.

Just as hedges, arbours and tunnels give architectural interest, so an element of clipped topiary adds a feeling of maturity and permanence to a garden, and does not take many years to look good. Shaping should begin when a plant is still young, although not for the first two years, and is at first usually done methodically with secateurs; later, as the outline becomes defined, electric clippers can be used. The more the plant is cut the more feeding it needs as it struggles to put out new shoots, so well prepared soil and plenty of moisture in the growing season are essential. Plants need feeding with organic humus-making fertilizers, as well as artificial compound fertilizers which should be given as growth starts in the spring.

Many of the larger topiary features are produced by planting a group of three or four together. It is essential that these should all be taken from the same clone. After the first two seasons, clip hard and feed liberally to encourage dense healthy growth, gradually tying shoots to a frame of stout galvanized wire or wickerwork to achieve a perfect shape. Leaders are chosen to grow on, and young shoots are tied into position or cut back to make bushy growth. The wicker or wire frame soon becomes completely concealed with boskage as the specimen matures. It is not difficult to keep the bush to the desired shape as long as cutting is done frequently; it can be a problem to reshape a very woody subject.

A frame is helpful even when training plants to make simple archways or recessed niches. At HARDWICK HALL a network of metal defines the recesses which frame statues in the *rond-point* where yew and hornbeam hedges meet. For elaborate shapes, special frames may be contrived. At MOUNT STEWART in Co. Down Lady Londonderry had shaped metal frames made by a blacksmith in Co. Fermanagh, on which she trained some of her topiary figures, including the complex Irish harp. The clipped bay bushes which frame the house terrace, on the other hand, were imported from Belgium in 1923 ready-shaped as mature specimens already 50 years old.

These topiary techniques for clipping and trimming of woody plants can be applied to making hedges more complicated, with shapes cut out along the top, sometimes in scallops or battlemented as at CASTLE DROGO. Buttresses project to make frames for statuary or flower beds. Single plant specimens (or groups of the same plant) are cut to represent cones, balls, birds or beasts. A fox hunt in yew runs along the broad top of a yew hedge at KNIGHTSHAYES, and finials and spheres in holly protrude from the hedges which line the water canals at WESTBURY COURT. Simple solid rectangles of box outside the west door at MONTACUTE HOUSE (planted 1973), the 'grand pianos' in yew at BLICKLING HALL, and the 'drums' at WIGHTWICK MANOR seem to anchor the garden with the house into the landscape, and seem an essential part of the framework of the overall design.

The great yew shapes at POWIS CASTLE date from the end of the seventeenth century; the topiary yews at CHIRK CASTLE were planted only at the end of the last century, but have grown high with wide bases to resemble Welsh hats. More elaborate representational topiary such as the Hidcote or Wightwick peacocks, the elaborate 'crowns' which frame the Italian fountain at NYMANS, and the chase at KNIGHTSHAYES have been made only in this century.

At WIGHTWICK MANOR the formal garden, designed by Alfred Parsons, is a series of yew enclosures, the hedges themselves with protruding buttresses and strange acute angles, emphasizing light and shadow effects. At the entrance to the rose garden, large cylinders of yew are topped with clipped peacocks.

The green alley, flanked by stone crowns, is 70 m (some 75 yd) long and 3–4 m (10–13 ft) wide and carries the eye to a wooden seat at the end. The yew had grown to 2.4 m (8 ft) in width and almost 6 m (20 ft) high. This has been reduced to a more manageable 90 cm by 2.1 m (3 × 7 ft). At cross entrances the yew arches are accentuated by being framed in a solid clipped box-like shape which projects forwards and upwards over the long line of yew. The designer Thomas Mawson also worked here later, and the drum-shaped golden yews in the rose garden are part of his contribution. Mawson liked to contrast leaf colours in topiary, budding a golden-leaved yew to the leading shoot of a clipped hemisphere in plain green, and training and clipping this golden cap to complete the sphere. Similar tricks are played when variegated holly is contrasted with a plain green form, and shaped into a ball on top of a solid base. At Wightwick Mawson also planted bushes of brightly coloured variegated holly along a walk edging the orchard. These are now clipped into domed cylinders.

Perhaps topiary is most pleasing when it seems to belong quite simply to its context. In the pillar garden at HIDCOTE each soaring yew shape springs from a solid cube which anchors it firmly to its place, a stabilizing foil in flower beds packed with extravagant plant shapes. At POWIS the 300-year-old yews, now 9 m (30 ft) high, have a monumental scale in keeping with the castle's grandeur, an additional bastion to its fortifications. At LYTES CARY where a garden path is flanked with cottage-loaf yews, large mounded cylinders of box against a stone wall quietly echo the rounded dome of a seventeenth-century dovecote in the parkland beyond. More fanciful contrived ornamental shapes, appropriate in a period garden, seem decoration rather than permanent garden features. The quiet solidity and flowing smooth clipped lines of more architectural structures add a stabilizing quality to a garden scene and, because topiary grows slowly and take years to mature, its presence implies a belief in the garden's continued development.

Knots and Mazes

Knot designs in gardens derived from embroidery and the medieval passion for intricate patterns. The 'over and under' worked in silk or wool was imitated in the garden by using foliage plants with distinct leaf colours. Similarly, the intricate designs of Persian carpets, the strapwork in wooden panelling and plaster ceilings in Elizabethan and Jacobean great houses were copied in the garden in the forms of interlacing knots. The idea is much the same as making a framework with some low-growing plant, usually box, santolina, rue or germander, small-leaved and dense in habit, and then further subdividing the framed area into smaller flower beds. Early ecclesiastical gardens would have had a simple and quite functional pattern, dividing herbs for cooking and medicine from each other; later the patterns became more elaborate and developed into the French *parterre de broderie* where there were no inner flower beds, but elegant scrolls of box were laid out on a background of plain or coloured gravels.

A simple knot pattern of box at Beningbrough Hall divides beds into triangles for planting contrast.

In the garden a continuous interlacing line of one plant, like a weaving thread, would be called a 'closed' knot, while when the plants remained in separate distinct areas each section would be termed an 'open' knot. These patterns, usually of low clipped evergreen bushes, outlined miniature flower beds, in which flowering herbs or even coloured sands or brick dust were placed. Essentially these patterns were most effective if they could be viewed from above; many knots were in garden areas directly outside the house window or sometimes in a sunken plot to be viewed from a terrace or steps. The Elizabethan raised walk and the mount not only allowed the countryside to be glimpsed from within the security of the garden, but also gave the elevation necessary to appreciate the complicated designs laid out like a carpet within the garden perimeters.

The maze or labyrinth, as a conception, probably came first from the mythological tortuous windings of the minotaur at Knossos. Later representing the path the Christian believer must follow to reach a spiritual goal, it became a common religious symbol marked out in church floors or outside pavements, during the late Middle Ages. The journey through a maze became a substitute for a pilgrimage to the Holy Land, and as a penance the faithful might follow its meanderings on their knees. An early maze in masonry is recorded in the twelfth century at Woodstock, where Henry II chased the 'fair Rosamund'. At first mazes were cut in stone, rock or turf; later they were delineated with low hedges.

At GREYS COURT a modern turf maze was commissioned by Lady Brunner in 1980 and designed by Mr Adrian Fisher. Basically dictated by Christian symbolism, it represents the 'Chemin de Jerusalem', the pilgrim's path to the Holy Land, and his ultimate salvation. The maze is a puzzle with choices at the cruciform junctions. The entire maze can be walked once and once only, by crossing over each of the diamond-shaped thorns, and this path becomes the Path of Life or an allegory of the pilgrimage through life and death to the beginning of Eternal Life, then judgement and finally Salvation when all is reconciled. Although the maze is only 25 m (85 ft) across, the total length of path is exactly a quarter of a mile. The seven rings of paths represent the seven days of creation; the diameter of the centre is nine times the span between each part, and represents the ninth hour of agony; the two arms of the Byzantine cross from finial to finial total 33 feet, the age of Christ at his death. The overall design represents the Crown of Thorns.

A shallow track or pathway is set in the grass turf. Three bricks on edge make the pathway 13 inches wide; 4,500 bricks are used to complete the 350-yard stretch. The pathway starts across a bridge in the orchard and leads a traveller into the maze of seven rings to the east, and ultimately to a central sundial. The sundial consists of a wrought-iron globe on a stone pillar. Brass strips set into the stone represent the continents of the world. A golden shaft represents the Light of the World, and protrudes out of the globe. A series of numerals runs round the globe, indicating the hour as the shadow of the golden shaft reaches them. The pillar itself has four faces, each containing an inscription carved in slate set into the pillar. The pillar stands at the intersection of two superimposed crosses; one, a plain Roman cross of native hardwood, lies within the second more elaborate Byzantine cross, which is of coloured marbles and stones.

Although grass-cutting is simple as a rotary mower slides smoothly over the 13-inch path, edging neatly is a problem. The curve of the sunken

Greys Court

The little Cromwellian Garden lies between three high walls, with a laburnum hedge at the south end. Inside a geometric frame of box hedging, basically shaped by two rectangles enclosing a circle, brick paths meet at a central point. Standard bushes of box stand as verticals on the four corners of the inner box rectangle. Spring and autumn bulbs push up between variegated London pride, silver-leaved anaphalis and grey-foliaged grass.

Because of its situation the garden receives very little sun in the winter; in summer, with the sun high in the sky, the garden is scorched. Plants such as the auriculas find these conditions difficult, but many of the small bulbs thrive. Although the area is small the garden is comparatively labour-intensive as, in spite of the plants being tightly packed in the beds, hand-weeding is necessary. Plants also tend to droop over the box edging and have to be 'tidied' back to prevent the low hedges being damaged.

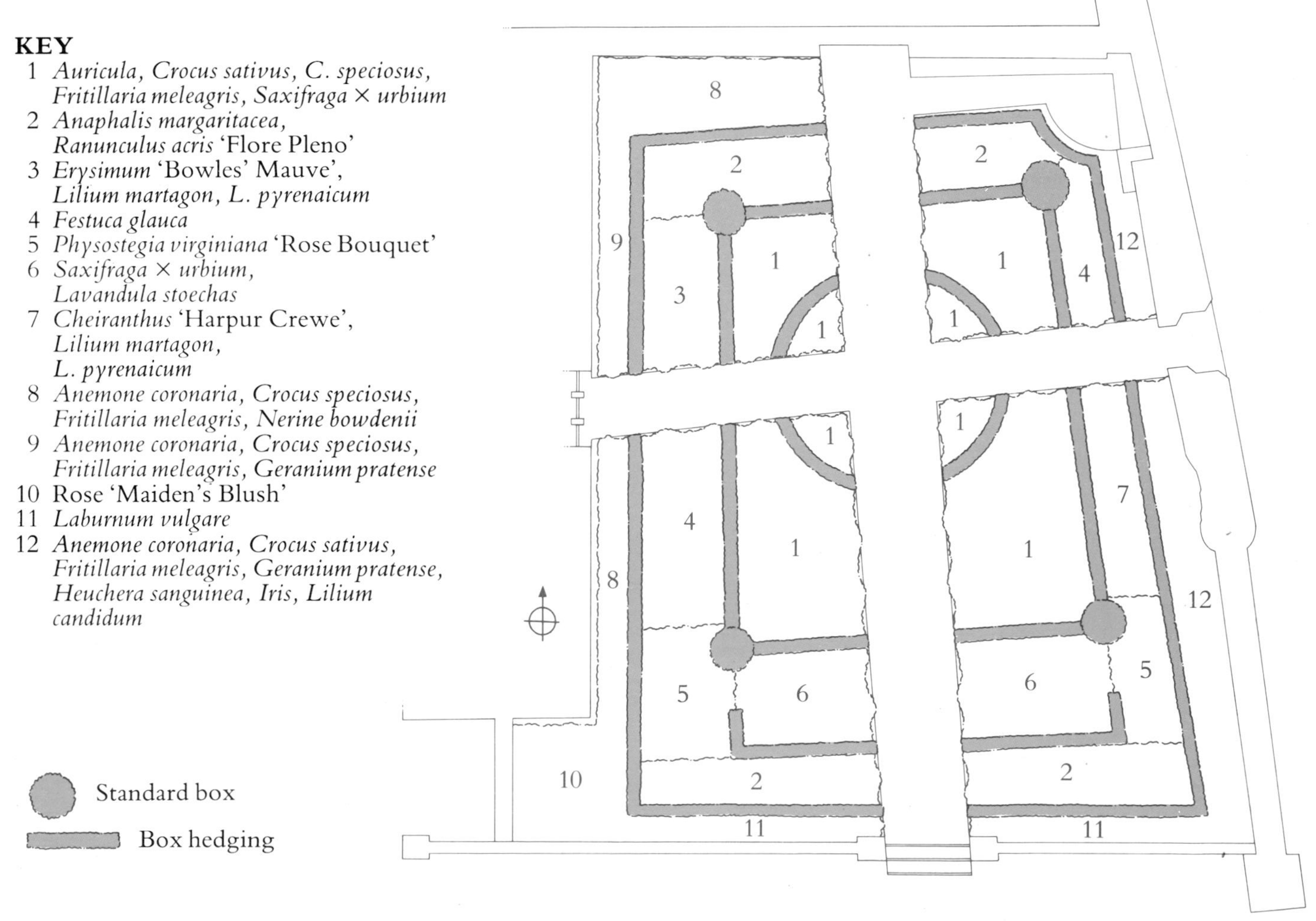

pathway or channel is too tight for a conventional edging machine. Instead, a Wolflawn Flite edger, basically a knife on a stick with wheel blade, is used, but the process takes eight hours a week. The bricks were set in soft pointing, eight buckets of sand to half of cement, which was brushed between the bricks and then wetted. As a result weeds can get a foothold and, again because of the narrowness of the gully, maintenance is time-consuming. Mr Ray Oliver, the Gardener-in-Charge at Greys Court, uses a weed wiper, a long tube with a wick impregnated with a contact herbicide.

Mazes in the Middle Ages derived from ritual or religious ideals, but by the fifteenth century, they lost their more philosophical significance and came to be used as ornamental features in Italian and French gardens. A book published in Venice in 1499 *Hypnerotomachia Poliphili* (The Strife of Love in a Dream) probably by the monk Francesco Colonna, influenced the development of Renaissance garden design. It included sections of fantasy on different garden themes. Ideas from Christian tradition and

Above: The laurel maze on the steep slope at Glendurgan has no logical pattern or philosophical meaning, but introduces formality into a woodland garden.

Opposite: At Moseley Old Hall (top) the garden is seventeenth-century in style. The knot garden in box and coloured gravels has been copied from a design of 1640. Bottom: A twentieth-century knot at Mottisfont Abbey was designed by Mrs Norah Lindsay. Beds edged with box and dwarf lavender are filled with colourful annuals.

pagan myths were united to describe intricate knots, labyrinths in water, forests and 'flowery medes', fine wooden arbours twined with jasmine, ruins and strange sculptures, all illustrated with precise woodcuts. After its publication, no European Renaissance garden could be without a maze or some other of the features described. As in the 'Dream', the garden labyrinth and flower bed was linked with astrology. The square represented earth and all its elements; the circle became a symbol of heaven, and each herb had to have a 'correct' position in its new environment, sometimes worked out with mathematical finesse. The labyrinth with its richness of magical and Christian meaning became the basis for designs for intricate garden beds, divided into precise geometric patterns. These early mazes were cut low, with no obvious intention to confuse; like the knot, they were meant to be viewed from above. The taste for these garden features, later developing into French *broderie* and *parterres*, remained a fundamental part of garden design through the sixteenth and seventeenth centuries.

It was not until the end of the seventeenth century that the head-high maze was introduced, as at HAMPTON COURT in 1690, with the deliberate idea of amusement through confusion. At Hampton Court the maze, made in yew, is trapezoid in shape, and measures some 66 × 25 m (222 × 82 ft). A rectangular beech maze at TATTON PARK measuring 34 × 18 m (114 × 60 ft) was planted in 1890. It lies almost at the centre of the pleasure gardens, and its presence is hidden by trees and shrubs. Although almost a copy of the maze at Hampton Court, the surroundings are thus quite different. The seventeenth-century original that inspired the Tatton maze would itself have been surrounded and framed by a rectangular compartment as part of a formal garden layout.

At GLENDURGAN in Cornwall the Trust maintain a maze with an unusual design. The hedges are of cherry laurel (*Prunus laurocerasus*) and stand at waist height. First planted in 1833 by Alfred Fox, whose descendants still live at Glendurgan, there is no evidence of the inspiration behind its conception, execution or meaning. In his journal for 5th October 1833 Mr Fox wrote, 'Began the preparation for a labyrinth at Glendurgan.' On 1st November: 'I rose at 5 a.m. and went on the water till breakfast. The men still busy with the labyrinth.' On 1st December: 'Nearly all the laurels planted to form our new labyrinth,' and on the 20th of the month he 'examined the apple and pear trees planted near the labyrinth.'

The maze lies on a steep slope leading down to the valley of the River Helford below. Strange in its asymmetrical shape, it seems almost as exotic as the rare magnolias, tree ferns and American agaves, much later additions, which today thrive in this almost frost-free garden. By 1979 the laurel had become weak and bare at the base and was infested with sycamore, brambles and other woody weeds. It was pruned back hard and fed liberally and the brushwood was cut out and painted with Roundup. At the same time the land-drains which had become blocked over the years were cleared.

Little Moreton Hall

The Trust based its design for a knot garden to frame the sixteenth-century house on a pattern found in Leonard Meager's *The Complete English Gardener* (1670). Areas of grass and of gravel are outlined by hedges of box (*Buxus sempervirens*), kept clipped low. Four clipped yew obelisks placed symmetrically provide a vertical accent to the pattern, and the area is enclosed by yew hedges. The beds on the periphery of the knot feature traditional herbs and a mixed planting which sustains the garden's period atmosphere.

A A
C C
B
B
C C
PATH

KEY

Yew obelisks

Box edging

Yew hedges

Gravel

Grass

A Mixed planting
B Ground cover on banks
C Herbs

Because they are precise, existing plans for elaborate flower beds, published in sixteenth- and seventeenth-century books, are relatively easy to follow. In some Trust gardens where a complete reconstruction is necessary, knot gardens have been made typical of the style of the period of the house. At MOSELEY OLD HALL a simple knot in box has been laid out. Taken from a 1640 garden plan found in a manuscript at Magdalen College, Oxford, the box pattern is emphasized by different coloured gravels and large pebbles, and the whole area is surrounded by a boxwood hedge. A layer of plastic under the gravel and close to the base of the box reduces maintenance to an annual clipping and periodic raking.

At HAM HOUSE a reconstruction of the garden as it was *circa* 1670 has been carried out. To the east of the house a vast pattern of box-edged beds is divided by diagonals and filled with a mass of trimmed silvery *Santolina chamaecyparissus* all clipped to one even height. Box pyramids accentuate the corners. Maintenance consists of annual tight clipping.

On a more intimate scale, at MOTTISFONT ABBEY a small knot garden where box and dwarf lavender intertwine was designed by Mrs Norah Lindsay at the turn of the century. This is on a scale suitable for a small modern garden. Incidentally, at both LITTLE MORETON HALL and FENTON HOUSE, lavender has been trained to make standards in reconstructions of seventeenth-century formal garden patterns, an ideal space-saving technique.

In the small west formal garden at BENINGBROUGH, a disarmingly simple modern knot pattern has been laid out by the Trust. A surrounding low box hedge makes a square which encloses another square at an angle across the corners. In the centre lilies grow through golden origanum, and the remaining triangles are planted with orange-brown tagetes and slate-blue violas, making solid blocks of colour.

Opposite: The knot garden at Little Moreton Hall is based on a seventeenth-century design appropriate to the period of the house. Grass and gravel patterns are edged with box. The garden is shown under construction in 1972.

Parterres

Of French origin, the *parterre de broderie* is an extension of earlier knot patterns and labyrinthine flower beds which were generally enclosed by walls and hedges. Traditionally they are an invention of the royal gardener Claude Mollet, working in the sixteenth century for the Italian Queen of France, Catherine de Medici. In the parterre, usually on a level area (often the terrace near a house), plants and possibly ornaments are arranged in a perfectly symmetrical way, more carefully balanced than in knots, on a larger scale and often as foreground to limitless formal vistas. In the French *broderie*, edging plants and continuous ribbons became scrolls and arabesques, often arranged on a bed of gravel, everything on a grander scale, and much less intimate than the knot or simple parterre pattern with fewer different types of plant and less emphasis on flowers. The dwarf box (*Buxus sempervirens* 'Suffruticosa') developed in Holland towards the end of the sixteenth century, was the perfect plant for these displays, which became ever more magnificent, with baroque arabesques and curves instead of geometric squares and circles. *Broderie* patterns in flower beds taken from textile designs and architectural motifs united a whole area in quite a different way from the separate knots. Often, like knots, designed to be looked at from above, these schemes were particularly suitable for the grand scale of French gardens, where in a flat landscape, the château dominated its site.

First in Holland in smaller gardens and then in England, designs were adapted to the terrain. At WESTBURY COURT in the flat fields of the Severn valley a so-called Dutch garden with water-canals has been reconstructed by the National Trust. Simple parterres, using plants available in 1700, are arranged in grass, which is cut at different levels to give the effects of further beds. On either side groups of small trees and clipped evergreen shrubs are arranged in a quincunx pattern, like fives on dice. At Westbury *Phillyrea angustifolia*, clipped into a rounded dome, is the centre bush; it is surrounded by Portugal laurel (*Prunus lusitanica*). Near by a simple box parterre in the Dutch style has low box (*Buxus sempervirens* 'Suffruticosa') hedges which define flower beds where marigolds (*Calendula officinalis*) mixed with *Echium plantagineum* and purple beetroot, *Iberis sempervirens* with purple-leaved sage (*Salvia officinalis* 'Purpurascens') and golden variegated sage (*S.o.* 'Icterina') grow in a sea of

grey-leaved grass (*Festuca glauca*). In the centre of each bed finials and balls of clipped box give height. This is a very simple pattern, known as a 'cut parterre'; somewhere between a knot and the much more elaborate sort of garden 'embroidery' which was practised in France.

At OXBURGH HALL the Trust has restored the intricate French *broderie*, based on a pattern from a French garden book, first published in England in 1712, but in fact not executed at Oxburgh until 1845. Designed to be seen from a raised terrace walk or from the house, it was described as a *parterre de compartiment*. Today the box edges are renewed and the *compartiments* filled with a permanent planting of santolina and blue-foliaged rue (*Ruta graveolens* 'Jackman's Blue'). Summer bedding plants include ageratums, French marigolds and, in the centre bed, 'Paul Crampel' pelargoniums amidst grey foliage. The gravel is kept weed-free with a simazine-based chemical applied once annually. The box is given a slow-acting fertilizer at the end of the winter and is cut in the summer; santolina and rue are cut after the last frost, in May. Annual cuttings of both the latter plants are held in reserve, in case of a severe winter.

At ASHDOWN HOUSE, where the Trust took over a Restoration house but no garden, a box and gravel parterre adapted by Mr A. H. Brookholding Jones from a seventeenth-century pattern book was laid out in 1955. Viewed from the windows of the house, the simple scrolls of box and plain dark gravel are the foreground to lime avenues which stretch across the landscape in French style. When it is established in a weed-free site so that the gravel is easily groomed, this sort of simple parterre involves little maintenance, and patterns are easily adapted to suit a smaller space.

In England many early parterres were swept away during the eighteenth century, when surrounding parkland came right to the windows of a house, regardless of whether it was of an earlier period. The National Trust sometimes reconstructs a garden appropriate to a house's architecture when no original records exist.

In Victorian England the bedding system was introduced. In a way this was a new type of parterre design, exploiting the availability of many new tender or half-hardy plants, the extension of greenhouse use and the growth of technical gardening knowledge. Above all, bedding out depended on the cheapness of labour. These bedding displays, often more a meretricious and competitive means of ostentatiously demonstrating new wealth than based on any aesthetic composition, might even be rated by the numbers of plants annually raised according to social rank. About 10,000 plants might be adequate for a country squire, but an earl or duke

Opposite: Beside the great water canals at Westbury Court a simple pattern of box edging encloses flower beds which are given height with clipped box topiary. Flowers in the beds are restricted to those known in English gardens before 1700.

At Oxburgh Hall (left) and at Ashdown House (below) patterns of box in curving shapes are derived from French parterres of the late seventeenth-century. At Ashdown box is set in gravel; at Oxburgh scrolls contain flower beds where colourful annuals are changed twice yearly.

should deploy 30,000 or even 50,000. It became a virtue in plants to be tender. In the grandest gardens, after a storm, a band of gardeners would have replaced all damaged plants by breakfast time the next day, adequate replacements being kept healthy in the glasshouse. As well as these massed displays of colour, inspiration came from the Italian Renaissance garden. So-called 'Italianate' parterres in box and coloured gravels became once more the fashion, and were placed on broad terraces. Sometimes a family's coat of arms formed the basis of a pattern; at others, scrolls and feather designs aped those of the seventeenth century. More often the new tender bedding plants replaced coloured gravels between the box.

By the mid-twentieth century these schemes had vanished from most private gardens, as fuel and labour costs made propagation on such vast scales impossible. Municipal parks still continue the tradition, massing spring bulbs such as tulips and hyacinths; anemones and tuberous-rooted ranunculus extend the display. Fortunately the Trust is now the custodian of several Victorian gardens, and by using new labour-saving techniques, manages to implement many old schemes, sometimes achieving exact replicas. At WADDESDON MANOR, golden yew hedges frame beds where a fountain of Pluto and Proserpine is surrounded by parterres laid out for Baron Ferdinand de Rothschild by the French landscape designer, Lainé. Plants in the beds were changed at least twice a year. Today 5,000 tulips and 4,000 wallflower plants are put in each autumn for spring colour; 3,500 pot-grown zonal pelargoniums and the same number of ageratums, sown under glass in spring, make an impressive summer display. Few private gardeners can attempt this sort of deliberate historical reconstruction. Nevertheless, in many modern gardens, bulbs, hardy and half-hardy annuals and tender bedding plants have become part of the seasonal planting pattern. In fact more bedding-out plants are sold each year than any other type of plant material, yet a coherent planting scheme is often lacking. Much of the planting, whether of bulbs or other plants, is in mixed colours, provided by nurserymen without discrimination. (Today it is getting difficult to obtain seed of many of the best annuals and biennials except in mixed colour packets, but as nurserymen and seed nurseries exist to satisfy demand it would seem possible to influence what they provide.) Narrow ribbons of wallflowers edge rose beds, followed later by trailing lobelias making a characterless and insipid colour scheme. From Waddesdon the aesthetic value of massing one or two colours together in solid-seeming blocks can be learnt. Because of its size, few garden owners can attempt a similar scheme; however, by keeping the relative planting proportions but working on a much reduced scale, it is possible to capture some of its spirit. Growing both annuals and tender bedding plants well needs dedication and most poor results are due to inadequate conditions: the right temperature, the correct compost, potting on at the desirable moment, are all things easier to provide and do on a large scale where one man gives the task his full attention. It is much more difficult to succeed when greenhouse space has to be shared with plants requiring different culture.

At ANGLESEY ABBEY, another grand-scale bedding-out area laid out as recently as the 1930s is a source of inspiration. Four thousand blue and white hyacinth bulbs scent the enclosed Hyacinth Garden in spring. As foliage dies down, orange and deep scarlet dahlias are planted in their place, the whole area enclosed now with a yew hedge: formerly the hedging plant was a form of thuja. Another garden where bedding on a large scale is practised is the newly restored KINGSTON LACY. Here the Edwardian scheme for a parterre in 'red, white and blue' seen in 1986, composed of pink begonias and blue heliotrope with an edging of snow-in-summer (*Cerastium tomentosum*) is a deliberate return to a scheme used by the Bankes family in the 1930s.

Many other ideas are offered by Trust parterres. At GAWTHORPE HALL, a modern scheme has been designed with a Victorian flavour. Because there is only one gardener, it is out of the question to consider planting these large Victorian beds with bedding plants as was originally intended. Now golden privet (*Ligustrum ovalifolium* 'Aureum') is edged with dwarf purple berberis (*Berberis thunbergii* 'Atropurpurea Nana').

Opposite: At Anglesey Abbey the Hyacinth Garden, blue and white with scented hyacinths in spring, becomes flamboyant with red and orange dahlias in summer.

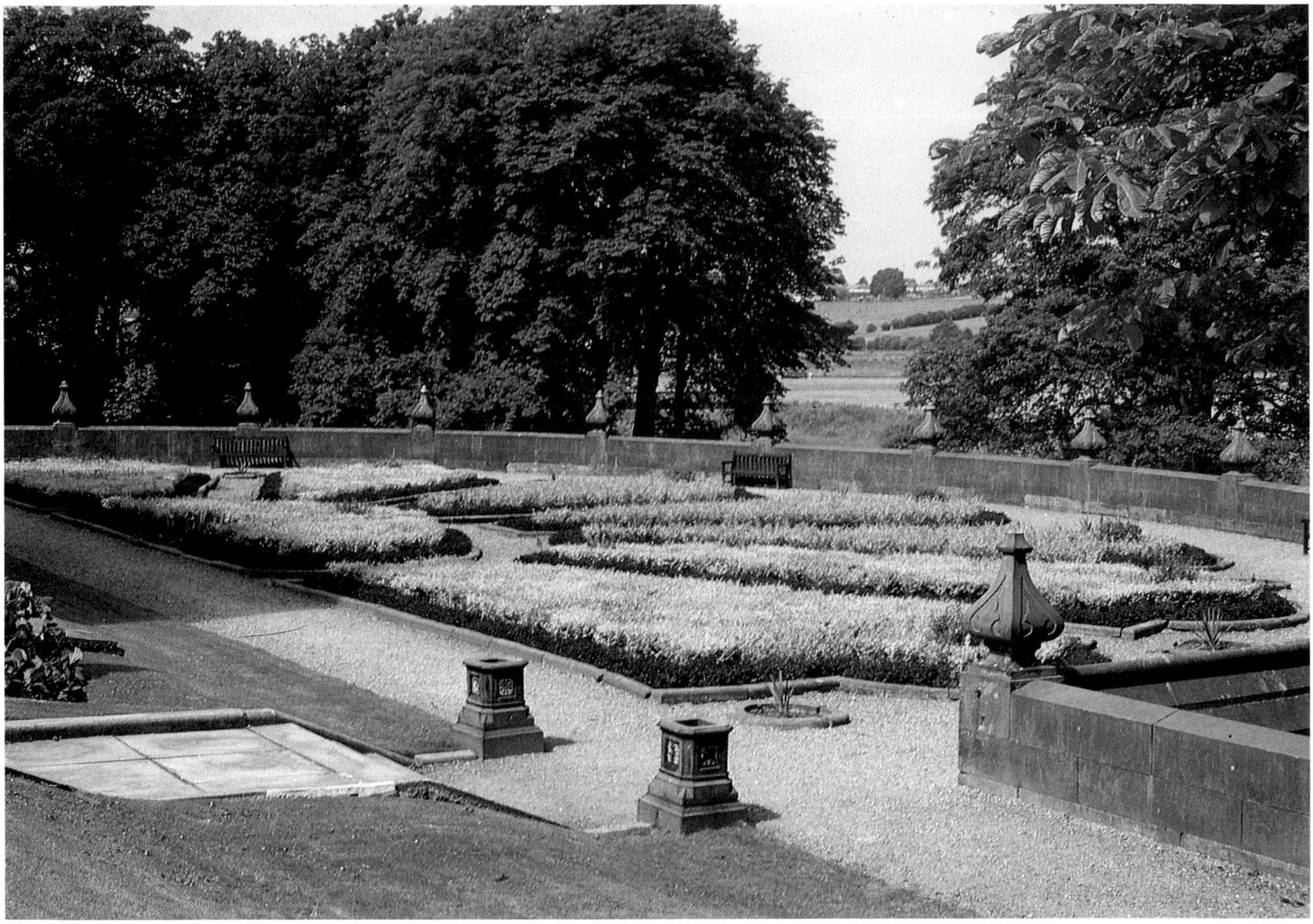

Gawthorpe Hall

At Gawthorpe Hall a modern parterre with a strong Victorian flavour has been laid out behind the house. Plants of golden privet are massed in seven wedge-shaped beds radiating from a central hemispherical bed. All the beds are outlined with purple dwarf berberis. Pampas grass (*Cortaderia selloana* 'Pumila') and grey leaved *Senecio* 'Sunshine' were included in the original planting, but neither did well, and green privet has taken the place of the pampas grass. The stylish *Yucca gloriosa* is still used as a 'dot plant'.

Opposite: A modern parterre at Gawthorpe Hall has an edging of dwarf purple-leaved berberis which surrounds wedge-shaped beds of golden privet.

At ERDDIG, a formal parterre surrounds a moss-covered Victorian fountain in front of the house. Planting is simple and easily copied in smaller garden areas. Some beds are planted twice yearly in the traditional way, while to save work others are laid out with silvery cotton lavender (*Santolina chamaecyparissus*) and the slow-growing *Ophiopogon planiscapus nigrescens*, a small grassy plant with almost black leaves. Domes of box mark the corners and give height.

On the north side of the Elizabethan house of LANHYDROCK, a Victorian-style parterre was laid out in 1935 to commemorate the jubilee celebrations of George V. Originally gravel pathways separated the intricately designed beds all edged with dwarf box (*Buxus sempervirens* 'Suffruticosa'), but now mown grass is more restful and links the area with surrounding smooth lawns. The formal gardens today are enclosed with battlemented walls, an addition made in the 1850s when George Gilbert Scott altered and enlarged the house for Lord Clifden. Originally high walls connected to the superb gatehouse contained garden courtyards typical of sixteenth- and seventeenth-century style, but in the eighteenth century all was swept away and parkland reached up to the walls of the house, until the Victorian alterations once more reinstated a more formal setting.

Round the parterre beds a higher 90 cm (3 ft) box hedge of the species, *Buxus sempervirens*, is carefully cut to slope inwards to a 38 cm (15 in) top. During war years the hedge was allowed to grow with vertical sides, preventing light from reaching the base, which became bare and woody. The Head Gardener, Mr Peter Borlase, emphasizes that it took nineteen years to restore the hedge to health and vigour. Now clipping is necessary only once a year; an annual dose of a compound chemical fertilizer promotes growth.

In the beds plants are changed twice during the year. In November the summer bedding is cleared away and the soil dug and manured in preparation for spring bedding plants. The soil is acid (pH 4.5) and the very high rainfall of 130 cm (52 in) washes away nutrients, so there are no short cuts to a careful annual routine of double digging incorporating humus-making material. In the smaller beds trenching is impossible, so the top layer of soil is first placed in a wheelbarrow while the compost is spread; a plastic sheet laid on grass is equally effective and tidy, but the narrow grass paths here do not allow of this solution. Compost at Lanhydrock is made from a mixture of fallen leaves from the woodland garden area, lawn mowings and farmyard manure. Stored in bulky heaps, the compost is turned in winter months when pressure of work allows. Mr Borlase changes plants and colour schemes almost annually. In the winter/spring scheme for 1985 dark blue and pink hyacinths ('King of the Blues' and 'Queen of the Pinks') were planted in the eight round beds, which resemble Victorian basketwork in shape; each bed of a single colour making for the best effects. Darwin and scented lily-flowered tulips interplanted with pansies complete the planting, the colours covering a range of white, ivory, pink, scarlet and yellow, but each bed with a separate single colour scheme. In other years Siberian wallflowers and polyanthus have been used instead of pansies. From 1933 to 1966 all the beds were planted with a carpet of forget-me-nots through which pink, yellow and red tulips grew in very traditional style, but repetition of this kind leads to disease. Mr Borlase still uses this simple spring planting in another bed on a higher terrace. Forget-me-nots are grown from F_1 hybrid seed to ensure perfectly consistent and even colour throughout.

At the end of May the beds are cleared and replanted. In 1984 fibrous-rooted begonias, petunias and F_1 impatiens grown from spring-sown seed were used. In the summer of 1985 begonias, blue ageratum, antirrhinum, marigolds, bright red verbena and heliotrope made a change. Again, no colours are mixed in any bed, but actual colour schemes will change from year to year. Plants quickly grow together and except for regular dead-heading need little summer maintenance. The parterre remains full of flower until the end of the season.

As in a private garden, the National Trust will try out different schemes and colour combinations, and will only repeat a planting pattern without some variation if there is a strong historical reason. Some gardens such as WADDESDON, ANGLESEY ABBEY and KINGSTON LACY will have a definite colour scheme for each time of year, but often it is appropriate to use different plants to give variety from year to year.

Although LANHYDROCK has a mild climate, these bedding schemes are suitable for any area, although in the colder northerly regions flowering times will be later, and the danger of late frosts prevents planting out summer bedding until the beginning of June. Gardeners are often strongly tempted to plant out tender spring-sown annuals or other tender plants much too soon, and today some garden centres offer boxes of plants in early May. Unfortunately, cold nights, even without actual frost, so damage plants at this stage that they seldom make an adequate recovery, and it is advisable to wait the extra few weeks necessary, allowing the soil to warm up as well as letting all danger of frost pass. Of course, in the microclimates of larger cities it is possible to plant earlier. Every gardener learns to know his own situation, and can discover small pockets in the garden which remain virtually frost-free.

The most effective planting is often simple. Often colour is badly used, usually because too many different colours are dotted about. In a private garden (if overall space permits) it is easier to set aside areas for seasonal colour; parts of the garden hardly visited during 'out of season' periods. In Trust gardens open to visitors for many months, each area must look its best for as long as possible. As in any planting schemes bedding out must be carefully thought out and prepared for months ahead. Sometimes perennials rather than bedding annuals form the basis of parterres. In the white garden at SISSINGHURST, some of the beds are rectangular and edged with low box. In spring white lily-flowered tulip 'White Triumphator' pushes through a low-growing evergreen carpet of *Lamium maculatum album*. There are many variations of such a scheme,

At Lanhydrock the Victorian style parterre was laid out in 1935. Planting inside the box-edged beds is changed twice a year but different colour schemes are used annually.

Lanhydrock

The main parterre on the wide terrace to the north of the house is an intricate pattern set in grass and surrounded by box hedging. A smaller series of beds lies on a second narrower terrace above. Spring and summer bedding is planted. The choice of plants and colours may change almost annually, but each bed is a block of single colour planting.

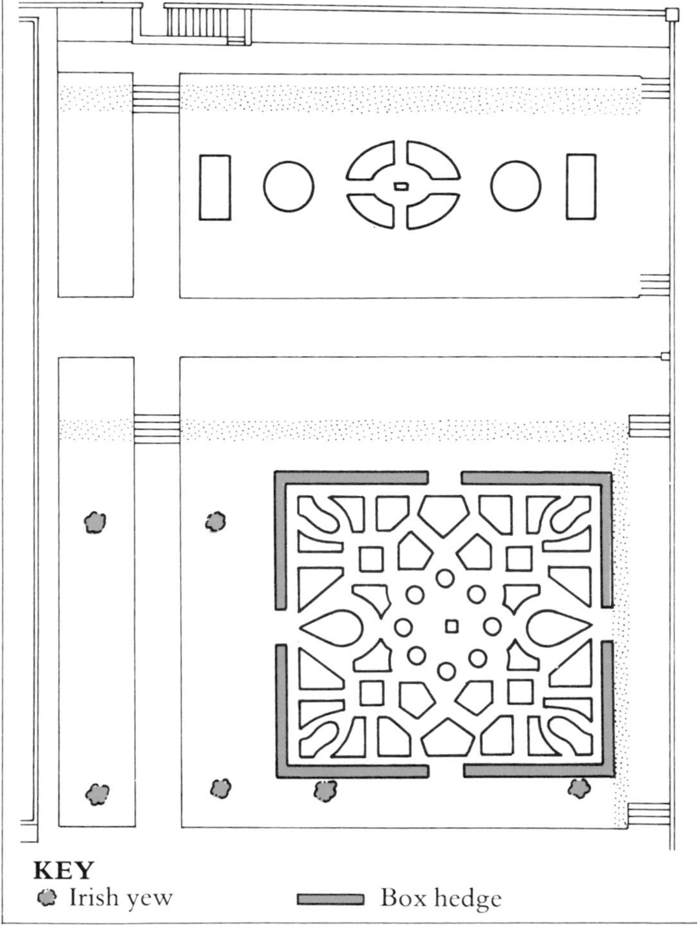

combining spring bulbs with later-flowering perennials, which quickly hide the dying foliage once flowering is over.

At KNIGHTSHAYES COURT the formal terrace planting is dependent for its success on the use of pale grey and silvery foliage. Pink and mauve flowering plants mix and blend through the carpet of grey. This is not strictly a parterre, as most of the plants stay in the ground as permanent features; the beds are covered and protected in winter by raised glass frames, more useful in preventing the plants getting too wet at the roots than necessary against frost. This careful treatment ensures the attractive appearance of the silvery-leaved plants even in spring when most such foliage looks the worse for wear.

This sort of 'formal' planting is useful to contrast with the deliberately cottage-type relaxed planting of many of the enclosures at both SISSINGHURST and HIDCOTE. In many beds planting is deliberately dense and weed-suppressing, plants growing into and over each other. At Hidcote, box-edged beds are bright with blue scilla in spring, and hardy fuchsias give summer colour. The fuchsia garden at Hidcote is an area enclosed by a 3 m (10 ft) mixed hedge of beech, yew and holly in which two symmetrical parterres face each other. Box-edged beds contain a carpet of spring-flowering *Scilla sibirica* 'Spring Beauty' planted tightly between bushes of hardy fuchsias. In March the scilla leaves emerge, followed quickly by three or more stems up to 15 cm (6 in) on which the bright blue flowers are borne. Dying foliage suppresses emergent weed seedlings, but a moisture-retaining mulch is sometimes given towards the end of early summer. The circular middle bed in each section is planted with 70 bushes of *Fuchsia magellanica* 'Variegata', with drooping flower-heads of red and purple and a mass of pale cream-margined leaves on arching 1.2 m (4 ft) branches. In each of the four front beds nearest the central brick path, 50 *Fuchsia* 'Tom Thumb', with cherry-red sepals surrounding mauve petals, make compact bushes, with a height and spread of 30 cm (12 in), hardly rising above the surrounding box hedge. In the beds behind, the taller *F.* 'Lady Thumb' with darker flowers is equally reliable.

These hardy fuchsias, flowering from July until October, are sub-shrubs, whose woody stems die to the ground each winter, new shoots coming from the base in early summer. They need little attention except for annual removal of dead wood (usually not done until the spring, since the woody stems protect the crowns in a severe winter). Although pot-grown fuchsias need regular feeding, these open-ground bushes will continue to flower for many seasons with little attention. They make ideal plants for permanent bedding, with the early-flowering scillas to give massed colour in spring.

Above: The fuchsia parterres at Hidcote are underplanted with spring-flowering scillas.

Ornamental Features

The focal point in a garden picture is often something man-made: a statue, an urn, a seat – or a container of plants. Ornaments and container planting have certain properties in common as design features: their appropriateness for their surroundings in terms of style, scale, colour and material, and their positioning at an axial point or against a backdrop where these qualities can be fully appreciated. Ornaments at focal points can be emphasized by architectural perspective. They can be framed by a doorway or flanked by a pair of objects. They can be set into stark relief against a contrasting plain background, perhaps a dark hedge. Equally, but with a subtler effect of contrast, the hardness of a stone urn or wooden seat can be softened by the presence of surrounding loose-textured leaves.

Strategic positioning means that an ornamental feature looks not only right but indispensable to the garden. These criteria can apply equally to a simple terracotta pot of tulips and to a classical stone statue. Either, in its place, should look essential: there is no such thing in good garden design as 'mere' ornament.

Ornaments in National Trust Gardens

Mr Michael Calnan, one of the Gardens Advisers to the National Trust, contributes an appraisal of the objects to be enjoyed in some of the many gardens:

❧ The National Trust's collection of gardens represents almost every period of British gardening history from the seventeenth century onwards, and includes perhaps the greatest collection of garden ornaments ever held in single private ownership. These range from statues, urns, fountains and furniture to temples and triumphal arches – objects other than plants placed deliberately to enhance garden design. They represent the changing fashions, tastes and influences of owners past and present.

The majority of ornaments in Trust gardens are works commissioned or purchased at the time when the garden was made, although mass-produced pieces of high quality are not uncommon. In a few instances modern sculptures and furniture represent the taste of the most recent owners, as at SCOTNEY CASTLE and DUDMASTON.

Throughout the history of gardening and in particular since the eighteenth century, carved stone has accounted for the largest number of garden ornaments to be seen in Trust gardens. No stone weathers better than quarried Portland stone, which takes on delicate shades of green and grey with age and exposure to the elements. Perhaps the finest stone urns are to be seen at WIMPOLE HALL and CLIVEDEN. Stone seats of the nineteenth and twentieth centuries are regular features of formal gardens. Like any stone seat, these tend to be uncomfortable as outdoor furniture, only being endurable on the warmest of days. A good example can be seen at GAWTHORPE HALL.

By the early nineteenth century a substitute for stone manufactured by the firm of Coade and Seely became popular. The composition remains unknown but its weather-resistance was better than that of natural stone. The designs were mostly admirable; a pair of obelisks and six caryatids at ANGLESEY ABBEY are dated 1792. A 'Coade stone' urn can be seen at ARDRESS HOUSE in Northern Ireland. There are also two fine large urns of this material at KILLERTON.

Today a good range of reproduction ornaments and seats is available, though care should be taken in selecting those that weather well and have not lost any of the fine details of the originals in the process of being cast or carved. Some of the better pieces are those created from reconstituted limestone with a surface texture resembling quarried Portland stone.

Of all the quarried stones used for garden ornaments and statuary, marble has never quite looked at home under our often overcast skies; only under the clear blue skies of its native Europe does it look its best. Furthermore, in our atmosphere pollution dissolves its surface, turning the milky sheen of polished marble to a granulated or pitted surface. Nevertheless the cost of marble statuary today is perhaps the major limiting factor on its popularity. There are still many fine examples in Trust gardens. Mozzani's group of Pluto and Proserpine make a central fountain for the south terrace at WADDESDON MANOR. At CLIVEDEN a huge marble fountain sculpture by Ralph Waldo Story depicts the Fountain of Love and marks the turning point in the main drive. Marble was equally popular for seating, especially in the seventeenth

Above: At Knightshayes Court, eighteenth-century ornaments decorate the raised terrace. The lead cistern is planted with silvery-leaved trailing plants in summer.

Left: At Ascott bedding-out is elaborate to match the formality of the scalloped pool, Italian fountain and massive hedges of golden yew.

Top: A basket-weave terracotta pot sits on the stone balustrading at Powis Castle.

Above: A fine urn on a plinth is framed by pink brick. The terraces at Powis are enriched with fine statuary and ornamental containers.

Opposite: Stone statues flank a view down the Long Garden at Cliveden. Statues and topiary are pure decoration but need careful siting.

and eighteenth centuries. Handsome benches at KNIGHTSHAYES COURT and TATTON PARK remind us of the delicate detailing that it can achieve. The supply of marble features today is almost exclusively limited to originals, which tend to achieve high prices when put on the market.

Terracotta has been used for garden pots from the sixteenth century. Popular external decorative detailing includes the basket weave of which there are good examples at POWIS CASTLE. Green and brown glazed pots are at OVERBECKS, appropriate to semi-tropical planting, while traditional pots from the South of France are at ARLINGTON COURT and an extremely handsome early-twentieth-century pair is at WALLINGTON HALL. Only pots which have been well fired can be considered safe for exposure to our climate. Some pots imported from abroad, although of high quality, are not always frost-proof and should be treated with caution if to remain outdoors in winter.

Throughout the history of gardening, bronze has been one of the most widely used materials. The natural deep rich brown patina of this alloy turns to a powdery green on exposure to the elements, a modern phenomenon resulting from atmospheric pollution. A fine nineteenth-century bronze Worshipper and Faun can be seen at HUGHENDEN MANOR, and a pair of twentieth-century bronze nymphs at CHIRK CASTLE.

A modern group in pure bronze by Henry Moore adorns an island in the lake at SCOTNEY CASTLE. Today artificial bronze ornaments can be manufactured from powder mixed with a resin cured in moulds to produce delicately detailed sculptures. Such a process has been used with success at STUDLEY ROYAL in making a copy of a Roman bust of Nero.

Increasing demand for statuary in the seventeenth and early eighteenth centuries gave rise to the use of moulded lead, which being easily worked, was capable of reproducing fine details. Unfortunately many of these works have been lost owing to the collapse of supporting internal iron frameworks. These internal frames are generally replaced nowadays by costly stainless steel structures. Lead figures by John Cheere *circa* 1718 of a Shepherd and Shepherdess can be seen at CHARLECOTE PARK.

Lead figures were often painted white to look like marble or stone, or perhaps in naturalistic colours. Conservators nowadays advise the painting of lead figures to ensure the total sealing of

the entire surface against water penetration. A fine group of lead sculptures on the terraces at POWIS have recently been repainted white, as they were originally. A charming group adorns the walls of the old kitchen garden at WALLINGTON.

Original lead ornaments are hard to come by nowadays, though a number of nineteenth-century reproductions can still be found in auction catalogues and at specialist garden ornament dealers. Few firms manufacture lead ornaments today, though it is possible to acquire good-quality reproductions in addition to modern works, which may be more suited to the private garden.

From about 1760 wrought iron was often used for making garden furniture and during the Regency period many graceful seats were produced. Today mild steel is often used as a substitute, although it cannot match the fineness of detail of originals.

Cast iron was increasingly used in the nineteenth century, especially in the mass production of garden furniture, often embodying popular motifs such as ferns, ivy, oak and vine leaves and Gothic or rustic themes. Florid cast iron seats are to be seen at ICKWORTH, CHARTWELL, CLIVEDEN and PLAS NEWYDD, while simpler designs are at KINGSTON LACY, THE ARGORY and ARLINGTON COURT. Cast iron has to be painted to protect the metal. Traditional colours would be various shades of green; black (MOUNT STEWART); blue/green (PACKWOOD); and chocolate. Often seats were painted to resemble a different material of construction (bronze for example). Today's reproductions tend to be manufactured in lighter aluminium alloys and painted white, ignoring this tradition.

Wood, which has always been widely available and is easily worked, was probably the earliest material used for garden ornaments. In Tudor gardens and earlier, wood was used for statuary, fences, *treillage* and, of course, garden implements. Wood carvings tend to lose their finer details with exposure to weathering. For this reason it is as furniture that wood has chiefly been used in gardens for many centuries.

Seats and benches have usually been constructed from a lasting hardwood such as oak, elm and iroko; cedar, although softer, is also popular. Rustic seats of the eighteenth and nineteenth centuries were often fashioned in yew, pear, larch and apple. Designs in outdoor furniture, particularly in this period, often followed from indoor counterparts, generally drawing inspiration from pattern books and abroad. Styles included Chinese, Gothic, classical and rustic. Good examples of these are to be seen at WESTBURY COURT, TATTON PARK, FARNBOROUGH HALL,

Top: An eighteenth century cistern at Barrington Court is framed by soft foliage shapes.

Above: A copper container is a foil to scarlet tulips at Sissinghurst.

WALLINGTON HALL, SALTRAM, CHARTWELL and HAM HOUSE. Traditional colours include 'eggshell' (matt) white, grey, blue and various shades of green.

Perhaps the best-known seat designs of the early twentieth century are those by Sir Edwin Lutyens. His seats were elegant and always solidly constructed. Reproductions can be seen at CLIVEDEN, painted white (as he often specified). Unpainted seats turn a pleasing silvery-grey with exposure to the elements, as can be seen at CHIRK CASTLE. On the circular croquet lawn at CASTLE DROGO a pair of Lutyens seats are painted a delicate green. Today Lutyens seats are still being made and the modern version can be seen at MONTACUTE HOUSE. At SNOWSHILL MANOR Charles Wade used a paint of a powdery blue with a hint of turquoise for all woodwork including seats, tubs, doorways and window frames; these are still to be seen, the paint renewed as necessary.

The quality of ornaments in Trust gardens, often contemporary with the house in style and material, is matched by their suitability of scale. Fine design, detailed workmanship, surface colour and texture all contribute to the unity of a garden layout which is set in a definite historical period. Ornaments become part of the architecture of a garden; if in scale and in the right position they are part of the framework and not additional features distributed haphazardly through the garden. The placing of these often exceptional works of art in the great Trust gardens may seem irrelevant to modern gardening. In fact in an age when mass produced ornament can be lacking in detail and harmonious finish it seems imperative for garden makers to take the opportunity to get their eye attuned to the 'best' in every period; thus developing a critical faculty which they can adapt when choosing something for their own. Unlike ornamental planting schemes which can be more or less copied or adapted on a lesser scale, exact replicas of these bronze, lead, stone and marble embellishments may be impossible. Nevertheless, appreciation of their design and judging how they are placed and contribute to an overall design, leads to a greater awareness of architectural detail and its use in gardens. A fine statue or ornament must compel a glance in passing, implying what Mr Hugh Johnson aptly calls the 'command to look'. Wood is much more easily copied and reproduced, and today garden seats frequently make focal points in place of statuary, their situation chosen either as an invitation to rest, or to stress an accent of design.

Seats become focal points in a garden as well as being invitations to rest. On the theatre lawn at Bodnant (top left) a painted seat is framed by a dark background of tightly clipped yew, while at Blickling (middle left) and Mottisfont (left) golden ivies and climbing roses respectively make a softer frame. At Hardwick Hall (top) a painted seat is silhouetted where hedges stretch to make a quiet walk. At Felbrigg (above) the scene is more functional, a movable wooden seat, forcing pots for rhubarb and protective glass cloches were all garden 'tools' before modern mechanization.

Container Planting

Much of what has been written in the last few pages relates equally to ornamental containers in which plants are grown – that is, as far as materials, scale, proportion and style are concerned. But two further elements affect the subject of container planting: as well as working well in their context, the plants and the container need to look good together. And finally, the dimension of time plays its part, as the containers perform their various seasonal roles with ephemeral or long-term displays of flowers and leaves.

Where it is traditional, the Trust continues a routine practised in the great Victorian and Edwardian gardens, when bedding-out plants and pots were planted twice a year, for summer and winter effects. Today most gardens are open to visitors for six summer months and sometimes more, so that planning and planting follows the same pattern. Plants for spring display are prepared and planted by the autumn. Those for the summer months are prepared during the early spring and placed in the containers or beds when conditions are right, often towards the end of May, and when most spring-flowering bulbs or biennials have finished flowering. The summer selection may well include more unusual and tender shrubs and perennials as well as annuals grown from seed that February.

In their heyday some of these grand gardens provided a display only for a very limited period, to coincide with the only time that the house was annually occupied, but preparations were intensive to ensure that enough 'reserve' plants were kept in readiness in case of unforeseen weather conditions At WADDESDON after a storm *all* the bedding plants would be replaced for visitors to admire the next morning. Some Trust gardens, however, stay open the whole year, and, like most private gardens today, were designed by resident owners who wished for and achieved an integrated garden, perhaps with separate definite areas of particular seasonal interest, but which basically 'performed' all through the year. In these gardens, although the emphasis may still be towards ensuring 'colour' in pots for April, pansies which perform well during 'open' winter weather may be combined with small winter-flowering crocus, iris (especially forms of *reticulata*), scillas and snowdrops.

Ornamental containers and ephemeral flowers can add interest, especially at times when parts of the garden tend to be dull. In a garden which is primarily planned for spring with permanent woodland planting of bulbs and flowering shrubs, pots filled with summer-flowering annuals, or permanent containers of later-flowering lilies or other bulbs will extend the season. Equally, a 'summer' garden can be given earlier interest with containers planted in the previous autumn with spring-flowering bulbs, pansies and wallflowers. An area with a strict colour theme can have this extended by accompanying containers full of appropriate flower colour.

A predominantly green foliage garden with perhaps grand ranks of topiary can be related to a more human scale by a series of punctuating containers of suitable 'weight' and visual strength. At SHUGBOROUGH, on the main lawn, where the golden-domed yews are a feature, stone pots are all planted with a summer display of dark-flowered heliotrope and pale blue trailing lobelia – rich sober colours relating to the existing yellows and greens and introducing no jarring colour contrasts. The plant combination is similar in the east formal garden at BENINGBROUGH, where the colour scheme is blue and white: there a container is planted with standard dark heliotrope and, this time, with dark blue trailing lobelia. Decorative stone urns on the outer terrace at KNIGHTSHAYES are planted with scented heliotrope and forms of pink-flowering diascia among grey foliage, and stand out against a background of dark yew. This relates to the pink and grey theme on the raised terrace. An eighteenth-century lead tank, flanked by a pair of standard wisteria, overflows with the pink trailing *Sphaeralcea munroana*, the silvery foliage of *Helichrysum petiolatum* and its smaller-leaved form *Plectostachys serpyllifolia* (formerly *Helichrysum microphyllum*).

Shrubs or small trees (especially evergreens), perhaps trimmed into topiary shapes, look well in pots, and can be wintered undercover to be in perfect condition when the garden is first visited in spring. At SALTRAM the lemon and orange trees, especially imported from Spain and Italy, are over-wintered in the orangery and brought out at the end of May, exactly as was practised in Renaissance gardens. In contrast, the Portugal laurel (*Prunus lusitanica*) in Versailles cases which line the view to the water canal at ERDDIG, only appear to be planted in the containers, but actually have their roots in the ground. In the seventeenth century clipped bay trees (*Laurus nobilis*) were used at this site, and given winter shelter.

Other permanent plants unsuitable for the particular soil of the garden can be given a specially mixed compost in a container. Camellias thrive in pots where an alkaline soil would not allow them to be grown successfully in open ground. They need little winter protection and their architectural form and spring flowers make a satisfactory arrangement of pots grouped in some shady place in a garden.

Both pots and plants become strong design additions to the furnishing of a garden, and increase its range. At TINTINHULL four large pots planted with July-flowering regale lilies are features on the west front of the house. Both stone container and exotically scented lily are part of the garden scheme, the lily growing to flower at eye-level, each group much more imposing than if growing in a flower bed. Some exotics look wrong if given a site next to more ordinary plants in a bed; putting them in a container accentuates their difference and proclaims the artificiality of gardening effects.

At HARDWICK a stone container under the house walls is planted with the dark-leaved *Fuchsia* 'Thalia', the old-fashioned *Pelargonium* × *hortorum* 'The Boar', which has a vigorous spreading habit and delicate pink flowers, and silvery-leaved *Lotus berthelotii*. The pelargonium, now rarely available in commerce, is a feature also at MOUNT STEWART in Northern Ireland. The lotus has scarlet flowers which appear in the leaf axils of the trailing shoots, and since these grow to 1.5–1.8 m (5–6 ft), the plant needs to be positioned at an adequate height for the stems to clear the ground. It is tender, but cuttings are easily taken and can be over-wintered in a greenhouse where the temperature is just above freezing.

The more ephemeral flowers and leaves of seasonal annuals, biennials or tender bedding plants can be different each year, and can be changed at least twice annually. Quite often the Trust has inherited the care of gardens where specific plants, by tradition, are always used. This historical continuity of planting is exactly the same as in all aspects of Trust gardening. Sometimes over the years an original tree or hedge grows to maturity and changes the aspect of a site, from one in full sun to shade. Then planting is adjusted to the new situation; plants tolerant of shade are substituted for sun-loving annuals.

Fortunately many of these gardens possess a good selection of decorative containers. In many Trust gardens well-designed old stone urns or weathered terracotta pots are already in use and any replacements or additions have to be appropriate in style

Top: In Mrs Winthrop's garden at Hidcote ornamental pots contain tender cordylines.

Above: A stone pot at Tintinhull House is planted with trailing ivy and the tender foliage plant *Melianthus major* which enjoys full sun and good drainage.

Top: Containers round the pool at Snowshill Manor are painted 'Wade Blue'.

Above: Wooden Versailles-type pots hold scented summer heliotropes and silver-leaved *Helichrysum petiolatum* at Beningbrough Hall.

and material. Nowadays many shapes in different materials are available in garden centres. Old and elegant designs are copied in modern concrete, terracotta, wood and plastic. Unfortunately the best are very expensive. Concrete or powdered stone mixed with cement can be very harsh in texture, but can be improved by frequent dousing in liquid cow manure, to encourage growth of lichen. Terracotta and earthenware made from clay are often reddish-brown when new, and being porous dry out quickly (a glazed surface is easier to clean and retains more moisture); unless they are of good quality and kept dry in winter, they are subject to frost damage. The untextured surface of coloured plastic is glaring and colours are often garish.

It is worth considering scale as well as design and colour. In very small gardens a collection of small pots is less effective than one or two large ones, but good results can be obtained by placing a collection of identical pots together all filled with the same plant to make a massed colour or foliage effect. For ease of maintenance light plastic pots containing the plants can stand inside the more elegant stone or earthenware. At TINTINHULL, again, the tender shrubs for drawing-room ornament are all now grown in easily moved plastic pots, which rest in willow baskets or in stone-glazed containers when indoors. Only the plastic inner pots are taken out of the house for regular feeding and watering, much reducing the labour of handling heavy pots and the risk of damaging ornamental ones.

All pot plants growing in the open are subject to greater extremes of climate than if their roots were safely buried in a flower bed. Choosing a site with the right amount of sun, shade or shelter is very important. If roots get too hot in summer all growth will stop, and in winter containers are especially vulnerable to cold winds and low temperatures. In dry weather, and even after rain if foliage is tightly packed together, a daily or twice-daily watering routine is necessary. Today moisture-retentive granules help keep the soil from drying out and lessen the burden of watering. In a private garden an owner may be able to water at weekends; in many of the smaller Trust gardens this is not possible, and plants easily wilt after two days (or three if a Bank Holiday Monday is included) of hot sun and dehydrating wind. Plants which have a setback when newly put out seldom recover to give of their best.

Soil condition, together with watering, feeding and 'growing' the plants well, is vital, and in fact determines how effective are these other routine horticultural tasks. If the soil becomes clogged, water may not drain freely and plants will have their roots permanently in damp stagnant soil; this is a much more frequent cause of poor plant performance than any other. All containers must have plenty of drainage holes and these must somehow be kept open, quickly becoming blocked if in direct contact with soil particles. To make certain of free drainage all pots should always be slightly raised on bricks or slates. There are many schools of thought on the best media for adequate drainage. Coarse drainage materials (in the past, old crocks from broken earthenware vases) are usually put in first, followed by a layer at least 6 mm (¼ in) deep of chippings or gravel, followed by a layer of leaf-mould, moss or chopped-up fibrous turf. Then a compost chosen for the type of plant is added; it should be of good texture, and have the correct balance of lime or acidity. Most planting is done with a formula based on a John Innes No. 3 mix, with adjustments for plants requiring specific conditions. This is loam-based with added nutrients and can be made in the garden. A mixture containing two parts loam, one part peat and one part grit makes a useful planting medium. It is stronger than the No. 1 and No. 2 mixes in which the plant will have been reared from seedling or cutting to the stage for planting out.

If the amount required is small it is easiest to buy a ready-mixed compost, specially modified for acid-loving plants if required. For plants which need very dry conditions an extra proportion of grit is added to improve drainage even in this top layer. Do not store a bought-in compost for many months because the balance and strength of the added nutrients may change and ceases to have food value. Soilless composts can also be used. Usually peat-based, these are cheap, light and easy to handle, and very useful in the earlier stages of plant propagation.

When pots are used only for annuals there is no problem about making certain that the soil is always in good condition; if necessary it can be changed with the plants. But most Trust gardens, as with private owners, want to maximize periods when the containers are decorative, so, instead of complete change-overs, planting is mixed, decorative trailing ivies, for example, remaining as permanent features. This means there is no obvious moment to make complete soil changes as some plant is always 'coming on'. During a garden year when any plants are added or replaced, some of the surface layer of soil can be scraped away, and some more mixed compost with artificial or organic fertilizers placed on top. This sort of top-dressing is sufficient for several seasons if adequate drainage has been ensured. Broadleaf P4, a moisture-retentive granule, can be added later and will reduce the need for watering.

All the plants in a container must have broadly similar requirements of soil type, water and feeding.

Left: The pink flowers and silvery foliage of *Convolvulus althaeoides* in the yard at Tintinhull House. In spring white tulips give interest and do not disturb the roots of this twining plant.

At Sissinghurst ornamental containers are chosen which are suitable for individual planting schemes. A copper container holds orange-flowered *Mimulus aurantiacus* which needs moisture and an Italian terracotta pot is tightly packed with drought-resistant petunias and *Helichrysum petiolatum*.

Planting can be of one plant only or can be exactly like a flower bed in miniature, planned to give a succession of interest with even some permanent evergreen shrub in the composition. A single myrtle, clipped bay or holly gives all-year-round interest and height, while many annuals and biennials with attractive colourful flowers lack individual architectural quality and need to be viewed in a mass. Ivies with interestingly shaped or variegated leaves trail over the edge. In the courtyard at TINTINHULL some of the pots contain permanent planting. The grey-leaved *Convolvulus althaeoides*, a sun-lover from southern Europe, proves surprisingly hardy, and its running roots are contained in a stone pot over the sides of which trail glaucous-leaved *Euphorbia myrsinites*. The euphorbia flowers early with lime-green bracts; the convolvulus bears its single pink flowers through the summer.

Achieving a good container display at the right time depends on a certain amount of strategic planning, and different gardens display different techniques. Small spring bulbs and corms such as species iris and crocus, although very suitable in ordinary gardens, flower early in the spring, before most Trust gardens are open. A practice in many Trust gardens is to interplant two different types of tulip, each chosen for a definite flowering season. It is possible to know from experience of a site in a garden the exact week when tulips will open and thus plan ahead to maximize their impact. The first lot, perhaps a group of the *fosteriana* hybrids which flower in early April, can be followed in May by lily-flowered tulips. By the time the first group needs dead-heading, the May tulips are already in bud, and their foliage, slightly greyish-green, is at its best. The bulbs are then removed; sometimes they are kept in a trench until the foliage dies down and then dried off, but it is now said that this is unnecessary. Another option is to plant the bulbs straight into a kitchen 'cutting' area, where they remain and are used for house decoration the following season.

If there is enough space, bedding pansies, which flower in winter when the weather is not too severe, make spreading plants whose foliage protects the emerging tulip shoots. It is best to keep some boxes of pansies in reserve in a frame, in case those already planted out (grown from seed sown in the previous July) suffer during a severe winter. Ideally, if pansies are to flower through the winter months, they need to be placed in their pots by the end of September; in practice, because most Trust gardens remain open until the beginning of October, it is seldom convenient to throw out the summer bedding so early. Most private owners will sacrifice *some* late-summer display, in order to have flowers in the garden in winter.

At SISSINGHURST elegant terracotta pots, which are covered up in winter to protect them from frost, are unwrapped in early spring and planted with forget-me-nots for 1st April; later they are filled with summer-bedding plants.

There is no doubt that keeping healthy plants in pots involves a lot of work. It is not only routine maintenance, but planning ahead is very important, especially today when seed packets often contain only mixed flower colours, which may not be appropriate. Without a heated greenhouse, as in many Trust gardens, those annuals which are sown in early spring for summer flowering are difficult to produce. For spring displays it is best to concentrate on biennials, such as wallflowers (forms of *Cheiranthus cheiri*), forget-me-nots and pansies sown the previous summer in open ground, and tulip bulbs. Many of the best 'tender' grey or silver foliage plants which, since they need little moisture, are ideal for growing in containers have to be propagated the previous autumn and kept free from severe frost. In a very favoured microclimate at MOUNT STEWART silver *Artemisia arborescens* and white-leaved cineraria are grown as tall standards, surviving the mild winters, their stems protected in the pots by a sea of blue forget-me-nots. All these 'silvers', flowing over the edges of containers, are the foil to flower colour and a valuable part of annual summer displays in appropriate gardens.

Mr Jimmie Hancock, the Head Gardener at POWIS CASTLE, specializes in growing uncommon plants in ornamental containers. Although he does grow bulbs, hardy annuals and annuals, he extends the range at Powis by growing many of the tender more woody plants which he finds he can put out earlier in the season, as once hardened off in their pots, they will withstand some frost. He writes:

Plants in containers have become a popular feature in our gardens. Gardens today are generally small and paved 'patio' areas give much scope for containers. Throughout the centuries plants in ornamental urns or pots have found favour even in our largest gardens, and were placed and the plants for them chosen with great care. To be a worthy feature in any garden scheme it must harmonize with other features, and should never appear as an afterthought or even perhaps an unsolicited gift which has been placed at random.

Containers

What about the container itself? In my opinion far too many containers are on the small side and not very practical. A container should have sufficient weight when filled to keep it in place in the strongest winds – this is particularly important when it has to be placed at any height. Containers should be large enough to hold sufficient compost for the needs of all the plants in them for one whole season. They should hold sufficient water to supply the needs of the plants for twenty-four hours, however hot or dry the weather. At Powis we have a good number of Edwardian terracotta pots which fulfil all these requirements. They are still in use and are a great asset to the gardens. When it comes to materials for containers there is little to compare with stone or pottery. It would be nice, perhaps, to add lead; but most of us have to have wood. The latter can be satisfactory but soon deteriorates unless used with an inner lining.

Planting

I have not found it very satisfactory to do permanent planting in containers, except in the case of two plant groups. Firstly, dwarf and slow-growing plants, including alpines, can be grown in shallow stone containers. These will thrive for many years, provided that plant associations are kept well balanced; any plants which tend to swamp others should be lifted as required and thinned out. Secondly, single shrubs can be grown permanently as specimens with ferns, ivies and so on round them. These can be placed in buildings or round the garden during the summer season. If left outside all winter containers, even those made of stone, are likely to suffer frost damage. In a long period of freezing weather the roots of the plants, unlike those of plants growing in the ground, will get frozen solid. In my view it is much more satisfactory to replant containers annually. They can be emptied in November or December and stored safely under cover over the winter.

For this type of planting a wide selection of plants, many of them not fully hardy, can be used and a list is included here. It should be possible to get colour for a period of at least four months, and in some cases six months is possible. I like to have my containers ready for placing in their summer positions by the first week of May. By then the plants should be of good size and growing fast and vigorously, with some flowers already appearing. The weather can be very temperamental at this time of year, so one is looking for a calm settled spell. If the plants have been hardened off properly the frost will have to go down to −4°C (24°F) before doing any noticeable damage. Cold winds are far more damaging, particularly during the first week or so outdoors. After that the breezes and cooler air conditions will have darkened and firmed the foliage, making it less susceptible.

The choice of plants will be determined by size of containers, sun, shelter and aspect of site. You will get more harmonious displays by not overdoing variety; in fact I find I rarely use more than four different types in any one container, and quite frequently only one. For containers to be viewed at eye-level I find fuchsias difficult to better. If restricted to one genus for growing in pots in our climate, it would have to be fuchsias. As they come

POWIS CASTLE

Mr J. Hancock's list of less common plants or varieties which are useful for containers:

Plant	Colour	Size	Habit	Season	Aspect
Alonsoa	orange	m	spreading	May/frost	sun/any
Argyranthemum foeniculaceum	white	m	spreading	May/frost	sun/dry
A. maderense	lemon	t	upright	June/frost	sun/dry
Cheiranthus 'Moonlight'	lemon	s	spreading	April/Sept	sun/dry
Convolvulus cneorum	white	m	spreading	June/frost	sun/any
C. althaeoides	pink	t	twining	June/frost	sun/any
C. sabatius	blue	s	trailing	June/frost	sun
Diascia 'Ruby Field'	pink	s	spreading	June/frost	sun/any
D. elegans	pink	m	spreading	June/frost	sun/wet
D. rigescens	pink	m	spreading	June/frost	sun
Erysimum 'Bowles' Mauve	mauve	m	spreading	April/Sept	sun/dry
Felicia amelloides	blue	m	spreading	June/frost	sun
F.a. 'Variegata'	blue	s	spreading	June/frost	sun
Fuchsia 'Brutus'	red/purple	l	upright	June/frost	sun/wet
F. 'Checkerboard'	white/maroon	l	upright	June/frost	sun/wet
F. 'Mission Bells'	red/purple	l	upright	June/frost	sun/wet
F. 'Mrs Lovell Swisher'	white/pink	l	upright	June/frost	sun/wet
F. 'Ting-a-ling'	white	l	upright	June/frost	sun/wet
F. 'Charming'	red/purple	m	spreading	June/frost	sun/wet
F. 'Eva Boerg'	white/purple	m	trailing	June/frost	sun/wet
F. 'Temptation'	white/carmine	m	spreading	June/frost	sun/wet
F. microphylla	pink	m	spreading	early/late	sun/wet
Gazania 'Cookie'	orange/red	s	spreading	June/frost	sun/wet
G. 'Freddie'	yellow/green	s	spreading	June/frost	sun/wet
G. 'Primrose Beauty'	lemon	s	spreading	June/frost	sun/wet
Heliotropium 'Princess Marina'	purple	m	upright	June/frost	sun/dry

Far left: The annual scarlet flowered *Alonsoa acutifolia* from Peru is striking with silver-leaved helichrysum in a stone trough at Powis Castle.

Left: At Powis, fuchsias are planted in basketweave terracotta pots.

Plant	Colour	Size	Habit	Season	Aspect
Helichrysum petiolatum	silver leaves	l	trailing	June/frost	sun
H. p. 'Limelight'	lime/gold leaves	l	trailing	June/frost	sun/shade
H. p. 'Variegatum'	variegated leaves	l	trailing	June/frost	sun/shade
Lantana camara	orange/red	m	upright	July/frost	sun
L. selloviana	lavender/mauve	s	spreading	July/frost	sun
Mimulus aurantiacus	orange	t	upright	June/frost	sun/dry
Oenothera cheiranthifolia	yellow	s	spreading	June/frost	sun/dry
Osteospermum ecklonis	white	m	spreading	June/frost	sun/dry
O. 'Blue Streak'	white	t	upright	June/frost	sun/dry
O. 'Buttermilk'	buff	t	upright	June/frost	sun/dry
O. jucundum	pink	m	spreading	June/frost	sun/dry
O. 'Tauranga' (syn. 'Whirligig')	white	t	upright	June/frost	sun/dry
Pelargonium 'Mrs Kingsbury'	pink	l	spreading	June/frost	sun
P. 'The Boar'	apricot	m	spreading	June/frost	sun
Plumbago auricula (syn. *P. capensis*)	pale blue	t	upright	July/frost	sun/dry
Salvia bacheriana (syn. *buchananii*)	purple	m	upright	June/frost	sun
S. chamaedrifolia	blue	s	trailing	July/frost	sun
S. blepharophylla	scarlet	s	spreading	July/frost	sun
S. coccinea	scarlet	m	upright	July/frost	sun
S. leucantha	purple	l	upright	Aug/frost	sun
S. patens.	blue	m	upright	July/frost	sun
Senecio bicolor cineraria	silver leaves	m	upright	June/frost	sun/dry
Tanacetum densum	silver foliage	s	spreading		sun
Verbena 'Hidcote'	purple	m	spreading	July/frost	sun
V. 'Huntsman'	scarlet	m	spreading	July/frost	sun
V. peruviana	scarlet	s	spreading	July/frost	sun
V. 'Sissinghurst'	pink	m	spreading	July/frost	sun
Zauschneria 'Dublin'	scarlet	m	spreading	July/frost	sun

from several continents they can vary from fully hardy to quite tender, they cover an amazing colour range, and among them are those which perform well in hot dry weather and others which flower well in poor summers. All are capable of five to six months' flowering if treated properly. What else can one ask for?

Propagation and Growing on for Containers

Without facilities, it may be best to buy in plants each year. When dealing with large containers and displays you need space at all times of year. Unfortunately if you have to buy in, the choice of interesting plants is much restricted, unless you can go to specialist growers. Cuttings should be taken as early as possible when there is some good new non-flowering growth. Pelargoniums usually can be taken in August, other plants from mid-September to the end of October as material becomes available. We have, of course, selected many plants because of their ability to flower over a very long period, so it is fruitless to grumble if they continue to flower when we want propagating material. I aim to have any major large plants propagated and potted up before lack of light slows down plant growth, by the end of October if possible. Once potted, they should keep a steady growth, but are only watered when they indicate the need. Very little heat is needed; temperatures will vary from 5°C (40°F) to as low as −2°C (28°F). The greater one's skill as a grower, the more the temperature can drop without harm. With plants kept on the dry side, we had few losses in 1981–82 when temperatures under glass fell to −6°C (21°F).

During the middle of February you will notice the first new growth on many of the plants. Spring has arrived and light has reached a level of real value to the plants. At this stage I start to increase my minimum temperatures, but timing depends on the light and the response of the plants. There can be no rigid rule. There is a difference of about a fortnight between north and south of the country. I am dealing with Midland light values here. As activity grows, propagation is also started again; plants for the smaller containers and a few of the quick growers, including *Helichrysum petiolatum* and its forms, which can very easily get too large and unbalance a carefully planned arrangement. Potting on quickly follows, and I now do the final potting of my main container plants. There are still two months before they will be put into their containers and during this time they will quadruple in size. I use 1.5–2-litre pots, so roots are not restricted but will fill the space. For high-quality performance later, this is the most important and vital period. Space in the greenhouse soon becomes a problem, and we now have a large polytunnel to give us extra space. Many plants cope well with the cold once they are growing strongly; fuchsias are among the first to be moved, and make sturdy plants even if temperatures fall to −2°C (28°F). One sees many fuchsias in commerce with soft, drawn shoots, which shows they have had excess heat to encourage quick growth. These plants should be avoided.

Making up the Containers

I find the last two weeks in April work best in my system. I make them up in the polytunnel. We use a John Innes based compost, but with a very coarse grade of peat, and the loam also contains coarse particles. We add slow-release fertilizer now, and find no other feeding is necessary during the life of the container planting. By this time the plants begin already to intermingle and growth flops over the edge of the pots. We stake all tall plants at this stage even if they seem sturdy enough: gusts of wind can ruin all the work. Canes will not be visible by the time the containers go out, but new growth should not require further attention. The largest containers which cannot be moved are made up *in situ*, at an opportune moment when it is reasonably mild and there is little wind. A week is long enough to complete this task and I know all will be well. *Fuchsia fulgens* and its forms are our most tender plants; they go out last, in the middle of May.

General Summer Maintenance

If the preparatory work is well done success, whatever the weather, is now assured. There is little work from mid-May to November, except for watering and general picking over flower-heads and removing dead leaves. These maintenance chores are essential and keep the containers looking fresh.

One of the beauties of the complete change made each season is that it gives you a fresh opportunity to experiment and to rectify mistakes. Observe how the various plants compete with each other. Look closely at your colour mixtures, and look at arrangements in other gardens and keep an eye out for suitable new plants.

II
GARDEN FEATURES

Borders

In gardening, the term 'border' has not only been used to imply the edging to a garden area, but has also come to be synonymous with arrangements of groups of hardy herbaceous perennials, which are thus often referred to as 'border plants'. The traditional herbaceous border reached its peak of performance in high summer, clumps of strong hardy perennials all being geared to flower together in July and August. The border usually edged a lawn and was backed by the wall or hedging that enclosed that section of the garden; often, too, double herbaceous borders would edge a pathway or face each other across a broad panel of mown grass. This planting area was just as seasonal as a spring garden or an iris bed, and had little colour or interest in it for the other months of the year. Many of the old gardens had space enough to include such separate areas, which were at their best at different seasons – and could be ignored at other times.

Today, in a small garden, since the 'border' may well be almost the only available planting space, owners seldom wish to confine its season to midsummer flowering or its range to only one type of plant. Small trees, shrubs, bush roses, hardy and more tender perennials, bulbs, annuals and biennials can all be planted as part of a scheme, each on the right scale and in the right proportions for the site, to extend the season of interest right through the year.

In this practice, gardeners are keeping faith with a tradition which persisted through many centuries, when any plant that was reasonably decorative or useful was grown in the border against the house or around the edges of a lawn or courtyard. Many of these hardy plants were native in origin or had been introduced before the eighteenth-century landscape taste swept flowers out of sight. They continued to be grown in smaller manor-house, rectory or cottage gardens during all the years when they were out of fashion in the 'trendsetter' gardens. Even at the height of the Victorian bedding craze, hardier perennials were by custom grown in borders in kitchen gardens, where they were used as cut flowers for the house.

Paintings made by George Elgood at the end of the nineteenth century record borders in gardens of great houses now administered by the Trust, and these show typically 'mixed' planting. Borders were often a delightful mixture of roses, hollyhocks, mulleins, madonna lilies, tall annual sunflowers, and, at ground level, scented mignonette; they were not always massed with the fashionable annuals. Elgood painted a border in the forecourt at HARDWICK HALL in 1904. Backed with a high wall on which climbing roses, honeysuckle and clematis twined, planting includes a standard rose, macleaya, mulleins and Japanese anemones, with foreground planting of pinks, tufted pansies and mignonette. At MONTACUTE HOUSE Elgood painted a bright border which edged the east forecourt where sunflowers, evening primroses, border phlox and campanula, pansies and pinks were all tightly packed together. A large evergreen shrub gives bulk and solidity but is the only visible concession to the vast scale of the surrounding architecture. Planting in the borders of these two great Elizabethan houses at the turn of the century was essentially similar to that in the flowery cottage gardens painted by Helen Allingham. Today at Hardwick many of the same plants are still grown but the borders are given depth and density with large shrubs such as magnolias, clerodendrums and evergreen viburnums, and spreading shrub roses. Sculptured-leaved acanthus, bergenia, *Crambe cordifolia*, hostas and echinops, planted in massive groups, match the scale and anchor house and garden walls to the ground. There are still plenty of flowers from good hardy perennials, many of them already in garden use in 1900. Thalictrums, aconitums, macleaya, *Aruncus dioicus* and *Artemisia lactiflora* perform in season and clematis and roses still climb on the walls. In the shade of the cedar *Hosta sieboldiana*, with bluish almost corrugated leaves, is planted to fill the width of the border, making a pattern of ribbling waves. At Montacute the forecourt borders have recently been replanted. Badly infested with bindweed and other perennial weeds, the ground was treated with dazomet and replanted in 1982 to a plan adapted from one made originally by Mrs Phyllis Reiss after the Second World War. The creator of the gardens at TINTINHULL HOUSE near by, and interested in colour associations, Mrs Reiss used purplish foliage shrubs and bright flower colours to tone with the golden Ham stone, which she felt made paler tints and grey foliage seem insipid.

Garden writers such as William Robinson and Gertrude Jekyll are often credited with being the originators of the classical herbaceous border, but in fact they always used mixed planting. Even when the herbaceous flower border was at its height in the early years of this century, their planting was not always strictly confined to perennials: the design structure was often given bulk with permanent shrubs, and the length of season of flowering beauty was extended by bulbs and annuals. Then as now, the most effective border planting would include spring-, summer- and autumn-flowering bulbs interplanted between clumps of spreading perennials to extend both ends of the flowering period. Annuals, biennials and tender bedding plants such as dahlias succeeded each other in drifts or clumps throughout the summer months. The enthusiast kept in reserve pots of lilies, hydrangeas or fuchsias which could be sunk in the border at dull moments.

Then as now, the most successful mixed borders were those where planting appears to be in layers. Starting at ground level, small spring bulbs and early-flowering perennials nestle under the skirts of deciduous shrubs; between the shrubs summer- and later-flowering perennials, biennials and annuals – or even small woody plants – cover the ground with massed foliage but flower at different levels. As the shrubs grow in width and cast longer shadows as they become taller, these less permanent plants need shifting around: indeed, they need division as part of border routine maintenance, but the whole area may be taken over by the shrubs, which will eventually grow together. On a higher level, a small tree may also cast its shadow over the shrubs and plants in an area, but may contribute height and visual balance, especially when the border is not backed by a high hedge or a brick wall.

Although borders are not the invention of Robinson and Jekyll, their practice and teachings have perhaps altered our perception of them, and it is undoubtedly to Miss Jekyll that we owe the planning – and the appreciation – of a border in the pictorial sense. Borders are often carefully designed to be seen in their entirety from far away across a lawn, but they must retain their effectiveness when viewed from much closer, when the different planes of planting become clear. From a distance the composition blends like a painted canvas; from close to, hidden valleys and shadows appear between and behind the plants. In some cases borders along paths or against walls can be seen only as the viewer walks along them, and in any long stretch of planting, each new individual group or planting association only unfolds itself to the eye in passing.

However it is seen, the very word 'border' implies something continuous. In any form of decoration a

Above: Where an old greenhouse stood at Wallington against a sunny wall, the border is edged with clumps of glossy-leaved bergenias, and buddlejas give height and colour in late summer.

Page 73: In the walled garden at Wallington, a double border has plants with predominantly blue and yellow flowers throughout the summer. Metal arches frame the view.

border is an ornamental edging to a usually plainer central part. So a flower border will edge an expanse of lawn, an area of stone paving or gravel, and will often be given a firm backing by a wall or hedge. This background vertical will provide a continuous coloured surface, behind foreground planting. A hedge such as dark yew acts as a foil to flower and foliage colour in front of it, while a stone or brick wall, although equally continuous, often itself becomes covered with growing plants, so that as a curtained backdrop it participates in the colour scheme of the design. These visual effects are accompanied by others of a more practical kind. Hedges steal moisture and nutrients from the plants near by; walls cast rain-shadows and plants at their base often lack moisture.

In border planning the planting is envisaged in its different planes, heights and depths, so that a whole three-dimensional picture is built up. Each individual plant has its own quality, and groups and clumps are put together so that a balanced composition results, an artistic masterpiece as well as a convincing demonstration of horticultural skill. A whole picture or a series of pictures is revealed, never a flat and level expanse of flower or foliage.

The conventional modern border composed traditionally of hardy perennials will still have the lowest-growing plants at the front, with careful gradation of heights towards the back. Extra interest can be given by making sure that some good foliage plants are brought right to the front, and if lower-growing plants are just glimpsed at the back of others. When planting is more mixed, a small tree, some shrubs, bush roses, bulbs and annuals for foliage or long flowering season require a freer mode of planting, lower-growing plants being suitably placed around the base of a tree or shrub, rather than immediately in the foreground. Spring bulbs show colour under the canopy of spreading deciduous shrubs, extending the season of interest. Perennial plants need to be grouped in clumps of sufficient size to compare with more woody plant material, and must be divided and replanted frequently not only for their own good, but to keep the whole composition in balance and harmony.

If it is possible to walk behind the border using a pathway between a narrow wall-border or separating the main border from its background hedge, a whole new area of planting is revealed, at the base of taller plants set at the back of the bed. Flower beds, as opposed stylistically to borders, were usually set into a lawn and could be walked round, so both back

Opposite: A dark hedge at Chirk Castle makes a background for a mixed border where scarlet roses and perennials flower over a long period.

Hot colours blend together in the border at Tatton Park (top) while the 'cool' pale colours at Barrington Court (above) are set off by the mellow brick path in basketweave pattern

Opposite: In the walled garden at Mottisfont a central double border is planned to give its maximum June performance at the same time as the rose collection.

Above: A border composition at Lytes Carey in Somerset. The mixed planting of roses, shrubs and sprawling perennials such as traditional catmint and alchemilla ensures a long season of interest.

and front were planted with low edging plants. Traditionally these islands, which might be forms of box-edged parterres or some sort of pattern, would have had 'bedding' plants grouped together all at one height. It is only recently that even these free-standing beds have been treated in a more pictorial way. In many Trust gardens borders and beds on the fringe of woodland, which might originally have been diversely planted, now frequently contain only evergreen shrubs, holly, aucuba and laurel having taken over as the shorter-lived plants died out. These are often made more interesting and lightened by the introduction of paler-leaved deciduous flowering bushes and an underplanting of perennials which not only contribute flowers in season but growing tightly together reduce maintenance costs by preventing the weed-germination that would take place in bare soil. Sometimes these plants will be chosen primarily for their foliage colour and texture, usually in tones of green or grey.

It was Gertrude Jekyll's training as a painter that led her to treat her flower beds as a canvas and she developed certain colour 'rules'. She found that the warm bright oranges, reds and crimsons – colours situated next to each other on the rainbow – would also associate most pleasingly in the garden in the same basic order of gradation; the paler 'cooler' colours she liked to plant with grey and silvery foliage plants so that the pastel tints seemed brighter, and she used colour opposites such as blue and orange, yellow and violet, in deliberate juxtaposition to make each colour more telling.

At CLIVEDEN Mr Graham Stuart Thomas designed two long and wide herbaceous borders which face each other across the lawn to the north of the house. Both borders have much the same dimensions as Miss Jekyll's own at Munstead Wood. Stretching north and south 60 m (200 ft), each is 5.4 m (18 ft) wide and backed by high walls where wall shrubs and climbing plants make a backdrop to flower and foliage colours in the borders. At Munstead pale flowers and grey-leaved foliage plants were placed at either end, and there was a careful build up to stronger 'hot' colours in the centre. At Cliveden one border is of strong vibrant colours; the other has misty pale flowers. Nevertheless the 'pattern' of careful graded colour expresses much of Gertrude Jekyll's teaching and practice. She liked to plant her groups as drifts, so that her colour schemes were like a pattern of weaving, rather than in more conventional blocks or triangles where plants in threes, fives, sevens and nines made clear colour divisions

and were less likely to blend in the eye as in a pointillist painting.

This practice of pairing beds or borders where one has bright, intense colour tones and another 'quieter', more subtle and muted colours recurs in a number of Trust gardens. An example is at TINTINHULL HOUSE, where two 'colour' borders were planned by Mrs Phyllis Reiss in the years immediately after the last war. Her nephew was killed as a fighter pilot, and the area which had been a tennis court was turned into a garden as a memorial to him.

In the main borders of this Pool Garden, tulips emerge early to flower at the beginning of May and give a hint of the colour theme of each area. In the west (east-facing) border where summer flower colour is predominantly 'hot' – deep yellow, orange, scarlet and crimson – tulip 'Queen of the Night', with subtle velvety-maroon, almost black, flowers sets the tone. Orange summer-flowering tiger lilies (*Lilium lancifolium fortunei* syn. *L. tigrinum fortunei*) push up through the evergreen leaves of *Iberis sempervirens*, and groups of *L. henryi* with orange-yellow flowers in late summer grow behind the scarlet *Potentilla* 'Gibson's Scarlet'. Scarlet dahlias such as 'Grenadier' and 'Bishop of Llandaff' extend the season which starts in June with groups of bush rose 'Frensham', still one of the best performers, and, if dead-headed, ready to give a further burst of flower in late August and September. Other reds include the tender *Salvia fulgens*, which does well in a wet year but performs poorly in drought conditions, and reliable penstemons such as 'Scarlet Fire' and 'Garnet'. Crimson nicotiana were bedded out in 1985 and flowered almost continuously for three months, introducing a 'bluer' pigment into the scheme. Yellow flowers, especially forms of *Compositae* with daisy-flowers, are used freely, but paler lemon-yellow of *Hemerocallis citrina*, lime-yellow *Alchemilla mollis* and fluffy cream flowers of *Artemisia lactiflora* cool down the whole scheme. A clump of *Sisyrinchium striatum* with cream flowers and architectural iris-like leaves is next to a suckering bush of *Symphoricarpos orbiculatus* 'Foliis Variegatis'. Where the border breaks in the middle and frames steps down to a pink and blue border in the kitchen garden, grey-foliaged *Senecio* 'Sunshine' and *Artemisia* 'Powis Castle' edge the beds.

In the opposite, west-facing border pastel colours, linked by grey and silver foliage, predominate.

Hot colours from the same section of the spectrum blend in the eye. At Tintinhull House this mixed border has flowers of yellow, orange, scarlet and crimson through a long season.

Today a purple-leaved *Prunus cerasifera* 'Pissardii' towers from behind the tall yew hedge which backs this border to the east, so some darker purple and violet-flowered plants have been introduced to link the tree to the bed below it. In May clumps of a pink Darwin tulip 'Queen of the Bartigons' grow among the later-flowering perennials, to coincide with the white blossom of a horizontal branching *Viburnum plicatum* 'Mariesii' across a corner. *Deutzia gracilis* and the Warminster broom (*Cytisus* × *praecox*) make a glorious show at the same time. Grey and silver foliage plants are planted at regular intervals along the front and pink and mauve penstemons make groups between salvias such as *Salvia* 'Superba', *S. haematodes* and drifts of the annual *S. farinacea*

'Victoria' with dark violet flowers carried for a long season. At the back purple-flowered delphiniums grow next to pale blue-flowered *Campanula lactiflora*. For later in the summer *Aster × frikartii* 'Mönch', *A. sedifolius acris* 'Nanus' and *Achillea ptarmica* 'The Pearl' flower with phlox and tall clumps of *Eupatorium purpureum*. Good foliage plants such as the spreading *Acanthus mollis latifolius* grow beside the elegant grey-leaved *Romneya trichocalyx* which produces its papery white poppy-flowers in summer.

Any border plan, unlike a finished canvas, does not present the same picture all through a season – let alone through different years. Each plant assumes many different aspects; some grow quicker than others, altering balance and proportion; flowering time can vary each year, and plants react to weather variations in different ways. The gardener making a border needs not only the skilled eye of a painter to plan the composition but also all the horticultural knowledge possible to ensure that the results are as predicted. In a mixed border shrubs may be single or in groups to suit the scale, but perennials are generally in clumps (hardly less than three of any one kind, and often many more to make an effective 'splurge' of colour) which spread and need dividing every few years. Gardening in this way is a highly skilled craft. In the case of herbaceous plants, which come quickly to their full maturity to give a peak performance, planning begins at least a year ahead, but a shrub will take much longer to develop its true quality.

Today the range of plants available through hybridizing and breeding is hugely increased, yet many original species are getting increasingly difficult to obtain. Nurserymen breed new hybrids or cultivars to satisfy the public's desire for longer flowering periods, for new colours, to make a plant short and sturdy (sometimes at the expense of elegance) in order to save garden staking, or simply for novelty. The cost of nursery work makes it economic to produce only plants which are quick and easy to propagate. Because of historical context many old species and cultivars have been collected and grow in National Trust borders, and several of the gardens have good plant selling areas where these almost 'vanished' species can be obtained.

In a small garden it may not be possible to have separate areas for separate seasonal interest, but as each part of any planting scheme depends for its success on plant association, there is still much inspiration to be gained from the larger garden. A border of spring-flowering bulbs can have neighbouring plants with striking leaves, which bear flowers later in the summer: veratrum, with strange pleated emerging foliage, euphorbias of all classes, *Iris pallida dalmatica* with grey sword-like spikes all year, and architectural yucca. Deciduous-leaved shrubs shelter small blue-flowered *Anemone blanda* or *A. apennina*, cyclamen species, scillas and erythronium, all woodland-type plants which benefit from the light shade given through the summer months. Tulips, often with fine green or striped leaves, can grow in clumps between hardy perennials which reach their peak in full or late summer, and little edging iberis and alyssum, flowering in early spring, later contribute pleasant leaves to set off the bright colours of summer. Mid- or late-season lilies welcome some protection for their emergent shoots in spring and grow happily interplanted with any similar low-growing shrub or shrubby spreader.

In larger gardens there can be whole garden areas for just one season. Plants which flower early but have strong or untidy leaves later are particularly suitable for separate garden compartments, which are visited only at one season of the year. Peonies, iris, oriental poppies, delphiniums and lupins, besides winter or spring 'gardens', are all possible. At POLESDEN LACEY, where the large walled garden is subdivided into sections, there is a peony garden, an iris garden and a lavender collection, each reaching its peak at a different time. The great summer border would have plants arranged for display for only a few months, but for that short period all the plants could flower together, simplifying planning. Later, Michaelmas daisies, perhaps edged with silvery foliage of *Stachys olympica* or dianthus, as in Miss Jekyll's own garden at Munstead Wood, flowered in October in another part of the garden. At UPTON HOUSE a collection of asters has been assembled in a 'late' border, and is formalized by the repetition of massive clumps of pampas grass (*Cortaderia selloana*). At NYMANS a curving border against a yew hedge has very simple planting. Bright red dahlias such as 'Bishop of Llandaff', 'Crimson Flag' and 'Breakaway' are interplanted with groups of the tall invasive *Anaphalis yedoensis* (syn. *A. cinnamomea*).

At TRERICE two borders both backed with walls face each other across the west forecourt. Plants with leaves of purple and gold and blue flowers are planned for summer interest. The soil is limy, rainfall is high at about 92.5 cm (37 in) and winters near the Atlantic coast of Cornwall relatively mild. Both borders are planted similarly, but with adjustments for the difference in aspect. Purple foliage shrubs such as *Cotinus coggygria* 'Royal Purple', *Prunus* 'Cistena' and berberis underplanted with *Lobelia cardinalis*, with almost translucent red-bronze leaves in spring, give the darkest colouring (the scarlet flower-heads of the lobelia are cut off later because they do not fit into the scheme and this also helps to keep the foliage bright and glowing). Golden *Philadelphus coronarius* 'Aureus' and *Spiraea bumalda* 'Gold Flame' have bright leaves in spring, although these become green as summer advances.

Delphiniums, specially selected from seedlings in a dark purplish shade, flower at the end of June with the twining mauve-flowered *Solanum crispum* 'Glasnevin' on the wall, later followed by dark velvety blue flowers of *Clematis* × *jackmanii*. Paler blue caryopteris with attractive grey leaves flowers towards the end of summer. Yellow flowers are contributed by the winter-flowering evergreen *Mahonia japonica*, which helps to give structure to the border, and the more delicate grey-leaved *Coronilla glauca*, which may flower all through the year. In mid- to late summer the perennial *Anthemis sancti-johannis* has golden-orange daisies rising above lacy grey-green foliage. Against the wall at the back of the border *Vestia lycioides*, bearing pale yellow drooping tubular flowers has a long flowering season, and the new yellow-flowered form of *Phygelius aequalis* is grouped effectively behind the purple-bronze-leaved little *Prunus* 'Cistena'. The soil is fertile and the only regular feeding is bone-meal in spring. Bushes of lavender, both 'Munstead' and 'Twickel Purple', are grouped to make a regular pattern along the border, which is 28 m (90 ft) in length and nearly 3 m (10 ft) wide. The border plan is labour-saving, even the delphiniums needing no staking, and only needs attention in late autumn and spring, when shrubs are pruned and herbaceous perennials divided and replanted to make larger groups.

In a lower enclosure to the south, the colour scheme is based on bronze or variegated leaves and white, purple and pink flowers. The architectural sword-like leaves of New Zealand flax (*Phormium tenax purpureum*) and bronze foliage of libertia, with underplanting of *Lamium* 'Beacon Silver' glowing and white in shade, are effective foils to flower colours. The tender *Abelia floribunda* and *Buddleja lindleyana* both have purplish-pink flowers carried over a long period, and thrive against the sunny south-facing wall.

The motive for designing and planting a border is not always the painterly inspiration to manipulate colour in plants in a satisfying visual composition. It may be an idea, an intellectual conceit – although, of course, the plants still need to make a pleasing picture. At WIGHTWICK MANOR, with associations with the Pre-Raphaelite Brotherhood and the Arts and Crafts Movement, borders under a terrace wall are divided by buttresses of yew, and in each the planting is only of shrubs or flowers mentioned in the works of Tennyson, Shelley and Dickens, Kempe (the craftsman and glassmaker), and plants grown at Kelmscott Manor, the home of William Morris. The results are not very visually interesting but the idea is a stimulating one, and might well serve as an inspiration to garden owners.

At POWIS CASTLE the south-east border in the Edwardian formal garden is mainly planted with various colour forms of phlox for late-summer flowering. Pink, mauve and white flowers blend together behind an edging of box 45 cm (18 in) high and 30 cm (12 in) across. For the early season onions, including *Nectaroscordum siculum* and *Allium aflatunense* are grouped with dodecatheons and *Camassia esculenta* in pale blue and white forms. The phlox have been subject to eelworm but treatment with aldicarb seems to solve this problem.

At PACKWOOD, famous for yew topiary, there are also some fine borders, which are readily adapted to gardens of a more modest scale. A sunken garden with raised beds of mainly hardy perennials augmented with annuals and tender pelargoniums and a colourful wall border show how close-packed planting of many different varieties, in very small groups, can ensure the good colour effects for many months. The planting style is traditional and distinctive, on the lines of that called by Loudon the 'mingled' border. The Head Gardener, Mr Ellis, plants in threes, or might even use a single plant of something like catmint; the large species, *Nepeta gigantea*, can stand alone. In the border raised by four courses of brick which make a supporting wall, phlox, golden rod, grassy-leaved crocosmia, heleniums and *Coreopsis verticillata* are interplanted with drifts of dahlias and pelargoniums. Grey-leaved alyssum, a smaller catmint and lavender bushes at the entrance fall over the brick, and are planted at regular intervals to hold the design together. At the back tripods provide a frame for some of the old forms of sweet pea including 'Primadonna' and 'Painted Lady', which are heavy with fragrance. Delphiniums at the back are staked in spring but many of the other

plants grow sturdily and the close planting obviates the necessity for meticulously supporting each one with twigs or bamboos.

In the wall-border taller plants such as the unusual creamy-yellow *Salvia glutinosa* with coarse hairy leaves and different yellow daisy-flowered plants keep colour going until late in the summer. Tall *Aconitum napellus* in different garden forms with their dark purple hooded flowers complement the bright yellows, while paler mistier blues are at the front. Mr Ellis says there is no particular colour scheme but by August yellows and blues predominate with splashes of scarlet pelargoniums drawing the eye. Many of these plants are propagated from the originals used by Mr Baron Ash, who gave Packwood to the National Trust in 1941. He created the sunken garden and central lily pond to add colour to a garden primarily of architectural yew and box.

At Packwood House raised beds round a sunken garden are planted with hardy perennials and summer annuals. Groups of each plant are small, colours designed to blend rather than being identifiable in separate blocks or drifts.

At BENINGBROUGH HALL a pathway running north and south is flanked by a double border of shrubs (including a large number of hybrid musk roses), herbaceous plants and bulbs, designed to give interest from early summer to the end of September. Perennials such as *Crambe cordifolia*, hostas, *Cimicifuga cordifolia* and Japanese anemones have been chosen to contribute good foliage effects even when not in their flowering season. The sword-like leaves of yucca and iris contrast with more rounded soft shapes. On the east the border is backed by a wall of the old kitchen garden, and on this clematis, honeysuckle, roses and an old Teinturier grape (*Vitis vinifera* 'Purpurea') are trained on wires attached to vine eyes to make a backdrop of foliage and flower colour throughout the summer. In the original plans the planting effects were for summer only, the borders coming into flower with the first roses and early perennials such as peonies and irises. Now drifts of tulips have been added to give a colourful display in May, growing beside emerging hosta and alchemilla leaves, and lily bulbs, Japanese anemones and *Buddleja* 'Dartmoor' prolong the season into autumn. Other plants more recently added include

Beningbrough Hall

The double facing borders stretch north and south. The wider border to the east is backed by a high wall; to the west the border is partly backed by an old box hedge. Both are given a formal pattern with repeated planting of *Buddleja* 'Dartmoor', and shrub roses and other shrubs give structure. The planting plan shows a section some 27.5 m (75 ft) long, towards the northernmost end of the 45 m (150 ft) border.

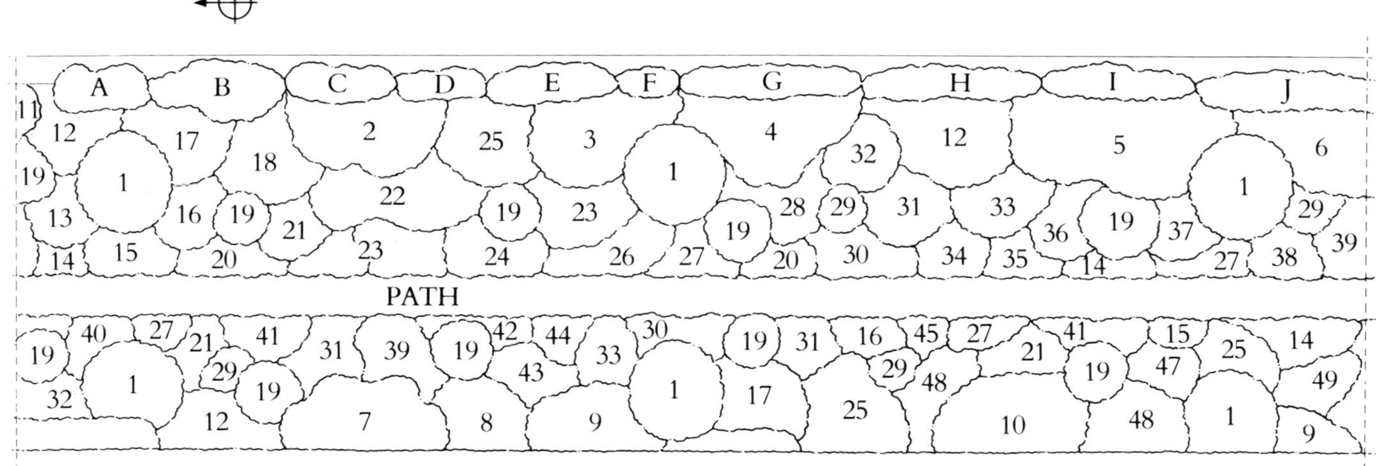

KEY

On wall

- A *Clematis* 'Perle d'Azur'
- B *Lonicera japonica halliana*
- C *Clematis* 'Etoile Rose'
- D Existing yellow rose
- E Existing pink rose
- F *Clematis* × *triternata* 'Rubro-marginata'
- G *Clematis* 'Venosa Violacea'
- H Existing pink rose
- I *Clematis* 'Comtesse de Bouchaud'
- J Rose 'Allen Chandler'

Shrubs

1 *Buddleja* 'Dartmoor'
2 Rose 'Felicia' (2 plants)
3 *Cotinus coggygria* 'Royal Purple'
4 *Rosa glauca* (3)
5 *Rose* 'Penelope' (3)
6 *Philadelphus* 'Erectus' (2)
7 Rose 'Iceberg (5)
8 *Berberis* × *ottawensis* 'Superba'
9 *Deutzia* 'Magician'
10 Rose 'Escapade' (5)
11 *Philadelphus* 'Belle Etoile' (2)

Perennials

12 *Cimicifuga cordifolia* (3)
13 Clump of lilac *Iris germanica*
14 *Dianthus* 'Charles Musgrave' (5)
15 *Stachys macrantha* (5)
16 *Campanula glomerata dahurica* (5)
17 *Miscanthus sinensis* 'Variegata' (3)
18 *Geranium psilostemon* (3)
19 Peony
20 *Alchemilla mollis* (6)
21 *Anemone* 'Prince Heinrich'
22 *Crambe cordifolia* (2)
23 *Geranium endressii* (5)
24 *Hosta fortunei hyacinthina*
25 *Thalictrum delavayi* (5)
26 Clump of purple/maroon *Iris germanica*
27 *Anaphalis triplinervis* (5)
28 *Campanula persicifolia* – blue (5)
29 *Lilium candidum* (5)
30 *Nepeta gigantea* (5)
31 *Achillea* 'Moonshine' (6)
32 *Miscanthus sinensis* 'Gracillimus'
33 *Anemone* 'Honorine Jobert'
34 *Sisyrinchium striatum* (5)
35 *Lamium* 'White Nancy' (5)
36 Clump of yellow *Iris germanica*
37 *Lychnis coronaria* (7)
38 *Penstemon* 'Garnet' (5)
39 *Hosta sieboldiana elegans* (2)
40 *Geranium pratense* (5)
41 *Nepeta* × *faassenii* (5)
42 *Geranium* 'Russell Prichard' (6)
43 Clump of lilac *Iris germanica*
44 *Penstemon* 'Pink Endurance' (5)
45 *Geranium* 'Johnson's Blue' (3)
46 *Salvia* 'Superba' (7)
47 Clump of lavender *Iris germanica*
48 *Thalictrum aquilegifolium* 'Album' (5)
49 *Penstemon* 'Castle Forbes' (5)

Thalictrum aquilegifolium with fluffy lilac-pink flowers in early summer, and *T. delavayi* which bears its rich lilac, creamy-centred small flowers in July and August.

Mr David Beardall, who is Head Gardener at Beningbrough, writes about the maintenance programme for the year:

❧ Once the border was established the soil is enriched annually with Growmore and a thick mulch of cow manure (or any available mulching material) is added to improve the texture, keep in moisture through the summer and prevent weed germination. The soil, which is alkaline, is never dug; worms and bacteria do the digging. The leaves of *Prunus* 'Tai-Haku' do occasionally show magnesium deficiency and the soil is treated with magnesium sulphate. Otherwise, the tasks for the year consist mainly of pruning shrubs, dead-heading roses, and cutting down herbaceous foliage in autumn or early spring. The hybrid musk and floribunda roses are given an additional 'shaping' when the dead-heading is done after the first flowering flush in June. This keeps them to a reasonable size, especially in relation to the scale of other plants. All the herbaceous geraniums are clipped over with shears after flowering to encourage a repeat performance later in the summer. The deciduous shrubs which flower on the new wood such as *Buddleja* 'Dartmoor' are hard-pruned in winter. When grown among other plants rather than as a specimen this particularly good cultivar with very dark purple flower-trusses and a semi-prostrate habit needs to have its lower branches removed to raise the head. The purple-leaved *Cotinus coggygria* 'Royal Purple' will benefit from spring pruning if foliage effects are required; its typical smoke-bush flowers will then be sacrificed. For maximum leaf colour and size the previous year's shoots are cut back to the lowest two buds. Those deciduous shrubs which flower on old wood, such as deutzia and philadelphus, have their flowering shoots removed immediately after the flowers fade. The bushes can be shaped at the same time. Penstemons flower almost continuously, but need to have their dead flower-spikes regularly removed. Cuttings of these are taken every year in case the winter is severe.

On the wall to the east the climbing roses are pruned in early autumn, carefully tied back to horizontal wires attached to the wall by vine eyes. The large-flowered and late-flowering clematis are pruned towards the end of winter. Also on the wall the semi-evergreen honeysuckle with fragrant whitish-yellow flowers (*Lonicera japonica halliana*) benefits from cutting back in spring, long shoots sacrificed and dead wood and 'ends' removed. ❧

The double border at Beningbrough Hall is planted with shrubs, roses, perennials and bulbs to cover most of the summer season.

At MOUNT STEWART beds in the Italian Garden to the south of the house are in carefully thought-out colour patterns. The soil is acid and moisture-retentive and humidity is, in general, high. Rainfall is 87.5 cm (35 in) but does not approach that of the Cornish gardens, and periods of drought are not unknown. Because of its situation on Strangford Lough, exceptionally mild winters are normal. Nevertheless many of the plants grown in these beds would thrive in a colder garden, and most of the plants are not fussy about a more alkaline soil. To east and west groves of tall *Eucalyptus globulus* give wind protection and make a frame for this part of the garden. From the terrace above, a gap in the tree planting permits a view to the Mountains of Mourne.

Groups of beds laid out in strict colour patterns as formal as a parterre surround a fountain on either side of the lawn. Each planted area is divided into four sections, each of which is further subdivided into three parts. All follow a definite colour scheme to which both leaves and flower-heads contribute in season. This is further emphasized by the foliage of a surrounding low hedge, which has been mentioned before. The hedge marks out a strong pattern and holds the designs together, giving a formal character to a scheme where the main planting is in a free style with the billowing soft foliage growth of herbaceous plants. To the east the predominating colours are bright and 'hot'; to the west grey and glaucous foliage sets off pale flower colours.

To the east a bed of standard and bush yellow roses, 'Whisky Mac' and 'Yellow Pages', is underplanted with scarlet perennial *Potentilla* 'Gibson's Scarlet' and edged with a 45 cm (18 in) hedge of clipped *Erica erigena* 'W. T. Rackliff'.

A companion bed is mainly of perennial plants with creamy-yellow, orange, vermilion and crimson flowers, but is given height with golden-leaved elder (*Sambucus racemosa* 'Plumosa Aurea'), which can be pruned back hard each year to prevent it from dominating other plants. In June a delphinium with creamy-yellow flowers and tangerine-coloured *Papaver pilosum* are effective with the glowing young foliage of the elder, and penstemons, including *Penstemon* × 'Schönholzeri' and *P. gloxinioides* 'Rubicunda', both scarlet-toned, begin to flower. Later the recently introduced yellow form of *Phygelius aequalis* flowers beside a citron-flowered montbretia making a cool contrast to the 'hot' colours of bronze-leaved *Lobelia* 'Scarlet Cardinal' and yellow-flowered *Rudbeckia maxima*, both of which need the moisture-retentive soil and high humidity which exists in this garden. The low surrounding hedge is of a dwarf berberis, *Berberis thunbergii* 'Atropurpurea Nana'.

Planting in the third bed is also mainly of herbaceous perennials with flowers of scarlet, bronze, citron-yellow and apricot, with a purple-leaved cotinus (*Cotinus coggygria* 'Royal Purple') as a feature plant. *Monarda didyma* 'Cambridge Scarlet' flowers early with a dark purple delphinium and the even darker carmine-flowered *Paeonia* 'Monsieur Martin Cahusac', while clumps of strong day-lilies, including *Hemerocallis* 'Stafford' and *H.* 'Burning Daylight', have mahogany-bronze flowers in July. Corms of *Watsonia beatricis* flourish in the mild climate at Mount Stewart and add an exotic note by late summer, growing between clumps of *Rudbeckia subtomentosa*, with black-eyed yellow daisies, and the brilliant scarlet blooms of *Penstemon* × 'Schönholzeri', which will continue to flower from mid-summer to October if regularly dead-headed. In gardens with a less favourable climate other watsonias, forms of *Watsonia pyramidata*, mainly with pink or white flowers, can be lifted and stored for the winter. However, *W. beatricis*, its grassy foliage almost evergreen, does not like to be dried off. This bed is edged round with a low hedge of a golden-leaved cultivar of *Thuja occidentalis*.

On the western fringe of the lawn the eucalyptus trees cast light shade over the beds where paler pink, blue and white flower colours predominate, with occasional strong accent given by the magenta-crimson flowers of the tall *Geranium psilostemon* in June and July, followed by the bright blue spherical heads of *Agapanthus inapertus pendulus* in August. All the 'reds' here have distinct bluish pigment and none of the flaming almost vermilion touches found in the east beds. The only plants used in both the east and west parterres are the purple-leaved cotinus and, round the roses, the same Mediterranean heather (*Erica erigena* 'W. T. Rackliff') is used for a hedge. The cotinus is a feature to contrast with silvery-grey foliage of *Artemisia ludoviciana*. Standards of the creamy-white rose 'Pascali' give height above 30 bushes of 'Dame Edith Helen', a 1920s hybrid tea double pink rose, underplanted with pink-flowering *Potentilla* 'Miss Willmott'. Near the cotinus iris, astilbe, hemerocallis and dicentra contribute foliage shapes, while mauve and pink flowers from thriving perennials succeed each other through the summer. The white form of martagon lily, *Veronica virginica alba* and *Astilbe* 'Bridal Veil' have flower-heads tinted rather than a pure 'laundry-white', to blend gently with the overall colouring. Shining young leaves of the toad lily (*Tricyrtis formosana stolonifera*) are welcome in spring, and their tall stems bear spotted reddish-mauve flowers in late summer. The glaucous-leaved Jackman's rue of the surrounding hedge begins to resent the overhead eucalyptus canopy, but its particular foliage contribution is hard to replace.

In the third section, hedged by grey-leaved *Hebe albicans*, planting is dominated by the California tree poppy (*Romneya coulteri*), with soft greyish-green foliage and papery white flowers. To extend flower colour until the first cold spell pink-flowered *Dahlia* 'Gerrie Hoek' is planted to make a strong group. *Olearia moschata*, a rare shrub, reflects the micro-climate at Mount Stewart. With silvery greyish leaves, the bush grows here to 90 cm (3 ft) and as much across, and is covered in white daisy-flowers in July. Different coloured border phlox and late-flowering Japanese anemones finish the season.

Mount Stewart

The Italian Garden at Mount Stewart is divided into two distinct colour themes. To the east colours are 'hot'; to the west flowers and foliage are pale. Detailed planting is shown for a representative quarter-section of a parterre in either colour scheme.

North-east corner of the West Parterre

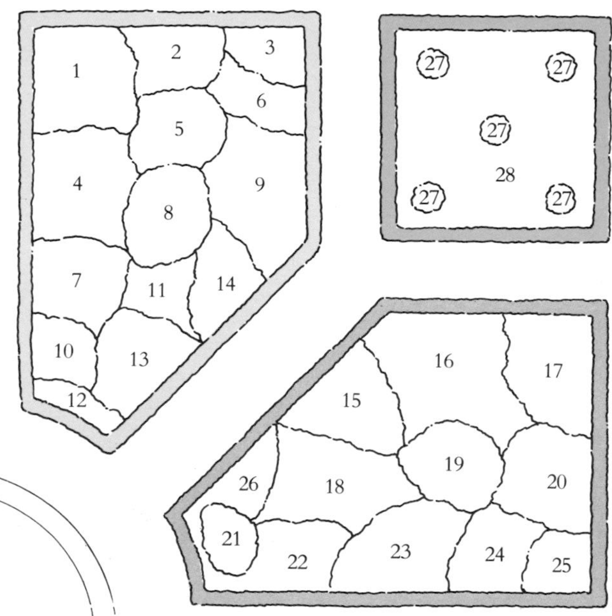

Low hedges round 1–14: *Ruta graveolens* 'Jackman's Blue'; round 15–26: *Hebe albicans*; round 27–28: *Erica erigena* 'W. T. Rackliff'

North-west corner of the East Parterre

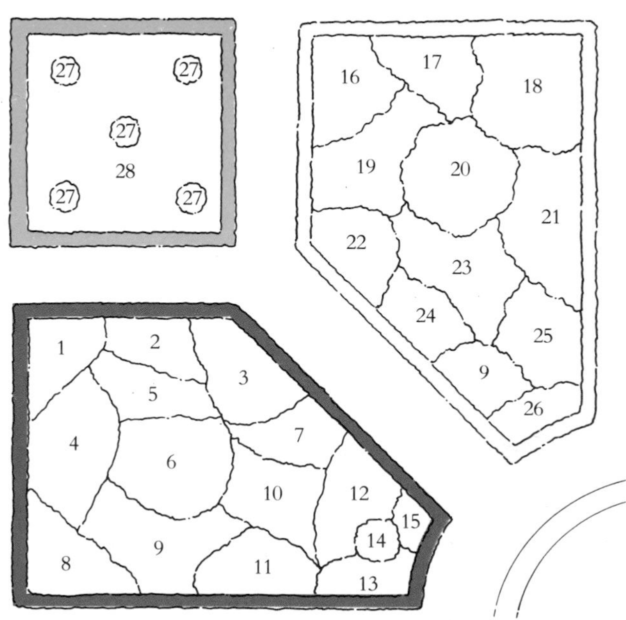

Low hedge round 1–15: *Berberis thunbergii* 'Atropurpurea Nana'; round 16–26: gold-leaved *Thuja occidentalis*; round 27–28: *Erica erigena* 'W. T. Rackliff'

West Parterre
KEY

1. *Cotinus coggygria* 'Royal Purple'
2. *Artemisia ludoviciana*
3. *Anemone* 'Hadspen Abundance'
4. *Geranium psilostemon*
5. *Veronica virginica alba*
6. *Iris* 'Jane Phillips'
7. *Agapanthus inapertus pendulus*
8. *Delphinium* (lilac-pink)
9. *Dicentra spectabilis*
10. *Tricyrtis formosana stolonifera*
11. *Astilbe* 'Bridal Veil'
12. *Hemerocallis* 'Pink Damask'
13. *Filipendula purpurea*
14. *Lobelia* × *vedrariensis*
15. *Salvia* 'East Friesland'
16. *Polemonium foliosissimum*
17. *Romneya coulteri*
18. *Anemone* 'September Charm'
19. *Delphinium* (white)
20. *Dahlia* 'Gerrie Hoek'
21. *Olearia moschata*
22. *Iris* 'White City' with *Allium christophii*
23. *Dictamnus albus*
24. *Phlox* 'Elizabeth Campbell'
25. *Astilbe* 'Amethyst'
26. *Monarda* 'Prairie Night'
27. Standard Rose 'Pascali'
28. Bush Rose 'Dame Edith Helen' & *Potentilla* 'Miss Willmott'

East Parterre
KEY

1. *Lobelia* 'Scarlet Cardinal'
2. *Phygelius aequalis* (yellow)
3. *Crocosmia* 'Citronella'
4. *Phlox* 'Harlequin'
5. *Rudbeckia maxima*
6. *Delphinium* (creamy)
7. *Lobelia* × *vedrariensis*
8. *Crocosmia* 'Carmine Brilliant'
9. *Penstemon* × 'Schönholzeri'
10. *Phlox* 'Prince of Orange'
11. *Potentilla recta macrantha*
12. *Inula hookeri*
13. *Penstemon gloxinioides* 'Rubicunda'
14. *Sambucus racemosa* 'Plumosa Aurea'
15. *Papaver pilosum*
16. *Phlox* 'Red Indian'
17. *Monarda* 'Cambridge Scarlet'
18. *Cotinus coggygria* 'Royal Purple'
19. *Centaurea ruthenica*
20. *Delphinium* (purple)
21. *Watsonia beatricis*
22. *Hemerocallis* 'Stafford'
23. *Rudbeckia subtomentosa*
24. *Heuchera* 'Greenfinch'
25. *Paeonia* 'Monsieur Martin Cahusac'
26. *Hemerocallis* 'Burning Daylight'
27. Rose 'Whisky Mac'
28. Rose 'Yellow Pages' & *Potentilla* 'Gibson's Scarlet'

Mr Nigel Marshall the Head Gardener at Mount Stewart, provides a season-by-season summary of the maintenance work in these formal beds:

✤ Autumn and Winter Work

Certain vigorous plants such as *Veronica virginica*, *Geranium psilostemon*, hemerocallis, kniphofias, border phlox and *Campanula lactiflora* need to be lifted and divided approximately every three years, or they begin to dominate the various colour combinations and groupings of plants. The foliage is cut down prior to lifting. The ground is dug over incorporating garden compost and well-rotted farmyard manure. This is also a good time to remove any persistent perennial weeds such as bindweed or couch grass. After digging the ground should be well firmed by treading with the feet prior to planting. The plants are then divided, usually with two forks back to back. The divided pieces should have three to four crowns; this will ensure nice-sized clumps for flowering in the following season.

This is a good opportunity to make any necessary adjustments in the planting plans, altering shapes and relationships of groups. Also by planting plants in different places over a period of years the incidence of 'replant sickness' is lessened. This applies particularly to roses, which cannot be replanted in the same beds in which they have been for many years. Border phlox also seem to benefit from being moved to a new site every few years.

At this time of year most of the foliage may be cut down and the ground generally tidied up and lightly forked over. However, the stems and leaves of tender plants such as fuchsias, penstemons and salvias should not be removed until the spring. This will help to protect the base of the plants from severe frosts through the winter. In addition bracken or other fern foliage can be worked into the ground round the base of the more tender plants. Cannas, dahlias and any other plants with tubers are best if lifted from the ground and stored in a frost-proof shed over the winter. *Lobelia cardinalis* and its various garden hybrids are also vulnerable and best lifted and 'boxed' up, then placed in a cold frame for the winter, where the foliage is kept dry. These plants, completely hardy in their own habitat where winters are much more severe than in Britain, suffer most from alternating periods of cold weather and wet followed by mild spells which encourage premature growth. Further cold will then nip new shoots and weaken the plant's constitution. In north-east America their crowns often remain in frozen wet ground all through the winter and emerge healthy in the warmth of spring. The young basal growths of

other plants such as delphiniums will be attacked by slugs during any mild spells in the autumn. This may seem unimportant, but often they lay eggs round the crown of the plant and new shoots are ravaged in the following spring, causing real havoc. Either slug pellets or liquid slug killer should be applied to keep these pests at bay.

Spring Work

In the spring work starts when ground conditions allow, and any still outstanding winter tasks are completed as soon as possible. The remainder of last year's foliage may also be removed before any young shoots start to emerge, as otherwise they may get damaged in the process of cutting back. Some plants such as *Aster amellus* varieties, ornamental grasses and kniphofias are best lifted and divided in early spring and not during the autumn. Apply a general garden fertilizer at two ounces per square yard at this time of year and lightly fork it in and generally tidy up the soil. This is a good time to apply a mulch of compost or spent mushroom manure before too much growth appears on the plants. In the past mushroom compost was 'lime'-based and would tend to make the soil more alkaline over a period of years, so that some nitrogen would have to be added, but the composition of growers' compost now normally does not bring this side-effect.

During April and May plants such as fuchsias, lobelias, young penstemons (taken as cuttings the previous season) and salvias can be safely planted out. They will stand the occasional overnight frost if properly hardened off. Dahlias and cannas are best left for a further few weeks until all danger of spring frosts has passed. As growth proceeds certain plants should be either staked or supported with bushy twigs, cut to about two-thirds of the expected height of the flower-stems. For staking strong plants such as delphiniums use 1.5 m (5 ft) bamboo canes, allowing two flower spikes to each cane. Shoots on delphiniums are best thinned out to give good-quality flower-spikes. This should be done when shoots are about 23 cm (9 in) in length, allowing seven or eight spikes per each established clump. Each stem will need two or three ties before actual flowering time.

Opposite: At Mount Stewart in Northern Ireland the flower beds in the Italian garden are in strictly arranged colour schemes. To the east the flower colours are warm: vibrant yellows, oranges and reds.

Spraying Operations

Herbaceous plants are not often bothered by garden pests. In some areas capsids can be troublesome and will spoil fuchsias, puncturing foliage and stems and preventing flower-buds from opening. One spray with a systemic insecticide should be sufficient control, if applied when foliage growth is well advanced but before any capsid damage is visible. Delphiniums are often subject to mildew attack, especially in areas of high humidity. This can be prevented by spraying with benomyl once or twice in the growing season. If lilies (and some other *Liliaceae*) and peonies are grown, watch for *Botrytis*, especially in a wet season, as this can ruin the plants. Benomyl will also counteract this, and a systemic insecticide added to the mixture will control the aphids which carry certain virus diseases fatal to lilies in particular.

Routine Summer Work

This consists mainly of removing spent flower-heads on plants to prevent seeding and to allow later flowering. After flowering, forms of anthemis should be cut down to about 15 cm (6 in) to encourage basal growth before the autumn, which is then left on for flower production the following season. August is a good time to lift and divide the bearded iris, *Iris germanica*. This is necessary roughly every five or six years. After lifting, incorporate garden compost or well-rotted farmyard manure into the soil and apply a handful of bone-meal. In gardens where the soil is acid, add two handfuls of hydrated lime per square metre (or per square yard). When replanting select the strong young rhizomes from around the outside of the old clumps. These should not be buried, but planted with the top half above soil level. Heucheras are best if divided and replanted in September rather than in the following spring. Plant the woody rootstock well below soil level to prevent them drying out.

Dwarf Hedges around the Beds

Low-growing hedges round the edge of the beds conform with the two distinct colour schemes. At the east end where there are strong flower colours of red, orange, yellow and purple, the hedges are of plum-coloured *Berberis thunbergii* 'Atropurpurea Nana' and a golden cultivar of *Thuja occidentalis*. To the west, where the colouring is much softer, the plants with pink, mauve, lavender, white and cream flowers predominating, the low hedges are of grey-leaved *Hebe albicans* and the glaucous *Ruta graveolens* 'Jackman's Blue'. All the hedges are clipped over twice a year, in spring and mid- or late summer to keep them approximately 45 cm (18 in) high and 30 cm (12 in) wide. Even at Mount Stewart there are occasional losses of rue, which is probably due to the fact that this west end of the south lawn is shaded and overhung by nearby trees (which would have been newly planted when the colour schemes were first devised in the 1930s), especially during the afternoons, which makes the plants 'drawn' and young stems and foliage soft and susceptible to cold winters. Being a Mediterranean plant, rue thrives where open exposure to sun will ripen and harden the wood. The cool damp atmosphere experienced in this Irish microclimate encourages excessive growth, and this combined with wet soil conditions, makes such a plant vulnerable to frost.

There are various other problems associated with these 'colour' beds. In original planting plans bergamot (forms of *Monarda didyma*) were used, but did not prove a success in this maritime climate. They suffer from dry spells in summer, and humidity causes mildew. Border phlox, while invaluable for colour display during August, all have to be protected by rabbit netting. Rabbits are a severe trouble but fortunately netting need only be 45 cm (18 in) high and by midsummer it is completely hidden by foliage. It is interesting to note that forms with variegated leaves, 'Harlequin' and a new white-flowered cultivar from the USA, 'Mt Fujiyama', are ignored by the rabbit population and never need protection.

Japanese anemones provide a long season of colour in late summer but are rather invasive. These have to have their roots chopped round with a spade quite frequently to keep them within bounds. It is not advisable to lift them regularly and replant as they take a few years to settle down again after disturbance. *Echinacea purpurea*, with mauve-crimson daisy-flowers on strong branching stems, has also not been a success at Mount Stewart. Unfortunately nurserymen usually distribute this plant in autumn when they only do really well if transplanted in spring.

Rose Beds

In the four corner beds of both parterres hybrid tea and floribunda roses are planted to conform with the colour schemes in neighbouring beds. Five standard roses are underplanted with some three dozen of the bush type. These in their turn have groups of low-growing herbaceous potentillas planted beneath them as ground cover. In spring tulips, chosen to give a hint of the colour patterns which come later in the season, provide interest in the rose beds. The rose beds are surrounded by hedges of shrubby *Erica mediterranea* (now correctly *E. erigena*) 'W. T. Rackliff', which has dark green leaves carried very densely and white flowers with conspicuous brown anthers. The erica is clipped over annually after flowering and the hedging is kept to a height matching the material used round the flower-beds. ✤

BLICKLING HALL in Norfolk has quite a harsh climate compared to that of Mount Stewart, but many of the same hardy perennials are used in the famous 'square' beds on the main lawn east of the house. Rainfall is much lower as you would expect in a garden in East Anglia, and a moisture-retaining mulch of well-rotted farmyard manure is essential. Although topiary yew specimens mark the corners of each square and outside beds edged with catmint are planted with roses, the rest of the planting is of herbaceous plants only, carefully graded for size and colour. Interestingly, when originally laid out by W. A. Nesfield for Constance, Lady Lothian, the parterres, although many more in number and much more elaborate, were filled with hardy plants rather than the tender 'bedding' plants favoured in most grand gardens in the Victorian era. By the 1930s many of the smaller beds were swept away and Mrs Norah Lindsay, a well-known amateur designer, prepared plans for planting the remaining squares which we see today. Although roses such as the pink 'Else Poulsen' and scarlet 'Kirsten Poulsen' are original floribundas dating from 1924, it has not been thought necessary to use only plants which would have been available to Mrs Lindsay. New garden cultivars which prove healthy and flower for long periods are used in addition to older varieties which need more maintenance. Basically the colour schemes are as she planned them.

Mr Charles Simmons, the Head Gardener at Blickling, writes about the planting and upkeep of these beds:

✤ In the early 1930s the fussy and complicated network of small beds and topiary, laid out in 1872, was drastically reduced and simplified, leaving four large square corner beds, now flanked by rectangular island beds of roses and catmint. At each outer corner, and actually positioned in the

Mrs Norah Lindsay designed the square beds at Blickling Hall in the 1930s. Colour schemes are strict. In the two beds farthest from the house flowers are predominantly yellow and orange with a touch of red; in the other two squares colours are blue, mauve, pink and white with a touch of crimson.

rose bed, a yew bush, acorn-shaped and about 3.7 m (12 ft) in height, stands in military fashion. After fifty years depressions in the grass still mark the position of many of the smaller beds which were levelled and turfed over at the time. The dense yew blocks shaped like grand pianos were also retained, and these stand aloof on their own areas of grass beyond the four square beds.

In the two beds nearest the house the flower colours are a blend of blue, mauve, pink and white, with a touch of crimson from the Rose 'Else Poulsen'. In the two beds beyond the colour

Blickling

In the east lawn at Blickling four square beds are arranged in blocks of carefully graded colour. All are surrounded by a symmetrical planting of roses edged with catmint, with clipped yews marking the corners. Detailed planting plans are shown for one bed in each of the colour schemes.

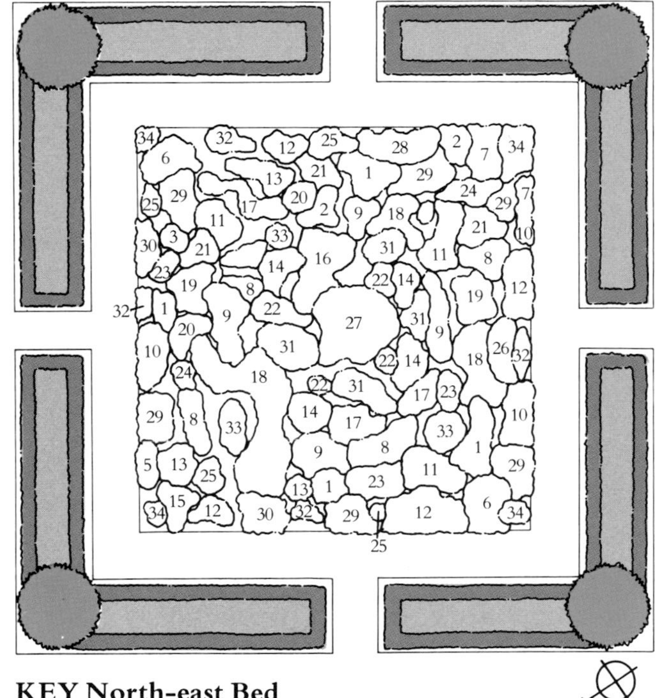

KEY North-west Bed

1 *Aconitum × bicolor*
2 *A.* 'Bressingham Spire'
3 *A. napellus carneum*
4 *A.* 'Spark's Variety'
5 *A. vulparia*
6 *Anaphalis margaritacea*
7 *Astrantia major*
8 *A. maxima*
9 *Campanula lactiflora*
10 *C. persicifolia* 'Telham Beauty'
11 *C. trachelium* 'Albo Plena'
12 *Delphinium*
13 *Dictamnus albus purpureus*
14 *Echinops ritro*
15 *Erigeron* 'Quakeress'
16 *Eupatorium purpureum*
17 *Galega officinalis*
18 *Geranium endressii*
19 *Lactuca plumieri*
20 *Lavatera cultivata*
21 *Leucanthemum maximum* 'Phyllis Smith'
22 *Liatris spicata*
23 *Limonium latifolium*
24 *Lychnis chalcedonica*
25 *Lythrum salicaria* 'Brightness'
26 *L.s.* 'Robert'
27 *Macleaya cordata*
28 *Monarda didyma* 'Cambridge Scarlet'
29 *Phalaris arundinacea* 'Picta'
30 *Phlox* 'E. Campbell'
31 *Bistorta amplexicaulis* 'Atrosanguinea'
32 *B.* 'Superba'
33 *Salvia* 'Superba'
34 *Sanguisorba* sp.
35 *Sidalcea* 'Croftway'
36 *S.* 'Croftway Red'
37 *S.* (own)
38 *Stachys olympica*
39 *S. macrantha*
40 *Thalictrum delavayi*
41 *Veronica spicata*
42 *V. virginica alba*
43 *V.v. japonica*
44 *Yucca filamentosa*

KEY North-east Bed

1 *Achillea* 'Coronation Gold'
2 *A.* 'Moonshine'
3 *A. ptarmica*
4 *Aconitum napellus*
5 *Anaphalis margaritacea*
6 *Anthemis* 'E. C. Buxton'
7 *A.* 'Grallach Gold'
8 *Antholyza coccinea*
9 *Artemisia lactiflora*
10 *Campanula trachelium* 'Albo Plena'
11 *Centaurea macrocephala*
12 *Erigeron* 'Quakeress'
13 *Helenium pumilum*
14 *H.* 'Riverton Gem'
15 *H.* 'The Bishop'
16 *Heliopsis scabra* 'Bladhams'
17 *H.s.* 'Incomparabilis'
18 *H.s.* 'Zinniiflora'
19 *Ligularia dentata*
20 *Lilium × testaceum*
21 *Lychnis chalcedonica*
22 *Macleaya cordata*
23 *Phalaris arundinacea* 'Picta'
24 *Potentilla nepalensis* 'Master Floris'
25 *Rudbeckia fulgida deamii*
26 *R. nitida* 'Goldquelle'
27 *R. maxima*
28 *Sisyrinchium striatum*
29 *Solidago* 'Goldenmosa'
30 *S.* 'Lemore'
31 *Solidago*
32 *Stachys olympica*
33 *Verbascum chaixii*
34 *Yucca filamentosa*

Catmint edging
Rose beds

scheme is yellow, pale orange and red. Certain plants such as grey-leaved *Stachys olympica* are used as edging in all four beds, and a single specimen of *Yucca filamentosa* stands at each corner, effectively linking the two schemes and ensuring that they seem part of an integral design. Groups of the double white-flowered *Campanula trachelium* 'Albo Plena' are also repeated in all the beds. The planting schemes and colour associations for each pair of beds is similar but not identical. For instance clumps of *Eupatorium purpureum*, *Lactuca plumieri* and pink-flowered lavatera take central positions in both of the beds to the west, nearest the house.

Aconitum napellus is in the middle foreground and *Erigeron* 'Quakeress' is at the edge of both the beds. In the yellow and orange beds to the east *Rudbeckia maxima* and golden rod (an old form of *Solidago* – unidentified) dominate both beds in late summer, occupying the central position, but other plants are repeated in more random positions. Mrs Lindsay understood how colours will appear to change when used in different associations and she never hesitated to use an identical plant with different neighbours to produce her desired effects.

In the beds grading of heights was carefully thought out. The immediate impression is that the soil towards the centre has been raised by 60–90 cm (2–3 ft). In actual fact the difference in soil level is no more than about 23 cm (9 in). In the beds nearest the house height in the centre is obtained by using plants such as *Lavatera* 'Olbia Rosea', the blue-flowered globe thistle (*Echinops ritro*), *Campanula lactiflora* and delphiniums. Sloping away from the centre and providing intermediate height are various veronicas, *Lythrum salicaria* 'Robert', *Astrantia major* and *Salvia* 'Superba'. Towards the extreme outside edge are groups of *Geranium endressii*, mauve-flowered *Stachys macrantha* and silvery-leaved *Anaphalis margaritacea*. In the two beds farthest from the house rudbeckias and tall macleaya are flanked with lower-growing cream-flowered *Artemisia lactiflora* and *Ligularia clivorum*. At the edge the forms of the shorter *Rudbeckia fulgida* stand in front of the lemon-flowered *Anthemis tinctoria* 'E. C. Buxton'. These are only a few of the plants used in the four beds and by careful choice of plants which flower successively through the summer the overall picture conveys the defined colour scheme from June to early autumn.

Bordering the west beds are pink and crimson polyantha roses, 'Else Poulsen' and 'Kirsten Poulsen', their colours blending with massed flowers in neighbouring beds. Catmint (*Nepeta mussinii*) contributes soft grey leaves and mauvish-blue flowers most of the season, cutting back in midsummer preventing it swamping the rose bushes and ensuring repeat – almost continuous – flowering. In 1985 severe winter frosts killed many catmint plants, and these had to be replaced in the spring. The further beds are bordered with polyantha roses, crimson 'Locarno' and orange-red 'Gloria Mundi', and similar planting of catmint.

Maintenance of these four colourful beds and the long border near by follows a similar annual pattern, and is a procedure which works well. All plants are cut down in November to within 12–15 cm (5–6 in) of ground level, and the beds are raked clean. Because of the density of plants there is no serious weed problem in the summer, although weeds do germinate at the outer edge where there is light and space. Digging is always done in the autumn, but again, can only be done when plants have to be divided or moved, as there is no space even for forking over. Farmyard manure is spread thickly over the surface of the soil as space permits. Some plants are split and replanted in the late autumn but, in this relatively cold climate, it is safer to leave division of many until the spring. This also allows an assessment of winter losses.

Staking the taller plants is carried out through May and June, as the plants grow, and at Blickling traditional pea-sticks are still used in preference to more modern methods. They are effective and unobtrusive. Another old practice still adopted here is the use of white painted wooden labels. These may last only two seasons, but they seem in keeping with the atmosphere of the garden, and are much appreciated by the many visitors.

At FELBRIGG HALL, near the coast in Norfolk, a double border runs east–west through the centre of the old walled garden. A box hedge contains the edge and planting is of shrubs only, including a good mixture of old and modern shrub roses, except for a ribbon of autumn-flowering colchicums along the front on either side, inside the boxwood. Much of the original planting was experimental and over the years changes have been made. Lilacs make a formal rhythm along the back of the border, although they have developed some problems.

Planned for minimum maintenance, the shrubs have grown together so that almost no bare soil is visible. Although some winter pruning is necessary (followed after a bad winter by cutting back dead shoots) and an organic mulch given occasionally to help conserve moisture, very necessary in this area of drying winds and a rainfall of 62 cm (25 in), the borders are much less labour-intensive than ones where perennials need dividing and reshuffling every few years, or where pockets of annuals are added to give a long season of flowering colour. The shrubs were chosen to give balanced interest through most of the summer months, some even when not in flower having good textured or col-

Felbrigg Hall

The shrub borders in the old walled gardens are edged with box, behind which autumn-flowering colchicums make a ribbon of mauve in September. These double borders are backed with lilac bushes (marked 'A' on the plan), and strong bushy shrubs such as buddlejas or shrub roses are planted at regular intervals in the central part of each border ('B' and 'C' on the plan). The larger shrubs are single specimens and the smaller ones are planted in groups to cover approximately the same spread. These shrubs include berberis, cistus, hardy fuchsia, hebe, hydrangea, hypericum, potentilla and some groups of bush roses. In the front lower-growing shrubs extend the flowering season and are chosen for their flower and foliage. All these woody plants are planned to grow together and interlock: the plan is formalized with regular outlines but, in reality, most of the bushes have more flowing shapes. This plan shows, from the western end, approximately half the 42 m (45 yd) length of the twin borders: the rhythmic planting continues throughout the border.

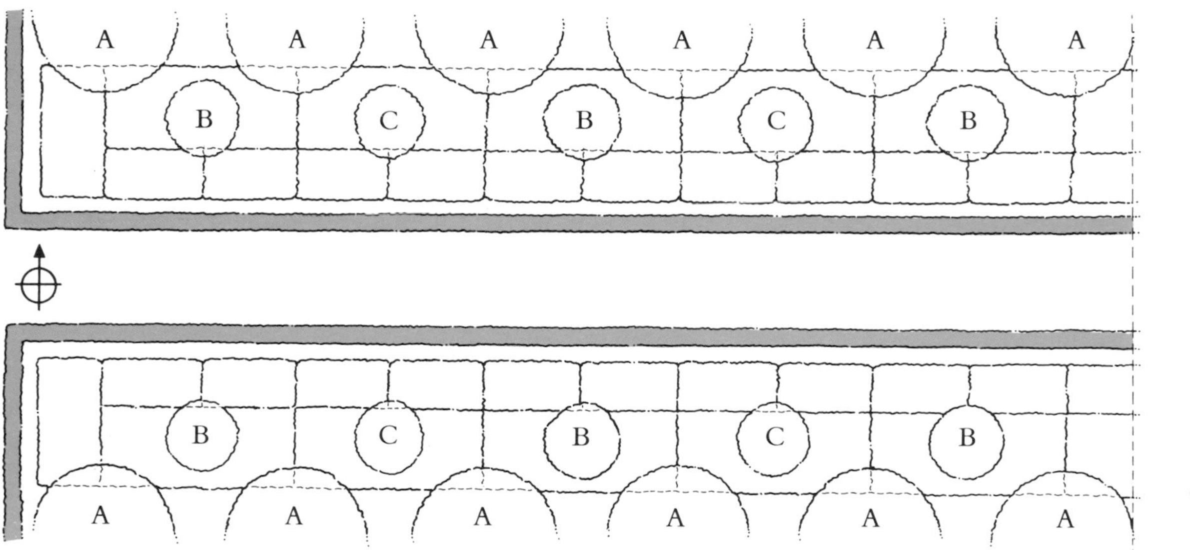

List of Plants in the Borders

Roses
'Nova Zembla'
'Lavender Lassie'
'Little White Pet'
'Anna Zinkeisen'
'Golden Wings'
'Bright Smiles'
'Bonn'
'Fairy Damsel'

Buddlejas
Buddleja 'Black Knight'
B. fallowiana alba
B. 'Harlequin'
B. 'Lochinch'

Shrubs
Berberis 'Rose Glow'
B. thunbergii atropurpurea
Caryopteris × *clandonensis*
Ceratostigma willmottianum
Cistus albidus
C. creticus
C. 'Silver Pink'
C. 'Sunset'
Cotinus coggygria 'Royal Purple'
Cytisus × *beanii*
Daphne 'Somerset'
Euonymus fortunei 'Silver Queen'
Fuchsia 'Chillerton Beauty'
F. magellanica 'Molinae'
F.m. 'Versicolor'
F. 'Mrs Popple'
F. 'Riccartonii'
F. 'Tom Thumb'
× *Halimiocistus* 'Ingwersenii'
Halimium lasianthum
H. ocymoides
Hebe 'Amy'
H. 'Autumn Glory'
H. 'Great Orme'
H. 'Marjorie'
H. 'Mrs Winder'
H. 'Spender's Seedling'
H. 'Waikiki'
Helichrysum splendidum
Hydrangea serrata 'Blue Bird'
H.s. 'Preziosa'
Hypericum beanii
H. 'Hidcote'
H. kouytchense
H. moserianum
Phlomis fruticosa
Phygelius capensis
Potentilla 'Beesii'
P. davurica veitchii
P. 'Farrer's White'
P. 'Katherine Dykes'
P. 'Manchu'
P. 'Primrose Beauty'
P. 'Tangerine'
P. 'Vilmoriniana'
Romneya coulteri
Ruta graveolens 'Jackman's Blue'
Salvia officinalis 'Purpurascens'
Senecio 'Sunshine'
S. 'Anthony Waterer'
Spiraea 'Gold Flame'
Weigela florida 'Foliis Purpureis'
W.f. 'Variegata'
Zauschneria cana (tender)

At Felbrigg Hall late-summer colchicums are a feature of the shrub borders in the walled garden. Planted as a strip inside the formal box hedge, they need little attention except for removal of dying foliage in early summer.

oured foliage. The colour scheme begins with soft colours at either end and works through to strong colours in the centre.

Height and flower given by shrub roses in early summer is followed by strong growing buddlejas, which need hard pruning each February, and will flower on the young wood late in the year. The original plan made in 1977 has been modified as some hebes, cistus, the silvery-leaved *Dorycnium hirsutum*, *Senecio compactus* and ericas have proved unsuitable. *Cotinus coggygria* 'Royal Purple' has been substituted for purple-leaved *Prunus* × *cistena*.

Massed planting of bergenia at the back of the border has been temporarily abandoned because the ground was infested with perennial couch grass, which invaded the bergenias and made weeding impossible. The soil is now clean after an application of dalapon.

The colchicums (*Colchicum lusitanum*, *C. tenori* of horticulture) along the front of the border produce their fresh green leaves in early spring and for the good of the bulbs it is essential not to remove the dying foliage until the end of July, when it comes away easily in the hand. Damage to the tip of the bulb may well prevent the stemless flowers from developing for display in September. At Felbrigg the low box hedge partly hides the browning leaves as they die down. The National Collection of colchicums, organized by the NCCPG, is at Felbrigg (see Appendix).

Mr Ted Bullock, the Head Gardener, writes both of the routine maintenance of the border plants themselves, and of the more troublesome care of the lilacs behind the border:

❦ Well-rotted manure is applied only to the roses. A dressing of a balanced general fertilizer is given to the other shrubs in the border in spring. The density of shrubs seems to keep most of the weed at bay, so we only lightly fork over exposed areas. We don't mulch very often. Generally I keep fertilizers away from colchicums. It doesn't seem to be necessary where they are grown in relatively clean ground. If they were growing in grass, I would probably consider the application of organic fertilizers such as dried blood, hoof-and-horn or bone-meal.

The shrub roses are pruned only once a year, and up till now this has proved sufficient to keep the height and relative scales in the right proportions. I should mention that 'Little White Pet' has not been pruned for some years. We like the effective mass, now approaching 1.5 m (5 ft) in height, at the back of the border. The same rose in the garden at the front of the hall at Felbrigg is kept in check at about 75 cm (2 ft 6 in) maximum by two prunings a year, a main spring pruning and the lighter autumn cut-back, to reduce wind-rocking during the winter.

The lilacs behind the border at Felbrigg were originally obtained from Hilliers, L. R. Russell and Sunningdale Nurseries. Fifteen varieties of lilac were grown at Felbrigg. First planted in December 1973, they were obtained either growing on their own roots or grafted on to privet stock (*Ligustrum ovalifolium*). This was in order to avoid the problem of suckering shoots.

The varieties grown on the privet have not been successful due to rootstock incompatibility, which becomes apparent after a few years. Whole tops of trees gradually die back and the bush can become detached from the rootstock, especially in the high winds which prevail at Felbrigg.

It is therefore now thought advisable to avoid lilacs which have been grafted on privet, and instead obtain trees growing on their own roots or grafted on common lilac (*Syringa vulgaris*), carefully removing any suckers which do appear by cutting as close as possible to the main roots in summer.

Maintenance of lilacs otherwise is fairly routine. Faded flowers are removed as early as possible. In winter weak thin branches are cut out and old overgrown leggy growth can be cut back to approximately 90 cm (3 ft) from the ground, in order to rejuvenate them.

An occasional spray of liquid seaweed is given during the growing season, and an application of fertilizer is beneficial when the lilacs come into growth in spring. A layer of leaf-mould 7.5–10 cm (3–4 in) thick is applied every two or three years, acting as a weed suppressor and mulch.

In the spring of 1985 the tips of the lilac shoots developed a nasty wilt, which appeared very worrying. Plant pathologists, however, agreed that it was due to excessive moisture, the high humidity causing *Botrytis*. By late in the summer, growth and foliage looked healthy again. ❧

Opposite: At Nymans annuals for summer display are arranged in triangular groups in the double borders. Preparation of plants in spring is labour-intensive but results are spectacular.

In the walled garden at NYMANS a central grass path has a border on either side in which the main planting is of groups of summer-flowering annuals which keep a good display from the end of June until October. Aligned more or less north and south, the double borders are in two sections, separated by an Italian marble fountain and by topiary yew shaped into elaborate crowns. Growing in rough grass behind the borders, spring- and summer-flowering trees and shrubs give interest and height through the whole season. Buddlejas and the late-flowering shrubby chestnut (*Aesculus parviflora*) become part of the summer scene, joining with groups of tall strong-growing perennials planted at the back of each border to give structure and depth. Many of these perennials have architectural foliage, so that even when not in flower they make a good backdrop. Among the perennials are echinops, macleaya and tall day-lilies. Groups of dahlias, specially chosen for colour and height, help keep the borders colourful until late autumn.

The groups of annuals are planted in blocks of 20–30 plants, all of which are grown from seed in February. The total number of seed trays exceeds 600, and these, started in heat, are then pricked out with 30 small plants to each box. Fourteen boxes of each plant are divided up between the four borders, three for each and two are put aside in reserve: for no obvious reason annuals can 'miff' off at the pricking out stage or later. Sometimes all plants of one variety do not thrive; at others it may only be some, and the reserve boxes make up the difference. In 1985 all the trays of the pure white *Lavatera* 'Mont Blanc' were failures, and **Mr David Masters** filled in gaps with *Salvia patens* with luminous blue flowers and *Hibiscus trionum* with wide white mallow-shaped flowers with deep black centres. Both of these plants have been a success, and, in fact, if there is time for dead-heading, continue to flower over a much longer period than the annual lavatera. Both groups of white and red nicotiana are planted and the larger-flowered *Nicotiana alata* (syn. *N. affinis*) 'Grandiflora' whose white flowers are tinted greenish-yellow. In 1985 the early-flowering species *N. langsdorfii*, with sulphur-yellow flower tubes, has been used to increase the range. Seed of this was obtained from Sissinghurst and, interestingly, appears to have hybridized with some neighbouring plants of *N. alata*, as the tubular-shaped blooms are wider and larger than those of the true species. The taller F_1 hybrid antirrhinums in single-colour packets are getting increasingly hard to obtain.

Nymans

Plants used in 1985 include:

Ageratums: 'Spindrift', 'North Sea', 'Tall Wonder' and 'Blue Mink'
Antirrhinums: 'Kim', 'Coronette White', 'Coronette Pink', 'Coronette Bronze', 'Coronette Crimson', 'Coronette Yellow', 'Doublon', 'Leonard Sutton', 'Polar', 'Lyra', 'Tall Rocket Mixed' and 'Madame Butterfly Mixed'
Cleome hassleriana (syn. *spinosa*)
Convolvulus 'Dark Blue'
Godetia grandiflora 'Sybil Sherwood'
Hibiscus 'Sunny Day'
Hollyhock 'Summer Carnival'
Impatiens 'White Tilt', 'Mixed Tilt'
Lavatera 'Silver Cup', 'Mont Rose', 'Mont Blanc'
Nicotiana langsdorfii and *N. alata* 'Nicki Red' and 'Nicki White'
Petunia 'Red Joy', 'Blue Joy', 'Sugar Daddy'
Perilla frutescens, P. nankinensis, P. laciniata
Rudbeckia 'Green Eyes', 'Goldilocks', 'Gloriosa Daisy Mixed' and 'Marmalade'
Tanacetum parthenium 'White Stars'
Viola 'Chantreyland', 'Giant Yellow', 'Prince Henry', 'Blue Heaven'
Zinnia 'Envy'

Groups of cannas and *Lilium* × *parkmannii* are also planted.

Dahlias

Cultivar	*Colour*	*Height*
'Australia Red'	dark red	1.20 m (4 ft)
'Baby Rose'	pink single	1.50 m (5 ft)
'Baby Royal'	pink single	1.20 m (4 ft)
'Baldere'	orange/pink	0.75 m (2 ft 6 in)
'Cherry Wine'	red	1.50 m (5 ft)
'Cobham G'	bright orange	1.35 m (4 ft 6 in)
'David Howard'	deep orange	1.20 m (4 ft)
'Doxy'	white	1.00 m (3 ft 4 in)
'Edith'	pink/orange	1.50 m (5 ft)
'Future'	light pink	1.05 m (3 ft 6 in)
'Gerrie Hoek'	light pink	1.50 m (5 ft)
'Klankstad Kerkrade'	yellow	1.35 m (4 ft 6 in)
'Kochelsee'	red	1.00 m (3 ft 4 in)
'Large Red'	red	1.80 m (6 ft)
'Margaret Appleyard'	orange	1.20 m (4 ft)
'Murillo'	pink	0.30 m (1 ft 8 in)
'Nellie Geerlings'	red	0.30 m (1 ft 8 in)
'Pink Cactus'	light pink	1.50 m (5 ft)
'Polly Peachum'	dark pink	1.35 m (4 ft 6 in)
'Rothesay Castle'	light pink	0.90 m (3 ft)
'Sneezy'	white	0.30 m (1 ft 8 in)
'Wraybury'	white	1.20 m (4 ft)
'Zonnegoud'	yellow	1.00 m (3 ft 4 in)

Planting takes place at the end of May or even the beginning of June. Wedge shaped areas are outlined with a trickle of sand for each group of plants and a label is placed *in situ*. No prepared plan is used, but taller plants such as antirrhinums in a single colour are usually repeated in a regular pattern down the middle of the borders, and the same colour and plant combinations are used in the facing beds. Corner planting groups are also symmetrical. Groups of foreground plants are kept well away from the grass edge so that they will not fall over and make mowing and edge cutting difficult. The general effect seems to be carefully thought out, yet on close examination very variable. This is because the 'key' plants establish a formal rhythm and repetition of colour groups is restful to the eye and gives a sense of satisfactory order. Any plant which grows to more than 45 cm (18 in) needs staking. Fortunately bundles of pea-sticks of hazel or beech are obtained through another Trust property, and 40 bundles of both 2.25 m (7 ft 6 in) twigs and 1.2 m (4 ft) twigs are necessary. The tops of the sticks are bent over tidily in traditional style. David Masters finds that rabbits are a real worry immediately after the plants have been put out, and the area is too large to use netting, which would anyway look unsightly.

In late autumn the annuals are thrown away after any seed required is saved, the dahlia tubers lifted, cleaned off and stored in a frost-free shed, and the ground is then dug over and plenty of farmyard manure dug in. An artificial compound fertilizer, with an NPK ratio of 5.3:7.5:10 and containing chelated trace elements, is also added. There is neither winter nor spring bedding in these borders, which are kept for their spectacular three-months' summer display.

BARRINGTON COURT gardens, although attached to a National Trust property, are entirely maintained and run by the Lyle family who have lived at Barrington Court since 1923. The Lyles created the series of gardens we see today using designs by Forbes and Tait, the architectural firm already involved in the restoration of the house, but with some planting plans by Gertrude Jekyll. The resulting inner gardens have a strong Jekyllian flavour, with separate areas at their best in succeeding months throughout the summer, and colour schemes carefully graded to an overall plan.

Miss Christine Middleton, the Head Gardener at Barrington Court, writes about the maintenance of borders where annuals extend the length of flowering displays with strict colour themes:

❧ The gardens were planned within the existing walls of some old cattleyards. Four flower gardens were designed with quite distinct permanent plants. Summer and winter bedding schemes increased the length of flowering periods over the year. Through the years two distinct colour schemes have predominated in two separate walled enclosures. In one the colouring is hot and bright, mainly in yellow, orange, red and white. In the other more subtle tints are used, mainly pink, mauve, blue and white. By limiting colours grown near each other to those closely related in the spectrum the eye finds considerable satisfaction, and there are no jarring effects.

The colour plan is adhered to each year, but different plants may well be used. It is not intended to make the garden a 'museum' piece, planted to a strict design, repeated annually, but rather to allow the idea of successful colour combinations to develop further and further. Many visitors return to Barrington to study the colour associations and how they continue to evolve.

Summer Bedding in the Lily Garden

Against the wall the evergreen *Viburnum tinus* flowers in winter and early spring. On the wall the climbing rose 'Dublin Bay' has rich blood-red flowers and abundant glossy leaves. Permanent plants include *Lilium pardalinum* with orange-red purple-spotted flowers, *Helenium autumnale* 'Moerheim Beauty' with bronze daisies, the shrubby *Potentilla fruticosa* 'Katherine Dykes' and in the front plants of *Helianthemum* 'Wisley Primrose' with small grey leaves and pale yellow flowers. Summer bedding plants are *Dahlia* 'Top Affair', *Rudbeckia* 'Irish Eyes', African marigolds (*Tagetes erecta* 'Moonshot' and *T.* 'Paprika'), *Antirrhinum* 'Orange Glow' and *Nicotiana* 'Lime Green'. These plants cover a colour range of pale yellow through

Barrington Court

Planting schemes for two seasons in two garden areas show how permanent shrubs and perennials maintain the structure of the bed and in season appropriate bedding plants sustain the hot, bright colours of the Lily Garden and the subtler misty mauves and blues of the Lavender Walk.

Lily Garden

Summer

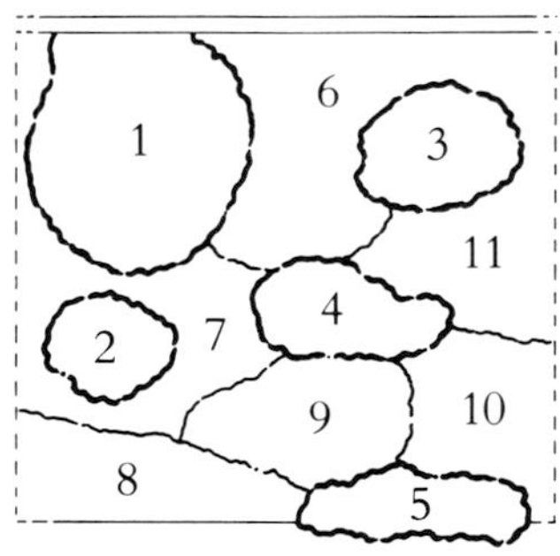

Winter

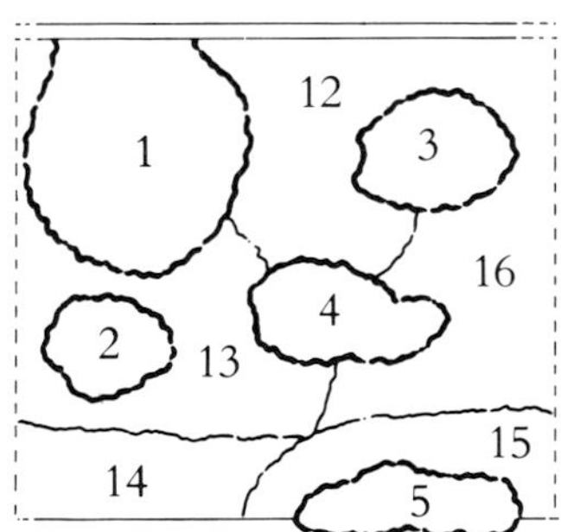

KEY

Permanent Planting

1 *Viburnum tinus*
2 *Potentilla* 'Katherine Dykes'
3 *Lilium pardalinum*
4 *Helenium autumnale* 'Moerheim Beauty'
5 *Helianthemum* 'Wisley Primrose'

Summer Bedding

6 *Dahlia* 'Top Affair'
7 *Nicotiana* 'Lime Green'
8 *Tagetes* 'Paprika'
9 *Antirrhinum* 'Orange Glow'
10 Marigold 'Moonshine'
11 *Rudbeckia* 'Irish Eyes'

Winter Bedding

12 Wallflower 'Orange Bedder'
13 Wallflower 'Golden Bedder'
14 Pansy 'Mount Everest'
15 Pansy 'Coronation Gold'
16 Wallflower 'Primrose Monarch'

Lavender Walk

Summer

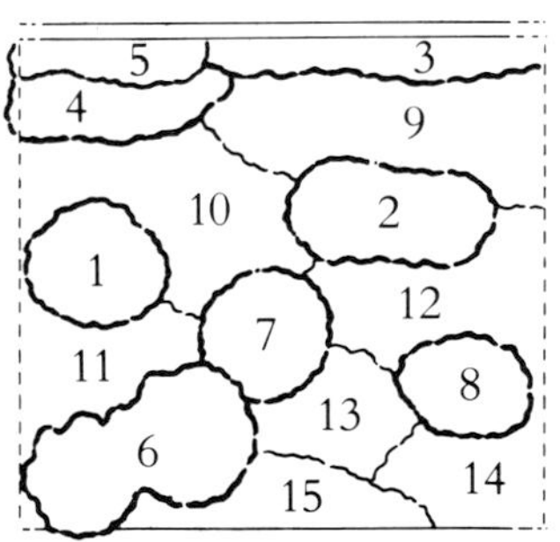

Winter

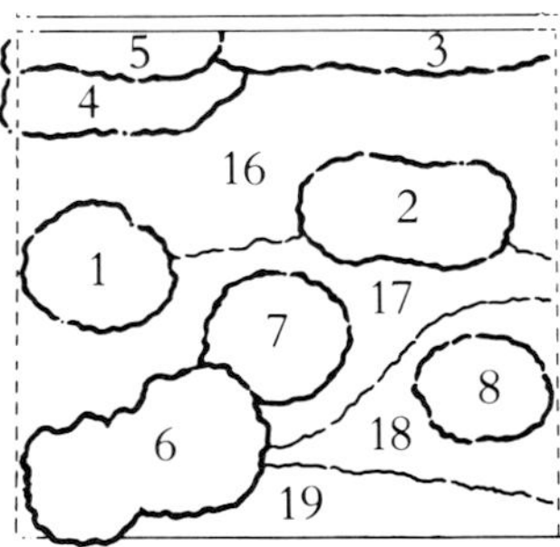

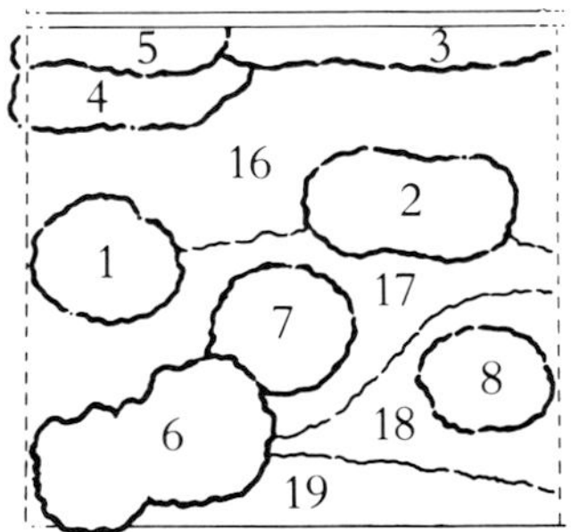

KEY

Permanent Planting

1 *Perovskia atriplicifolia*
2 Shrub Rose 'Penelope'
3 Rose 'Coral Dawn'
4 *Chaenomeles* 'Moerloosii'
5 *Clematis armandii*
6 *Lavandula angustifolia*
7 *Artemisia ludoviciana*
8 *Phlox* – white

Summer Bedding

9 *Cleome hassleriana* 'Pink Queen'
10 *Salvia horminum* 'Bouquet Mixed'
11 Heliotrope 'Marine'
12 *Verbena venosa*
13 *Petunia* 'Pink Joy'
14 *Aster* 'Milady Mixed'
15 *Ageratum* 'Blue Mink'

Winter Bedding

16 Wallflower 'Giant Pink'
17 Wallflower 'Carmine Icing'
18 *Myosotis* 'Royal Blue'
19 Pansy 'Ullswater'

orange to red, with greens and whites occasionally added. Blues and pinks are confined to other areas of the gardens. Although essentially this scheme is 'bright', by being confined to a definite range colour clashes are avoided and the composition is 'easy' on the eye.

Raising of Summer Bedding

Dahlias can be either potted and started into growth in a cold frame or planted straight into the ground in late April.

All other plants are raised in a glasshouse with a minimum temperature of 5°C (40°F). Seed is sown in trays of peat-based compost and kept in a propagating case at 10–18°C (50–65°F) until germination occurs. Trays are then removed to a glasshouse bench where they are grown on until large enough to be pricked off into John Innes No. 1 potting compost. Apart from the cleome and heliotrope, which are potted into 9 cm (3½ in) pots, seedlings are pricked into trays. They are then grown on until large enough to be transferred to cold frames for hardening off before planting out.

Beds are prepared by forking over, giving a dressing of a balanced fertilizer and raking after a firm treading. Plants are put in and watered and slug pellets are scattered near by.

Dahlias will need staking, but all the other plants should be self-supporting, with the exception of the cleomes, which might need some support if in a wind funnel or an exposed position. Antirrhinums, dahlias and marigolds in the Lily Garden will need regular dead-heading to keep them flowering continuously, but hoeing is the only task needed to keep the bedding scheme in the Lavender Walk tidy throughout the summer, from May to September.

Raising of Winter Bedding

Winter bedding in the Lily Garden consists of 80 plants each of the wallflowers 'Golden Bedder', 'Orange Bedder' and 'Primrose Monarch', and 35 plants each of pansies 'Mount Everest' and 'Coronation Gold'. In the Lavender Walk there are 80 plants each of wallflowers 'Giant King' and 'Carmine King', 15 *Myosotis* 'Royal Blue' and 35 pansy 'Ullswater'.

All seed is sown in drills in open ground in the nursery area at the end of May or the beginning of June. The plants are transplanted as soon as they are large enough into open ground in the kitchen garden, planted 23–30 cm (9–12 in) apart and with 30 cm (12 in) between the rows. They are grown on until the middle of October, when they are lifted and moved into their flowering positions.

Garden compost and fertilizer is added and the beds are forked over. The soil is consolidated and plants are put in 23 cm (9 in) apart. They are watered and slug pellets are scattered near by.

Summer bedding in the Lily Garden

	raising of bedding plants					bedding out		
plant	sown	germinated	pricked off	outside	planted	distance apart	eventual height	quantity
African marigold	4 Apr	7 Apr	15 Apr	7 May	28 June	23 cm (9 in)	30 cm (12 in)	25
Rudbeckia	5 Mar	10 Mar	29 Mar	29 Apr	28 June	30 cm (12 in)	60 cm (2 ft)	12
Antirrhinum	8 Feb	17 Feb	15 Mar	15 Apr	28 June	23 cm (9 in)	30 cm (12 in)	40
Nicotiana	28 Mar	10 Apr	18 Apr	7 May	28 June	23 cm (9 in)	60 cm (2 ft)	25
Tagetes	4 Apr	7 Apr	28 Apr	11 May	28 June	15 cm (6 in)	23 cm (9 in)	40
Dahlia						90 cm (3 ft)	135 cm (4 ft 6 in)	3

Summer bedding in the Lavender Walk

	raising of bedding plants					bedding out		
plant	sown	germinated	pricked off	outside	planted	distance apart	eventual height	quantity
Ageratum	5 Mar	9 Mar	7 Apr	7 May	25 June	15 cm (6 in)	23 cm (9 in)	25
Aster	28 Mar	30 Mar	18 Apr	7 May	25 June	23 cm (9 in)	23 cm (9 in)	30
Cleome hassleriana	15 Mar	22 Mar	5 Apr	28 May	25 June	60 cm (2 ft)	90 cm (3 ft)	9
Heliotrope	5 Mar	13 Mar	1 Apr	7 May	25 June	30 cm (12 in)	30 cm (12 in)	7
Petunia	19 Feb	26 Feb	15 Mar	15 Apr	25 June	23 cm (9 in)	23 cm (9 in)	20
Salvia horminum	28 Mar	31 Mar	7 Apr	28 Apr	25 June	30 cm (12 in)	45 cm (18 in)	25
Verbena rigida						23 cm (9 in)	45 cm (18 in)	25

There are few easily accessible guides to plants which will thrive in the milder counties, and today few nurseries stock plants which are not in general demand. Nevertheless many smaller plantsmen's nurseries can be searched out where stocks of the more unusual and perhaps 'difficult' plants are available. Every garden inside every region will have areas in it with a more favourable microclimate, caused by sheltering walls, overhead canopies or good frost drainage. Some gardeners are able to take the extra trouble necessary to get young plants through their first seasons in the open when they are at their most vulnerable, and protective shields put round them in winter will keep free from icy winds and frost (see 'Practical Maintenance' chapter).

It seems right, therefore, to include descriptions of two favoured borders where plants usually accepted as tender and difficult grow successfully.

At OVERBECKS, on the Devon coast, where the climate is exceptionally mild, terraced gardens giving superb views out to the Salcombe estuary contain trees, palms, shrubs and many small plants which will not normally grow without protection. Unlike most of the woodland gardens in Cornwall, Overbecks has alkaline soil, a pH of 7.5, so rhododendrons and camellias do not flourish here, leaving room for other seldom-planted exotics which take advantage of the Mediterranean-type climate. A specimen camphor tree (*Cinnamomum camphora*) overhangs a cliff edge, and *Euonymus fimbriatus* (or possibly the very similar *E. lucidus*) with shining red young spring foliage towers 9 m (30 ft) above beds filled with tender fuchsias, irises, osteospermums, eucomis, fascicularias and both *Puya alpestris* and *Beschorneria yuccoides*. The New Zealand tree fern (*Dicksonia antarctica*) grows alongside *Astelia nervosa* and the difficult Chatham Island forget-me-not (*Myosotidium hortensia*). American agaves are being encouraged to establish themselves as permanent features.

There are so many rare plants at Overbecks that it is tempting to describe them in detail. Instead a plan is shown of just one typical border where flowers and jungly foliage give a tropical effect.

Mr Tony Murdoch, the Gardener-in-Charge for the National Trust, has drawn out a detailed plan of the west Museum Border which lies on the main lawn next to the house. With the warm climate and high rainfall plants tend to grow luxuriantly, so planting schemes cannot remain static. A rock face forms a backdrop to the bed and on it the tender early roses, pink-flowered *Rosa* 'Anemone' and *R.* 'Cooperi', the Burma rose, both forms of the Cherokee rose, *R. laevigata*, make a jungle of flower and foliage. The late-flowering *Clematis* 'Abundance' twines among the rose branches, its pinkish-red nodding flowers sporting creamy stamens.

Overbecks

The west Museum Border lies against a rock wall which gives added protection to an already favourable microclimate in the mild south-west. Plants grow vigorously and the foliage of many creates an almost tropical luxuriance.

Watsonias and gladiolus in clumps throughout the border

KEY

Herbaceous Perennials

1 *Mahonia acanthifolia*
2 *Phormium tenax* 'Purpureum'
3 *Matteuccia struthiopteris*
4 *Symphytum grandiflorum* 'Hidcote'
5 *Nicotiana langsdorfii*
6 *Zantedeschia* 'Green Goddess'
7 *Crinum* × *powellii*
8 *Kniphofia galpinii*
9 *Ricinus communis*
10 *Tithonia rotundifolia* 'Torch'
11 *Hedychium*
12 *Schizostylis* 'Viscountess Byng'
13 *Rudbeckia* 'Goldilocks'
14 *Viola* 'Irish Molly'
15 *Crocosmia* 'Jackanapes'
16 *Hemerocallis* 'Contessa'
17 *Helianthus* 'Autumn Beauty'
18 *Echium pininana*
19 *Hedychium greenei*
20 *Rudbeckia* 'Marmalade'
21 *Cosmos* 'Bright Lights'
22 *Phlomis russeliana*
23 *Phormium tenax* 'Firebird'
24 *Agapanthus* 'Headbourne White'
25 *Fuchsia cordifolia*
26 *Phlomis chrysophylla*
27 *Iris confusa*
28 *Adonis aestivalis*
29 *Cosmos* 'Sunset'
30 *Hemerocallis dumortieri*
31 *Gladiolus*
32 *Cortaderia selloana* 'Pumila'
33 *Astelia nervosa*
34 *Argyranthemum* 'Jamaica Primrose'
35 *Kniphofia northiae*
36 *Canna*
37 *Osteospermum* × *ecklonis*

Climbers

C1 *Rosa* 'Anemone'
C2 *Clematis* 'Abundance'
C3 *Rosa* 'Cooperi'

At the shady southern end of the border a clump of ostrich plume fern (*Matteuccia struthiopteris*) grows in front of the large-leaved *Mahonia acanthifolia* which bears its scented mimosa-yellow flowers in autumn and through early winter. The purple-leaved New Zealand flax (*Phormium tenax* 'Purpureum') makes an architectural background, its huge sword-like leaves contrasting with the delicate lime-yellow tubular flowers of the species *Nicotiana langsdorfii*. In front *Zantedeschia aethiopica* 'Green Dragon' makes a strong group. The half-hardy *Tithonia rotundifolia* 'Torch' from Mexico with orange daisy-flowers grows next to ricinus and tender hedychium species, including red-flowered

At Killerton planting groups are of generous size but the relative scales of mixed perennials and annuals in the main border require careful planning ahead.

Hedychium greenei. The tall blue echium, *Echium pininana* flowers and seeds itself through the border, above white agapanthus and soft grey-leaved phlomis bushes, which include *Phlomis russelliana* and *P. chrysophylla*, the latter with a golden tint to the foliage. Canna, the tender *Argyranthemum* (syn. *Chrysanthemum*) 'Jamaica Primrose', the silvery *Astelia nervosa* and the desirable *Kniphofia northiae*, the flower-spikes of which open yellow from buds of coral-pink, between tall grey-green leaves. Towards the house end of the border a clump of pampas grass (*Cortaderia selloana* 'Pumila') carries silky plumes in autumn. Groups of watsonias from South Africa grow luxuriantly throughout the bed, and in this favoured climate survive the winters.

At KILLERTON in east Devon, where the soil is lime-free and frosts are not uncommon, a warm border against the house was replanted following repairs and repainting by **Mr Richard Fulcher**, then Head Gardener. The border, rich in botanical interest, expresses the tastes of a plantsman.

Facing west and hardly more than 45 cm (18 in) wide the bed is crammed with plants which give each other protection. A large *Fremontodendron californicum* makes a background curtain, and eccremocarpus and the annual Canary creeper, *Tropaeolum peregrinum* with lemon-yellow flowers and fresh green leaves, clambers against the wall and through other plants.

There is a good collection of salvias, which include *Salvia rutilans*, the pineapple sage *S. fulgens*, *S. leptophylla*, *S. discolor* with grey leaves and purple-black flowers, *S. greggii*, *S. juriscii*, *S. leucantha*, *S. bacheriana* with dusky purple flowers and glossy leaves, and the bright blue-flowered *S. patens*, which is normally grown annually from seed or cuttings. Good foliage plants include the silvery-leaved *Argyranthemum foeniculaceum* (syn. *Chrysanthemum foeniculaceum*), grey-leaved gazanias, the trailing *Euphorbia myrsinites*, *Convolvulus cneorum*, a small plant of the slow and rare *Pachystegia insignis*, related to the olearias, *Othonnopsis cheirifolia* with bright yellow daisies and *Hebe* × *franciscana* 'Variegata', all of which provide a good balance of ornamental leaves. A collection of diascias with pink or mauve flowers, *Agastache mexicana* with sage-like pink to crimson flowers, *Anisodontea hypomadarum* and *Malvastrum lateritium*, *Sphaeralcea fendleri* and *Penstemon centranthifolius* with bright carmine flowers carried on tall 90 cm (3 ft) stems are all flourishing. *Lobelia tupa* has dusky rich-red flower spikes.

At CHARLECOTE PARK soil is alkaline and dries out easily. The climate is much more severe than that of Cornwall. **Mr David Lee**, the former Gardener, writes about the border which runs along the edge of woodland to the north of the house:

✾ The 'Shakespeare Border' is situated on the site of an old pleasure-boating canal, which finally fell into disrepair in the eighteenth century. The water-bed was finally filled in with soil, possibly taken from the river's edge when it was being widened, and planted up as a shrubbery with evergreens such as box, holly, phillyrea and yew, and later the snowberry (*Symphoricarpos albus*) from North America, which spreads rapidly in the neutral dry soil. It was left as a shrubbery until 1973 when it was decided to plant it, as far as possible, with plants mentioned in Shakespeare's plays. In 1558 Shakespeare when still a youth had been caught poaching and arraigned before Sir Thomas Lucy, whose descendants finally gave Charlecote to the National Trust in 1946. Heartsease, dog and sweet violet, columbine, burnet, the poisonous hemlock and aconite, saffron and cuckoo flower have been encouraged to spread through the bed.

Preparation

Before planting, all other plants which had crept in over the years had to be removed, and the existing box hedge running along the west side of the border (*Buxus sempervirens*, not the dwarf form) which had grown distorted and unkempt had to be severely cut back into the old wood to encourage a better shape. After many years of neglect the soil was in poor condition. Both perennial and annual weeds were a problem, and it was important to eradicate ground-elder and enchanter's nightshade before planting any of the perennials. It is extremely difficult to use contact herbicides on a weed such as ground-elder once it is growing thickly round the crown of herbaceous plants without damaging the plants themselves. After initial clearance heavy mulches of well-rotted garden compost have been applied annually to improve the structure of the soil, provide nutrients and to help suppress annual weeds. In an old garden seeds of nettles, brambles and others will remain dormant in the soil for many years, only germinating when conditions improve.

The new border is essentially a mixed one, where woody shrubs such as rosemary, lavender, sage and rue mingle with herbs which were of medicinal or culinary use. Other shrubs which were known to Shakespeare, and mentioned in Gerard's *Herbal* of 1597, include the cabbage rose or rose of Provence (*Rosa centifolia*), the damask rose (*R. damascena*), myrtle (*Myrtus communis*), broom (the native *Cytisus scoparius*) and the spiny gorse (*Ulex europaeus*). These are permanent feature plants in the border and give height and solidity. Most of the herbs grown for use before the seventeenth century tend to become woody and grow untidily, giving a border an uncared-for look, so particular trouble is taken to dead-head spent flowers and to cut back the more straggling shoots all through the growing season. When plants such as wormwood (*Artemisia absinthium*), burnet (*Sanguisorba officinalis*), chamomile (*Anthemis nobilis*) and forms of pinks – in Shakespeare's time known as gilly flowers – are regularly cut back they make strong bushy plants.

In early autumn flowering stems are removed from all plants where flowering has finished and the seed, if required, has been collected. Plants such as hemlock (*Conium maculatum*), burnet and columbine (*Aquilegia vulgaris*) will all seed too prolifically if allowed, and become as much of a nuisance as any weeds.

An essential part of the management of this border is replacing groups of plants every three to four years. Cuttings from semi-ripe wood are taken from lavender bushes (*Lavandula angustifolia*), rosemary (*Rosmarinus officinalis*), the common sage (*Salvia officinalis*), thyme (*Thymus officinalis*) and marjoram (*Origanum vulgare*) in August and propagated in a cold frame. Seed is collected from the hemlock, pot marigolds (*Calendula officinalis*), cowslips (*Primula veris*) and oxlips (*P. elatior*), or they are allowed to seed in moderation *in situ*. The seed from double daisies (*Bellis perennis*), the common broom and wild primroses (*Primula vulgaris*) can be sown in seed pans the following spring and the young plants pricked out in rows to be given permanent situations in late summer. Other plants such as chamomile can be increased by division, best carried out in spring. Thyme and marjoram can also be divided in this way. ✤

Mr Lee also points out that the plants grown in the border do not include *all* of Shakespeare's plants, but only those which might reasonably have been found in English herb gardens towards the end of the sixteenth century. Gerard, of course, lists more than two hundred in his *Herbal*.

Charlecote Park

A section of the Shakespeare Border at Charlecote Park, where plants mentioned by Shakespeare grow against a box hedge backing on to the deer park.

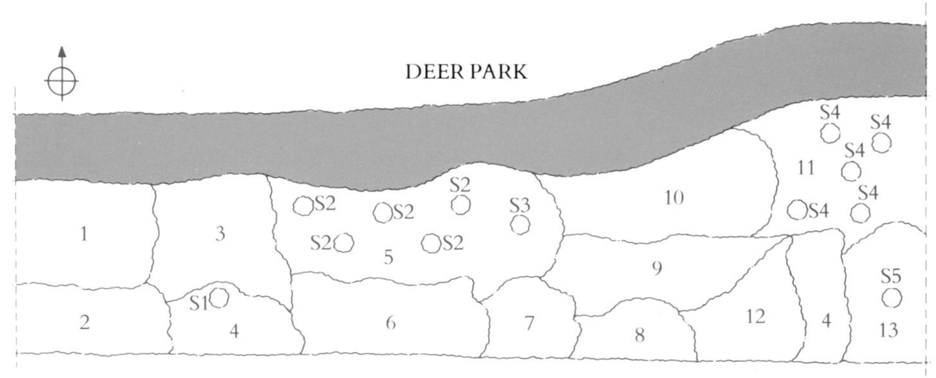

KEY

Herbaceous perennials

1 Rosemary (*Rosmarinus officinalis*)
2 Lavender (*Lavandula angustifolia*)
3 Burnet (*Poterium sanguisorba*)
4 Double daisy (*Bellis perennis*) 'Flore Pleno'
5 Oxlip and madonna lily (*Primula elatior, Lilium candidum*)
6 Wild strawberry (*Fragaria vesca*)
7 Pink (*Dianthus*) 'Old Clove Red'
8 Camomile (*Anthemis nobilis*)
9 Columbine (*Aquilegia vulgaris*)
10 Wormwood (*Artemisia absinthium*)
11 Cowslip (*Primula veris*)
12 Sage (*Salvia officinalis*)
13 Rue (*Ruta graveolens*)

Shrubs

S1 Myrtle (*Myrtus communis*)
S2 Gorse (*Ulex europaeus*)
S3 Rose (*Rosa centifolia*)
S4 Broom (*Cytisus scoparius*)
S5 Rose (*Rosa damascena* 'Versicolor')

Rose Gardens

The conventional modern rose garden depends on the established regularity of growth, repeat-flowering habit and bright eye-catching colours of the modern hybrid roses. Perhaps fortunately, the Trust, in the main, looks after gardens where roses are either in separate garden areas, part of a mixed border scheme or have some definite historical association which sets a guide to the type of rose to be grown. The modern bush roses which need hard pruning each season have little decorative value through the winter months so, if space permits, are ideally sited behind a hedge or enclosed in a separate compartment where they are visited only in summer. The more vigorous types of bush rose and both old and modern shrub roses fit into planting schemes where other shrubs, herbaceous perennials, bulbs and annuals crowd next to them in happy association. In the third category are rose gardens which represent a particular style, where the roses planted are those that were readily available and fashionable at a definite date. The rose garden can be a complete unit in itself; it may or may not be linked with other garden themes or be in a style appropriate to the house.

Because Trust gardens are usually large it is often possible to fit these rose gardens with an historical context into an existing scheme. Nevertheless there are problems which arise because the visiting public have come to expect roses to have longer and more repetitive seasons of flowering than is possible if strict historical accuracy is maintained. By keeping or introducing architectural motifs with a strong period flavour the Trust has found it possible to extend the range of the rose plants without losing the authenticity of the design. Pale flower colours where pinks and mauves predominate; avoidance of 'salmon' or the more modern vibrant orange or vermilion hues; use of roses with clustered flower-heads rather than large florist's blooms – these are all considerations when planning a rose garden with a Victorian or Edwardian style. A rose garden of the 1930s will have the then new floribundas such as 'Else Poulsen', its flowers bright rose-pink carried in clusters above glossy bronze foliage. The popular hybrid tea 'Peace' was first introduced in 1939, the floribunda 'Frensham' in 1946. Most varieties have been superseded by modern roses, longer-flowering and disease-free. Trust period rose gardens are

In the Edwardian Rose garden at Polesden Lacey there are still many of the old varieties.

generally a judicious mixture of some old roses which represent the period and style, but with the addition of the more practically satisfying top performers available today.

At POLESDEN LACEY rose pergolas and beds date back to the Edwardian era, when Mrs Greville laid them out as a section within a walled garden. Now a large collection, it remains much as Mrs Greville made it. Some of the roses such as the ramblers 'Dorothy Perkins' and 'American Pillar' were raised in America in 1901 and 1902 respectively. For no good reason these roses seem now rather despised, but it is still a pleasure to discover them in an old garden. 'Dorothy Perkins' has small double pink clustered blooms; 'American Pillar', more strident, has large single flowers in a vivid carmine pink, with a pronounced white eye. Both have large glossy leaves, which need spraying to prevent mildew.

Elsewhere the Trust has constructed rose gardens or replanted them with roses appropriate to the period of the house or to the style of the garden, which may have been later. A Victorian rose garden at SHUGBOROUGH matches the period of the terraces, and at TATTON PARK a Gertrude Jekyll-type rose garden is planted with roses mainly in the pale tints she preferred. So far there has been no need for the Trust to attempt to reproduce gardens based on Thomas Robins' paintings of the eighteenth century, where he depicted roses on pillars and palings in very flowery settings, quite remote in style from the prevailing fashion of the landscape park. Nor has the Trust embarked on any design based on Repton's for Ashridge Park in 1813 where he planned a circular rosary with seventeen beds and surrounding trellis and garlands of roses. The nearest approach to an early-nineteenth-century rose garden is the collection at MOTTISFONT ABBEY, covering a wider range than the famous Malmaison roses of the Empress Josephine, immortalized individually by Redouté.

Modern or old shrub roses can be planted as bushes in mixed borders, or in beds of their own, often in the latter case with underplanting of suitable herbaceous plants and bulbs. At SISSINGHURST CASTLE the rose garden itself is filled with early gallicas, centifolias and newer hybrids and old species, all of which associate well with other plants – pinks, *Saponaria ocymoides*, alliums with spherical heads and grey foliage, colourful herbaceous geraniums and many others. Elsewhere at Sissinghurst roses are part of the typical 'cottage'-type planting, play-

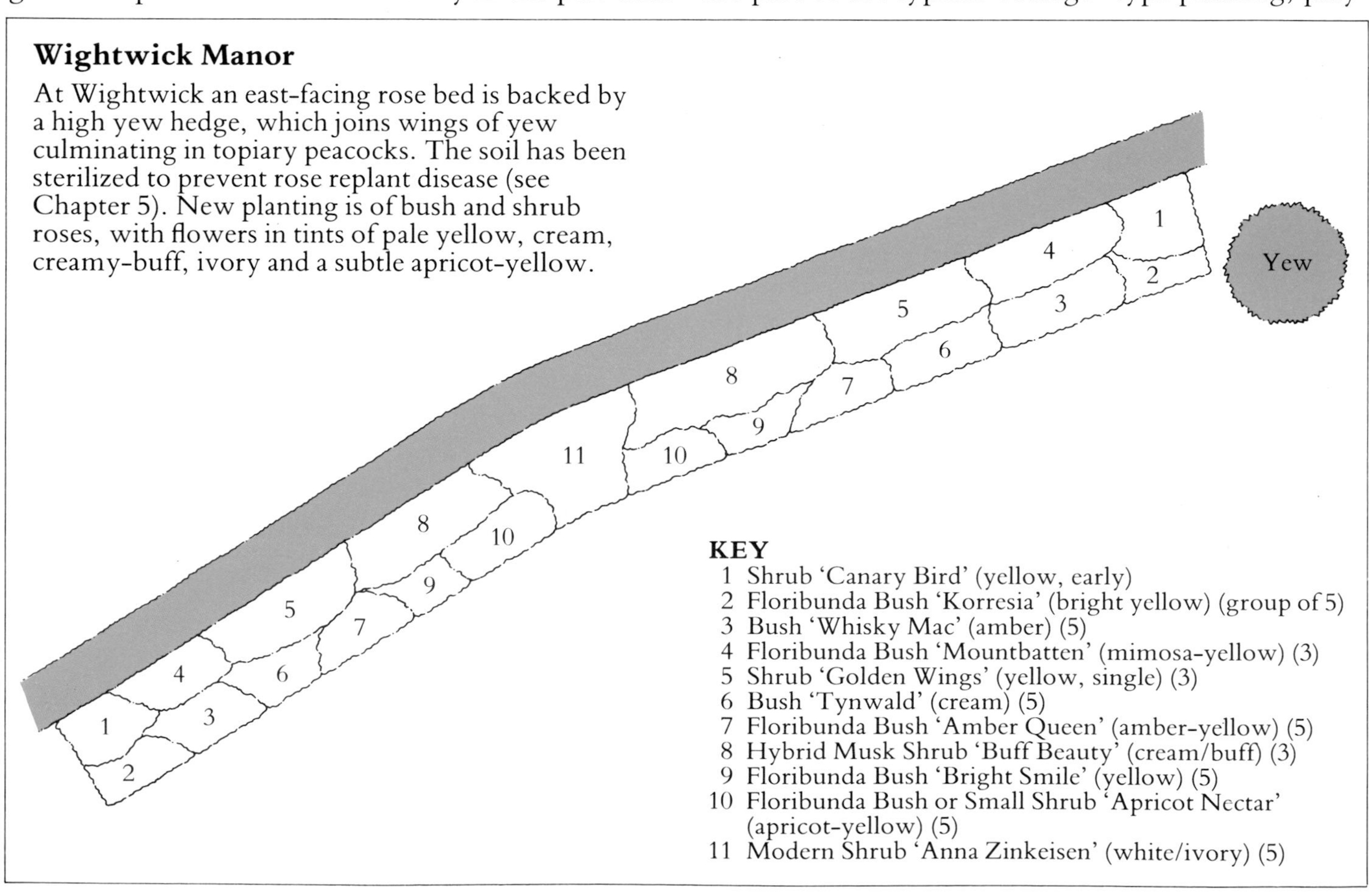

Wightwick Manor

At Wightwick an east-facing rose bed is backed by a high yew hedge, which joins wings of yew culminating in topiary peacocks. The soil has been sterilized to prevent rose replant disease (see Chapter 5). New planting is of bush and shrub roses, with flowers in tints of pale yellow, cream, creamy-buff, ivory and a subtle apricot-yellow.

KEY
1 Shrub 'Canary Bird' (yellow, early)
2 Floribunda Bush 'Korresia' (bright yellow) (group of 5)
3 Bush 'Whisky Mac' (amber) (5)
4 Floribunda Bush 'Mountbatten' (mimosa-yellow) (3)
5 Shrub 'Golden Wings' (yellow, single) (3)
6 Bush 'Tynwald' (cream) (5)
7 Floribunda Bush 'Amber Queen' (amber-yellow) (5)
8 Hybrid Musk Shrub 'Buff Beauty' (cream/buff) (3)
9 Floribunda Bush 'Bright Smile' (yellow) (5)
10 Floribunda Bush or Small Shrub 'Apricot Nectar' (apricot-yellow) (5)
11 Modern Shrub 'Anna Zinkeisen' (white/ivory) (5)

The walled garden at Mottisfont Abbey contains the national collection of old roses.

ing their part as neighbours to other shrubs or lower-growing plants. They are on walls and cascading out of old fruit trees in the orchard; in the white garden the central arbour of *Rosa mulliganii* dominates the planting scheme at the beginning of July, while white 'Iceberg' roses are set in frames of box to formalize the arrangements.

Mr Graham Stuart Thomas's rose collection at MOTTISFONT now includes 300 different forms, and occupies the old kitchen garden, where walls of mellow pink brick are a perfect background to the predominantly pastel tints of the older roses. Mottisfont is now a garden to be seen for one glorious moment in June, with an herbaceous border running up the centre; flowering plants chosen partly to coincide with the main 'flush' of rose bloom also have similar pale colours and nestle between foliage plants of silver and grey.

Under the main terrace at Montacute House shrub roses are underplanted with clumps of weed-suppressing hostas.

At MONTACUTE HOUSE a shrub rose border to the north of the broad terrace is underplanted entirely with groups of hostas, their sculptured leaves a perfect foil to the lax growth and arching stems of the rose bushes above them.

At ACORN BANK a border against a south-east wall has been planted with mixed shrub roses, among which foxgloves are encouraged to seed. Roses include an assortment of rugosas, the single white 'Alba' and the increasingly rare 'Belle Poitevine' with bright almost magenta flowers. Single-flowered rugosas usually have freely carried hips, so this border is colourful in autumn. Other roses in the bed are the shell-pink Alba rose 'Céleste', the yellow-centred single pink 'Complicata', and a moss rose 'William Lobb'. The edge of the bed in full sun is carpeted with *Stachys olympica*.

Roses are difficult to grow successfully in the acid soil and moist clean atmosphere of the south-west. At LANHYDROCK in Cornwall the formal box-edged beds on the south terraces within the walled court garden contain bush roses which need renewing every ten years. Some lime is added every year and feeding is given with a fertilizer which contains a higher proportion of potash to nitrogen than a normal balanced NPK brand. In this very wet and warm climate nitrogen tends to encourage growth and foliage rather than good flowering. Pruning is done twice, once in the winter to tidy the bushes and make them less subject to root-rock, and again in March to remove any frosted tips. The bushes are cut back very severely. A programme of regular spraying primarily against black spot starts as soon as the roses come into leaf, usually in mid- or even early April in this comparatively mild garden, where spring comes much sooner than in the north or east of the country. Mr Peter Borlase, the Head Gardener, prefers to change the brand of fungicide used fairly frequently; this and an insecticide are sprayed on at ten-day intervals until the end of the summer. Foliar feeds are also given towards the middle of the season and prove very effective.

On the lower terrace triangular beds at four corners are planted with floribunda-type bush roses including 'Lilli Marlene', with semi-double crimson-scarlet flowers carried in large open clusters, and bronze leaves. These beds surround a diamond shape in the centre where pale magenta-flowered 'Escapade' tones down the colouring, and contributes fragrance. On the second terrace a modern rose 'Bright Smile' has replaced massed planting of 'Allgold'. This bush rose is shorter than 'Allgold', and has slender buds which open buttercup-yellow. The foliage is glossy and healthy and is a great success at Lanhydrock.

On the third and highest terrace a rectangular bed of 'Else Poulsen' is surrounded by corner beds of 'The Fairy'. The former, one of the oldest floribundas (1924), has handsome dark glossy bronze leaves and bright rose-pink flowers in good trusses; unfortunately it is rather prone to mildew and is being replaced in several Trust gardens by the healthier and very vigorous China rose 'Nathalie Nypels' with flowers and foliage of very similar colouring. 'The Fairy' has small double pink globular flowers borne in large clusters, and glossy green foliage, and seldom grows to more than 60 cm (2 ft) but has a useful spreading habit.

Originally at POWIS CASTLE shrub roses were a separate feature on one of the terraces, but the heat and excellent drainage in these beds, set against high walls, were found not to be ideal. Recently rose beds have become a successful feature in the lower garden, and are outstanding for the interest and variety of low-growing flowering plants among the rose bushes; plants carefully chosen and massed in groups to complement the colour scheme found in each bed. The more vigorous hybrid musk roses (moved from one of the upper terraces) include substantial clumps of 'Buff Beauty', 'Penelope', 'Danae', 'Moonlight', 'Prosperity', 'Cornelia' and 'Felicia', all arranged in a bed facing south-west across the lawn. At the back of the border runs an original holly hedge which will be replaced in the next few years by English yew, to match the other hedges in this part of the garden. The vigorous bronze-leaved *Tellima grandiflora purpurea* and grey-leaved *Anthemis sancti-johannis*, with pure clear orange daisies, are planted in groups towards the back. In front, clumps of *Primula* Garryarde 'Guinevere', bergenia, the creeping South African *Diascia elegans* with delicate pale pink flowers, and the small white-flowered *Epilobium glabellum* give foliage or flower interest for much of the year, disguising the base of the rose bushes.

Beyond the end of the vine pergola, still facing south-west, a selection from the modern shrub Chaucer roses bred by the David Austin rose nursery is underplanted with clumps of the small glaucous-leaved grass *Festuca glauca*, another diascia, *Diascia cordata*, and *Allium karataviense* with striking foliage and globular flower-heads in early summer. These roses have been bred for fragrance and, unlike most of the older roses, continue to flower all the

Lanhydrock

In the walled court garden a pair of symmetrical rose beds lies on each of the three terraces that flank the path leading up from the gatehouse to the house itself. The formality of the scheme is emphasized by pillars of clipped Irish yew.

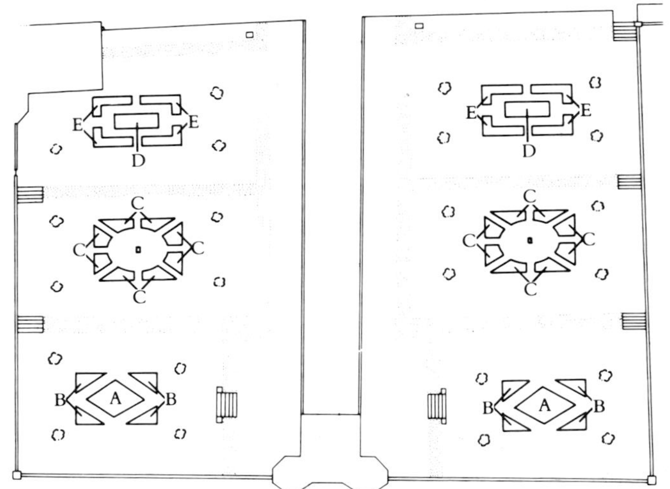

KEY

○ Irish yew

▫ Granite plinth with urn

Lower terrace:
A 'Lilli Marlene'
B Floribunda 'Escapade'

Middle terrace:
C 'Bright Smile'

Upper terrace:
D Floribunda 'Else Poulsen'
E Polyantha 'The Fairy'

Overleaf: Formal box edging surrounds the rose beds set in the main lawn at Lanhydrock. The rose bushes, in separate colour blocks, are sprayed and fed regularly.

Opposite: An enclosed garden area at Nymans contains a collection of old roses at their best in June. A rambler rose 'Goldfinch' covers the entrance archway.

Above: A rose border at Chartwell. Yellow roses are underplanted with alternating clumps of catmint and grey-leaved *Stachys olympica*.

summer. One of the best is 'The Friar', which has apricot-pink flowers of tea rose shape and scent. These shrubs remain about a metre (3–4 ft) in height and spread, and are suitable for the front of wide borders or make a feature bed in a modest-sized garden. The size of the rose bed here is 3.7 by 15 m (12 by 48 ft).

Mr Hancock reports that the soil is enriched with an annual mulch of leaf-mould mixed with straw, grass mowings and horse manure. He says that the fertile heavy soil with a pH of 7 'does' roses well, but a regular maintenance spray programme through the summer is necessary to keep the roses clean and healthy.

Along the back of a thick yew hedge another rose bed, this time formally box-edged, faces north-west. In this planting the colour schemes are bright gleaming yellows and the 'hot' colours of orange, scarlet and deep crimson. Here bush roses of floribunda type are hard-pruned in late spring. Yellows such as 'Allgold', which keeps its strong yellow tone even as the flowers fade, 'Arthur Bell' and 'Yellow Cushion', with paler yellow fading to cream, move round the spectrum towards the vibrant orange-flame colours of 'Zambra' (semi-double, 60 cm or 2 ft), the vermilion 'Orangeade', the scarlet 'Eye Paint' (1.2 m or 4 ft) and 'Lilli Marlene', and the deep crimson of 'Europeana' (60 cm or 2 ft). The roses are underplanted with *Mimulus* 'Whitecroft Scarlet' and the fiery *Alonsoa warscewiczii*, a half-hardy perennial from Peru, with dark green leaves and scarlet flowers 2.5 cm (1 in) across carried freely from June to October. The latter is easily grown from seed each year, to be set out in May. Another rose bed in more sober colours adjoins to the north and has its flowering season extended by the bronze-leaved *Primula* Garryarde 'Guinevere' with pale mauve flowers, and clumps of shooting star (*Dodecatheon meadia*) with rose-purple flowers carried on tall stems above a rosette of green, both of which thrive in the moist lush setting.

At NYMANS a shrub rose garden is representative of the best of those roses known before the First World War. Trellis arches and metal tripods are curtained with ramblers, and the bushes are underplanted with catmint, *Artemisia ludoviciana* and *Alchemilla mollis*, which harmonize with the pale mauves, pinks and creamy yellows. The planting is arranged round a circular brick well-head. Another planting of roses at Nymans is simple. Between double curving stone steps a whole bed is filled with *Rosa gallica officinalis*, with hydrangeas to prolong

the season. An outer bed is edged with *Euonymus* 'Silver Queen'.

At TINTINHULL HOUSE a pair of rectangular beds, tucked behind and north of 2.4 m (8 ft) yew hedges, is planted effectively with the same rose, its light crimson flowers carried towards the end of June for a spectacular three weeks. The rose foliage is subject to black spot and mildew, so the bed is regularly sprayed with a fungicide even after flowering is over. Earlier in the season, and beginning towards the end of March, when all the roses are cut down to a bud 15 cm (6 in) from the ground, blue scillas make a carpet of flower. Later the summer snowflake (*Leucoium aestivum*) flowers in April and May, thriving in the damp shade, with a few *Fritillaria meleagris* that have escaped from neighbouring beds.

In many Trust gardens, bush roses and shrub roses are used in mixed borders; shrubs, perennials, annuals and bulbs give a long-lasting display. In the kitchen garden at Tintinhull, where the theme is pink and misty blue, narrow double borders, divided into two sections by a cross-path, are backed by espalier pears which face each other across a stone-flagged path. When first planted by Mrs Phyllis Reiss in the 1940s, the floribunda pink rose 'Else Poulsen' was used, interplanted with bushes of August- and September-flowering *Caryopteris* × *clandonensis*. It was found that this bronze-leaved rose is prone to mildew, so recently the polyantha China rose 'Nathalie Nypels' (1919) has been substituted. With equally glossy bronze-tinted leaves, this rose flowers all summer if the dead-heads are regularly removed and it seems disease-free. The bushes are pruned hard at the end of March, and given a good mulch of farmyard manure or garden compost. As they come into leaf a regular spraying programme commences and they are given a sprinkling of Growmore as buds form and swell. In each of the four borders ten roses flank each side of a 10 m (11 yd) path, in flower beds 1.5 m (5 ft) in width. Between each rose but set at the back of the beds are bushes of the blue-flowered caryopteris and along the front the small catmint *Nepeta nervosa* bears its blue spikes all summer.

In 1985 the bedding *Ageratum* 'Blue Danube' was planted between the catmint and contributed a new

Above: At Peckover House in Wisbech rambling roses such as 'Paul's Scarlet Climber' and an old pink-flowered cultivar grow on arches above a gravel walk.

Opposite: In the kitchen garden at Tintinhull House a double border of pink roses is backed by espalier pears.

subtle shade of blue at ground level. *Verbena bonariensis* with 1.2 m (4 ft) tall branched stems and flat heads of violet has been allowed to seed at random throughout the bed. This verbena, hardy in some gardens, will flower readily in one season from self-sown seed. At the four farthest corners silver-leaved artichokes (*Cynara scolymus glauca*) are architectural, and eight pillars are clothed in scented honeysuckle (*Lonicera japonica halliana*), which has to be ruthlessly cut back each April.

Although this rose walk is chiefly dependent on the performance of 'Nathalie Nypels' and the pink and blue colour scheme, the season starts with the flowering of double rows of single early orange-scarlet *Tulipa* 'Prince of Austria' in late April. Clumps of tulip bulbs fit neatly between the plants of catmint along the front edge, and the grey leaves hide the dying foliage of the tulips.

Climbing roses are another feature at Tintinhull, and **Professor John Malins**, the tenant at Tintinhull House, describes how he prunes the roses on the brick and Ham stone walls which partly surround the garden and on the walls of the house itself:

❦ At Tintinhull walls abound and there is ample opportunity to study the habit of the various roses which are grown on them. Their height varies from 1.5 to 5.4 m (5 to 18 ft) and it is soon clear that 1.8–2.4 m (6–8 ft) makes for the easiest pruning. Wall plants are trained to horizontal and vertical wires (2 mm gauge), spaced at 50 cm (20 in) and made fast to wall nails which have a vine eye and are driven in at intervals of 2 m (6 ft).

Climbing roses vary a good deal in vigour and the yellow Banksian rose which produces long and slender shoots in profusion is the most difficult to prune. Its flowers are borne on wood which is at least two years old and pruning is confined as far as possible to the complete removal of older shoots. This particular plant overhangs a footpath and there has to be some extra pruning up to 2.4 m (8 ft) and tying in of long shoots above this, the work being done immediately after flowering.

We find that 'Paul's Scarlet Climber' and 'Guinée' on the west wall of the house need very little pruning beyond shortening of lateral shoots. 'Climbing Lady Hillingdon' will reach 4.5 m (15 ft) or more and to reduce this to 3.7 m (12 ft) is the limit of comfort on a ladder and does encourage flowering at a lower level, near to the eye and nose. We have three plants of 'Madame Grégoire Staechelin' on the north wall of the house and they need very little pruning to keep them below 3.7 m (12 ft) while the rather lax growth is not much disturbed as it gives support to the frail shoots of *Tropaeolum speciosum*, which do not climb until the roses' flowering period is over.

Very old plants of 'Climbing Crimson Glory' and 'Climbing Shot Silk' on a 2.4 m (8 ft) south-facing wall are fan-trained, avoiding at all costs any crossing over of branches. The laterals are shortened to three or four buds. With age, the main stems produced fewer laterals, and then one must hope to find one low down which can be trained as a replacement.

In this relatively mild climate pruning takes place in November and December of all roses other than the Banksian. Further action in the spring is rarely necessary, and never for those grown on walls. ❦

Rudyard Kipling's Rose Garden at Bateman's before flowering. The beds are edged with mossy saxifrage.

Rudyard Kipling loved the garden at BATEMAN's and took a considerable interest in its design. He is responsible for the pear alley already described, yew hedges, and the small formal rose garden which lies in the lower part of the garden beyond a pond screened with pleached limes. A channel from the pond draws water and feeds the rose garden's central fountain. Modern bush roses of floribunda type have replaced the original polyantha roses which were available when Kipling planted the garden. First bred in France at the end of the nineteenth century, polyantha roses, with clustered flower-heads, lost their popularity when the taller more vigorous floribundas were introduced between the two wars.

Mr Alan Champion, the Gardener-in-Charge at Bateman's, describes how the rose garden is maintained today:

❧ The rose garden was planned and planted by Rudyard Kipling. His original plan is on display in his study and is dated 1906.

The roses are of the floribunda type, now called cluster roses, but which when planted were called polyantha. Cluster roses are pruned at about the beginning of April. The reasons for pruning are to allow light and air into the bush and to fight pests and diseases. First of all you should make sure that your tools are in good order. Secateurs are used, but loppers for anything thicker than about 2 cm (3/4 in). First remove all dead wood and all crossing wood. This type of rose is cut back by at least a third of the last season's growth to an outward-facing bud. Always make a diagonal cut away from this bud. The bushes should then be sprayed with fungicide.

At Bateman's once pruning is completed the beds are edged with shears, weeded and dug lightly over with a border fork to a depth of a few inches. Care is taken not to dig too close to the rose bushes as this can loosen roots – if a bush starts to rock to and fro this will, in time, kill it. Damage to the roots also causes suckers to grow. These can be recognized by a different growth, leaf and habit to the bushes themselves. Removal of suckers is best achieved by pulling up by hand, wearing thick gloves; cutting only makes them grow more vigorously. After weeding is completed the beds are mulched. You can use pulverized bark, which is very effective and looks good but is expensive. Steamed mushroom compost looks attractive, too, but it should not be used continuously on soil unless it is clay, because it can contain too much lime. Ask when buying it what the pH level is; pH 7 or below should be fine.

After this initial work in the spring, the beds are kept weed-free and edged regularly. The roses are underplanted with spring bulbs, including narcissus and muscari. The inner beds are edged with London pride (*Saxifraga × urbium*), and the outer beds with a red-flowered mossy saxifrage. These need cutting back from time to time to keep them from invading the beds.

The roses are sprayed once fortnightly with fungicide, alternating between two types. This helps prevent resistance to one formula from building up. In between the fungicide spraying they are also sprayed with an insecticide, unless there are a lot of ladybirds present, in which case we leave them to do the work for us.

When in flower the roses are regularly dead-headed which helps to promote more flowers and gives a longer flowering season. This can be done every day but we normally do it once a week because of lack of time. ❧

Although the estate at CLIVEDEN is in essence a large eighteenth-century landscape, there lie within the main design several gardens on a relatively small scale. One such area occupies what was laid out in the 1720s as a circle of yew trees measuring about 60 m (200 ft) in diameter. The land in this circle has, over the years, been treated in many ways; as a bowling green, a tennis court, and later as a rose garden on a formal plan rather like a cartwheel. **Mr Philip Cotton**, the Head Gardener at Cliveden, writes about the rose garden in a wood which Sir Geoffrey Jellicoe designed for Lord and Lady Astor in 1959, and about the adjustments and changes which have been necessary over the years since:

❧ It was this rose garden that Lord and Lady Astor decided in 1959 should be altered to provide an intimate and secluded place in which to enjoy peace and tranquillity. Accordingly, they sought the advice of Sir Geoffrey Jellicoe to create a less formal design. It is said that he had in mind the tortuous path by which man progressed through life when suggesting the layout for his 'Glade Garden'. The resulting scheme was of beds contained by irregular sinuous curves which flow in a delightful way into one another to create six beds of different areas with grass paths between. These paths pass, at intervals, under delicately constructed painted wooden arches, clothed in clematis, honeysuckle and roses. A statue of Hercules was placed at the centre of the design, and is a focal point seen from the entrance to the garden as one passes under a more elaborate arch, also of painted wood. It appears that Jellicoe envisaged the beds being planted with a mixture of roses and herbaceous plants.

By 1976 this garden had developed into a 'secret garden' filled with fragrant blooms in the rose season. It is true that this design occupies approximately half an acre, but it could be smaller, and all the work we have carried out, the principles on which our decisions have been founded, and the practical methods employed could just as easily apply to a few square yards. So I think it will be of interest to discuss the work done and the reasons lying behind it.

Some of the rose species and cultivars of the 1959 planting had proved suitable to the site while others had outgrown the original scheme, for example *Rosa californica* 'Plena'. Others had not fared so well, so that the intended undulations in plant height (related also to the width of the bed, tall where wide, shorter where narrow) had been lost. Another important fact was that the surrounding broad-leaf trees, some planted, some self-sown, and many of them within the original yew circle, had cast shade over the garden and restricted air movement, thus encouraging mildew and black spot.

Accordingly, a start was made to remedy some of the disadvantages by the removal of the poorer surrounding trees (many by this time diseased and one or two definitely unsafe), and the coarser-growing roses were replaced by plants of smaller ultimate size more in keeping with the intended design. Many of the plants were just renewed, as although admirably suited to their positions, they were old plants of failing vigour.

As the shape of the beds is so important a feature of this garden, it was decided to use ground-cover plants to draw attention to these shapes in contrast to the mown grass. Highland Hybrid dianthus grown from seed, *Veronica incana, Ajuga reptans* 'Jungle Beauty', *Viola labradorica purpurea, Geranium endressii* 'Wargrave Pink' and the golden creeping jenny (*Lysimachia nummularia aurea*) were all used. The lysimachia proved to be a lesson in how not to use ground cover under roses. It was planted next to a patch of *Ajuga reptans* 'Variegata' to clothe a bed of yellow-flowered roses. The lysimachia throve rather better than the ajuga, which it overpowered, and the resulting yellow carpet made it almost impossible to see the blooms of the roses against it. All gardeners learn from their mistakes.

For six or seven years we continued, as labour was available, to clean up the surrounding wooded area. Dutch elm disease had caused us to fell some large trees to the west, and the clearing created was planted with evergreens – hollies, viburnums, aucubas, vacciniums etc – and a gravel path was constructed from the secondary rose garden entrance to the ilex grove, to replace the constantly worn grass. Some planting was established in the beds surrounding the garden to increase the flowering season: indigofera, exochorda, buddleja, weigela, eucryphia, cytisus, ceanothus and autumn foliage colour provided by acers and berberis among others.

By about 1980, although the foregoing changes were making a difference, we were still not satisfied with the rose garden, and felt able to devote more effort to further developments. The National Trust is always keen to preserve historical features if they are of value, so it was decided to reinstate the circle of yews dating back to the 1720s. The survivors were now some 9 m (30 ft) high and with a spread of 6 to 9 m (20 to 30 ft). These were reduced to stumps of some 2.4 m (8 ft), which will produce green columns (a technique practised both here and on other Trust properties before) and will therefore be more equal in size to the newly planted trees which now complete the circle where losses had occurred over the years.

A few words about planting methods may be of interest. Cliveden stands on a gravel hilltop overlaying chalk, so drainage is very rapid and the 'soil' is impoverished. So we find it necessary to excavate pits about a metre (3 to 4 ft) in diameter and 45 to 60 cm (18 in to 2 ft) deep to accommodate each tree, filling each in with good topsoil, leaf-mould and manure. Even then we have to irrigate in dry periods, so recently we have been using a water-retentive additive (an agricultural polymer called Broadleaf P4) to add to the planting medium.

In order to give more importance to the Jellicoe design we decided to make the outer edge of the grass surrounding the rose beds as near as possible concentric with the yews. We could not achieve a true circle because there now exist one or two trees of considerable importance in the outer planting, especially a holly through which clambers a huge

Cliveden

The sinuous shapes of the rose beds cut like stencils in the grass are emphasized by the colour of the pulverized bark used as mulch. The winding paths pass under painted wooden arches clothed in honeysuckle, clematis and climbing roses.

KEY

- Statue of Hercules
- Entrance archway
- Rose garden archway
- Yew

A *Rosa* 'Bobbie James' climbing through holly
B *R. filipes* 'Kiftsgate' on dead tree
C Summer-flowering shrubs

1 Polyantha 'Little White Pet'
2 Hybrid Rugosa 'Schneezwerg'
3 Hybrid Perpetual 'Ferdinand Pichard'
4 *R. primula*
5 *R. moyesii* 'Geranium'
6 Floribunda 'Moon Maiden'
7 Alba 'Alba Semiplena'
8 Hybrid Rugosa 'Sarah van Fleet'
9 Hybrid Rugosa 'Fru Dagmar Hastrup'
10 *R. rugosa* 'Alba'
11 Hybrid Musk 'Felicia'
12 Hybrid Spinosissima 'Maigold'
13 *R. multibracteata*
14 Bourbon 'Adam Messerich'
15 Bourbon 'Commandant Beaurepaire'
16 Floribunda 'Marlena'
17 Hybrid Spinosissima 'Stanwell Perpetual'
18 Hybrid Musk 'Lavender Lassie'
19 Polyantha 'The Fairy'
20 Rambler 'Bleu Magenta'
21 Modern Shrub 'Golden Wings'
22 Floribunda 'China Town'
23 Hybrid Spinosissima 'Lutea Maxima'
24 Floribunda 'Baby Bio'
25 Hybrid Tea 'King's Ransom'
26 Hybrid Sweet Brier 'Goldbusch'
27 *R. hugonis*
28 Floribunda 'Allgold'
29 Floribunda 'Arthur Bell'
30 Polyantha 'Yvonne Rabier'
31 Hybrid Tea 'Pink Favourite'
32 Bourbon 'Madame Lauriol de Barny'
33 Floribunda 'Iceberg'
34 Modern Shrub 'Aloha'
35 Bourbon 'Madame Ernst Calvat'
36 Hybrid Musk 'Wilhelm'
37 Centifolia 'Fantin Latour'
38 Floribunda 'Lilac Charm'
39 Floribunda 'Ripples'
40 Hybrid Tea 'Blue Moon'
41 Bourbon 'Variegata di Bologna'
42 Rose 'D'Orsay'
43 Hybrid Tea 'National Trust'
44 Floribunda 'Frensham'
45 Hybrid Musk 'Erfurt'
46 Alba 'Great Maiden's Blush'
47 Gallica 'Belle de Crécy'
48 Hybrid Musk 'Cornelia'
49 Centifolia 'Tour de Malakoff'
50 Floribunda 'Tambourine'
51 Bourbon 'Zigeuner Knabe'
52 Hybrid Rugosa 'Roseraie de l'Haÿ'
53 China 'Nathalie Nypels'
54 Floribunda 'Chanelle'
55 Bourbon 'Souvenir de St Anne's'
56 Hybrid Sweet Brier 'La Belle Distinguée'
57 Gallica 'Président de Sèze'
58 Hybrid Tea 'Papa Meilland'
59 Hybrid Perpetual 'Ulrich Brunner Fils'
60 Hybrid Tea 'Josephine Bruce'
61 *Potentilla* 'Manchu'
62 Damask 'Celsiana'
63 Modern Shrub 'Fritz Nobis'
64 Alba 'Koenigin von Danemarck'
65 Floribunda 'Else Poulsen'
66 Hybrid Tea 'Rose Gaujard'
67 Hybrid Rugosa 'Blanc Double de Coubert'
68 Floribunda 'Escapade'

Rosa 'Bobbie James', but a reasonable compromise was reached. This entailed increasing the width of grass in places, and has helped to reduce wear.

In 1959 the 'Jellicoe' beds were created by digging out the natural gravel to a depth of just over a spit, and filling it with imported Cranleigh loam, obviously with the idea that roses would prefer the heavy soil. It certainly retains moisture better than the surrounding area, but when wet it is sticky and difficult to work, and in summer it bakes hard and cracks. These conditions made the weeding of ground cover (yes, weeds do grow in ground cover) very difficult. This planting also prevented us from using powder or granular fertilizers properly, and we had to spray on formulations. For these reasons we have removed the ground cover, and we are using pulverized bark as a mulch. This, while retaining moisture and suppressing weeds, has the added advantage of contrasting the shape of beds with the lawn. The rose beds themselves have now been planted more thickly, and a few new cultivars introduced which agree in colour with the general scheme. Some poor growth has led us to think that 'rose sickness' is now present in the soil, and we have sterilized the worst (yellow) bed with dazomet. The improvement, after planting with new roses, is marked, so we shall be doing other beds in future.

When doing this sterilizing we have to be careful that the gas released by the chemical does not contaminate the surrounding lawn, so a trench is dug 38 cm (15 in) deep, and the vertical side of the lawn is lined with polythene, the trench backfilled, and the same polythene sheet then laid over the surface after dazomet is incorporated and the surface sealed by watering and rolling.

It cannot be denied that the old and new shrub roses do have a relatively short flowering season, although some repeat-flowerers help in this respect. It is for this reason that we have planted early-flowering bulbs among the roses. *Tulipa praestans* 'Fusilier', *Narcissus* 'W. P. Milner' and *Muscari* 'Blue Spike' give early interest.

The eastern perimeter of the garden between the grass and yews has recently been replanted. Most old roses have been removed to concentrate all roses in the 'Jellicoe' beds except for 'Bobbie James' in the holly and 'Kiftsgate' in a yew opposite. All the new plants are chosen to extend the flowering season of the garden. *Fritillaria imperialis* and narcissi start the display, followed by spiraeas, kerrias, ceanothus, daphnes etc, followed by eucryphias, hydrangeas and then autumnal acers.

One of the most recent additions is a second large wooden arch, like the existing one, placed at the secondary entrance/exit leading to the Ilex Grove. Now both entrances are equally defined.

While all the above alterations and developments have been carried out, the annual routine maintenance has always been in progress. The major pruning is generally done in March. New roses are cut down hard to help them establish a good root system, but the other shrub roses are pruned more lightly, really shaping, removing weak growth and flowered wood, and keeping the framework of branches well spaced to allow air movement and to promote vigour. Every few years the stronger growers like the rugosas are cut down hard to keep them in scale.

We are often taken to task for not dead-heading our roses as much as we should. Quite frankly, we do not have the time. I am sure it would be done and be a benefit if we lived in a more leisured age, and today's staffing levels do not allow for such luxuries. Throughout the summer a spray programme is followed using fungicides (triforine, benomyl, maneb) and a systemic insecticide (diazitol). We use either a wheelbarrow-type sprayer, the pump driven by a petrol engine, with a lance on a long hose, or an 18 litre (4 gall) knapsack type with a manual pump.

The lawns are mown and the edges trimmed on a regular basis with the rest of the estate, and all is weeded as necessary. Fertilizer is applied to the rose beds after pruning and worked into the mulch, which is itself replenished as necessary. We use Vitax Q4, as we find the trace elements contained in this formulation are beneficial. During the flowering season a top dressing is given at intervals and watered in as necessary.

All the thought, planning and hard work is devoted to presenting just one small area of this estate to the public, where they can enjoy the colours, form and scent of the flowers in a peaceful atmosphere, sitting perhaps, on one of the seats carefully placed by Jellicoe, the design chosen to harmonize with the whole concept. What better surroundings for peaceful contemplation? ❧

Opposite: The rose garden designed by Sir Geoffrey Jellicoe in the wood at Cliveden. Trellised archways invite exploration of a complicated ground-plan, and undulations in plant height match the varying widths of the beds.

At TATTON PARK an inner garden, almost surrounded with walls, is known as Her Ladyship's Garden. A tea house set in a wall with access to a tennis court beyond, looks over the enclosed area where pool, pergola and rose beds are remote from the rest of the garden. Tradition has it that gardeners had to finish work in this area before 10 a.m. in Edwardian times, so that Anna, the last Lady Egerton, should not be disturbed. Stone steps lead down to the pool and a low balustrade and wall, over which climbers such as *Rosa mulliganii* (formerly *R. longicuspis*) clamber, separate the garden from the thickly planted Tower garden beyond.

The rose beds have recently been planted in pale pastel colours very much in Gertrude Jekyll's style, although she rarely used the salmony tints such as those in 'Margot Koster', which was not introduced until 1931. Two symmetrical 9m (30 ft) square areas are planted in different patterns. In one to the east an outer bed almost surrounds the entire square, leaving a stone paved path for access to a central sundial. The first bed is planted with 180 bushes of the fragrant white-flowered 'Katherine Zeimet'; the second and smaller bed with 'Margot Koster'. Both these roses are polyantha pompons, with small rambler-type flowers held in close clusters. They are low-growing and compact and flower through most of the summer. The planting is in irregular lines, the bushes spaced at approximately 45 cm (18 in) apart.

Opposite: At Tatton Park two square rose bed areas are laid out in formal patterns.

In the western section the garden is divided into eight segments, each individual segment massed with equally small, compact roses – 'Baby Faurax' with violet almost blue-tinged flowers, or 'Cameo' with china-pink small double blooms. There are about fifty plants in each bed.

In both sections standard bushes of 'Little White Pet' are arranged symmetrically to give height and interest. This rose, an 1879 introduction bred in America, is bushy with double white well-formed petals. Round the edges and breaking the harsh line of stone paving glaucous-leaved dianthus make an elegant and neat ground cover, about 30 cm (12 in) in width, reminiscent of some of Miss Jekyll's plans for rose gardens made in the first 30 years of this century. The dianthus supply the fragrance lacking in these roses.

At SHUGBOROUGH a rose garden was constructed by the National Trust in 1966, just below the main terrace west of the house. A Victorian design includes roses swinging as garlands on ropes between pillars, trellis-work arches and pyramids for roses and clematis. The period flower-colouring is in a range from white, pink, purple to dark red, but does

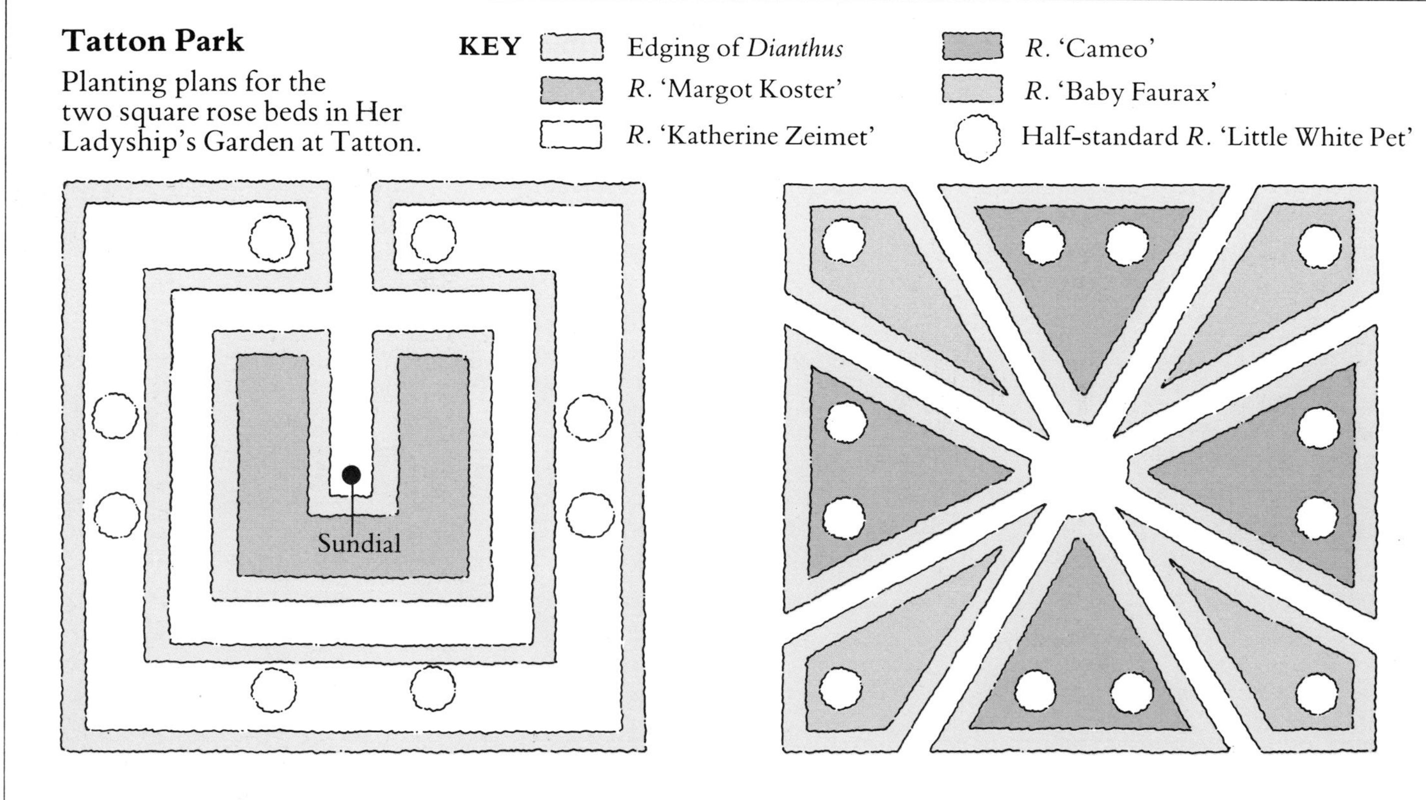

not include any flowers with a more modern 'salmon-pink' tint. At first only roses which were available at the end of the nineteenth century were used, but more recently, to get better performance in this cold soil and poor site, healthier bushes and modern roses with a longer flowering period have been added to the scheme. In the main beds towards the centre, beds of the polyantha China rose 'Nathalie Nypels' face each other diagonally across a sundial. With semi-double china-pink flowers carried all season and healthy foliage with bronze tints to the young shoots, this massed planting is matched by two beds of 'Madame Louise Laperrière' (1951), a rose with larger fragrant deep crimson flowers. Blue clematis flower on arches above a bed of the modern hybrid tea rose 'Innoxa Femille' (1982) with flowers of deep burgundy.

Bush forms of 'Little White Pet' grow under standard 'Ballerina' with shell-pink clustered heads, and 'New Dawn', 'Mary Wallace' and 'Violette' link the outside framework. 'Zéphirine Drouhin', the thornless rose, and its sport 'Kathleen Harrop', with clear pink flowers, both find a place. Rugosa roses, both 'Fru Dagmar Hastrup' and 'Roseraie de l'Haÿ' surround 'Souvenir de la Malmaison' and are wonderfully resistant to disease and very free-flowering. 'Crimson Showers' is grown formally to make a weeping standard.

Above: At Shugborough Hall a Victorian-style rose garden was designed by the National Trust in 1966. Garlanded roses swing on ropes between trellis-work arches and pyramids where clematis intertwine.

Herb Gardens

Perhaps because the earliest gardening books were herbals, where plants were described for their medicinal or culinary use rather than for their ornamental flowers or leaves, herb gardens not only have a poetic and historical attraction but seem important because they are useful. Herbs seem evocative of fragrance and pot-pourris, faintly ecological as so many of them are original 'unimproved' species, and if used infrequently today for cures, are still a vital ingredient of the cookpot. Today when privately owned gardens are mainly small a herb garden remains a popular feature.

In Tudor gardens (and earlier walled monastery gardens) the herbs were grown with the root and leaf vegetables, and each herb needed a separate plot to avoid confusion when harvested. Herbs were necessary not only for flavouring dishes but for curing and 'scenting' to disguise disagreeable odours. In these early herb gardens no attention was paid to attractive forms of growth, and the knot of ornamentals was in a separate part of a garden. In a modern herb garden plants from both areas are included. Rosemary, santolina, thymes, hyssop and germander (*Teucrium chamaedrys*), essential ingredients of the knot, are included for their aromatic foliage, and quite often are used to make low surrounding hedges or patterns in beds, separating herbs and protecting them (and their fragrance) from drying winds.

In the eighteenth century, when flowers were banished to a distant walled kitchen garden, herbs went with them, and it was not until the first years of this century that interest in their ornamental possibilities was re-awakened. One of the most successful herb gardens, and one which has proved a lasting influence, is that at SISSINGHURST CASTLE, a property of the Trust since 1967. Here Vita Sackville-West (Mrs Harold Nicolson) not only gardened but also wrote articles about her gardening interests. She helped popularize the idea of making a herb garden an ornamental feature, and giving it a garden compartment of its own.

At SCOTNEY CASTLE Mrs Christopher Hussey and Lanning Roper together made a herb garden in a sunny area inside the ruined walls of the originally fortified mediaeval castle. Designed in a circle, the planting includes many herbs that would have been essential when the castle still housed a community which on occasion would be isolated from the outside world. Sage, including the ordinary culinary *Salvia officinalis* and its golden and purple-leaved forms, fennel (*Foeniculum vulgare*), marjoram (*Origanum vulgare*) and its silver and golden forms, and thyme all have highly aromatic leaves. Among this basic planting white and yellow tulips and polyanthus give colour in spring, and any bare earth is covered during the summer with heliotrope 'Marina' and with scented-leaved pelargoniums.

An open sunny site by the ruined Scotney Castle provides a bed for mixed planting of herbs and perennials.

In the mid-1970s the original herb beds at HARDWICK HALL were extended by the Trust into a large herb garden. In the formal layout, hops, both the green *Humulus lupulus* and its golden-leaved form *H.l. aureus*, are grown on tripods as draped pyramids to give height and form, at the corners of beds. Only plants likely to have been in the original Elizabethan garden are grown. Divided into two sections, each with a square central bed surrounded by a gravel path, with further beds of herbs on all four sides, the garden grows mainly culinary herbs and a pamphlet describes their uses.

North-east Section of the Herb Garden at Hardwick Hall: Plan

The northern section of the herb garden at Hardwick Hall has a symmetrical layout within which planting, especially of the low-growing and annual herbs, may vary from year to year. Perennial hops on tripods accentuate the corners and massed low-growing plants are used for edging.

Mr Robin Allan, the Head Gardener at Hardwick, has indicated in the plant key/table (opposite) which herbs need to be cut down in autumn, and the method and frequency with which they are propagated.

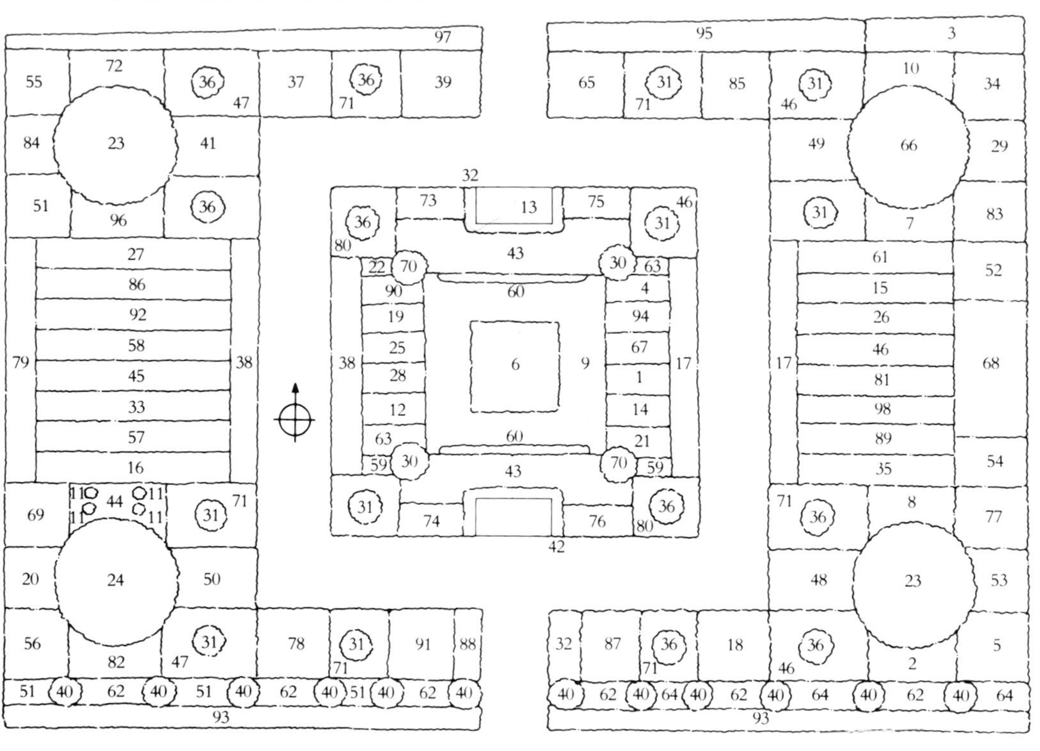

The herb garden at Hardwick Hall was redesigned in the 1960s. Many herbs are prolific seeders and have spreading root systems.

Mr Robin Allan, the Head Gardener at Hardwick, writes about maintaining the herb garden:

✤ We deal with spreading roots by digging out the excess, which are then potted up to sell to the public. Soapwort is not responding to this treatment and it will be necessary to sink plastic sheeting to make vertical containing edges in the soil. Herbs need little feeding and at Hardwick a general fertiliser is only given when plants are put out and at seeding time.

Some of the seed is raised under glass, including parsley, sweet marjoram, basil, and tobacco. Some plants are allowed to seed *in situ* and are thinned out into a row in spring: orach, with bronze-purple leaves, opium poppies, and marigolds. Some plants we do not allow or are reluctant to let seed over the garden. These include angelica and good King Henry. We cut off the flower-heads of some plants in August, partly to keep them tidy but also because they will sometimes flower again.

The hop shoots need constant cutting back as they invade the borders. Juice from the cut stems will make a brown stain on clothing. We constantly suffer from flea beetle on young seedlings of borage and find that bromophos is an effective control. In autumn when we cut down the plants we find that sheep shears are often very effective. ✤

North-east Section of the Herb Garden at Hardwick Hall
Plant Key and Cultivation Notes

Key no	Common name	Botanical name	Propagation frequency (years)
1	Alecost	*Tanacetum balsamita*	cutting/ division 3/5
2	Alkanet	*Alkanna tinctoria*	seed/division★
3	Allium	*Allium moly*	division
4	Anise	*Pimpinella anisum*	seed
5	Basil	*Ocimum basilicum*	seed
6	Bay	*Laurus nobilis*	cuttings
7	Bergamot red	*Monarda didyma*	division★
8	Bergamot pink	*M. didyma*	division★
9	Blackcurrants	*Ribes* cultivars	cuttings
10	Borage	*Borago officinalis*	seed
11	Broom	*Cytisus scoparius*	cuttings
12	Caraway	*Carum carvi*	seed
13	Chamomile	*Anthemis nobilis*	cuttings
14	Chervil	*Anthriscus cerefolium*	seed
15	Chicory	*Cichorium intybus*	seed★
16	Chinese artichoke	*Stachys affinis*	division★
17	Chives	*Allium schoenoprasum*	division 3/5★
18	Comfrey	*Symphytum officinale*	division 3/5★
19	Coriander	*Coriandrum sativum*	seed
20	Cotton lavender	*Santolina chamaecyparissus*	cuttings 2/3
21	Curry plant	*Helichrysum angustifolium*	cuttings 3/5
22	Dill	*Peucedanum graveolens*	seed
23	Elecampane	*Inula helenium*	division★
24	Fennel	*Foeniculum vulgare*	seed★
25	Feverfew	*Tanacetum parthenium*	seed★
26	Florence fennel	*Foeniculum dulce*	seed★
27	Foxglove	*Digitalis purpurea*	seed
28	Garlic	*Allium sativum*	division 1/2★
29	Geranium	*Geranium macrorrhizum*	division
30	Giant fennel	*Ferula tingitana*	seed★
31	Golden hops	*Humulus lupulus* 'Aureus'	division
32	Golden thyme	*Thymus vulgaris* 'Aureus'	cuttings 3/5
33	Good King Henry	*Chenopodium bonus henricus*	seed
34	Hellebore	*Helleborus atrorubens*	seed
35	Hemlock	*Conium maculatum*	seed★
36	Hops	*Humulus lupulus*	division★
37	Horehound white	*Marrubium vulgare*	seed
38	Hyssop	*Hyssopus officinalis*	cuttings 3/5
39	Italian lavender	*Santolina pinnata neapolitana*	cuttings 3/5
40	Lavender	*Lavandula angustifolia*	cuttings
41	Lemon balm	*Melissa officinalis*	division 3/5★
42	Lemon thyme	*Thymus × citriodorus*	cuttings 3/5
43	Lettuce	*Lactuca* cultivars	seed
44	Licorice	*Glycyrrhiza glabra*	division
45	Linseed	*Linum usitatissimum*	seed
46	Lovage	*Levisticum vulgare*	seed★
47	Marigold	*Calendula officinalis*	seed
48	Marjoram pot	*Origanum onites*	cuttings/ division 3/5
49	Marjoram sweet	*O. marjorana*	seed
50	Marjoram wild	*O. vulgare*	cutting/ division★
51	Mint	*Mentha × alopecuroides*	cuttings 2/3★
52	Mint apple	*M. rotundifolia*	cuttings★
53	Mint apple variegated	*M. villosa* 'Variegata'	cuttings★
54	Mint peppermint	*M. piperita*	cuttings 2/3★
55	Mint pineapple	*M. × gentilis*	cuttings 2/3★
56	Mint spearmint	*M. spicata*	cuttings★
57	Monkshood	*Aconitum napellus*	division 5★
58	Mullein	*Verbascum thapsus*	seed
59	Musk	*Mimulus moschatus*	division 3/5
60	Opium poppy	*Papaver somniferum*	seed
61	Orach	*Atriplex hortensis*	seed
62	Orris root	*Iris* 'Florentina'	division
63	Parsley	*Petroselinum crispum*	seed
64	Pennyroyal	*mentha pulegium*	cuttings 1/2
65	Pineapple sage	*Salvia rutilans*	cuttings: tender
66	Purple fennel	*Foeniculum vulgare purpureum*	seed★
67	Purslane	*Portulaca oleracea*	seed
68	Rhubarb	*Rheum rhaponticum*	division★
69	Rock hyssop	*Hyssopus aristatus*	
70	Rosemary	*Rosmarinus officinalis*	cuttings
71	Rue	*Ruta graveolens*	cuttings
72	Saffron	*Crocus sativus*	division
73	Sage	*Salvia officinalis*	cuttings 3/5
74	Sage golden	*S.o.* 'Icterina'	cuttings 3/5
75	Sage purple	*S.o. purpurascens*	cuttings
76	Sage tricolour	*S.o.* 'Tricolor'	cuttings
77	St John's wort	*Hypericum perforatum*	seed
78	Savory summer	*Satureja hortensis*	seed
79	Savory winter	*S. montana*	division
80	Soapwort	*Saponaria officinalis*	division★
81	Sorrel	*Rumex acetosa*	division 3/5
82	Southernwood	*Artemisia abrotanum*	cuttings
83	Stinking hellebore	*Helleborus foetidus*	seed
84	Sulphur lavender	*Santolina rosmarinifolia canescens*	cuttings 3/5
85	Sweet Cicely	*Myrrhis odorata*	seed★
86	Tansy	*Tanacetum vulgare*	division 3/5★
87	Tarragon	*Artemisia dracunculus*	division 3/5★
88	Thyme	*Thymus vulgaris*	cuttings 3/5
89	Tobacco plant	*Nicotiana tabacum*	seed
90	Tree onion	*Allium cepa proliferum*	division 3/5
91	Valerian	*Valeriana officinalis*	division 3/5★
92	Vervain	*Verbena officinalis*	division 3/5★
93	Wall germander	*Teucrium chamaedrys*	division 3/5
94	Welsh onion	*Allium fistulosum*	division 3/5
95	Wild strawberry	*Fragaria vesca*	division 3/5
96	Woad	*Isatis tinctoria*	seed
97	Woodruff	*Galium odoratum*	division 3/5
98	Wormwood	*Artemisia absinthium*	seed★

★ Denotes cutting back in autumn

The paths in the herb garden are of crushed limestone, rolled in and very hard. In summer they become very dusty; dust which the constant traffic of visitors' feet distributes over the plant leaves. In winter frosts tend to lift the surface and lime sticks to boots. Nevertheless, the paths look nice, remain neat and are not rough or noisy for walking or wheelbarrows.

In other Trust gardens, herbs occupy areas of a kitchen garden. At GUNBY HALL culinary and medicinal plants surround a bay tree, and at FELBRIGG HALL in Norfolk where the Trust has restored the kitchen garden, a hot sunny south-facing border backed with a high wall is used for growing herbs, which thrive in the hot dry climate of East Anglia.

The herb garden at ACORN BANK was begun in the 1960s, but mainly developed in the 1970s to replace a small vegetable garden. A special feature is the Trust's largest selection of herbs and medicinal plants, including a large variety of aromatic-leaved trees and shrubs as well as the usual perennial herbs. Annuals such as calendula, chervil, borage and basil are encouraged to seed freely, and height is given to the beds by quince trees and damsons.

Mr Christopher Braithwaite, the Gardener at Acorn Bank, writes about the conditions in which the herbs are grown:

❧ The herb garden contains culinary and medicinal herbs grown in three different beds, separated by gravel paths. Most are woody shrubs or perennials but annuals such as calendula, chervil, borage and basil are encouraged to seed freely. Some, in fact, such as thornapple (*Datura stramonium*) and poppy resent being transplanted even as seedlings. Against the south-facing wall, in the past heated with flues to protect fruit blossom from late frosts, the bed is hot and gets baked in summer. The central bed is half-shaded but the bed along the south-west wall is in the dense shade cast by canopies of quince and damsons. Many plants used for medicinal purposes, among which are many British natives, require rich soil and good drainage rather than the full sun associated with the aromatic-leaved Mediterranean-types. Fortunately at Acorn Bank, on the site of the old kitchen garden, soil is deep, light and loamy and slightly alkaline, and remains rich and fertile. Only the shaded bed where moisture-loving plants include trilliums, veratrums and ferns is given even an annual mulch. ❧

Chris Braithwaite finds that the thirteen different varieties of mint, and soapwort and danewort (*Sambucus ebulis*) are the most invasive, spreading by underground roots. He finds that by planting

Opposite: Tripods are used as frames for perennial hops at Hardwick Hall. Herbs grow untidily and architectural features help hold the design together.

Below: At Felbrigg Hall a south-facing border backed by a wall is planted with herbs. A fig tree thrives in the poor soil.

annuals around them, rather than other perennials, he has a chance to discourage the creeping rootstocks at the end of the season, and thus prevents them from spreading through the bed. Mints do best if allowed a free root run and are seldom happy if grown in drainpipes or containers sunk in the ground. Each year he keeps some of the young rootstock and cuts off the older central crowns on one side or the other.

Most of these plants with fragrant leaves come from warm Mediterranean-type climates, where they thrive in well-drained sunny positions. Many prefer alkaline soil and few need rich feeding. Herb gardens are at their best in the early to mid-summer, inevitably becoming blowsy and overgrown later. Many different designs for herb gardens exist, some based on an historical concept. Others evolved as it became obvious that plants with such 'wandering' qualities needed firm control and separating by paving of brick or stone, hidden strips of slate or metal, and low-growing hedging plants. For marking a frame or pattern box, lavender, sages, rosemary and

Acorn Bank

The herb garden at Acorn Bank lies in a sheltered walled garden. Three long beds stretch east and west and the western edge has a large greenhouse built against the stone wall. The detailed plan shows the most sunny bed under the high north wall; the other beds are equally tightly planted and the south bed is partly shaded by small trees and shrubs such as damson, cherry laurel, brooms and guelder rose. Plants are both native and foreign, and are for both medicinal and culinary use.

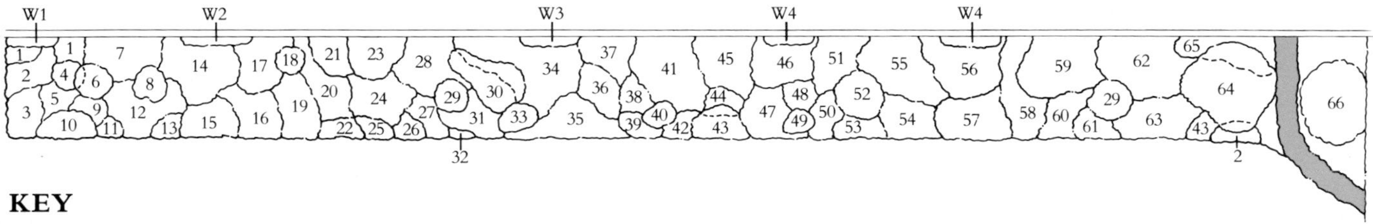

KEY

Hedge of *Thuja occidentalis*

1 Rosemary (*Rosmarinus officinalis*)
2 Lavender (*Lavandula angustifolia*)
3 Thyme (*Thymus vulgaris*)
4 Fringe tree (*Chioanthus virginicus*)
5 Dill (*Peucedanum graveolens*)
6 Laburnum (*Laburnum × watereri* 'Vossii')
7 Danewort (*Sambucus ebulis*)
8 Witch hazel (*Hamamelis virginiana*)
9 Summer savory (*Satureja hortensis*)
10 Rock hyssop (*Gratiola officinalis*)
11 Sea holly (*Eryngium maritimum*)
12 Cranesbill root (*Geranium maculatum*)
13 White asphodel/bugbane (*Asphodelus cerasiferus*)
14 Elecampane (*Inula helenium*)
15 Basil thyme (*Acinos alpinus meridionalis*)
16 Sweet basil (*Ocimum basilicum*)
17 Chicory (*Cichorium intybus*)
18 Bay (*Laurus nobilis*)
19 Musk mallow (*Malva moschata*)
20 Clary sage (*Salvia horminum*)
21 Globe artichoke (*Cynara scolymus*)
22 Scotch chamomile (*Anthemis nobilis*)
23 Goat's rue (*Galega officinalis*)
24 Mountain spinach (*Atriplex hortensis*)
25 English chamomile (*Anthemis nobilis* 'Plena')
26 Golden sage (*Salvia officinalis* 'Icterina')
27 Redspur valerian (*Centranthus ruber*)
28 Angelica (*Angelica archangelica*)
29 Damask rose (*Rosa damascena trigintipetala*)
30 Hercules club (*Aralia spinosa*)
31 Sweet Cicely (*Myrrhis odorata*)
32 Lawn chamomile (*Anthemis nobilis* 'Treneague')
33 Bilberry (*Vaccinium myrtillus*)
34 Deadly nightshade (*Atropa belladonna*)
35 Thyme (*Thymus vulgaris*)
36 Cone flower (*Rudbeckia*)
37 Clematis
38 Thorn apple (*Datura stramonium*)
39 French lavender (*Lavandula stoechas*)
40 Dogwood (*Cornus stolonifera*)
41 Evening primrose (*Oenothera biennis*)
42 Cotton lavender (*Santolina chamaecyparissus*)
43 Marjoram (*Origanum marjorana*)
44 Wild indigo (*Baptisia tinctoria*)
45 Great mullein (*Verbascum thapsus*)
46 Cup plant (*Silphium perfoliatum*)
47 Bitter candytuft (*Iberis amara*)
48 Virginian pokeweed (*Phytolaca decandra*)
49 Mezereon (*Daphne mezereum*)
50 Black root (*Leptandra virginicum*)
51 Yellow loosestrife (*Lysimachia vulgaris*)
52 Juniper (*Juniperus communis*)
53 Golden thyme (*Thymus vulgaris* 'Aureus')
54 Horehound (*Marrubium vulgare*)
55 Teasel (*Dipsacus fullonum*)
56 Woad (*Isatis tinctoria*)
57 Madder (*Rubia tinctoria*)
58 Variegated balm (*Melissa officinalis* 'Variegata')
59 Lovage (*Levesticum vulgare*)
60 Wood sanicle (*Sanicula europaea*)
61 Blue flax (*Linum perenne*)
62 Fennel (*Foeniculum vulgare*)
63 Southernwood (*Artemisia abrotanum*)
64 Hop tree (*Ptelea trifoliata*)
65 Caper spurge (*Euphorbia lathyrus*)
66 Almond (*Prunus dulcis*)

Wall Climbers

W1 Rose
W2 Hops (*Humulus lupulus*)
W3 Moonseed (*Menispermum canadense*)
W4 Honeysuckle/woodbine (*Lonicera periclymenum*)

santolina are ideal, usually needing to be clipped only once annually. If a taller dividing screen is desirable, yew or holly will provide a dark background to the predominantly pale leaves and pastel flower colours, or roses with scented leaves (forms of *Rosa eglanteria*) can be trained on wires to make a barrier. The evergreens tend to grow too tall and they take away the essential light on which these sun-loving herbs depend, but even yew can be kept as low as 90 cm (3 ft) if pruned very regularly.

Other perennial herbs are also used for tracing the outline of beds. Violets, chives, London pride (*Saxifraga* × *urbium*) and pinks (forms of *Dianthus*) are suitable. Because each individual plant is not always top-grade, a bold design and some sort of repeated planting theme in beds of defined shape is advisable when the separate herb area is planned. Herbs can be divided up into types for different uses. Some are for cooking and flavouring. Some are for medicines and pot-pourri. Some are particularly suitable for the site. Gardeners with botanical interest like to grow herbs in their natural families, which might include beds for *Compositae*, *Labiatae* or *Umbelliferae*, while in other gardens the plants may be for dyeing or even may have traditional astrological significance.

Of course herbs do not have to be grown in separate areas. Even in Trust gardens herbs are scattered between vegetable rows, are found suitable homes among good perennials, or carpet soil or paving with matted growth. Angelica, fennel, lovage, bay, bergamot, rosemary, rue, various sages, sweet Cicely and thyme are all excellent ornamentals worthy of a place in the garden, without consideration for their more utilitarian qualities. In the warmer gardens bay trees and rosemary bushes are used architecturally, and bay can be shaped like topiary. At WESTBURY COURT clipped bays act as buttresses to the walls each side of the *clairvoyées*. In other gardens bay trees in pots are clipped into formal spheres or pyramids. Rosemary makes a corner plant, its woody branches straggling over steps or pavement. Forms of bergamot (*Monarda didyma*) actually prefer the rich manured border to the sunny well-drained sites. With scarlet flowers in the type, or with the pink flowers of some of its cultivars, it is a useful addition to a mixed border. Rue (*Ruta graveolens*), and particularly the form *R.g.* 'Jackman's Blue', is a valuable Mediterranean foliage shrub, its grey-blue leaves a foil to bright flower colour or blending with metallic 'silvers'. At Westbury Court the purple-leaved *Salvia officinalis* 'Purpurascens' and the golden-variegated *S.o.* 'Icterina' make patterns in the simple parterre. Thriving in hot sunny well-drained beds, these shrubby sages quickly grow woody, and if part of a formal foliage scheme, needs renewing every few years. Angelica (the biennial *Angelica archangelica*), the stems of which are preserved for cake decoration, fennel (both the common *Foeniculum vulgare* and its bronze-leaved form *F.v. purpureum*) and lovage (*Ligusticum officinale*) are architectural foliage plants of ornamental value in any part of the garden. Angelica is useful in a new border, which lacks 'body' in its first season, and can later be abandoned. Fennel seeds freely and as the seed-heads are attractive is often allowed to multiply while lovage tends to spread quickly by underground roots. The rampant double form of soapwort, *Saponaria officinalis* 'Roseo Plena', or bouncing Bet, needs its rhizomatous roots controlled by deep slates or sheets of corrugated iron. Restricted in this way at Westbury it is a useful and colourful addition to borders of plants all grown and known before 1700. Carpets of thyme are fragrant when trodden and are ideal plants for paving cracks. Forms of *Thymus drucei* make creeping mounds, and coloured-leaved forms of the lemon-scented *T.* × *citriodorus* will carpet the ground in light shade.

The south-facing border in the enclosed Herb Garden at Acorn Bank. The herbs are for culinary and medicinal use, and include many native plants.

Water

All great gardens of the world make use of water as an element in their designs, each country adapting its many qualities to particular climate and needs. Eighteenth-century landscapes with water such as those of FARNBOROUGH, PETWORTH, STOURHEAD, STUDLEY ROYAL and WEST WYCOMBE, where naturalistic lakes reflect sky, trees and classical buildings, are today in the care of the Trust. For many people these parks, and others privately owned, are the epitome of English garden design, where scenery has become linked with emotional response, the sites and source of poetic imagination, and their preservation more vital than any other gardening style. But the Trust has not only been influential in preserving landscapes where water is on a grand historical scale; more recently it has rescued and restored important almost forgotten and derelict gardens, where the element of water is dominant. At WESTBURY COURT, in the flat countryside bordering the estuary of the Severn, late-seventeenth-century water canals have been dredged, their walls rebuilt, parallel lines of yew hedging (with holly topiary) replanted, and the surrounding garden restored with plants of the period. At ERDDIG, water canals are reflecting mirrors for lime avenues, but have only very recently been restored to their contemporary appearance. In England these gardens are among the few which remain of this style (many other or earlier formal water gardens were swept away during the eighteenth century) and their faithful restoration enables historians and modern gardeners to trace the influences of fashion on the use of water in the garden.

At CLAREMONT an early landscape garden complete with lake and island was given to the Trust in 1949. The property, associated with Vanbrugh, Bridgeman, Kent and Brown, has a green amphitheatre carved out of the hillside, overlooking a lake and island. Completely overgrown with small trees and cherry laurel, the amphitheatre was re-seeded, the lake dredged and water-lilies planted. Interestingly, the mud and rubbish taken from the lake bottom was 'campshedded': close-driven posts of elm were placed in the water behind which the spoil was dumped. The size of the lake was reduced by a metre or so around the edge, top-soil added, and grass was sown to consolidate this new bank. This commonsense approach can easily be copied when cleaning out any pond or lake, provided the edging makes naturalistic curves.

SHEFFIELD PARK, a great landscaped arboretum has eighteenth- and nineteenth-century lakes which reflect the exotic trees planted on their banks. A 7.5 m (25 ft) waterfall of Sussex sandstone and clay, with no retaining cement, connects the lake areas; it has been carefully restored, and planting at its edge is suitably naturalistic.

Water in gardens is not always represented by an expanse of still reflecting surface, stimulating the mind to contemplation (the double meaning of 'reflection' suiting the eighteenth-century interest in man's inner life as well as alluding to water in a landscape). Moving water awakens the senses by its constant movement whether from fountains which fill the air with sparkling drops and murmuring sound (which by association suggests coolness), or natural or man-made cascades of rushing water, slow- moving streams or narrower- fast-running rivulets. The essence of all water garden design lies in appreciating these dual qualities, and using them to evoke moods as well as visual satisfaction. Any expanse of still water increases the feeling of space, reflecting the sky, the changing patterns of sunlight, and moving shadow and cloud. In Britain's humid atmosphere reflections fade away into misty distance giving gardens a mysterious quality seldom realized in hotter countries where water appears dark in contrast to bright sunlight. By planning and manipulating the level of water and the angle of vision, Le Nôtre, in seventeenth-century France, extended his garden dimensions by exact reflections; under grey changeable skies these effects are less predictable. The great landscape lakes reflect the surrounding woodland and, as at WEST WYCOMBE, classical temples seem to float on misty water. The fluidity of water provides contrast with the stability and immobility of architecture, its depths providing tranquillity and a living place for fish, and a still surface a reflecting mirror for swooping swallows.

In many gardens now owned by the Trust water is not only used for display but provides a site and setting for growing a wide range of aquatic and moisture-loving plants. Sometimes these gardens have been made where natural streams could be shaped and dammed to provide the still water around which plants could thrive. It is the skill of the plantsman which determines appropriate planting beside the naturalistic lake, such as STOURHEAD or

SHEFFIELD PARK, or the more domestic ponds at UPTON HOUSE or ARLINGTON COURT. The water garden at CLIVEDEN, complete with newly restored Japanese pagoda, has been cleared in part of plants which choked the surface, and surrounding beds simplified with moisture-loving plants in broad sweeps of each sort. At HIDCOTE, in a garden renowned for its series of enclosed 'garden rooms', a further area of stream and open woodland allows informal planting.

In gardens where water seems to be merely ornamental, it often has a secondary, more utilitarian purpose. The formal lily pond, itself kept filled by channelled rain-gutterings or main water supply, doubles up as a water receptacle for storage and can be dipped into for hand-watering.

In the history of gardens the earliest were the oasis

At Westbury Court late-seventeenth-century canals have been restored.

enclosures of the Middle East, set in harsh desert surroundings, where water was canalized for irrigation as well as to express man's symbolic progress through life. Fountains, out of fashion in the landscape period for being too contrived and artificial, were originally designed to clear the water surface of insects rather than to please, and their development as garden ornament in classical and then Renaissance times was a secondary function. The use of water as 'jokes' came from sixteenth-century Italy and demonstrated ingenuity and a grasp of hydrostatics. At DYRHAM PARK, the formal ponds and cascades remain in the garden west of the house, but the original formal garden was very much larger with cascades and water canal. It included a rustic sitting area where the unwary could be doused by the turn of a water cock. Moving water moistens and cools the air (perhaps less important in British gardens than in hotter climates) and in Victorian times fountains were back in favour, providing a chance and reason for monumental statuary.

In a small modern garden water pressure (or an electric circulating pump) makes it possible for sparkling water drops to fill the air from a simple concealed jet. Large holes give single water spouts, held together by surface tension, while a network of tiny perforations makes a haze of mist. Sometimes the effect we see today is not the original intention.

For instance, a fountain jet originally designed with large holes becomes clogged and instead produces a fine spray. At TINTINHULL the fountain has changed its performance in just such a way, and is not easy to clean out, but its subtler effect is also pleasing.

Even the smallest garden where there is no room for any expanse of water surface can safely introduce some water feature. A small electric pump can force upwards a huge jet of water, giving both movement and sound, and, if falling into a surrounding pool, an ever widening series of ripples. Piped water through a hole in a wall can run over a decorative surface, or drip over a ledge as in an eighteenth century grotto, taking up little space yet breaking the silence with its continuous murmur. Monumental sculptured fountains such as the Victorian one at the end of the avenue of limes as the house at CLIVEDEN is approached, or the earlier statue fountain at WADDESDON, may seem to have little relevance for the modern gardener, but the largeness of their scale reminds one how necessary it is to fit any feature into an appropriate space. From visiting these great gardens it is possible to acquire a feeling for the relationships of size which later becomes instinctive. A garden designer is manipulating and making use of space in his basic plan, long before he uses his horticultural knowledge to furnish the garden with plants.

Like all garden features water must be planned appropriately, its scale and relationship to the rest of the garden as important as how it itself is shaped or used. The nature of a garden site generally determines what sort of water is suitable. National Trust gardens, reflecting taste and fashion covering all periods of garden development, give inspiration and guidance. Lessons absorbed from larger gardens, which may be supreme examples of style, simplify decisions in smaller garden areas. Sometimes in a small garden, as at SNOWSHILL, the pleasant gentle sound of dripping water is sufficient to convey an impression of coolness. At TATTON in the Edwardian rose garden steps descend invitingly to a stone-balustraded swimming pool combining ornament with use. The raised carp pool at HIDCOTE was also originally designed for practical purposes as the family swimming pool, a pleasant reminder that even the greatest National Trust gardens were originally for living in as well as for display. Now the circular design where surrounding hedges make dark reflections has become an architectural feature in this famous garden.

Opposite: The sound and movement of water refresh the mind. At Stagshaw above Lake Windermere the stream is natural, the woodland planting in keeping.

Above: Sheffield Park in autumn. The smooth surface of the lake reflects the exotic trees planted round its edge.

Formal Water

Formal water proclaims artificiality; tanks, canals, rills and pools are contained in geometric shapes, straight lines and curves edged by stone parapets or paving, sometimes steps leading down to the water level, the surface of which gives the best reflections if it is as high as the surrounds. These water features can be near buildings, often constructed on a level terrace, the main feature of a sunken garden open to the sky, or reflecting light and shadow in some secret garden corner. In some gardens water lies as a formal geometric mirror, between grass panels and intensive border planting. At BODNANT a long rectangular canal set in green lawn reflects the eighteenth-century Pin Mill, which faces the raised green theatre at the far end. In the Pool Garden at TINTINHULL, on more modest scale, the rectangular tank 17.5 by 3.7 m (25 by 4 yd) stretches south from a modern summerhouse built as a memorial just after the Second World War. Red- and yellow-flowered water-lilies link the dominating 'hot'-coloured border to the west with pale primrose and pastel tints to the east. At KNIGHTSHAYES tall yew hedges surround a centrally placed pool where only a silver-leaved weeping pear (*Pyrus salicifolia* 'Pendula') and a statue break horizontal and vertical lines. Here, just as with growing plants on water-surfaces, constant thinning of the pear tree ensures it will not take up the whole water surface with its reflection. Sometimes stonework alone is linked with a natural river by balustrading high above or by a water-gateway where steps lead to a landing place. At CHARLECOTE PARK Victorian balustrades, recently restored by the Trust, frame curving stone steps descending to the slow-moving Avon (the river was diverted by Brown in the 1750s), as romantically as in any Claudian landscape, where departing travellers are embarking from the steps of classical buildings. The Trust have plans to restore a simplified version of the elaborate parterres which would have been first revealed to a visitor approaching appropriately from the river. Moving water, canalized, at BUSCOT PARK descends to a lake by low falls and under bridges through a series of narrow and widening geometric pools, quiet reflection contrasting with constant gurgling sound and movement, just above or below. The designer Harold Peto aligned his formal water garden to stretch down the high hill on which the house stands, carrying the eye across the lake towards a classical temple on the further side.

At Buscot Park moving water, descending to a naturalistic lake below, was canalized by Harold Peto. Quiet reflections contrast with movement as geometric pools broaden and narrow.

Aquatics, plants physiologically adapted to airless

soil, thrive at varying levels in shallow or deeper water, their leaves and flowers floating on the surface in the summer. Some such plants even have air-ducts which carry air from the water surface to the roots deep below. Sometimes the roots of plants find sites in the mud on the bottom of a pond, but they are more usually planted in containers placed on bricks or masonry ledges. Water lilies (forms of *Nymphaea*), and cape pondweed (*Aponogeton distachyus*) spread horizontally to contrast with the vertical shapes of irises, rushes and grasses.

True aquatics will only flower and thrive in still water, and cannot survive changes in current and changes in water depth through the seasons. On the other hand, many plants such as Japanese iris (*Iris ensata*, syn. *I. kaempferi*), *I. laevigata* and its variegated form, and the so-called hardy arum lilies (*Zantedeschia aethiopica*), which dislike a position in moist soil where in winter roots become surrounded by frozen water, will survive very low temperatures if roots are safely below surface level.

Ornamental pots containing plants not suitable for growing in water are arranged near the water's edge. Venus' fishing rods (*Dierama pulcherrimum*) a bulbous plant preferring moisture-retentive soil, droops its grassy leaves over reflecting water and is a feature at TINTINHULL. There, its hanging bells in pale almost white to purplish pink tints, are draped over a lily-pond in the predominantly white-flowered Fountain Garden.

When choosing a site for a pool remember that full sunlight encourages algae, but that few aquatics will flower in shade. The formal pool has to become a happy compromise between planting with 'spreaders' such as water-lilies which prevent light reaching into the water depths, and the maintenance of clear areas of reflecting water. Ideally at least a third of the water surface should be clear. All aquatics are oxygenating plants but the most effective in controlling algae are those with very rapid summer growth, which by consuming carbon dioxide and mineral salts, help to filter and clarify the water. Once a balance has been reached, pool gardening does not involve constant attention to spread and density of plants, but most aquatics will need thinning and replanting every few years. The more formal the garden the more essential it is to spend some time removing unsightly dying leaves. In a hot summer many large flat water-lily leaves wither and give a very unkempt appearance.

Ornamental fish can only thrive if they have enough oxygen so care must be taken not to clean out the most vigorous oxygenators. If fish appear to gasp, running water from tap or hose pipe will quickly restore a balance. Most plant life produces enough food for fish, but it is often recommended to give some food before the winter, so that the fish build up a reserve of fat. When ponds become completely frozen across, air-pockets should be made by thawing small circles with hot water; on no account break hard ice as this can be dangerous to aquatic life.

Plants would grow most luxuriantly if the bottom of the pond were covered with suitable soil, but the results would quickly become a tangle of unsightly growth. It is much better to use some form of perforated container, plants then becoming confined to their allotted root area, and easily lifted when soil needs renewing or roots need dividing. Broad-based stable wooden crates with low sides, perforated plastics made specifically for the job, or even hessian sacking containing root balls can all be used. Rich, heavy loam is ideal, but do not add peat or organic fertilizers which encourage algae and pollute the water. The use of weed-killers in ponds is now strictly controlled, and one of the best remaining methods of dealing with persistent 'natural' weed is to use granules of an aquatic formulation of dichlobenil, Casoron-GSR, which sink to the bottom and prevent root growth. This can be done only if no ornamentals are to be retained.

The lily terrace at BODNANT is dominated by two old cedars, to the north the glaucous-leaved *Cedrus atlantica glauca* has sweeping skirts which almost brush the surface of the central pool, and on the south side the more sober dark green cedar of Lebanon (*Cedrus libani*) casts its shade. These two great trees, planted in 1876, had already begun to dominate the steep slopes below the house at Bodnant when the terraces were completed in the years before the First World War. As a result steps and balustrading are aligned not on the house as might be expected, but in such a way as to allow the cedars to give symmetry and balance to the whole architectural scheme.

The lily pond, on the third of a series of five hanging terraces, is reached from steps at the side, and yew hedges are cleverly placed on the outer edge so that the view, even from a higher level, cannot reach into the Pin Mill canal and long herbaceous borders below, but only out to the Welsh hills beyond the garden perimeter across the valley of the Conwy river. Thick planting of evergreen oaks to

At Bodnant the lily pond is emptied, cleaned, repaired and the water lilies replanted every few years.

the north, and deciduous trees to the south of the terrace, further increase a feeling of being in a remote secret part of the garden and, more practically, protect this planting area from cold winds.

The lily pond is a basic rectangle, 33 × 16.5 m (110 × 55 ft), but on its western edge a complete semi-circle, with a radius rather less than half the width of the pool, completes the outline. The design is such that the whole facade of the house above is reflected in the calm surface of the water, and planting of water-lilies and other aquatics is planned to ensure a wide central patch of clear empty surface, with the rafts of floating lilies to either side. The water is 1.5 m (5 ft) deep, its surface almost 20 cm (8 in) below the overhanging coping of large York stone slabs with which it is edged, and the water, fed from the hills above and channelled through a series of canals and basins, is constantly renewed and fresh. An overflow outlet releases the surplus water into the long rectangular pond on the canal terrace below. A round raised pool, with rustic stonework and a shell basin, at the back of the terrace, built against the high retaining walls, allows water to feed the pool along a narrow stone-edged rill, and the constant sound of running water is cool and refreshing.

Much of the planting is done in brick containers on the base of the pool, but plants such as water-lilies which need shallower water grow in wooden receptacles on raised brick supports. On the western edge a stone ledge 60 cm (2 ft) below the coping stone allows more shallow planting to a depth of about 25 cm (10 in) of water, and it is here that the graceful stems of clumps of *Cyperus longus* give some vertical accent in contrast to the 'floating' lily rafts and the horizontal water surface. On a corner a vigorous clump of native flag iris (*Iris pseudacorus*) with vertical sword-shaped leaves and yellow flowers in early summer give interest, but the main planting is of hardy water-lilies, placed in varying depths of water to suit the types. The pattern of planting is dominated by the eight squares of lilies in the deepest water. Some have glossy green leaves, others have purple-bronze foliage. The water depth is rather more than that usually recommended in text books, and flowering tends to be later than when plants are in shallower water which heats up early in the season. The flowers are mainly crimson and pink and include the most brilliant red of *Nymphaea* 'Escarboucle'; *N.* 'James Brydon', with maroon leaves and rose-crimson blooms; and *N.* 'Colossea', which bears flesh-pink flowers. There are also some white, cream and yellow-flowered lilies, but these are less striking; planted near the water's edge, they allow the eye to be drawn towards the brighter reds at the centre, flanking the space kept empty for reflections. Each of the main squares which in summer has a spread of approximately 3 m (10 ft) is occupied by 15 plants.

Contrary to what is often said, the climate at Bodnant is quite harsh, and in most winters the temperature falls to as low as −12°C (10°F) and ice 15 cm (6 in) thick forms on the pond. The lowest temperature recorded is −14°C (8°F); combined with a wind of gale force 8, this created a great chill factor, hence causing much damage. In summer during periods of extreme heat algae can build up, but rainfall is high (an annual average of 100 cm or 40 in) and periods of drought seldom prevail long enough for this to cause serious problems. Water remains clean and sweet due to the constant movement and replenishment, but if for some reason the natural water reservoir supply is temporarily suspended, evaporation is very rapid. Fish in the pond are attractive golden orfe and they were selected because they are hardy and have a streamlined shape. They survive periods of a few weeks or more when the water has a 15 cm (6 in) crust of ice; cold is not a problem as long as enough oxygen is trapped under the ice.

Oxygenating weed is kept at a low level in proportion to the numbers of fish and volume of water, since the constant supply of running water provides the fish with sufficient oxygen. In a still pond more of this vegetative plant would be necessary. Water-lily leaves provide shade and keep the fish cool even in periods of excessive summer heat.

The pond is cleaned out approximately every three or four years, in April, before temperatures increase enough to start growth. The bottom 22.5–30 cm (9–12 in) of mud is cleared (and used as a mulch on neighbouring flower beds), the base and sides repointed where necessary and water-lilies and other plants divided and replanted.

Mr Martin Puddle, the Head Gardener, treats the operation with military precision. In his family he is the third in succession to hold this position; his grandfather Frederick Puddle, coming from Yorkshire in 1920, was succeeded by his father Charles, from whom he took command in 1983. Experience and continuity is thus remarkable, and tasks which might be daunting to a newcomer become routine. Over the years it was established how important it was that the thick rootstock and long tough lily roots should never be allowed to dry out, so the maximum time allowed for the entire cleaning programme is eight days.

Eight men are part of a team, one being in charge of the lower water outlet, where a filter prevents fish being washed away. The plug over the lower outlet is pulled out at three a.m. and the water is emptied slowly. As the level is lowered, fish are caught by hand or scooped up in buckets, great care being taken not to allow the bottom mud to cloud the water, and make location difficult. When the level at the lower end is about 15 cm (6 in), fins of the last 50 fish are just visible and they can be easily caught. All the fish are immediately put into other pools, where water-temperature and conditions will be similar. After the fish have been removed the sludge has to be excavated by wheelbarrow and shovel; no heavy machinery can be allowed in or on the edge of the pool. The plants are taken up and covered by plastic bags to prevent evaporation.

The cedar and the pool on the lily terrace at Bodnant.

The whole surface is brushed in one direction, washed down with hoses and scrubbed with hard bristle brushes before drying out so that any necessary repairs to the base or sides can be effective. Frost and melting ice have usually caused minor leaks and crevices. The large square brick bases are then lined with turf sods, upper surface downwards, and the containers tightly packed with fine loam, given bulk with small chopped turf. The soil is beaten down with wooden hammers, and rammed so firmly that no air pockets can remain, which might later fill with water and 'float' the soil up. The lilies are then split with forks and knives, and are carefully replanted in the top 10 cm (4 in) of soil using a hand-trowel. The pool is filled gradually and the golden orfe returned, breeding rapidly to increase their numbers. Oxygenating weed does not need replacement but appears naturally.

Most National Trust water features were made before plastics existed, and there are expensive maintenance bills when concrete linings crack and edges leak under pressure from an expanding sheet of ice, or from movement of subsoil. Restoration of water canals at WESTBURY, where containing sides were of brick, needed skilled masonry pointing, and few owners today would use materials such as brick if starting from scratch. Actual construction of a formal pool today is relatively simple and inexpensive using modern diggers, and some sort of plastic or fibreglass liner (although these are seldom available in large geometric shapes) is often cheaper and easier to install than traditional concrete. Swimming pool experts now usually use liquid concrete forced rapidly through a tube. Both laminated PVC and butyl synthetic rubber last for many years, and are easily repaired if accidentally punctured. The flexible type of plastic sheet, with folds at the corners, can be draped in an excavated hole and its overlapping edges covered with soil and stone or modern composite paving.

Informal Water

In the eighteenth century the contours of parkland were reshaped to create hollows where rivers were dammed and widened to make placid expanses of water in which surrounding woodland and classical temples were reflected. When not fed by natural rivers these lakes had densely planted sides which curved out of sight to hide the furthest shores. In the same way, but on a much reduced scale, the smallest garden pond will simulate reality, and must lie at the lowest point of a garden site to which water would flow of its own accord. The most fortunate owner may have, if not a broad river to be adapted into the landscape, a stream where moving water can be dammed to make quieter pools or canalized to make narrow rills. Rock garden pools can be constructed between slabs of rock making miniature cascades and faster currents, where water broadens out to allow bog and moisture-loving plants to thrive in the damp soil at the edge, and alpines, secure in a well-drained niche, get their roots down to water.

Any expanse of water increases the feeling of space in a garden. At The Courts the leaves of giant gunnera and peltiphyllum give a semi-tropical atmosphere.

At SIZERGH CASTLE a storage lake feeds a string of rock pools below. Made in 1926 from local Cumbrian limestone, the rock garden covers a quarter of an acre, and lies in a hidden trough to the east of the house. Although planting round the edges is planned to look natural, the area is not part of a wider landscape, and except for the use of local stone, bears no relationship to the bleak countryside beyond the parkland. Originally Japanese maples, small conifers, alpines, and moisture-loving perennials were planted by the pool and today, surrounded by trees, it houses the best collection of hardy ferns in the country (see below). Many of the conifers have had to be removed and others have grown to tree size, and the planting covers a wide range of interest. Tall pines which provide shelter from wind cast shade at the back of the pool, and spreading dwarfer conifers and maples make pockets of light and shadow nearer the pond edges, increasing the planting possibilities. This sort of gardening is very labour-intensive and requires a sound knowledge of which plants need moist or comparatively dry conditions. The planting patterns should appear to be natural, some plants making drifts in clefts of rock, others thriving beside the water's edge and following its contours and cambered sides. In some areas dense planting excludes many weeds, but some of the more unusual small plants and ferns need to be constantly hand-weeded. Also there must always be a continual reshuffling of plant groups to adjust the balance between the 'rompers' and those naturally less vigorous.

Round the water giant-leaved skunk cabbage, both the American *Lysichitum americanum* with yellow flower spathes and the white Asian *L. camtschatcense*, thrive between groups of primula including *P. japonica* 'Miller's Crimson' and the later-flowering *P. florindae*. Higher on the banks groups of spreading tellima, geranium, epimedium (both *Epimedium rubrum* and *E.* × *versicolor* 'Sulphureum') and *Campanula poscharskyana* are interrupted by ferns among which are hart's tongue (*Asplenium scolopendrium crispum*) with goffered edges to the fronds, and the lady's fern (*Athyrium filix-femina*). A pendulous eastern hemlock (*Tsuga canadensis* 'Pendula') weeps above patches of bronze-leaved *Astilbe* × *arendsii* 'Fanal', golden grass and *Asarum europaeum* with shining kidney-shaped leaves. A white-flowered pulmonaria makes a good clump in spring, near the rarer *Glaucidium palmatum* with flowers of violet-lavender. *Oenothera tetragona* contributes dark foliage early; later crimson buds open to clear yellow. Tangled mats of saxifrages cling to the limestone rocks, including *Saxifraga aizoides* 'Ingwersen's Variety'. A group of ostrich plume ferns (*Matteuccia struthiopteris*) is architectural, with hostas, veratrum and sheets of blue omphalodes under a spreading Japanese maple. Rodgersias and day-lilies make large clumps in the moist soil while brunnera and bergenia are massed in drier conditions under a fine specimen of *Pinus wallichiana*. A clump of the now increasingly rare native oxlip, *Primula elatior* shows the interest of the Head Gardener, Mr Malcolm Hutcheson, in conserving native flora. Willow gentians (*Gentiana asclepiadea*) have seeded everywhere; clumps of royal fern (*Osmunda regalis*), summer snowflake (*Leucojum aestivum*), corydalis and dicentra spread in natural groups. This garden has developed over a period of 60 years; the wealth of botanical interest to be found at Sizergh can be maintained only with constant supervision.

A very different sort of water-gardening pattern can be seen at KNIGHTSHAYES where a natural pond is surrounded with casual planting to blend into the Devon landscape beyond. Here willows have been planted round a pond on the lower slopes of the outer garden. Forms with elegant leaves of green and grey, and with brown polished bark in winter, make an attractive and simple display; ideal for any water gardening scheme, its scale readily adaptable. At Knightshayes the pond lies in a bowl open-ended at the south-western extremity, but shaped at the sides like an amphitheatre, where green sloping lawn falls below clumps of English oak and Atlantic cedar. Frost drains freely and runs away into the valley bottom below. The pond itself still lies 120 m (400 ft) above sea level and is fed by natural streams from parkland rising to 235 m (780 ft) to the north. Many willows are not in fact very hardy, and even in this warm Devon garden the silver-leaved coyote willow (*Salix exigua*) from Western North America and Mexico, has succumbed to the severe winters recently experienced. Other willows which have failed here are *Salix acutifolia*, *S.* 'Melanostachys' and *S. pentandra*, the bay willow from northern Britain and Europe. With such plants from colder climates, the warm spells in winter experienced in gardens in a temperate region, which encourage sap to rise prematurely, are a factor to be taken into account when assessing general hardiness. Also the lowest ground temperatures experienced at Knightshayes may be only −10°C (14°F), but the chill factor caused by wind reaches as low as −21°C (0°F), and the willow garden is exposed to the prevailing south-west winds.

The finer the prospect, the more urgent it is to keep simple any gardening which encroaches in the foreground. From above, looking under the oak canopies (their heads were raised in 1970 to allow an outlook), the eye swings easily over the grouping of willows and the glint of water, to the Devon landscape of dairy farms and hedgerows which rises steeply above the valley of the Exe beyond. On the slopes of the natural bowl older trees, including a tall *Abies grandis* to the north and a western hemlock (*Tsuga heterophylla*) and a copper beech to the east, narrow and frame the distant view. Below the hemlock clumps of *Cornus florida*, the leaves of which colour richly in autumn, are planted in the grass, and giant gunnera leaves give scale and texture. Groups of pale-coloured spring-flowering azaleas on the contours above the water are sheltered by a new clump of Monterey pines (*Pinus radiata*) beyond. Two pink-barked Asiatic birches (*Betula ermanii*) stand above a bank of May-flowering bluebells stretching down to the grey-leaved *Salix lanata* and forms of *S. repens* on the water's edge. A weeping ash stands to the side on the lower slope, its pendulous cascading branches contrasting firmly with the horizontal water surface. At present a tall golden poplar sits obtrusively in the central well of the trough, but it proves too eye-catching and will be removed; a new specimen will be planted among the groves of trees on the east slope. To the west an old arboreum rhododendron looks exotic on the far rim of the natural amphitheatre, but its dark red flowers prove pleasantly muted.

Many of the willows, a gift from Maurice Mason, are unnamed, but they are grouped carefully in clumps of each species or variety. As you descend to the pool on the left large spreading bushes of the rosemary-leaved willow (*Salix elaeagnos*) make a silvery-grey mound above *S. hastata*, *S.* × *balfourii* and *S. aegyptiaca*, these separated by a path from further plantings of *S. lanata* and *S. repens*. To the right *S. sachalinensis* 'Sekka' is striking with slender pointed shining green leaves. It is framed by other tall willow bushes, and *Populus maximowiczii* grows beyond more azaleas. A fine clump of the tender *Salix exigua* is matched for its silver effects with a group of *Populus alba* further west. By the water between willow clumps the spreading evergreen *Rubus tricolor* has made a weed-proof mat, its shining dark green heart-shaped leaves contrasting in texture and colour with more delicate willow foliage. Near by, *Rubus lambertianus* also thrives, but might not do so in a less favoured garden. Its leaves are narrower and its branches arch elegantly rather than creeping over the ground.

Willows themselves, however densely planted, do not cast sufficient shade to suppress weeds and grass growing beneath them. The smaller creeping species cannot easily be underplanted, so maintenance to a high standard is difficult and proves more labour intensive than is expected. The moist acid nutrient-rich soil at Knightshayes that is so good for ornamental plants also encourages the spread of creeping and seeding weeds. Where water-plants with large thick leaves are massed round the edge of water, weed germination is controlled. Here the lighter willow canopies allow in light, but make it difficult to use contact herbicides to control perennial weeds or simazine products to prevent germination. Hand-weeding and occasional spot-spraying of persistent weeds is necessary. At Knightshayes the willows are cut back every few years. In a smaller garden with ample labour, they could be pollarded or cut to the ground annually. Many of those with shining coloured stems should be cut in March, after full winter effects have been gained, but others with especially striking summer leaves, such as *Salix sachalinensis* 'Sekka', can be cut at any time during the winter, to encourage regrowth of stems glowing with strong healthy foliage. Old bushes can be cut in two stages, leaving a year's interval for regrowth.

A new walk to the east of the third lake at SHEFFIELD PARK has been named the Queen's Walk to commemorate the Jubilee of Her Majesty Queen Elizabeth. Part of this walk is across a swamp, a silted area of lake where alders and other trees had grown into a jungle. A track was cut out and branches of trees cut into lengths which could be lifted by four men using two rope slings. The branches were laid end to end on each side of the proposed path, marking its width. Smaller branches and top growth twigs were packed in between, and then 'plastered' with thick mud and allowed to settle for a few weeks. The surface was then levelled and covered with Sussex hoggin, a sort of quarry rubble containing a high proportion of clay. When laid and rolled, hoggin makes a surface almost as hard as concrete, and will last a long time. A slight sloping camber allows rainwater to drain off.

At Cotehele water and planting round its edge give a naturalistic effect.

The moat surrounding the ruined castle at Scotney is planted with a mixture of hardy native and exotic plants.

At SCOTNEY CASTLE in Kent a moat surrounds the ruins of a fortified castle, which lies in the steep-sided valley below the Victorian house. A dramatic view from the bastion above frames the castle ruins in surrounding trees. Fortunately at the time of the building of the new house by Anthony Salvin advice on the garden was sought from William Sawrey Gilpin, nephew of the Rev. William Gilpin, the author of *Picturesque Tours*, rather than from W. A. Nesfield, brother-in-law of Salvin himself, who loved to design formal Italianate parterres on flat areas near a house. As a result the gardens made in the hanging valley above the old castle and moat are a supreme example of 'pictural naturalism'. Round the water planting has been enriched with large-leaved exotics and hardy natives, all of which could have been recommended by William Robinson or Gertrude Jekyll. Fortunately both Mr Christopher Hussey and his wife fully understood the true 'romantic' spirit of the place, and Mrs Hussey still manages the garden with the Trust, who acquired the property under Mr Hussey's will in 1970.

On descending from the bastion, the water garden is seen to be in two parts. A small island in one section, previously covered in ponticum rhododendron, was cleared and a statue by Henry Moore (a gift from the sculptor in memory of Christopher Hussey) placed in the centre. Planting near the statue is very simple, New Zealand flax (*Phormium tenax*), yellow and white rhododendrons and ferns. Drifts of *Primula japonica* 'Postford White', with flowers whorled round the stems, grow by a white-barked birch (*Betula utilis jacquemontii*), a thicket of evergreen *Lonicera pileata* and the creeping grey-leaved willow (*Salix repens*), and a patch of *Bistorta* 'Superba' drops down to the water edge. Near by tall swamp cypress (*Taxodium distichum*) take advantage of the moist conditions, their fresh bright green foliage turning dusky shades of pink in autumn.

Elsewhere round the moat's edge the leaves of gunnera, *Iris pseudacorus*, rodgersias and royal fern make architectural shapes, while king-cups (*Caltha palustris*), forget-me-nots, polygonum and astilbes give flowers in season. There are groves of rustling bamboo and giant lilies (*Cardiocrinum giganteum*) are grouped in the shade. The scale and artistry of water-planting at Scotney lies somewhere between the hidden elaborate rock garden at SIZERGH, deliberately planted as a complete garden in its own right, and the willow pool at KNIGHTSHAYES, where planting becomes part of the greater landscape, enhancing and not distracting from it. At Scotney plants romantically frame the old castle ruins, which give a domestic perspective to the wooded landscape beyond. The garden is designed to produce a series of pictorial views, where vegetation, water and centrally placed buildings build up a balanced composition, each dependent on the other.

At WALLINGTON the mean temperature for January is 3°C (37°F), but most of the kitchen garden slopes south and east so that water and frost drain away downhill. Many of the waterside plants which do so well at TRENGWAINTON (see below) also thrive here, although flowering in the north is probably three weeks later, and the summer growing season (the weeks in which the soil is warm enough for plants to grow and all danger of ground frost is past) much shorter: hence the wood of some plants does not ripen sufficiently to withstand the winter. The stream in the kitchen garden at Wallington ran through an underground culvert until 1962, when the Trust brought it to the surface in the upper part of the garden and made a feature of its banks, planting with alpines and small shrubs. The sides of the stream are built up with concrete so plants do not benefit from moisture at their roots. Planting is therefore mixed, since good drainage allows for a wide range, although as much as possible plants are chosen which look appropriate beside water. The stream runs down the centre of the walled garden in a conduit (known locally as a 'cundy'), and recently water from it was used to make a natural-looking pond where aquatics float and the margins are covered with bog plants. **Mr Geoffrey Moon**, the Head Gardener, gives the account of the making of this pond:

✤ When it was decided to make a new pond in a corner of the garden at a low place we did not know exactly where the cundy was located. We knew that parts of it were inside the walled garden because at three places it was open to the sky with steps down so that water could be scooped from a little chamber for watering plants. The cundy carries water from an outlet where the lake in the wood outside the walled garden overflows; in parts it runs under woodland and a field and in parts under the garden.

When we came to excavate the pond in the chosen site we hit right on top of the cundy. Because it is 1.2 m (4 ft) high and 90 cm (3 ft) wide with a curved top it was impossible to get the required 1.5 m (5 ft) for the deepest part of the pond without removing the cundy over this part. This was done and 5 cm (2 in) diameter pipes laid out side by side as a substitute. The water supply pipe was laid in a trench from the nearest open place in the cundy, 10 cm (4 in) plastic pipes being used; a small circular 'well', 60 cm (2 ft) in diameter and 1.5 m (5 ft) deep, was built over the pipe end. This was made of stone, the water filling from the bottom and splashing noisily out of a spout at the top into two small ponds set at lower levels; then into the pond proper. A similar stone well was built as an overflow in the deepest part of the pond with a short pipe into it at the base, fitted with a hand-operated valve for draining the pond, and a pipe out leading back down into the cundy.

Sand was laid over the bottom of the excavated area to the depth of 15 cm (6 in) and a butyl sheet in one piece laid out over it. It had to be adjusted to size on site by cutting off the surplus at the narrow parts of the pond and putting in folds and tucks to get it to follow the curves. Plastic bags filled with

Above: Two views of the pond made in the 1960s in the walled garden at Wallington by bringing an underground stream to the surface. Planting round the edges of the pond is mixed, and hoops of bent hazel sticks are sometimes used to protect vulnerable plants from visitors.

sand were used at intervals round the edge to hold the sheet in position. The water was turned on and the pond filled; each day the sand bags were lifted and the sheet adjusted so that the pressure of water carried the butyl sheet over the contours of the base and sides of the pond. When the pond had been filled for about a month and was nicely settled, the edges of the sheet were cut again more neatly to size, enough being left to turn about 60 cm (2 ft) into a trench 15 cm (6 in) from the edge of the water.

Two-thirds of the pond is planted with a narrow border around the edge, and the other third, where water and lawn meet, is left so that people can walk right to the water's edge. Plants were placed in the water and in the border; the area around was levelled to match the water's surface and sown with grass seed. After a short time the appearance of the site changed from that of devastation to order and visitors began to walk down to see our handiwork.

However, this happy state was not to last. Came the autumn rains in October and the pipes under the pond were too small to carry the volume of water. Pressure built back into the cundy and the joint between pipes and cundy fractured, causing water to burst through under the butyl sheet, which lifted up so that the pond emptied out and caused a flood lower down the garden. This caused a lot of disturbance to the plants in the pond and in the borders round its edge and it took some considerable time and labour to reinstate them.

The following summer the water surface was progressively obscured with spirogyra, the floating green blanket which grows rapidly in sunlight and despite strenuous raking and chemical treatment it persisted.

Came the autumn and again floods fractured the joints under the sheet which was badly torn and had to have patches glued to it. The plants in and around the water had again to be replanted. At this stage we seriously considered abandoning the pond altogether – filling it with soil and making it into a lawn. It was decided to make one last attempt to solve the problem of flooding. We dug exploratory trenches outside the garden wall and found the cundy; from here we excavated and laid big pipes to conduct the flood water away from the pond and down to the River Wansbeck which runs near by. This operation was successful and pond and plants settled down and took on a natural effect.

In 1973 we planted in the water. Submerged aquatics including *Callitriche stagnalis*, the water starwort (*Ranunculus aquatilis*), *Crassala aquatica* and the Canadian waterweed (*Elodea canadensis*). Floating plants were *Hydrocharis morsus-ranae* and the water soldier (*Stratiotes aloides*). Unfortunately the elodea has grown too successfully and has become a pest, choking the water and harbouring blanket weed. It proves very difficult and costly to remove and impossible to eradicate. The most successful water plants have been the white water-lily (*Nymphaea odorata alba*) and the yellow-flowered *Ranunculus lingua* 'Grandiflora'.

Round the edges of the pond we had some problems hiding the butyl sheet which tended to be visible above the water line. This problem was solved by raising the water level 7.5 cm (3 in) by adding stones to the top of the outlet 'well', and by planting with large-leaved plants in the borders so that they would grow right down to the water's edge. Here the most successful are the umbrella plant (*Darmera peltata*, syn. *Peltiphyllum peltatum*), the giant rhubarb (*Rheum palmatum rubrum*), *Rodgersia aesculifolia*, *Ligularia stenocephala*, *Iris pseudacorus* 'Variegata' and the grassy *Cyperus longus*. Where the bank is very steep a shrubby willow (*Salix fargesii*), with stout reddish stems and attractive buds, is decorative in winter. To break up the rather regular outline of the inlet 'well' we have planted the low horizontal-growing laurel *Prunus laurocerasus* 'Zabeliana', which sends out shoots across the stone work.

Near by a bed of willows includes the silvery-leaved coyote willow (*Salix exigua*) and the darker grey rosemary-leaved *S. elaeagnos*. They are underplanted with the willow gentian (*Gentiana asclepiadea*).

In some spots in the borders we have planted the spiny *Berberis wilsoniae* to deter people from walking on the borders to reach the water's edge. In other places for the same purpose we have used bent hazel sticks as hoops, inserting both ends into the ground.

Twenty-four fish, golden orfe, were put it the water and prove to be a great attraction for the 70,000 people who visit the garden every year. ❧

Today with modern excavators, electric pumps for raising and recycling water and suitable 'liners' or shaped fibreglass containers an informal water garden can be constructed relatively easily. It is all the more important to make sure it is an appropriate feature in any particular garden. Obviously, to appear natural, all artificial edges must be concealed by plants, water or soil: a hint of plastic or fibreglass destroys the natural effect aimed at. Surrounding banks should not be too steep for ease of planting or for access. Gertrude Jekyll, writing at the turn of the century, recommended a substantial flat ledge beside a pond. Conditions for different sorts of plants have to be planned. Bog plants are like aquatics and need soil permanently saturated and no drainage; their roots are specially constructed to need little oxygen. The swamp cypress (*Taxodium distichum*) as it grows to tree size, throws up 'knuckles' in order to breathe. Other plants love and need moisture, but the soil must also drain freely and it may be difficult to keep the conditions just right all through the year. It is obviously easier to make a 'bog' than provide a damp bed where with open porous soil, it becomes too dry in summer or too water-logged in winter. If the water table is high it may be necessary to raise soil level; if drainage is too good plastic sheeting will hold additional water, and some holes can be cut in it to allow excess to escape. When an artificial pond or stream is made it is difficult to ensure the right growing conditions; concrete edges or soil beyond a container will receive no benefit from the near-by water supply. Suitable moisture-loving plants will not thrive, and other planting looks inappropriate and unnatural beside water.

If space is restricted it is hard to make a water feature that seems to have occurred naturally. Just as planting in or near a formal pool is controlled and architectural, designed to complement and enhance the geometry in a restricted space, a 'natural' pond or lake provides a setting for groups of moisture-loving plants, which appear to grow as they would in nature in the transitional moist area between the water and higher, drier ground. Interesting exotics can be interspersed with indigenous plants which further enhance the natural aspect. Many of these plants which thrive in a temperate climate have large textured leaves, and their luxuriant growth gives a semi-tropical jungle effect, intensified by the smooth contrasting water surface. Gertrude Jekyll's recommendations here are still valid today, and have influenced National Trust gardening styles: 'It is as well as a general rule, in planting wild places . . . to keep exotics nearest to the home end, and to leave the native plants for the further part of the wild.' Giant gunnera, rheum and rodgersias contrast with the spikes of indigenous flags (*Iris pseudacorus*) and its startling variegated form (*I.p.* 'Variegata'). Astilbes, *Aruncus dioicus*, hostas and ligularias are solid perennials which can be planted in broad masses. In acid

soil drifts of Asiatic primulas give colour in spring, and in neutral or limy conditions the July-flowering *Primula florindae* contributes sheets of yellow. Plants growing on the margins of ponds should be allowed to grow freely and planting should look as unplanned as possible.

At CLIVEDEN the Trust has recently replanted much of the water garden, using larger areas of each plant group to suit the scale. Enlarged from a duck pond in 1893, the curving stretch of water surrounds a magnolia hillock, reached by a stone bridge where William Waldorf, later the first Viscount Astor, placed a genuine Japanese pagoda which had been exhibited in the Paris Exhibition of 1867. As in many so-called Japanese gardens of the late Victorian or Edwardian eras, planting was exuberant, making use of the many moisture-loving plants which were then available, rather than concerned with the deeper philosophical and symbolic meanings of the genuine Japanese water garden, such as that constructed in 1910 for Lord Egerton at TATTON PARK outside Manchester. At Cliveden clumps of small-leaved rhododendrons and azaleas make a solid background on the contoured sloping banks, giant king-cups (*Caltha palustris*), flowering also in spring, grow below at the water's edge. Later Asiatic primulas, moisture-loving iris, astilbes, hemerocallis and finally purple loosestrife provide flower and leaf interest through the rest of the summer season.

At TATTON a wide pond called the Golden Brook surrounded by dense woodland, including dark spires of conifers, many of them Japanese species, is densely planted to the edges, azaleas and rhododendrons overhanging and reflected in the water, contrasting with the large leaves of *Gunnera manicata* grouped by the pool's edge. On an island that is approached by a half-moon bridge a Shinto temple overlooks the Japanese garden, complete with the Master's tea house on a small central island. Here in a sunlit glade planting is simple and restrained, the moss-covered ground making a gentle carpet be-

neath spreading Japanese maples. In Japan there are more than 40 different mosses which are recommended in gardens. On the banks at the sides which rise steeply to frame this pocket of sophisticated planting, clumps of the native British royal fern (*Osmunda regalis*), also found growing wild in Japan, and the evergreen *Gaultheria shallon* from North America make a dense thicket.

The garden was built about 1910 by labour especially brought from Japan to erect the Shinto temple. The design incorporates many authentic scenes and is typical of a wealthy lord's garden. The success of design and layout of a Japanese garden with its intricate rules is perhaps finally proved by the quality of overall peace and natural tranquillity that it creates in the contemplative beholder.

Opposite: Moisture-loving plants are massed in large groups on the edge of the pond at Cliveden. On the island a Japanese pagoda gives the garden an oriental atmosphere.

Above: At Tatton Park, behind the Half-Moon bridge, a symbolic Japanese garden was constructed in 1910. A moss-covered glade is half-shaded by Japanese maples, and ferns clothe the sloping banks.

Stream Gardens

Quoting Miss Jekyll again: 'A natural running stream, especially if it flows fast over a shallow pebbly bed, with sides either naturally near the water-level or purposely made so, is one of the very best settings for beautiful plants. It can often be so arranged that the path shall cross it from time to time, either by well-set stepping stones or by a simple plank or log bridge. But it is most desirable, especially in places that have a natural character . . . that a wise restraint should be observed about the numbers of different plants that are to be seen at a glance.'

Trust stream gardens with plant associations that can be copied or adapted easily to a smaller scale, are those of DUNHAM MASSEY near Manchester, SHEFFIELD PARK in West Sussex and TRENGWAINTON in the mild climatic conditions found in Cornwall.

At DUNHAM MASSEY, after clearance of brambles and nettles, drifts in large masses of any one specimen have been planted along the edge of a broad stream. Mr Harry Burrows, the Head Gardener, described the work done in this area of the garden. The banks of the stream had suffered from years of neglect when the Trust took over the property. The stream runs more or less from east to west and to the south woodlands of oak and birch are still being gradually cleared and replanted. Old hollies, gaunt and disfigured with age, grew along the northern bank, and in many cases have needed rigorous cutting back to force rejuvenation. On the southern, more gently sloping, stream edge a few good moisture-loving plants remained, surviving between seedlings of oak, birch and rowan and old tree stumps. Brambles infested the whole area and as the ground was cleared and later dug, trailer loads of old brick were discovered and had to be hauled away. Although some of the best specimens of oak and birch were retained to provide a canopy, most of the tree seedlings were removed. Stumps were excavated, the brambles cut down and cleared away after having been killed by the herbicide triclopyr.

The stream itself was cleared out with a mechanical digger, and the sloping banks graded and smoothed down. The water-level is controlled by sluice gates, but occasionally these may block with leaves, so planting is kept away from the very edge of the stream, in case of flooding. The ground was first covered with leaf-mould and grass-cuttings from the lawns, and farmyard manure was incorporated as the soil was dug and levelled. Following a soil test the area was dressed with a balanced compound fertilizer and magnesian limestone was added to increase the lime content (the soil is very acid, as low as pH 4.2), to supply magnesium and to release other nutrients and make them available to the plants.

At Hidcote the banks of a woodland stream are carpeted with moisture-loving plants.

Most moisture-loving plants thrive in light shade and at Dunham, oak, which is relatively 'benign', and, to a lesser extent birch provide just the right conditions to prevent the soil drying out excessively in periods of drought, although manure and grass-cuttings are used as a mulch in the more open sections.

The new planting plans laid emphasis on foliage form, shape and colour as well as on the more fleeting seasonal flowers. Along the edge of the stream existing clumps of giant gunnera were reinforced with rheum, lysichitum, *Iris pseudacorus*, *I. laevigata* and *I. ensata* (syn. *I. kaempferi*) forms, and drifts of the royal fern (*Osmunda regalis*). Tall sword-like leaves of *Phormium tenax* near the tufted Chilean bamboo (*Chusquea couleou*) gave contrast. A drift of *Salix elaeagnos*, decorative with its rosemary-like foliage, white rugosa roses and the low-growing evergreen *Berberis candidula*, with shining leaves conspicuously white beneath, mark the corner and screen the stream and its planting from the entrance to give surprise. Herbaceous astilbes, ligularias, cimicifuga and lythrum are planted in wide clumps, and hostas and striped grasses give foliage interest. Along the path edge alchemilla, *Geranium macrorrhizum* 'Ingwersen's Variety', with scented leaves, pulmonaria and hostas thrive where the soil is drier. Since planting, the native bluebell has become invasive and, for this particular problem, digging out by hand is essential. Mares-tail is a perpetual weed and needs careful spraying with glyphosate. Wiping with an impregnated glove proves practical and effective in preventing the herbicide touching other plant foliage. Most other weeding is done by hand, but the soil is occasionally forked or cultivated with a hoe.

Dunham Massey

The stream or bog garden at Dunham Massey is sheltered by woodland of oak and birch to the south. A few of the trees remain in the planting area: the better specimens were retained when the overgrown south bank of the river was cleared. They provide a light canopy over drifts and clumps of moisture-loving plants, many chosen for their foliage interest.

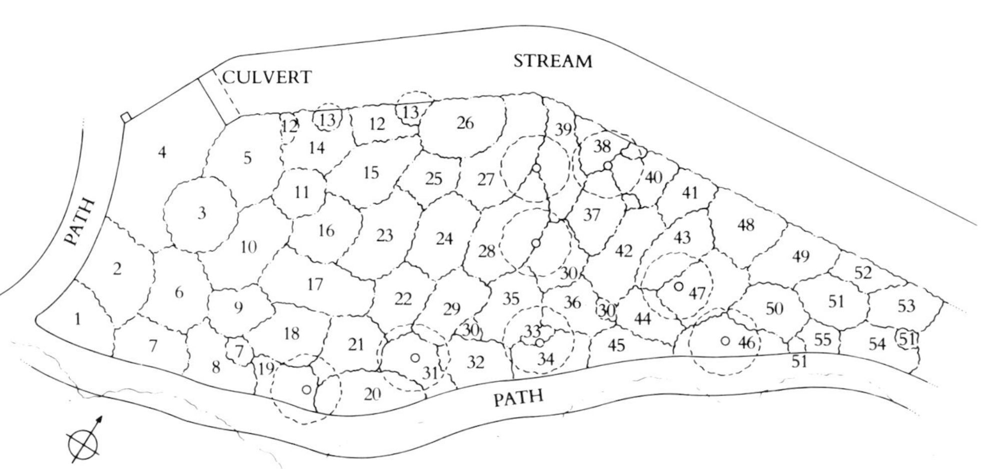

KEY

○ Existing birch or oak tree

Shrubs

1 *Berberis candidula*
2 *Rosa rugosa* 'Alba'
3 *Chusquea couleou*
4 *Salix elaeagnos*
5 *Physocarpus opulifolius* 'Luteus'

Herbaceous Perennials

6 *Lythrum salicaria* 'Robert'
7 *Hosta sieboldiana* 'Elegans'
8 *Rudbeckia* 'Goldsturm'
9 *Curtonus paniculatus*
10 *Centaurea macrocephala*
11 *Phormium tenax*
12 *Iris ensata* 'Snowdrift'
13 *Osmunda regalis*
14 *Polygonum campanulatum*
15 *Euphorbia griffithii* 'Fireglow'
16 *Eupatorium purpureum*
17 *Ligularia dentata* 'Desdemona'
18 *Veratrum nigrum*
19 *Alchemilla mollis*
20 *Hosta ventricosa*
21 *Anemone* × *hybrida*
22 *Rheum palmatum* 'Rubrum'
23 *Filipendula rubra* 'Venusta'
24 *Miscanthus sinensis* 'Zebrinus'
25 *Cimicifuga racemosa*
26 *Gunnera manicata*
27 *Aruncus dioicus*
28 *Inula magnifica*
29 *Cautleya robusta*
30 *Meconopsis* seedlings
31 *Phalaris arundinacea* 'Picta'
32 *Brunnera macrophylla* – white
33 *Brunnera macrophylla*
34 *Geranium macrorrhizum* 'Ingwersen's Variety'
35 *Astrantia* 'Margery Fish'
36 *Liriope* 'Majestic'
37 *Astilbe* 'Deutschland'
38 *Filipendula ulmaria* 'Aurea'
39 *Euphorbia palustris*
40 *Lysichitum americanum*
41 *Iris pseudacorus* 'Golden Fleece'
42 *Hosta fortunei* – own variegated
43 *Lythrum salicaria* 'Brightness'
44 *Aruncus dioicus* 'Kneiffii'
45 *Pulmonaria* 'Mrs Moon'
46 *Hosta* 'Royal Standard'
47 *Filipendula palmata* 'Elegantissima'
48 *Rheum officinale*
49 *Senecio tanguticus*
50 *Campanula latifolia* 'Brantwood'
51 *Gentiana asclepiadea*
52 *Iris laevigata* 'Rose Queen'
53 *Rodgersia tabularis*
54 *Bergenia* 'Silberlicht'
55 *Speirantha gardenii*

Above: At Sheffield Park a waterfall of Sussex sandstone and clay connects the two lakes; repairs have been carried out with Forest of Dean sandstone slabs which are more weather resistant.

Opposite: New streamside planting at Sheffield Park. An old drainage ditch has been opened up, dams constructed to give contrasting areas of still and moving water, and hardy plants make drifts to give flower and foliage interest.

At SHEFFIELD PARK water is on a very grand scale with Capability Brown and later lakes forming a landscape where native and exotic trees are planted. Nevertheless, some of the details at Sheffield are worth considering for adapting to gardens on less magnificent scales. The rocky falls between two lakes have lately been repaired with sandstone slabs from the Forest of Dean, which better resist the wear of water and frost than the Sussex stone originally used for its construction in the early years of this century (by Pulhams, the creators of the Wisley rock garden). A continuing flow of water is ensured by installation of an electric pump, but overhanging plants and moss make it all seem quite natural.

To the south of the main garden and lakes, and just beyond the rectangular gentian beds, an area containing many good conifers such as *Abies procera*, *Cephalotaxus fortuni*, *Picea likiangensis* and *Pinus pinaster* had become overgrown with brambles, bracken and sycamore seedlings. Fallen trees lay on the ground. In 1980 Mr Archie Skinner, the Head Gardener, started a clearance operation, a task mainly confined to winter when time was available from other more urgent maintenance jobs. During the work an old drainage ditch was discovered and this, with planting along its banks, has made an attractive stream garden. The bed of the ditch was widened and dug out, dams were put in to make contrasting areas of running and calm water, and to give the continual sound of water gently dropping to lower levels. The wood used was from sweet chestnut, made water-tight with blue-clay purchased from local brickworks. Once the ground was cleaned and prepared the stream margins were planted with moisture-loving hardy plants to provide foliage interest and flower colour through a long summer season. The hardy arum *Zantedeschia aethiopica* thrives in shallow water and mud. Bulbs of summer snowflake (*Leucoium aestivum*), a British native, make drifts, and interplanted ferns give interest when flowering is over. The giant lily *Cardiocrinum giganteum* from the Himalayas has its emerging shoots shaded and protected by more ferns and is planted in soil richly prepared with well-rotted manure and leaf-mould.

There are many good groups of hostas which include *Hosta fortunei* and *H.f.* 'Aurea', *H.* 'Honeybells', the latter with fragrant flowers inherited from *H. plantaginea*, but with faintly blushed lilac colouring instead of pure white, held above undulating leaves. The very similar *H.* 'Royal Standard' flowers late and has equally fragrant white blushed lilac

flower-heads, on 90 cm (3 ft) stems above broad heart-shaped rich green leaves. *H. rectifolia* 'Tallboy' also has lilac flower-spikes, held on 1.2 m (4 ft) stems above heart-shaped fresh green leaves, and is one of most rewarding and spectacular hostas. Hostas combine beautiful leaves with scented flowers and are effective in massed planting. Although normally quite hardy, they are slow to increase; any division necessary for named forms yields only a few plants after a couple of years. Mr Skinner likes to increase his stock before planting so that he can keep his groups in the right scale and proportion.

Drifts of Asiatic candelabra primulas such as *Primula pulverulenta* with tiered flowers in pink and mauve spread in the deep acid soil, and plants can be split up to make new groups. *P. bulleyana* has more striking orange flowers. Seedlings of the drumstick primula (*P. denticulata*) are encouraged to mingle between other plants. Mr Skinner is also making a collection of varieties of Siberian iris (*Iris sibirica*), which with vertical grassy foliage and tall stems topped with flowers in different blues will be planted in the moist soil along the stream edge. Plants planted 30 cm (12 in) apart quickly grow together and make effective ground cover.

At TRENGWAINTON, too, the stream originally ran underground, but it was brought to the surface and planted by Sir Edward Bolitho in 1897, more than sixty years before the Trust received the property. Here, near Penzance, rainfall is high – often as much as 115 cm (46 in) annually – and the climate is exceptionally mild. High humidity and warmth make perfect conditions for Asiatic primulas and blue meconopsis, yellow skunk cabbage from America (*Lysichitum americanum*) and white from the Far East (*L. camtschatcense*), and large-leaved rodgersias, many of which were introduced to gardens only in this century, and would have first been grown experimentally in these ideal conditions.

The stream runs down beside the main driveway to the house, and is overhung by a mature planting canopy of old ash, beech and sycamore which was opened up to start the woodland garden in the early years of this century. The Monterey pine (*Pinus radiata*), the Monterey cypress (*Cupressus macrocarpa*) and, since the late 1960s, new windbreaks of Leyland cypress (× *Cupressocyparis leylandii*) have been added for extra shelter as well as for their value as evergreens. As in many seaside gardens (and Trengwainton is only a few miles from the Cornish south coast) wind, and in this case prevailing wind from the south-west, is a major problem. At a lower level the rampant bamboo *Arundinaria anceps* was planted to make wind-filtering screens to protect a collection of fine rhododendrons and other good acid-loving shrubs, which would thrive in the mild climate, especially if given a good start. Planted to the south-west of the stream which carries peaty water through a farmyard higher on the slopes of the hill to the north-west, the bamboo also provided shelter for moisture-loving perennials which are placed in great drifts to match the shape of the winding stream-bed. At some points the banks are steep, at others the bed broadens out so that plants grow at water's edge, and take advantage of the boggy soil. High humidity suits many of these plants and growth is lush. Near the stream spreading tree ferns (*Dicksonia antarctica*), the even finer-leaved *Woodwardia radicans* and strong spreading clumps of *Blechnum chilense* flourish well between groups of hydrangea, olearia, rhododendrons and azaleas, together making a textured green backdrop through the seasons for the massed flowers of primula, crocosmia, astilbe, day-lilies and spires of white *Cimicifuga racemosa* in later summer.

In the last few years many of the bamboo plants have flowered and died, and when clumps have been removed it has been possible to extend the stream garden into a new area to the south-east, away from the edge of the drive. A pair of the evergreen *Podocarpus salignus* frames a view downstream to this newly opened section of woodland. Cascades have been made with flat local stone which quickly become moss-covered. As light is let in seedlings of brambles, nettles and docks start to germinate, and these are sprayed with triclopyr. *Primula pulverulenta* seeds prolifically and the elegant *Stipa arundinacea* (syn. *Apera arundinacea*) with soft reddish-brown arching stems and grassy flower-heads places itself in strategic sites. A new bed has been made in the woodland for the Chatham Island forget-me-not (*Myosotidium hortensia*) which needs a very mild climate and plenty of seaweed mulch. Its bright blue flowers above shining leathery leaves are worth every horticultural effort; the tender crowns with emerging shoots are protected from rabbits by wire netting.

Further upstream planting is mature and thick clumps often need dividing and splitting. The moist mild conditions also suit weeds such as ground-elder and the equally invasive creeping buttercup (*Ranunculus repens*). Mr Peter Horder, the Head Gardener, who has been at Trengwainton since 1970, finds that with today's shortage of much skilled help, his team will tackle stretches of the planting every few years, rather than attempting to keep the soil clean throughout the beds; especially true in an infested patch where plants are weak-growing.

Many of the plants by the stream have striking foliage which contributes as much to the beauty of the whole effect as the more fleeting seasonal flower-colour.

Plants include: *Aruncus dioicus*, astilbe, the double and single king-cup (*Caltha palustris* and *C.p.* 'Flore Pleno'), cimicifuga, crocosmia, including the bronze-leaved *Crocosmia* × *crocosmiiflora* 'Solfatare' and new groups of scarlet-flowered *C.* 'Lucifer', moisture-loving euphorbia such as *Euphorbia griffithii* 'Fireglow' and red-stemmed *E. sikkimensis*, fascicularia, many forms of hedychium with strongly scented late-summer flowers, hemerocallis in variety, *Bistorta* 'Superba' and a broad drift of *Aconogonum campanulatum*. Early spathes and giant

Opposite: The stream at Trengwainton runs at the edge of woodland. Planting is luxuriant. In the mild Cornish climate high humidity and warmth provide the perfect conditions for exotic waterside plants.

leaves of *Lysichitum americanum* make bold waterside groups, with effective foliage of rodgersias, peltiphyllums and variegated glycerias. A clump of *Zantedeschia aethiopica* 'Green Jade' has grown to 1.2 m (4 ft) in height. *Iris sibirica*, *Libertia ixioides* and groups of pampas grass in front of healthy bamboos such as *Arundinaria nitida* add foliage contrast. *Sanguisorba obtusa* has elegant pinnate leaves and bottle-brush flowers of soft pink in August after many of these plants have already finished their display. There is a good collection of kniphofias covering a long flowering season.

Mr Peter Horder writes about the maintenance of the stream garden:

During the winter we embark on ground preparation of preselected areas for replanting. The soil is well forked over to ensure the area is free of perennial weed before applying well-rotted farmyard manure 10–12.5 cm (4–5 in) deep. A quantity of carefully cleaned soil mixed with leaf-mould or peat may be brought in to top up the areas, then gently firmed according to the moisture content. A second firming will be given after raking in a basic general fertilizer prior to planting out primula seedlings in February and March. The splitting and replanting of subjects such as astilbes, day-lilies and irises is done between March and early spring when weather and soil conditions are suitable. Clumps are divided, old root stocks discarded and the stronger divisions replanted a foot or so apart.

Established plantings will benefit from a light dressing of bone-meal during a moist spell in April. During the flowering season which follows we rogue any candelabra primula seedlings which have strayed into the wrong group. We favour bold plantings of one variety for maximum effect, just as drifts and blocks are made in the planning of a good herbaceous border. By this time, weeds – hopefully only annuals – are appearing and an early clean through will save a lot of work later in the season. By June and July there may be empty patches where perennial weed is growing strongly enough to be eradicated by weedkillers. Creeping buttercup, couch grass and ground-elder are treated with glyphosate; the deeply rooting horsetail with ammonium sulphamate. The treatment is repeated if necessary in August. These areas must be thoroughly cleared before preparation for planting can be done during the winter. Where perennial weed is found growing among herbaceous plants, they are lifted, split and cleaned before replanting may be carried out.

In mid to late summer, when water-levels are at their lowest, we repair any leaking water courses and cascades. The water-level is controlled by damming higher up the stream and a grey-black colouring powder is added to the cement so that the alterations are not visible. In the damp climate moss soon forms on the new stonework, especially if liquid manure is brushed on to it a few times.

On one side, between the stream borders and a line of shrubs, is a narrow undulating strip of dry shaded ground where little grows well except weeds. Here the area is sprayed with paraquat probably twice in the summer to form a moss-covering. Our stream garden benefits from being fed naturally with liquid manure from the home farm above, but although good for the plants and ensuring lush growth, this can be a problem. A mass of pungent slurry accumulates in the wider pools, especially where there is insufficient moving water, and has to be raked downstream or removed with a shovel. It is too concentrated and thick to be spread around any plant material. While working on the stream-bed it is possible to reduce any rampant growth of plants such as yellow monkey-musk which have invaded the water-courses.

During August and September seed of the candelabra primulas is collected as it ripens and is sown as soon as possible after gathering. This ensures maximum germination. This is also a good time of year to look at the various plantings along the stream and make notes of any flowering plants which clash in colour with neighbours, and need regrouping in the following late winter or early spring. Most years when the ground is moist, soft or recently cultivated, we have trouble with moles and slugs. Traps and baits have to be used as the creatures soon eat the roots and leaves of the primulas and weaken the root systems of plants around their tunnels.

Dead-heading of flowers through the summer is kept to a minimum; many plants such as astilbes have heads which turn to lovely bronze shades, giving added value during the winter months. In the autumn as well as taking the leaves of beech and sycamore off the main stream, we clear the thickest accumulations from adjacent borders. Then we return to our notes to reflect on the current successes and failures in the stream garden and to plan for the following year.

Ferneries

It is rare today to find separate garden areas put aside for fern cultivation, yet any north-facing bed which has a reasonably moisture-retentive soil and pockets of dry-stone walling makes an ideal site for hardy ferns (many of them native) or their cultivars. Indeed, in an old neglected garden, ferns can be survivors when other fussier plants have been choked by rampant weeds or died from neglect. In fact ferns will also thrive in more open situations and contribute their delicate lacy foliage as ground cover in the light shade of deciduous shrubs and trees. Some of these natives reach the garden by wind-borne spores. One of the commonest is hart's tongue (*Asplenium scolopendrium*) which will find a place at the base of any wall in sun or shade. Almost evergreen, young fronds are shining and smooth and the only attention it needs is the removal of unsightly leaves in early spring. Many cultivars are 'crested', forms where the point instead of tapering becomes puckered and frilled; others have waved undulating margins. The native soft shield fern (*Polystichum setiferum*) and its cultivars, tolerant of bright sun and heat, will grow in pavement, its roots cool beneath the stone. *P.s. acutilobum* grows to 60 cm (2 ft), with pointed dark green divided fronds, and at NYMANS a fine group of *P.s. divisilobum*, with graceful dark green finely divided leaves, thrives on the edge of a shady bed in the lawn beyond the house.

For the enthusiast the best collection of ferns in any of the Trust gardens is at SIZERGH CASTLE, where they thrive in the rock-pool garden made by Lord Strickland in 1926. This is the National Collection of four genera. Today many of the dwarf conifers and maples planted at that time have grown to spreading dimensions, and the ferns grow in rocky niches between clumps of low-growing small perennials and more delicate alpines. Many have already been mentioned in the chapter on water gardens. Unusual forms of the more common polystichum include the sword fern from North America (*Polystichum acrostichoides*). The rare *Asplenium scolopendrium crispum*, a hart's tongue with undulate goffered fronds, grows beside the lady fern (*Athyrium filix-femina*). A fine group of ostrich plume ferns (*Matteuccia struthiopteris*) is found contrasting with the broad heavy foliage of neighbouring hostas and veratrum. Forms of the native male fern (*Dryopteris filix-mas*) and a dryopteris from Japan, *D. erythrosora*, superficially seem to have little in common except for being of the same genus. Fortunately the Head Gardener at Sizergh, Mr Hutcheson, has labelled most of the ferns so it is possible to learn.

The best-known fern in British gardens is the royal fern (*Osmunda regalis*), another native from damp acid bogs, and thriving along stream edges and by ponds. It is a feature by the lake at TATTON PARK and in the quarry at STANDEN, the leaves colouring to a rich tawny brown in autumn. This fern is surprisingly tolerant of lime, but must not have soil which dries out in summer. Rarer forms of it can be seen at Sizergh. A maidenhair fern, *Adiantum pedatum*, introduced from North America in 1656, has glossy black stems and the young foliage is a delicate pinkish brown, later turning a bright green in summer and remaining attractive as the leaf browns and dies in winter. It looks exotic but is reliably hardy; it is more likely to die from scorching sun than from low temperatures. Ferns certainly prefer partial shade and some degree of humidity, and grow best in good friable loam. Many will only thrive if the soil is acid, and some need calcareous soil.

At Standen ferns have been planted in the quarry behind the house.

Other hardy natives such as *Dryopteris filix-mas* and the more delicately made *Athyrium filix-femina* will thrive where soil is moist, and usually seed freely and need no special attention. The Japanese painted fern (*Athyrium nipponicum pictum*, syn. *A. goeringianum pictum*) has glaucous grey lacy fronds and is very desirable, not difficult to grow if it can be obtained.

One of the reasons that ferns are not grown more often is a general lack of knowledge about how to look after and to increase them. Perhaps also the Victorian fern craze of the 1850s has led gardeners to believe that all ferns need the closed humidity of a Wardian case or fern house, while, in reality, many are hardy natives. Ferns do not flower; they produce spores, usually on the undersides of their leaves. These spores drop off, take root, but do not become ferns themselves; instead they produce the seed from which new ferns grow. To save and germinate these spores watch carefully until spore marks become brown, and then collect them in clean paper. Sow them on compost, cover and keep moist and wait for the prothalli, the small heart-shaped growths which have both male and female organs, to appear. As fern fronds develop, pot on into suitable containers. In fact many hardy ferns can be increased by division with a sharp spade, a quicker and easier method than collecting and sowing spores, but only possible if the fern is growing in a bed rather than in the cracks of a wall. When replanting after division the root stock or rhizome should not be placed too deep; those in the wild generally sit on the soil, pushing down fibrous roots for nourishment. Some ferns such as hart's tongue and the lady fern will produce bulbils on the old fronds; these can be sliced off and pegged down in peat boxes.

At PENRHYN CASTLE on the Welsh coast, a sloping west-facing garden bowl, encircled by trees, provided a home for native British ferns described by William Robinson in 1900. Here they were massed in bold groups, combined for effect with hardy evergreen shrubs. Probably this grouping would have resembled Miss Jekyll's fern walk at Munstead

Above: The Victorian Fernery at Kingston Lacy has recently been restored. Dry stone walls support new soil for a collection of ferns.

Wood described in *Wood and Garden* (1899), where a mossy bank some 2.7 m (9 ft) wide was planted with a preponderance of dilated shield fern (*Dryopteris dilatata*) and lady fern (*Athyrium filix-femina*), with hollows for moisture-loving osmunda and blechnum. Although it was much neglected during the 1939–45 war, Penrhyn has been run by the Trust since 1951, and many plants in this old fern collection have been encouraged.

At STANDEN *Blechnum penna-marina*, a dwarf evergreen fern from New Zealand, acts as ground cover, among hart's tongues and low-growing epimedium. Here in West Sussex the natural sandstone rock and acid soil provide perfect growing conditions for this little fern: its horizontal fronds, copper-coloured when young, creep along the ground, while from its centre taller fertile richer bronze-coloured fronds rise to 15 cm (6 in). Its carpet allows in enough light for small hoop petticoat daffodils to flourish.

Less hardy ferns introduced from abroad grow in Trust gardens on the south Devon coast and in Cornwall. At TRELISSICK and TRENGWAINTON clumps of *Blechnum chilense*, with broad arching much-divided fronds, grow near the tender New Zealand tree ferns (*Dicksonia antarctica*) and thrive under the woodland canopy. If happy, this fern tends to spread rapidly and, given a protective mulch, it will survive in quite a severe climate. Coppery when young, the pinnate leaves become dark green and leathery in summer, and often remain so through winter months, needing little attention except for cutting away the old fronds as new growth begins. The walking fern (*Woodwardia radicans*) has arching 1.8 m (6 ft) lighter green fronds, at the tips of which are buds which take root in the right conditions. In places near the stream at Trengwainton it has almost made a colony. In the colder climate of Cheshire artificial heat is necessary for these plants: at TATTON PARK in the Fern House built by Paxton in the middle of the nineteenth century, both *Dicksonia antarctica* and *Woodwardia radicans* are a glorious sight. Smooth green leaves of agapanthus arch in front of the ferns and behind, clinging to the walls, the little creeping fig (*Ficus pumila*) makes a leafy curtain.

An Edwardian fernery has recently been completely restored at KINGSTON LACY in Dorset. In semi-shade winding paths run between raised beds contained by dry-stone walling. In each bed separate groups of hardy ferns grow in new topsoil.

Rockeries

A true rock garden, envisaged as a site for growing small mountain plants which need good drainage and simulated mountain conditions, is expensive to make and labour-intensive to keep. Today a modern alpine gardener is more likely to give these small colourful flowering plants the conditions they crave by building raised beds or 'screes'. The soil is specially prepared for those plants which come from limestone mountain ranges or for those which come from areas of non-calcareous rock. The soil is contained by dry-stone walling, railway sleepers, blocks of tufa (or peat for raised peat beds), and outside troughs, all of which can be wholly or partly protected in winter by glass or polythene lights. The alpine enthusiast will have a greenhouse with temperature and ventilation adjustment to provide almost perfect growing conditions.

Some of the earlier rock-work creations were bizarre attempts to simulate the landscape from which these plants derived. From a visual as well as a practical point of view it became apparent that rock-work was among the more difficult types of garden scenery to design and execute successfully. At Lamport in Northamptonshire Sir Charles Isham built a north-facing rock garden in 1848. Its south front was a vertical wall over 6 m (20 ft) high; its north face a steep slope with miniature crevices, rocks and chasms simulating an alpine hillside where dwarf conifers, ferns and ivy were grown, but few flowering alpines would thrive without the intense light of their own habitat. Stone gnomes were the forerunners of today's plastic dwarves. In the second half of the nineteenth century an amazing landscape was constructed at Friar Park, including miniature Matterhorn and glaciers.

Many of these early attempts were haphazard as sites for growing plants, only occasionally acknowledging the special needs of alpines. (Just as often they were frankly intended as landscape features, designed to evoke the sublime and awesome effects of mountainous terrain.) These mountain plants need to be both dry and freezing in winter (usually covered with snow). The temperate lowland garden is in general too damp and too mild, and average

An artificial rockery bank at Ascott (top) built in 1896 contrasts with the rock garden at Rowallane (above), where pockets of soil between the natural outcrops of whinstone provide perfect conditions for planting. Celmisias from New Zealand, with silvery leaves and daisy flowers, are often difficult to grow successfully.

Opposite: At Arlington Court levels are adjusted by a bank where rock garden plants are at home.

garden soil is often slow in draining and too rich in nutrients. At the beginning of this century the greatest rock-garden expert was Reginald Farrer, and his advice on construction and alpine growing still has much to offer today. He recognized that many other plants from all regions of the world would benefit from the same garden conditions as were required by plants from the Alps. He stressed the importance of so constructing a rock garden as to make it look as natural as possible. His famous dicta on 'almond puddings' (spikes and pinnacles of limestone as at Friar Park), 'dogs' graves' (puddings with stones laid flat), and 'devil's lapful', where cartloads of bald square-faced boulders were dropped about anywhere, are often quoted. In the twentieth-century rock garden, rock should be tilted backwards into the slope, with the largest surface to the ground, all nooks filled tightly with soil (so no questing root could find a vacuum and starve), and only a half or less of the rock showing above soil level. In the Alps and similar terrain, moisture is abundant yet sharp light grit allows good drainage: a foundation layer of clinker (or similar materials), topped up with stone chippings and a light sprinkling of loam and soil creates comparable conditions. More alpines die of defective drainage, water freezing round their crowns in winter, than from any other cause. To further simulate conditions of a natural mountainous habitat an underground water-pipe with minute perforations could be set at least 30 cm (12 in) below the soil, and water introduced in periods of drought.

Although Farrer recommended that a rockery should appear as a natural feature at the edge of a shrubbery, he also stressed the importance of sun and wind, and that shade should come from the rocks and not from overhanging trees. Over the years since some of these great rockeries were constructed, trees and shrubs have grown and much of the area is heavily shaded. Fortunately, although the small alpine flowers no longer thrive in these conditions, other plants such as ferns and the dwarf rhododendrons are in their element.

Nevertheless, where the Trust has inherited a craggy Victorian rockery – even of the kind deplored by Farrer – its policy is to conserve it in the spirit in which it was made rather than to convert it to the modern taste. At CRAGSIDE in Northumberland Lord Armstrong created, at the end of the last century, one of the greatest rockery–pleasure grounds ever made in these islands, partly by using the natural outcrops and partly by skilful construc-

tion to create the effect of tumbled disarray on a gigantic scale.

The scale of most of the rock gardens in Trust properties is much too great for easy adaptation to a garden of restricted size. Yet in many of the gardens a rockery area has evolved for reasons not strictly to do with providing conditions for growing alpines successfully. Sometimes a rockery has been established in the quarry first excavated to provide building stone for the house, as at COLETON FISHACRE, KILLERTON and SCOTNEY CASTLE. John Coutts, Head Gardener at Killerton between 1900 and 1909, before he left for Kew where he later became the curator, was responsible for clearing the quarry of old cherry laurel and planting interesting alpines and acid-loving small plants, suitable for shade. Today much of the quarry garden is overgrown but clearing is beginning, and recently drifts of blue-flowered meconopsis have been introduced at the approach, behind the rustic hut to the west of the great lawn and view into the park. At STANDEN the rocky dell behind the house where ferns thrive in shade beside a pool is called the Quarry Garden and was made when the sandstone hillside was quarried to provide stone for the house.

Most gardens in the hands of the National Trust are those which have been acquired as the surroundings of a house of historical importance; in a few cases the garden itself has been of such interest that it merited preservation regardless of the house itself (indeed, in some cases such as at SHEFFIELD PARK, house and garden are now separately owned). In either case the trust inherits a duty to keep the garden as nearly as possible as it was in its heyday, both for historical continuity and also quite deliberately to stress the history of garden design and plant introductions. As in all old properties, different layers of history become interwoven, successive generations of owners imposing the gardening fashion of their time on what was there before. The Trust has constantly to balance opposing interpretations of style against increasingly high cost of upkeep and the need to preserve a garden as an example of its period. Rock gardens are very labour-intensive to create, especially when they are made from stone specially imported in to the garden, and the Trust policy is rather to restore old ones than to create new features. The Trust cannot afford to expend countless man-hours in growing 'tricky' plants which need special conditions, but vast drifts of ground-cover quickly lose scale with existing rockwork or even hide it. It is a question of selecting plants that are neither fussy nor invasive, but are fairly dense and weedproof. Their scale and character should be appropriate for their site, and they should contribute variety and interest.

Fortunately among Trust properties are some with important rock garden areas which were developed just at the turn of this century and reflect the contemporary style and affluence. At WADDESDON MANOR a natural outcrop was moved and used as the basis of a rock garden, built of artificial 'Pulhamite' stone by the famous Pulham firm from Bishops Stortford. At SIZERGH CASTLE in the 1920s T. R.

Hayes from Ambleside used local Cumbrian water-worn limestone to construct the rocky pool garden mentioned earlier. At HIDCOTE MANOR local Cotswold limestone, unearthed when the garden was being made, was used to make a natural-looking rock bank, raised 30 cm (12 in) above ground level, thus increasing the range of plants which can be grown, but not restricted to alpines. At ARLINGTON COURT a raised bed acting as a retaining wall links two different levels in the terraced Victorian garden and is attractively planted with heathers and cistus. Filled with suitably draining composts, this type of rock bed, far from interrupting the coherence of design, unites separate garden areas.

At ROWALLANE in Northern Ireland the most spectacular of all Trust rock gardens has been made over the glacier-smooth natural outcrop of whinstone. Here where rock was never far from the surface, cartloads of acid topsoil were added to make planting pockets for Asiatic primulas, silver-leaved New Zealand celmisias, erythroniums, gentians and meconopsis. Small-leaved rhododendrons, heathers, philesias and other acid-loving shrubs give bulk and winter shapes as well as flower-colour later.

Mr Mike Snowden, the Head Gardener at Rowallane, talked about the problems he inherited in an old and established rock garden, and how he continues to tackle them. Planted at the beginning of this century by Mr Hugh Armytage Moore, this rock garden had by the 1970s become infested with perennial weeds. Ground-elder, bluebell and the little white wood anemone (*Anemone nemorosa*) grew densely and the soil had become a seed-bank, so that any disturbance brought fresh germination, even when roots and bulbs had been removed. All the plants were taken up, their roots were washed free of soil and they were then stored in a nursery area.

New growth of weed-leaves was then sprayed, using a hooded sprayer to prevent drift on to some of the shrubs which were retained *in situ*, with glyphosate, a contact herbicide which works through the foliage to the roots of a plant. Because effects are not immediately apparent, Mr Snowden uses a dye in the mixture so that it is clear which leaves have been sprayed. Later he uses a Croptex glove, impregnated with weedkiller and dye, to touch individual weeds which still recur.

After a couple of seasons the ground was clean enough to start replanting. Hand-weeding is done where residual weeds still appear, but is a relatively simple task. Formerly when weeding was done often only the 'tops' could be pulled off, because of fear of disturbing the root system of neighbouring plants, and much of the good topsoil disappeared over the years to the compost heap. Originally Mr Armytage Moore both excavated the rock, delving down between the natural outcrops where soil was deep enough for planting, and imported additional soil to fill up rock crevices. He also placed a rock or two to fortify a new pocket of soil. Nevertheless the rock garden remains a natural phenomenon, and the bare rock surfaces are as they were when the land was grazing pasture, which still exists just beyond the garden perimeter. The local name whinstone (also used in the north of England) indicates an acid outcrop where gorse (*Ulex europaeus*) naturalizes. The rock is exceptionally hard, and dates from the glacial period when softer limestones were pushed aside. The dramatic effect of the rock outcrop had also become blurred by an accumulation of overgrown 'dwarf' conifers, many of which have now been removed.

In replanting there is no 'drawing-board' plan. Rather, groups are instinctively placed to make the right patterns, and plants given just the depth of soil in which they will do well. No plan on paper could indicate the deep declivities and contrasting areas of shallow soil, or even areas of sun or shadow. Different faces of rock shade sections where Asiatic primulas and dwarf rhododendrons do well, and daphnes and potentillas will flower to extend the season. At the base of the rocks wide groups of self-seeding primulas and monocarpic meconopsis are a feature. Heathers have been collected on the face of the rocks which looks to open countryside, and at the lowest end more dwarf rhododendrons, pieris and ground-covering gaultherias grow tightly together, allowing little space for smaller plants. Pockets of soil in the centre are planted with more unusual plants, and, if necessary, Mr Snowden varies the pH of the topsoil to suit individual types. In places the soil is deliberately maintained as neutral where small herbaceous geraniums will flourish but gentians, maianthemums and celmisias like the acidity. Mulches of leaf mould are applied when possible, but Mr Snowden points out that today mushroom compost, which used to be based on alkaline ground limestone, now contains gypsum and will not make the soil more alkaline. He advises storing it for a year and not using it fresh. Falling leaves are a problem among the rocks, collecting in crannies, and Mr Snowden uses a leaf-blower extended with a length of plastic drainpipe to blow the leaves off the smaller plants and from under heathers.

III
GARDEN WALLS

Any wall, whether it is the side of a building or a boundary or compartmental wall, offers a third dimension in planting to serve as a frame or backdrop to the garden proper. The presence of a wall has an effect on local conditions and both extends and limits the choice of plants in its vicinity. Subdivision into separate enclosures and compartments, many of them walled, paradoxically gives even large Trust gardens a great deal in common with many ordinary domestic private gardens. The majority of town gardens, for example, are rectangular in shape and much of the planting is on the walls of any adjacent buildings. A town gardener, therefore, may draw much inspiration from wall planting schemes found in the larger Trust gardens: aspect and suitability, which dictate planting policies and plant choice, may correspond, even if the scale is widely different.

In decorative terms, wall planting falls into three categories. There is the 'architectural' planting, when foliage plants act visually as buttresses or grow in a bed at the base of a wall to link the buildings to the ground. There is the more ornamental theme (a Jekyll favourite) of softening hard masonry lines with a curtain of foliage. There is the practical role which walls play as supports for espaliers, for example, demonstrating that function and decoration are almost inseparable in gardening. Finally, and more generally, walls and walled enclosures provide shelter and protection for plants, often extending the planting range of the garden.

Walled gardens in classical times developed as an extension of the house, the enclosure being used as an additional room. The walled courtyards round many houses are still treated in this way, and are linked both with the architecture of the house and with the life-style of its occupants. Originally walls were for security and all gardening took place inside them. Gardens attached to ecclesiastical foundations grew mainly culinary or medicinal herbs during the Middle Ages, but gradually areas were set apart for places for retreat, the *hortus conclusus* where arbours and scented flowers offered refreshment. The Renaissance-type gardens of the seventeenth century were still based on a series of enclosures, as evidenced by William Lawson's plan first published in 1618 (but reprinted several times to 1683). The garden, divided into six compartments, provided spaces for completely individual gardening themes, with mounts at each corner from which the countryside beyond could be surveyed. In this sort of garden style raised walks and mounts allowed glimpses of the world beyond the garden walls, but glimpses to be snatched only from the security of an enclosed space. It was not until the eighteenth century that the idea of the garden being part of the greater landscape became accepted in England. Walls were relegated to making enclosures for the functional areas of the garden. By the end of the century, elaborate walled kitchen gardens, often placed some distance from the mansion, were established for fruit, vegetables

Above: At Tintinhull House wall borders are packed with shrubs, perennials, bulbs and irises.

Opposite: The walled garden at Westbury Court. Arbours and box-edged beds are planted with old roses and plants known in gardens before 1700.

Page 163: Walls provide protection for shrubs at their base, as well as vertical surfaces for climbing plants. At Cotehele *Euphorbia characias* grows next to Jerusalem sage, *Phlomis fruticosa*.

and for cut flowers and pot flowers for the house. They often also contained decorative flower borders. Those on the grandest scale were run as factories, with a team of gardeners, each one with an allotted role in seed-sowing, fruit and vegetable cultivation and the management of hothouses. Here tender pot plants were kept in winter and cuttings from the tender bedding plants were housed for the twice yearly change-over in Victorian schemes.

The Trust has inherited many such large walled gardens, which were built to provide for the great house and the numerous servants attached to it. Today fruit and vegetables are uneconomical to produce when employing paid gardeners, and few actual kitchen areas are open to public view. The sloping vegetable area at UPTON PARK still grows its early crops and there are vegetables to be seen at BARRINGTON COURT, FELBRIGG HALL and HIDCOTE MANOR. At BUSCOT HOUSE the old walled garden is being restored and replanted with trees, covered walks and borders. In several cases walled gardens have been largely converted for economy into ornamental orchards with climbing plants on the walls, for example CLUMBER PARK, LACOCK ABBEY and OXBURGH HALL. The transformation of the walled kitchen garden at MOTTISFONT ABBEY to house the National Collection of old (pre-1900) roses is mentioned in Chapter 2. Elsewhere there has been an even more abrupt change of usage within the walled areas: at BASILDON PARK, CLIVEDEN and MONTACUTE HOUSE the walled gardens proved to be conveniently sited for car parks.

By the end of the nineteenth century, in a return to the spirit of the Renaissance, architects again saw the ornamental garden as an extension of the house, designing a series of outdoor rooms divided by walls and hedges. This framework provided the perfect setting for 'cottage-type' informal planting, where hardy plants as advocated by William Robinson and Miss Jekyll were used to furnish the rooms abundantly and to soften hard lines of clipped hedges and of masonry.

Wall Planting

In a walled garden the vertical surfaces covered in climbing and trailing plants displaying ornamental flowers and foliage or more utilitarian espaliered fruits become curtained backdrops to planting in the beds beneath. When a garden is a series of enclosures in this way, the second side of the wall provides further planting space, but with distinct differences in aspect on either side, offering conditions to suit a different selection of plants. The gardener needs to take into account the special growing conditions that may prevail near any wall: perhaps a favourable microclimate where plants whose hardiness is doubtful will be able to thrive; possibly problems of wind turbulence, rain shadow or increased alkalinity. Plants can be chosen to suit the site. South-facing walls provide sites for tender sun-lovers and bulbs which need hot dry soil. The north side of a wall suits shade-lovers, although if the prevailing wind is south-westerly, the wall often acts as a rain shadow and the soil can be very dry at the base. The soil at the base of a wall also tends to alkalinity since mortar chippings add lime. In full sun this sort of poor soil suits plants such as the Algerian iris (*Iris unguicularis*), and many South African bulbs revel in the heat. The shady side provides a site for the ferns that do not need a lot of moisture, and for plants such as Lenten roses (*Helleborus orientalis*), if plenty of humus-making organic material is added. East-facing walls which receive the early morning sun should not be planted with spring-flowerers, since frozen buds will be damaged by the quick thaw after a night of frost: camellias and tree peonies are obvious examples.

Exploiting to the full the planting potential of a walled enclosure – such as an old kitchen garden – can be a plantsman's paradise, especially when the garden is in one of the more favoured regions. Even in colder inland northern and eastern areas differences of aspect expand the planting possibilities. At BENINGBROUGH HALL, for example, the old walled kitchen garden has been redesigned in a relatively labour-saving layout, with a refreshingly uncluttered atmosphere. It is now sown with grass and is used for events and as an informal play area for visitors. A central alley is formed where the original espalier pears which once lined the path are now trained to meet as archways. Against high walls ivies, climbing hydrangeas, vines and hops with golden leaves (*Humulus lupulus aureus*) are systematically arranged. Trained into fan-shapes, they act as flat green buttresses in architectural symmetry along the walls. Figs grow in full sun on the south-facing top wall and a glossy-leaved cherry laurel (*Prunus laurocerasus*) occupies the shady corners. White painted seats are arranged in a regular pattern. Outside the bottom wall plants which prove tender in this east Yorkshire garden have been given a protected site: facing south, choisyas, ceanothus, bay, *Jasminum beesianum* and *J. officinale* and *Actinidia chinensis* take advantage of reflected heat from the high walls.

At ROWALLANE the walled garden formerly used only for kitchen produce, fruit and as a nursery area for young plants going later into the woodland was gradually filled with exotics by Hugh Armytage Moore and over the years has developed into an interesting ornamental area. (An account of the recent weedkilling programme here is given by Mr Mike Snowden in Chapter 5.) Herbaceous borders with shrub roses and fuchsias, a spring blue and yellow garden and fine shrubs have grown into tall specimens against the walls. Until recently a *Cupressus cashmeriana* with blue-grey foliage carried on pendulous branches survived in a corner. Large hoherias, many magnolia and hydrangea species, *Pileostegia viburnoides*, the climbing *Schizophragma integrifolium*, *Drimys winteri* and *D. lanceolata*, *Itea ilicifolia*, and tender escallonias all grow here. Now mature, these plants, many of which are evergreen, have to be pruned hard, or in time their canopies will completely shade the planting beds below, where meconopsis, double-flowered colchicums and *Celmisia holosericea* from New Zealand give a good display. The national collection of penstemon cultivars is now held here. Incidentally, the walls date back to the 1860s, when they were built by the Rev. John Moore, who had recently bought the property. He devised a unique method of plant support, incorporating bands of projecting tiles pierced with holes to which to tie the plants – originally conventional kitchen-garden fruit but nowadays ornamental shrubs. These tiles are now getting old, but some replacements have been obtained in modern Kilmarnock glazed bricks. Elsewhere at Rowallane special wall ties are used which are forged in a smithy near Lanhydrock.

Mature trees, shrubs and woodland plants in the walled garden at Rowallane. The blue-flowered poppies are hybrids of *Meconopsis grandis*; they only thrive in an area of high humidity and will not tolerate alkaline soil.

At PENRHYN CASTLE in North Wales the sloping walled garden at some distance from the castle has a formal parterre on the upper terrace, and the walls give extra shelter to the tender plants that grow well there: spring-flowering *Cytisus maderensis* and *Clianthus puniceus*, daisy-flowered mutisias, *Holboellia coriacea*, lemon-scented verbenas, *Pittosporum eugenioides*, *Vitis vinifera* 'Purpurea', *Drimys aromatica* and smaller plants such as a selection of osteospermum. *Salvia patens* grows in the beds at the base of the walls. Other good plants include fremontodendron, *Solanum crispum*, various ceanothus, *Corokia virgata*, *Smilax aspera maculata*, and by the entrance gate for its scent in spring, *Azara microphylla*. In shade the coral plant (*Berberidopsis corallina*) produces its deep crimson flowers in late summer, and *Distylium racemosum*, with glossy leathery leaves, has petalless flowers in April.

At COLETON FISHACRE in the milder west-country climate near Dartmouth, where the woodland garden slopes down to the cliffs above the sea, the walled garden gives extra protection for tender plants. **Mrs Richard Taylor**, who until recently ran the garden, describes the planting:

❧ The garden at Coleton Fishacre was begun in 1925, while the house was being built for Rupert D'Oyly Carte (whose father Richard was the famous impresario). The architect, Oswald Milne, was a pupil of Lutyens, and both house and garden architecture show a strong Lutyens influence, which often leads visitors to wonder if Miss Jekyll was responsible for the planting. Not so; the landscape architect Edward White (who among other achievements was involved in the design of the rock garden at Wisley) was in some way that is not clear from the archives concerned with the initial design of the garden; Lady Dorothy D'Oyly Carte herself was largely responsible for the actual planting. The garden diary she kept shows a progression from fairly commonplace familiar shrubs and trees to a more adventurous approach, as, no doubt, she began to appreciate the climatic and edaphic potential of the site.

As in any coastal garden, the first requirement was shelter, and while the massive belts of pine were still small the garden was very exposed to violent sea winds. In these early days the walled rill garden, with its typically Lutyens central watercourse, must have been almost the only part of the garden sheltered enough for very tender plants. This symmetrically designed garden slopes gently, so that the narrow stone-lined rill drops over a series of small falls, filling the little garden with the sound of water. It is in effect three-sided, with walls facing roughly south, north and east. The north-facing wall, shady yet warm, offers ideal conditions for plants of Chilean origin, and both *Mitraria coccinea* and *Berberidopsis corallina* do well and flower freely. Camellias, too, appreciate these conditions – all too well, as they have grown far too large and have to be severely cut back. They provide additional shelter for a newly planted *Pentapterygium serpens*; other north-wall plants include *Bomarea caldasii*, *Lonicera tragophylla* and *Correa backhousiana*, which produces its limy-cream trumpets at all seasons of the year.

The upper, south-east-facing wall is occupied by two vast wisterias, to which we have added *Datura sanguinea*, *Cestrum* 'Newellii', *Salvia boliviensis* and *Grindelia chiloensis*, with *Fremontodendron californicum* in the corner – a harmony of soft and strong colours in the yellow-orange-red range.

The long south wall was originally the home of *Mandevilla suaveolens*, now surviving, and thriving, only on the house walls, and of *Wattakaka sinensis* with a campsis and an enormous *Feijoa sellowiana* still surviving. In place of the mandevilla we have planted *Araujia sericofera* and *Buddleja madagascariensis*; the latter survived the severe winter of 1984–85 and is growing away strongly. Another surprising survivor was the Australian *Hibbertia scandens*, cut to the ground but getting away again, as also *Salvia gesneriiflora* (an original planting, lost and now replaced).

The symmetrical beds on either side of the rill are planted with a selection of kniphofias, accompanied by silver- and grey-foliaged plants such as gazanias, by further salvias including *Salvia rutilans* and *S. blepharophylla*, with *Tropaeolum tuberosum* as ground cover. Other cover is formed by *Malvastrum lateritium* in terracotta and the coral-pink *Sphaeralcea munroana*, *Zauschneria californica* 'Dublin' and *Lobelia laxiflora*. The picture is completed by self-sowing annuals such as *Argemone mexicana*, *Calceolaria mexicana*, *Hibiscus trionum* with black-eyed cream flowers and *Collomia grandiflora* in harmonious colours of yellow, apricot, orange and scarlet.

Further west, in Cornwall, the walled bays at TRENGWAINTON, which were originally built for fruit and vegetables, now overflow with rare tender plants. Wall shrubs, climbers, bulbs and perennials,

Above: At Beningbrough Hall a small enclosed formal garden next to the house is backed by an old wall; low hedges give extra protection and warmth.

Opposite: At Gunby Hall in Lincolnshire mellow brick walls protect plants from east winds.

many from the southern hemisphere and introduced only in this century, have grown large and present an exciting collection to the plantsman. These walled areas and sloping walled vegetable beds (see below) were constructed in 1820 to allow the maximum heat from the sun's rays striking the 45-degree slope to stimulate production of early crops; today those in the lower garden walled area are planted only with ornamentals. Mr Peter Horder, the Head Gardener, points out that over the years many of the trees and shrubs have grown to shade sun-loving tender perennials, so since 1980 these

have been moved into an open central section of the inner gardens, part of a new scheme of development. Here the collection has been augmented with a wider range of tender, and above all, later-flowering subjects, which contribute interest when spring and summer displays are over. Mr Horder adds that the earliest planting of ornamentals dates from 1910 and includes *Podocarpus salignus*; *Magnolia campbellii mollicomata* was planted in 1926. However the majority of the planting, now mature specimens, has been done since the 1940s. He finds that although sheltered from winds, these walled areas are frost pockets, 15 degrees of frost having been registered on a few occasions since he became Head Gardener in 1971. When planting, care is taken to site tender plants in the higher beds and banks, preferably where the morning sun does not reach the buds while the frost is still on them.

It is hardly possible to include a full list of the interesting plants at Trengwainton, but the names of a few will stimulate interest.

Climbers include *Trachelospermum asiaticum*, a cultivar of the Chilean lapageria, *Lapageria* 'Rose Pink', *Berberidopsis corallina*, *Pileostegia viburnoides* and *Senecio scandens*. Asiatic magnolias include the *Magnolia campbellii mollicomata*, *M. nitida* and the related *Michelia doltsopa* with fragrant multi-petalled white flowers. Evergreen olearias from New Zealand, Tasmania and the Chatham Islands include *Olearia furfuracea*, flowering with daisy-heads in August, forms of *O. phlogopappa* and particularly the hybrid from Tresco, *O.* × *scilloniensis*, and *O. semidentata* with lilac daisy-flowers in June. *O.* 'Zennorensis', a hybrid of the rare *O. lacunosa*, which also grows here, and *O. ilicifolia*, which thrives on shady banks in the woodland at Trengwainton, has remarkable sharply toothed leaves and stalks covered in brown tomentum. *O. virgata* has wiry linear leaves carried very densely to give a grey cloudy effect, and although seldom seen is one of the hardiest of this ornamental genus.

Evergreen shrubs given the benefit of wall protection include *Abutilon* 'Kentish Belle', *Buddleja lindleyana*, *Cassinia vauvilliersii albida*, *Cestrum elegans*, *Cleyera fortunei* with marbled grey-green polished leaves, and *Rhododendron maddenii crassum* and *R.* × 'Fragrantissimum'. Ginger-plants include *Hedychium densiflorum* and *H. greenei*, and echiums

Moseley Old Hall

Planting in the walled courtyard at the entrance to Moseley Old Hall consists of shrubs, roses, climbers and herbaceous perennials that were known in the mid-seventeenth century. The lawns are decorated in period fashion with clipped cones and spirals of box.

KEY

Roses

- R1 *Rosa foetida bicolor*
- R2 *R. damascena trigintipetala*
- R3 *R.* 'Quatre Saisons'
- R4 *R. gallica officinalis*
- R5 *R. alba semi-plena*
- R6 *R.* 'Maiden's Blush'
- R7 *R.* 'Tuscany'
- R8 *R.* 'De Meaux'
- R9 *R. eglauteria*
- R10 *R. alba* 'Maxima'
- R11 *R. centifolia parvifolia*
- R12 *R. foetida*
- R13 *R. damascena versicolor*
- R14 *R. gallica* 'Versicolor'

Shrubs

- S1 Lilac
- S2 existing holly probably *Ilex aquifolium*
- S3 *Rosmarinus* 'Miss Jessop's Upright'
- S4 Chaenomeles
- S5 *Weigela* 'James Crawford'
- S6 Laburnum
- S7 Holly

Climbers

- C1 *Vitis labrusca*
- C2 *Clematis viticella* 'Rubra'
- C3 *Jasminum officinale*
- C4 *Lonicera periclymenum* 'Belgica'
- C5 *Clematis integrifolia*

Herbaceous Perennials

1 *Helleborus niger*
2 *Geranium striatum*
3 *Doronicum plantagineum* 'Excelsum'
4 *Aster amellus*
5 *Lilium croceum*
6 *Hemerocallis fulva*
7 *Ranunculus acris flore pleno*
8 *Polygonatum multiflorum*
9 *Physalis alkekengi*
10 Common fern
11 *Iris foetidissima*
12 *Corydalis lutea*
13 *Dianthus barbatus*
14 Auriculas
15 *Iris sibirica*
16 *Calendula officinalis*
17 *Artemisia abrotanum*
18 *Aconitum napellus*
19 *Iris florentina*
20 *Saponaria officinalis* 'Flore Plena'
21 *Astrantia major*
22 *Fritillaria imperialis* (bronze and yellow)
23 *Paeonia mascula*
24 *Hemerocallis flava*
25 *Centranthus ruber*
26 *Centaurea montana*
27 *Geranium sanguineum*
28 *Catananche caerulea*
29 *Clematis recta*
30 *Lilium candidum*
31 Iris *pallida dalmatica*
32 *Eryngium alpinum*
33 *Dictamnus albus purpureus*
34 *Paeonia officinalis*
35 *Campanula persicifolia*
36 Martagon lily
37 *Ranunculus aconitifolius*
38 *Tradescantia virginiana*
39 *Teucrium chamaedrys*
40 *Hypericum androsaemum*

such as the tall *Echium pininana* seed freely. *Rhaphithamnus spinosus*, a shrub rare in the British Isles but which flourishes at Tresco in the Scillies, has turquoise flowers and fruits.

Callistemons, clethras, tender escallonias and eriobotrya, *Dodonaea viscosa purpurea*, eucryphias, fuchsias and myrtles combine to give the effect of semi-tropical jungle.

In the new garden beyond the inner wall, an *Acacia cultriformis* has been trained back against the wall where it benefits from the extra heat. Tender salvias, *Hedychium forrestii*, *H. gardnerianum* and *H. thyrsiforme* normally grown in the heated greenhouse, kniphofias, *Lobelia tupa*, white and blue-flowered agapanthus and the large strap-leaved *Wachendorfia paniculata* all do well. Various species of eucomis give interest in late summer, and the sword-shaped leaves of New Zealand dwarf phormiums provide a permanent architectural element. Over the corner of an old rock garden an impressive clump of royal fern (*Osmunda regalis*) has formed a massive root system. A red grass (*Uncinia rubrum*) and golden-variegated *Hakonechloa macra* 'Aureola' give leaf colour.

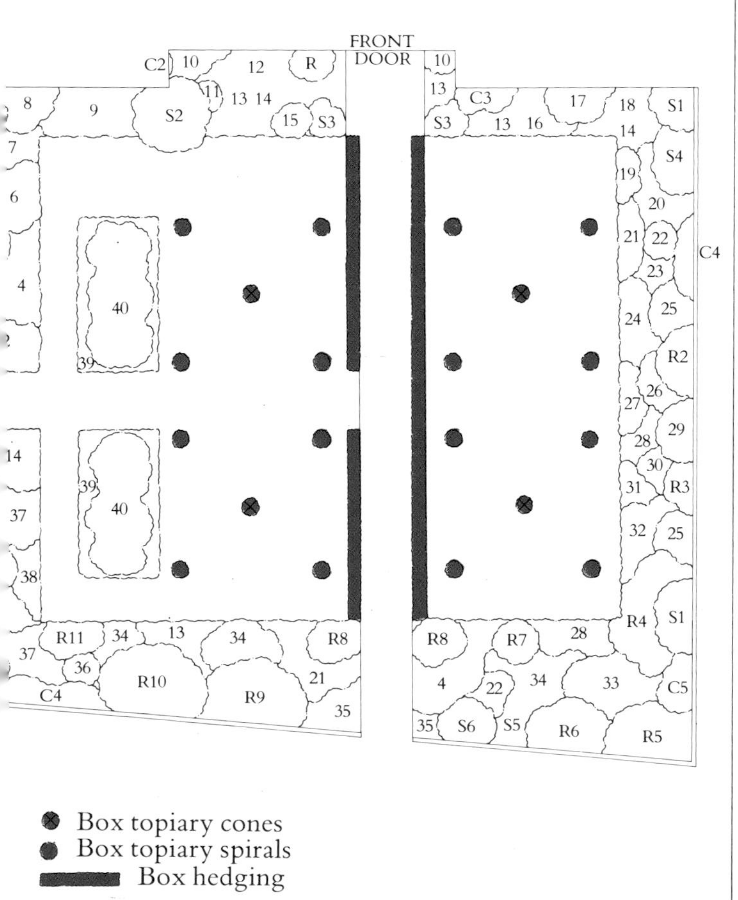

The National Trust found no garden existing at MOSELEY OLD HALL when it acquired the property in 1962: the partly walled enclosure at the front of the house contained only an old holly standing by the front door, and some of the lilacs which are seen today. Since the future Charles II sheltered at Moseley after the Battle of Worcester, garden features on a period theme were chosen as the basis for the reconstruction. In various parts of the garden contemporary style is manifested in the wooden arbour, knot garden and other features described in the appropriate places in this book.

In the recreated walled garden, box specimens clipped into finials and spirals which rise from the grass are typical of the seventeenth-century passion for topiary. In two rectangular beds groups of *Hypericum androsaemum* with bright red berries are surrounded by low hedges of germander (*Teucrium chamaedrys*). Lilacs and old shrub roses occupy the corners and give height, and honeysuckle clambers on the walls. Only plants that Charles might have found here in 1650 have been used in the borders, which were replanted in 1984.

Walled enclosures often have problems from wind turbulence. Wind, perhaps funnelled through a narrow opening, strikes the solid masonry and bounces off again making strong currents which are very damaging to plants in the vicinity. Moving air tends to rise above or go round any obstacle in its path, increasing its speed close to the highest point or at the sides. On the lee side of a wall there will be a vacuum, and turbulence produces swirling effects which can pull climbers down or rock established plants. Thick dense hedges will have almost the same effect as walls; the ideal barricade filters and diffuses the strength of the wind, providing sheltered areas on the lee side, where the speed of the current is much reduced. For gardening the optimum reduction of wind speed and turbulence is provided by screens with a ratio of about 60 per cent solid material to 40 per cent space; obviously it is difficult to measure density of hedges, but the general principle is easy to grasp.

A small walled garden such as that of the Chapel Garden at CASTLE DROGO, first designed and planted by Dillistone in the 1920s, is particularly vulnerable to wind currents. The sunken garden under the west walls of the house is reached by narrow entrances down steep granite steps. The house with its main terrace is situated on the eastern edge of Dartmoor above a precipitous slope to the river Teign, where it is exposed to the full force of south-westerly gales. Some of the original planting of evergreens remains, but in 1985 rose and lavender beds were renewed and the small lawn completely reseeded. The beds were treated with dazomet against rose replant disease. A glossy-leaved *Magnolia grandiflora* 'Exmouth', with *Garrya elliptica*, is trained back on strong wires against the stone. In the sunniest spot an old fig has been replaced. Ivy clings to the north-facing chapel wall and *Parthenocissus henryana* grows well, its veined leaves giving interest all through the summer, and colouring more brightly in autumn.

Castle Drogo

Steep steps descend from the upper forecourt to the little Chapel Garden, which is almost entirely surrounded by protective walls. Mature climbers soften the harsh granite. Modern planting is simple: blocks of 'Hidcote' lavender mark the corners and separate beds of low-growing bush roses, which are planted in single colour blocks. Box domes give further formality and strengthen the design.

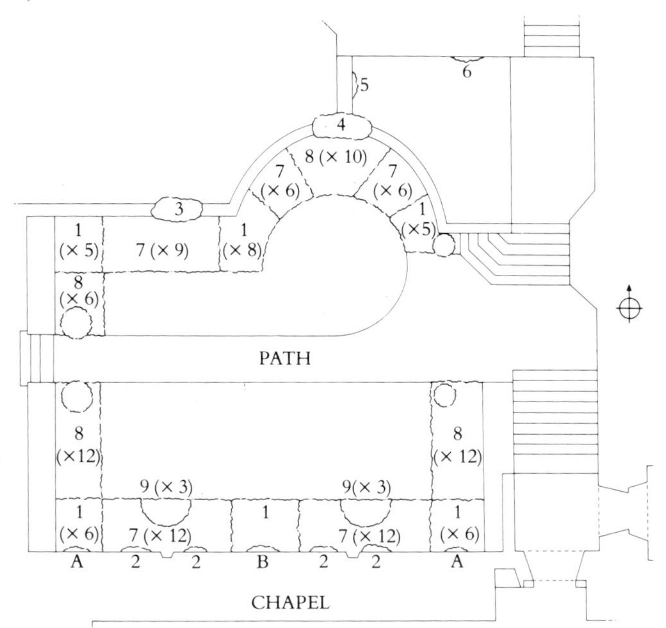

KEY

Existing Climbers
A *Hedera*
B *Parthenocissus henryana*

Shrubs
1 *Lavandula angustifolia* 'Hidcote'
2 *Viburnum plicatum*
3 Fig (*Ficus carica*)
4 *Magnolia grandiflora* 'Exmouth'
5 *Garrya elliptica*
6 Camellia
7 Rose 'Petit Four'
8 Rose 'Robin Redbreast'
9 Rose 'Yvonne Rabier'

○ Box dome

The roses in the more open flower beds were all chosen for their wind resistance and to smother the ground quickly. They are all suitable for growing in restricted beds or even in containers. More robust and taller than miniatures, they grow to 60 cm (2 ft): at this height, they withstand the gusts of wind that so often destabilize rose bushes. Most are of recent introduction, but an old variety dating from 1910, 'Yvonne Rabier', is on the right scale. It is of polyantha type; vigorous, and with scented flowers, it will perform all summer if regularly dead-headed.

The new rose planting echoes the original Dillistone colours. The modern red and pink roses in the Chapel Garden are now introduced in catalogues as patio types. 'Robin Redbreast' has dark red flowers with a yellowish white eye and bears its blooms in dense clusters, and 'Petit Four' has clear pink semi-double flowers carried all through the season from June onwards. In the more open bed, clumps of 'Petit Four' and 'Robin Redbreast' alternate with low-growing lavender, *Lavandula angustifolia* 'Hidcote', and box bushes framing steps and stonework. On the southern side more lavender bushes separate large groups of pink 'Petit Four', which surround clumps of the old double white rose 'Yvonne Rabier', mentioned above.

The National Trust is fortunate in owning houses which vary in size from the massive Elizabethan to the more modest elegant eighteenth-century, and even to quite humble cottages. Plants which grow upon the walls or in beds against the walls should match the scale of the building. The twining honeysuckle, jasmine and rambling roses appropriate to a cottage porch will look ridiculous on 18 m (60 ft) high stone and brick walls. Similarly bushes grown against these imposing walls, or in the beds at their bases, must match the scale. Strong evergreen shapes against the lower walls act as living and growing buttresses, and anchor a building securely to its site. Just as a house on a slope needs a flat terrace on which it can visually rest, so a great house benefits from dense-growing architectural plants which seem to prop it up. A variegated Persian ivy smothers a small section of the grey Mona marble of which PENRHYN CASTLE is built, Virginia creeper grows on the west side, and elsewhere the masonry is kept clear of planting. At GAWTHORPE HALL a recently planted narrow border at the base of the house walls is filled with evergreen shrubs which will create a solid base as they grow together. They include mahonias, the dense-leaved small cherry laurel (*Prunus laurocerasus* 'Otto Luyken'), evergreen berberis, *Euonymus fortunei* 'Coloratus', and low-growing periwinkle (*Vinca minor*). Rounded leathery leaves of bergenia and dark-foliaged *Euphorbia robbiae* spill over the edges of the beds.

Mounded yew topiary shapes match the architecture at CHIRK CASTLE and provide protective wings to stabilize the building. Behind these, climbers reach up the wall to flower in profusion in the light. *Hydrangea petiolaris* becomes a dense host plant to intertwining honeysuckle and climbing roses, which would look too fragile on their own. At both ICKWORTH and THE VYNE, elegant old plants of the evergreen 'farmyard' tree *Phillyrea latifolia* fill in space near the walls of the houses. Unfortunately very slow-growing, which is probably the reason for its scarcity, this is one of the best of small evergreen trees, making either a spreading canopy or responding to clipping into tight shapes.

At POWIS CASTLE the ancient yews extend the architecture, towering above the terraces on which many unusual plants thrive. Powis does not have a

Powis Castle

At Powis a small paved garden under the castle walls is open to the sun on the south side. The house walls have been clothed with climbers and mixed planting of shrubs and mainly low-growing perennials fill the three borders. The flowers are all white, cream, ivory or pale yellow, and variegated and grey foliage keep the theme cool. Many of the shrubs such as the myrtle (*Myrtus communis* 'Tarentina') have aromatic leaves, complementing scented flowers of honeysuckle and philadelphus. Near the narrow entrance an ornamental tub contains lemon-scented verbena (*Lippia citriodora*) conveniently placed for touching in passing.

KEY

Herbaceous Perennials

1 *Hosta plantaginea* (4)
2 *Viola septentrionalis* (5)
3 *Digitalis grandiflora*
4 *Dicentra formosa* 'Alba' (5)
5 *Aconitum vulparia* (2)
6 *Hosta* 'Thomas Hogg' (4)
7 *Corydalis thalictrifolia* (5)
8 *Gillenia trifoliata* (5)
9 *Sisyrinchium striatum* 'Aunt May' (4)
10 *Linaria dalmatica* (3)
11 *Epilobium glabellum* (5)
12 *Filipendula vulgaris* 'Flore Pleno' (3)
13 *Iris florentina* (3)
14 *Francoa ramosa* (4)
15 *Hemerocallis flava* (5)
16 *Oenothera missouriensis* (3)
17 *Clematis recta* (herbaceous clematis)
18 *Arum creticum* (3)

Shrubs

S1 *Lippia citriodora* (group of 3, in tub, with *Alyssum maritimum*)
S2 *Skimmia japonica* 'Rubella' (3 in group)
S3 *Philadelphus* 'Coupe d'Argent' (3)
S4 *P. microphyllus* (2)
S5 *Skimmia japonica* 'Fragrana' (2)
S6 *Myrtus communis* 'Tarentina' (3)
S7 *Pittosporum* (variegated)
S8 *Phlomis russeliana*
S9 *Lonicera syringantha*
S10 *Cistus* (own dwarf: 3)

Climbers

C1 *Clematis flammula*
C2 *Lonicera caprifolia*
C3 *Clematis rehderiana*
C4 *Lonicera periclymenum* 'Serotina'
C5 *Ampelopsis brevipedunculata* 'Elegans'
C6 *Jasminum officinale* 'Affine'

Alyssum maritimum and *Mimulus moschatus* in paving

particularly favourable climate, but the well-drained upper south-facing terraces, almost cut out of the pink limestone rock, provide microclimatic pockets where tender plants will grow in the wide beds and against the heat-retaining brick walls. Banksian roses and a fine white wisteria (*Wisteria floribunda* 'Alba') with long racemes decorate the roof of the aviary. Tender *Datura meteloides* dies down each winter but shoots again each spring. Frost drains rapidly down the steep slope, and Mr Jimmie Hancock, the Head Gardener, finds that many tender plants which he grows from cuttings each autumn and keeps in frost-proof frames all winter can be put out early in the season. On the lower terraces wide borders, edged with box, have unexpectedly moist soil suitable for lush herbaceous perennials, but the exposure to full sun can scorch foliage in summer. In all such terrace planting there is constant revision of border plans as different factors of frost, drainage, exposure and rainfall play their part in affecting the general aspect. Walls provide shelter and reflected heat to ripen wood, yet create rain-shadows close to the base of the wall; terraces provide free drainage for damp and frost, making perfect sites for many tender plants, yet some plants find the southern aspect too hot and welcome an overhead canopy of branches. A gardener like Mr Hancock gets to know the vagaries of his site.

In the lower garden, *Ceanothus* 'Jermyns' flowers well by an old espalier pear against a gable wall, above massed planting of Bowles' Mauve wallflower (*Erysimum* 'Bowles' Mauve' of gardens, perhaps now more correctly *Cheiranthus* 'Bowles' Mauve'). With its grey-green leaves, this bears its mauve flowers all summer if dead-heads are removed, but it is not reliably hardy.

In a narrow bed under the south wall of his own house which fronts on a corner of the lower garden, Mr Hancock grows the tender climber *Maurandya barclaiana* from seed each year, as well as *Fremontodendron californicum*, *Carpenteria californica*, the hardy form of the silvery-leaved *Artemisia arborescens* 'Faith Raven' and *Cistus* × *aguilari*. The florist's broom (*Cytisus maderensis*) survives mild winters here. Lower-growing plants include yellow *Linum flavum compactum*, *Othonnopsis cheirifolia*, a shrubby grey-leaved oenothera (*Oenothera cheiranthifolia*), with leaves like a wallflower, the silvery-leaved *Convolvulus cneorum*, and *C. sabatius* (syn. *C. mauritanicus*), with its trailing pale blue flowers. Mr Hancock also has a new form of this plant with much darker Oxford-blue saucers. Another Californian plant, *Zauschneria californica*, with scarlet tubular flowers and grey leaves, thrives here, but some less hardy salvias cannot survive the frosts. The dark red shrubby *Salvia blepharophylla* and the velvety-purple *S. bacheriana* (now the correct name for *S. buchananii*) both need to have cuttings taken in summer.

Trees and shrubs which grow large should not be planted too close to a house or garden wall. Poplars, which are deep-rooted but sucker easily, have a bad reputation for damaging foundations. The Trust has often inherited a property where fine old magnolias or other wall shrubs threaten wall stability, even where the foundations are substantial, and has had to sacrifice mature plants. Modern buildings and smaller houses are at even greater risk. In general this proves most destructive if the soil is a heavy shrinkable clay, from which roots take moisture and cause movement of the substructure.

Unless the plants being placed at the base of the wall prefer poor soil, it may be worth enriching the topsoil, or even replacing it to provide suitable conditions for plants going into a permanent site. Generally it is worth positioning plants at least 45 cm (18 in) away from the wall, rather than immediately against it, and then tying them back to supports fixed to the wall. However, it is possible to take advantage of even a narrow bed separating a wall from the gravel or hardcore surface of a path, since roots will spread beneath this and even benefit from the protection it gives from hot sun.

Climbing plants, except for those with adhesive root pads and those like ivy with aerial roots at the end of each shoot, need some sort of frame or support on a wall. Most having twining tendrils or twining stems which hook on to or twine around wires, trellis, or another plant which becomes its host. Many clematis will grow successfully through the branches and foliage of another climber or shrub. The silver-leaved *Senecio leuchostachys* will in a season clamber up through a 2.4 m (8 ft) trellis or into an established climber, but the delicate foliage dies back in winter. The rarer *S. scandens* which flowers in late summer can climb through a spring-flowering ceanothus without harming it. Annuals such as *Cobaea scandens* also climb high in a season if given some initial support. Climbing roses have specially recurved hooks which anchor them to supports or frames.

For most climbers some sort of galvanized wire support (a gauge of 1.6 mm is recommended), is permanently fixed on the wall and fastened to galvanized vine-eyes driven into the mortar. The wire comes in reels and can be stretched horizontally and vertically over the wall surface. The horizontal wires will usually be about 30 cm (12 in) apart and the vertical wires more widely spaced. The metal hooks or vine-eyes are inserted into a new wall while it is being built, but the Trust often has to repair old walls and drilled holes are needed to fasten these supports firmly and securely into the masonry.

At BODNANT under the south-facing high wall, where greenhouses stood until recently, tender climbing and wall shrubs are used to make a backdrop to a wide border. Although near the coast of North Wales, the climate is not as favourable as in many west coast or Cornish gardens, but nevertheless Mr Martin Puddle, the Head Gardener, knows the best spots which will allow the more tender plants to flourish. The wall bed is narrow, a path running along at the back of the border for easy access to shrubs and climbers. *Clematis armandii*, *C. tangutica* and the scarlet trumpet honeysuckle (*Lonicera* × *brownii* 'Fuchsioides') twine on the wall. Below them, bushes of shrubby azara, *Piptanthus laburnifolius*, *Cytisus battandieri* and *Abutilon* × *suntense* flower in early summer, while the border is full of drifts of scarlet poppy (*Papaver orientale*). Earlier, after a mild winter, the silver wattle (*Acacia dealbata*), the mimosa of florists, is covered with pale yellow fragrant flowers. Callistemons also take advantage of the warm wall where their wood ripens in full sun, to ensure flowering the following season.

At Bodnant the maximum advantage is taken of any factors which contribute to creating microclimatic sites. The steep fall of the ground, overhanging plants and pergolas, and the projecting masonry buttresses which support high walls all contribute. On a lower terrace where white wisteria hangs over the balustrade, *Photinia glomerata*, with mature leaves to 12.5 cm (5 in) long and bright red translucent young foliage, avoids frosts in its position tight against the wall. Schizandras, *Camellia reticulata*, crinodendrons, *Drimys winteri*, lespedeza and *Carpenteria californica* also thrive with some overhead protection from climbers on the pergola. In many smaller gardens some of these characteristics or features exist to be exploited to improve the microclimatic conditions.

Projecting wings give the great south-facing forecourt at LANHYDROCK three high walls, against which good evergreen shrubs are suitably bulky. Camellias are carefully trained back on to wires stretched against the wall. Pruning has to be done carefully to ensure flowering shoots, but when, after flowering is over in late spring, the plants spread jungle-like over the windows, ruthless cutting is in order. In these narrow 90 cm (3 ft) beds under the high walls the soil gets very dry. In periods of drought some of these evergreen shrubs which carry a heavy load of leaves can be reduced in size to prevent excessive transpiration. In the east-facing shady border skimmias are massed, contributing their bright berries by the middle of summer. *Pileostegia viburnoides*, an evergreen climber with self-clinging pads, will reach 6 m (20 ft) in a favourable climate, as here. The flowers are terminal creamy panicles and are useful in late summer when few other climbers give of their best. *Daphne odora* 'Aureomarginata' has scented flowers in spring while glossy-leaved sarcococca species start to flower in the middle of winter. Known as Christmas box, their flowers fill the air with fragrance. In the more sunny narrow bed against the stone walls of the house there is a large *Magnolia grandiflora*, also pruned back rather than permitted to make a 'bushy' shape. Besides encouraging flowering, pruning exposes more wood to the sun, and it hardens off to give frost protection. Potentillas in shade and hebes in sun give summer colour.

At TRERICE, not far away from the Atlantic north coast of Cornwall, a small sixteenth-century manor house retains its early walled and terraced enclosures. The alkaline soil conditions are comparatively rare in Cornwall, and lower rainfall – only 90 cm (36 in) instead of the average of at least 112 cm (45 in) in the gardens on the south Cornish coasts, makes this one of the few Cornish gardens where the style is not that of informal woodland. Rhododendrons, camellias and other acid-loving exotics do not thrive, but the mild climate and raised terraces encourage more Mediterranean-type planting.

In the sheltered and sunny wall borders, silvery-leaved *Convolvulus cneorum* and cistus are massed above creeping spurge (*Euphorbia myrsinites*), with glaucous leaves and sulphur-yellow flowers. Prostrate rosemaries, usually more tender than the type and vulnerable in more inland gardens, trail down terrace walls. Fuchsias are interplanted with grey-leaved hebes, both *Hebe albicans* and *H. colensoi* 'Glauca' in a narrow bed alongside a broad raised walk or bowling green. Pyramid-shaped *Drimys lanceolata* bushes are repeated in a regular pattern beside a wall. Abutilons, figs, *Abelia floribunda*, *Fremontodendron californicum* and the mauve-flowered potato, *Solanum crispum* 'Glasnevin', cover stone walls in sun with flower and foliage, each separate walled or terraced enclosure planned as a definite colour scheme. A modern fern-leaved rose 'Helen Knight' has been trained on one side of the projecting porch. Mr John Petry, the single-handed gardener, uses good ground-cover plants to suppress weeds. Forms of comfrey such as *Symphytum grandiflorum* and the less vigorous lamiums such as *Lamium* 'Beacon Silver' fill in gaps between clumps of day-lilies and the prostrate-growing evergreen shrub *Viburnum davidii*. In a newly constructed east-facing walled courtyard planting is very simple; a 'Mermaid' rose, *Trachelospermum jasminoides*, ceanothus, honeysuckle and chaenomeles are planted against the low walls. Across the yard, clambering against a farm building in full sun, the rare evergreen climber from South America, *Araujia sericofera*, thrives. Known as the cruel plant, its flowers trap the long probosces of night-flying moths in its native land. The creamy flowers held in short racemes are followed by grooved yellowish-green pods, sometimes 12.5 cm (5 in) long.

At NYMANS climbing plants grow against the ruins of the old house, and shrubs are planted at the base of the walls. *Clematis armandii* flowers early, followed by neighbouring yellow-flowered *Piptanthus laburnifolius* and *Abutilon vitifolium* 'Veronica Tennant', with papery white mallow flowers. *Genista cinerea* is a mass of golden yellow in June, beside bushes of crimson rose 'Fellenberg'. By July a form of *Lonicera etrusca*, 'Michael Rosse', is outstanding, its creamy-yellow flowers faintly tinged with pink. Other shrubs which benefit from the shelter of the high walls are lower-growing corokias and the spreading *Ceratostigma willmottianum*, which is covered with bright blue flowers in late summer.

In a corner made by low walls near by, *Clematis* 'Etoile Rose', with nodding silvery-pink flowers, and *Lonicera* × *brownii* 'Fuchsioides' make a group with a bush of the thornless rose 'Zéphirine Drouhin'.

At BENINGBROUGH HALL Siberian crabapples are planted outside the north walls of the old kitchen garden. Nearer the house, beds under the south-facing walls of soft pink brick provide a favoured situation for sun-loving perennials. Rainfall on the east of the Pennines is low and the soil is alkaline. *Limonium latifolium*, libertia, dorycnium, *Linum perenne*, sea kale, southernwood, *Achillea* 'Moonshine', an old rose 'Mrs Herbert Stevens', *Geranium renardii*, the shrubby silver-leaved *Artemisia* 'Powis Castle', *Hemerocallis* 'Marion Vaughn', and *Anthemis tinctoria* 'E. C. Buxton', all with pale flowers, enjoy the warm site, and the small shrub *Abelia chinensis*, with rose-tinted flowers in late summer, has a sheltered corner.

At BLICKLING HALL, at the bottom of the dry moat and well sheltered from cold winds, plants are grown against the east wall of the early-seventeenth-century house. The soil in the garden is lime-free, but under the brick walls it is likely to be more alkaline. The tender Cooper's Burma rose, a form of the Cherokee rose (*Rosa laevigata*) with white single flowers thrives here, and its success perhaps reflects the dry climate with plenty of hot sun in summer, which ripens the wood. Near by *Trachelospermum jasminoides* 'Variegatum', with strongly scented summer flowers, and the large-leaved *Buddleja farreri* are tender in many gardens, but here they seem safe out of the wind. Along the wall other climbers include *Vitis* 'Brant', which fruits freely, the yellow-flowered honeysuckle, *Lonicera* × *tellmanniana*, beautiful but unfortunately with no scent, *Clematis* 'Ville de Lyon' and some climbing roses: 'La Rêve', first introduced in 1843 as 'Laffy's Pink', 'Paul's Scarlet Climber', a 1916 rose with unfading cupped double blooms of scarlet-crimson, and 'Paul's Perpetual White'. Other shrubs include *Fuchsia magellanica* 'Versicolor', *Ceanothus* 'Gloire de Versailles' and *Caryopteris* × *clandonensis*, all of which are hard-pruned in early spring. *Hydrangea aspera villosa*, the evergreen *Abelia* × *grandiflora* and its golden-leaved form, and *Ceratostigma willmottianum* flower at the end of the summer. The tender sub-shrub *Salvia microphylla* (syn. *grahamii*) although sometimes cut to the ground in winter, carries its rich red flowers for a long period from June until the first frost.

At LYTES CARY in Somerset the narrow border at the base of the Elizabethan house is filled to overflowing with plants which could have been grown in Sir Henry Lyte's time: the pale pink form of *Lathyrus latifolius*, forms of *Clematis viticella*, southernwood (*Artemisia abrotanum*), Jerusalem sage (*Phlomis fruticosa*), catmint and myrtle (*Myrtus communis*) – although the Mediterranean evergreen is often cut sharply back in winter. Above this border a yellow Banksian rose of later introduction from China flowers in spring and needs pruning immediately afterwards. A summer-flowering passion flower (*Passiflora edulis*), which dies back to the ground

each winter, grows well against the warm grey stone.

At TINTINHULL the completely shaded north wall of the house supports vigorous plants of the early-flowering double pink rose 'Madame Grégoire Staechelin'. Although flowering only once, in June, this rose is outstanding and throws out long healthy shoots each year. Its pruning is discussed in the section on Rose Gardens. In the bed at the base of the wall a large plant of the free-flowering *Mahonia pinnata* and yellow and white single and double forms of *Rosa pimpinellifolia* are established in strong suckering groups, while other mahonias make evergreen clumps to frame a doorway which leads to the sunny west-facing court in front of the eighteenth-century facade of the house. By midsummer, and continuing until October, the flame nasturtium (*Tropaeolum speciosum*) bears its startling scarlet flowers among fresh green leaves, and twines over the prickly rose stems and up the wall. By the yard doorway, in deepest shade, the fern *Adiantum pedatum* carries its fronds of delicate beauty on black wire-like stems.

At CHARLECOTE PARK a north wall of the house is simply planted. The semi-herbaceous late-summer-flowering clematis, *Clematis* × *jouiniana*, with china-blue flowers, is annually trained up the walls to make a fan shape. At its feet glossy-leaved bergenias

Above: In the dry moat at Blickling Hall wall plants are protected from fierce winds.

shine through all the seasons, especially if their unsightly dying leaves are removed, and flower in early spring. This pattern is repeated along the wall three times. Maintenance in this bed consists of cutting down the dead clematis foliage each spring, training new growth on to fan-shaped wires, and of keeping the bergenias tidy all year round.

A stone wall faced with brick gives extra reflected heat. Facing due south at the top of a steep bank, the favourable microclimate permits unexpectedly tender climbers and wall-shrubs to be grown successfully at Sizergh Castle.

At SIZERGH CASTLE a high stone wall has been faced with brick, which retains more heat. The grey-leaved shrub *Senecio* 'Sunshine' has been tied back and hangs like a curtain on the warm wall. Also in the wall border are some normally tender shrubs: *Abutilon* × *suntense*, *Escallonia* 'Iveyi', ceanothus, *Genista aetnensis*, the grey form of *Buddleja alternifolia*, *Itea ilicifolia* and the difficult *Pileostegia viburnoides* all do well in this northern garden, the flower bed on a raised terrace giving the plants excellent drainage. Similarly, at WALLINGTON a double walled terrace runs along a wall of the old kitchen garden, giving extra drainage for tender wall plants in the bed above.

At SISSINGHURST CASTLE walls, hedges and fences divide the garden into compartments. Correct pruning at the right time of the year for wall shrubs and climbers is vital. Standards at Sissinghurst are impeccable. **Miss Sybille Kreutzberger**, one of the Head Gardeners there, sums up the essentials:

The pruning of shrubs and climbers trained on walls or fences is often a cause of concern and bewilderment to many people faced with a plant that has got too big, too old, or has fallen flat on its face. 'What can I do about it?' we are frequently asked. The question is – to prune or not to prune? Here, then, is a brief summary of what we do at Sissinghurst.

The first thing is to recognize whether a shrub or climber flowers on old or new wood; that is, wood made by the previous season's growth or wood made in the current season. This is almost more important than knowing and identifying the plant; once you know on which wood it flowers you are half-way to deciding how to act. For ease of recognition I shall divide them into the following categories:

a Those shrubs and climbers flowering before mid-June can only flower on growth made the previous season. If, therefore, these are cut in winter or spring the flowering will be reduced. The right time to thin or cut back these shrubs is immediately after flowering. This allows plants the maximum time possible for making new wood in preparation for flowering the following season.

Examples of shrubs and climbers in this category would be *Osmanthus delavayi*, *Buddleja alternifolia*, early-flowering clematis and true rambler roses. Some of these shrubs and climbers can be more easily managed by creating a spur system rather than allowing a free-for-all. If they are pruned immediately after spring-flowering, growth is very vigorous. Chaenomeles, schizandra and wisteria are plants which benefit from the new shoots being shortened to 15 cm (6 in) in July and then again in December–January, cutting back to two or three buds.

b Those shrubs and climbers flowering between midsummer and autumn, the majority of which will be flowering on the current year's wood. Any pruning is best done in winter or early spring to encourage new vigorous growth. Cut back flowered wood to the new shoots and tie in replacement shoots, shortening them by a third. Prune the laterals to two to three buds in early spring. In July vigorous new non-flowering growth can be shortened.

Examples would be deciduous ceanothus, most other buddleja species, *Campsis radicans*, *Solanum jasminoides* and *Vitis vinifera*. The latter should be pruned in mid-winter before the sap rises.

c Those climbers which are more or less herbaceous, i.e. dying down to a perennial rootstock each winter or being treated in the same way (this will include tender woody plants which will shoot from the base each spring). Examples of shrubs and climbers which are cut down to a few buds from their base each spring would be many clematis, tropaeolum species, *Humulus lupulus*, *Aconitum volubile*, eccremocarpus and tender perennials such as cobaea and maurandya.

d Those wall plants and climbers which require only intermittent pruning to keep them within bounds and to promote the continued production of new wood. This makes it possible to cut out an old leg from time to time, thereby invigorating and prolonging the life of the plant. This is particularly necessary for shrubs grown for their foliage effect. Examples in this category are *Carpenteria californica*, *Fremontodendron californicum*, coronilla, evergreen ceanothus. Ceanothus should ideally have their branches layed in to form a fan-shape. Weak and straggly branches can be removed from time to time, cutting back to a vigorous young shoot lower down, which is then used to 'lay' in. These shoots should be tied in very loosely as they can easily strangle. The climbing hydrangea (*Hydrangea petiolaris*) generally needs little pruning but, if flowering branches get too far from the wall, it is possible to cut a proportion of these back to encourage the production of new wood close to the wall surface. This would also apply to schizophragma species.

The care and maintenance of 'climbers' embraces more than just pruning. Feeding, mulching, adequate tying-in and possible watering and spraying (with fungicides and insecticides) all contribute to their successful performance. Here are a few guidelines:

1 Choose a good well-branched plant when you buy. If necessary, pinch out the tips of the stronger shoots to encourage several new shoots of equal strength, rather than a leader with side shoots.

A well-trained clematis at Sissinghurst demonstrates the importance of tying and training new shoots each season.

2 Prepare the planting hole generously, and not too close to the wall or fence: this is a dry spot. Water the pot or shrub before planting and again afterwards.

3 Provide adequate support in the way of wires, mesh or stout nails so that the plant can be trained in from the start.

4 In the case of tender shrubs, particularly evergreens, give protection during the first winter or two with a mulch over the roots and sacking or polypropylene netting. These materials let in air, but shield the foliage from drying winds and frost.

Clematis

Few climbers flower more profusely or give greater pleasure than well grown clematis.

Planting Prepare a good-sized hole and incorporate as much rotted manure, compost or leaf-mould as possible. Spread out the roots, and plant about 5 cm (2 in) deeper than the original soil level of the pot. Firm, water and mulch if you can. Most clematis are not fussy about aspect, and they like their roots cool and shady; the mulch will ensure this.

Pruning This is really much less complicated than it sounds, and you do not have to know the name of the clematis to get it right. If in any doubt of what to do leave it for a season and notice when it flowers, and *where* on the plant the flowers come.

1 As a rough guide, those flowering in April, May and early June need no regular pruning. If they get too large, contain too much dead wood or are straggly and out-growing their site, cut them back into the old wood. This can be done, cutting right back to the ground, if necessary, immediately after flowering is over. *Clematis montana*, *C. chrysocoma sericea* (syn. *C. spooneri*), *C. macropetala*, *C. alpina* and *C. armandii* all fall into this category and should be treated accordingly.

2 Large-flowered hybrids flowering on the old wood in May and June. These include the *patens* group, which flower early on short shoots from the previous year's wood. These require no regular pruning but spent flower-heads can be cut back to an active bud and dead wood removed. Every few years cut them right down after flowering, for complete rejuvenation.

3 Large-flowered hybrids which flower in June to October on old and young wood are treated in the same way. Some young shoots are thinned out in spring to encourage basal growth. These include the *lanuginosa* group.

4 Clematis which flower in July to October on the current season's wood. These include *CC.* × *jackmanii* and × *viticella* hybrids, *CC. texensis, tangutica, orientalis, flammula* and *rehderiana*. Cut back to 45 cm (18 in) or less from the base each spring. Cut out a proportion of shoots entirely, in order to promote a multi-stemmed plant.

Young clematis of all types should be pruned hard for the first year or two to encourage branching. Then, if wilt does strike, the plant will probably survive. If left unpruned these clematis will flower quite well, but the flowering starts high up and the base will become increasingly bare.

Training Clematis hate to swing about. Tie them in, spacing out the shoots before they get entangled, and do this several times during the growing season so that they are well displayed. A saddle of sheep- or pig-netting astride the wall will help to anchor the clematis when it reaches the top. Stem ties are good for fixing them and much quicker to use and safer than string. Always tie loosely.

At Sissinghurst we use a variety of training systems:

1 Direct on walls covered with wire-mesh, Netlon or pig-netting.
2 On tripods made of three stout poles, set firmly astride the plant, and tied together at the top some 1.8–2.1 m (6–7 ft) from the ground. Shoots are spaced out as they grow, so that the tripod is well furnished by flowering time.
3 On or through small trees or shrubs, choosing as hosts these which flower on the current season's wood.
4 The less vigorous clematis can be grown in large pots and will train downwards.

Feeding, mulching and watering Plants on walls get very little moisture. Clematis hate to be dry, and poor soil and dry roots are often the cause of failure. Mulching with compost, manure or bark will keep the soil moist, as well as shading the roots and cutting down the need for watering in dry periods. We feed each year with a general fertilizer.

Pests and diseases There are three main problems encountered when growing clematis: earwigs, mildew and wilt. Earwigs are controlled by application of a systemic insecticide; the earwigs usually make holes in the flowers in late summer. Fungicides are used against mildew. Wilt is the most serious and difficult to control. It is caused by a fungus and may suddenly attack a single shoot or the entire plant. It seems to occur most often when tying-in has not been done regularly, and shoots have been blown about and bent, perhaps restricting the flow of sap. We don't suffer much from wilt here. Enough moisture, good growing conditions and the minimum of handling, except for careful tying in, seem to help the plants resist its occurrence. Our regular sprays with bupirimate plus triforine or benomyl, used against mildew, may well also help combat wilt. If it does occur, cut out the affected part and hope for the best. Mice can sometimes be a problem, eating the young shoots as they emerge. ✤

Orchards and Kitchen Gardens

The introduction to this chapter touched on the fate of some of the old walled kitchen gardens: how the passage of time and contemporary needs have changed their use. Much as the Trust would like to keep kitchen gardens and orchards in their traditional productive role, in very few cases is it economically possible to do so. Instead these areas now provide other services rather than provisioning the inhabitants of the house. Where 'food-growing' garden areas still exist, walled or not, the Trust is often concerned with replacing old plants, especially old fruit varieties now seldom available in commercial nurseries. By this policy the Trust ensures that historic names are not lost for ever.

Sadly, however, such specific information is sometimes lacking. At GLENDURGAN in Cornwall new fruit trees are being planted in the upper walled garden, which in recent years was mostly planted with ornamentals. Here no record remains of the names of the apple and pear trees which were planted near the labyrinth in 1833 by the present Mr Philip Fox's great-grandfather, Alfred Fox. In this case the Trust advises using traditional Cornish varieties which have survived in other gardens.

Occasionally, the plants have distinct local associations. For instance, at WIGHTWICK MANOR on the outskirts of Wolverhampton there are old specimens of a pear called 'Tetten Hall' named for a house near by. These were planted before the garden was designed by Alfred Parsons at the turn of the century. Beyond, a nuttery dates the garden to the Edwardian era. Recently the Trust have added a weeping mulberry (*Morus alba* 'Pendula') to cascade on to the front lawn beside a Judas tree (*Cercis siliquastrum*) and a neighbouring medlar (*Mespilus germanica*).

Medlar and mulberry are also among the period plants chosen for the theme of the recreated gardens at MOSELEY OLD HALL, where planting is restricted to those plants already known and grown towards the end of the seventeenth century. A wooden framed walk leads to a corner arbour of hornbeam and to a nut walk; turning back towards the brick house the stone-flagged pathway is lined with pairs of quince (*Cydonia oblonga*), mulberry (*Morus nigra*) and medlar, which, like the orchard beyond, provide both spring blossom and later fruit.

In the enclosure in which the new herb garden and the flowers for cutting are grown at HARDWICK HALL, a very old walnut overhangs an original nuttery. Recently this has been expanded; young walnut trees have been planted and new nuts include filberts and 'Pearson's Prolific' (syn. 'Nottingham Cob'). Beyond the herbs a new mulberry (*Morus nigra*) walk runs down to the wilder orchards at the bottom of the garden.

To the east of the herb garden and the yew/hornbeam roundel an orchard containing many wellknown and tried varieties of old fruit trees was recently replanted with specimen pears which include 'Packham's Triumph', 'Marie Louise' and 'Pitmaston Duchess', all grown as standard trees. The damsons 'Merryweather' and 'Farleigh Damson' are also making good progress as standards, while original specimens of 'Oullin's Golden Gage' are also found. New trees of the two latter gages have been added. The apple 'Rev. W. Wilks', a seedling introduced to commerce by Veitch's Chelsea nursery and dating back to the turn of the century, grows in the rough grass beyond the east-facing shrub rose border. This apple for dessert or culinary use has large slightly conical fruit, white or very pale primrose with a few streaks of clear red. Beehives safely situated at the far end of the orchard make the scene pleasantly domestic.

Other old fruit trees in the orchards at Hardwick include 'Norfolk Beefing' and a newly grafted young plant, three 'Duke of Devonshire' apples (Hardwick was one of the homes of the Dukes of Devonshire) and a large ancient *Pyrus communis* with dark sooty bark. Today this original species, the common or garden pear, which is so ornamental, is almost unobtainable, since cultivars for specific purposes are much more frequently in demand. Probably itself a hybrid, it has been long cultivated and in April is smothered in blossom; later it bears small sweet-tasting fruit. The leaves often colour richly in autumn.

In one orchard many bulbs and wild flowers grow, and the grass is left long as a meadow. In this rough grass, in areas defined by mown paths which meet at the centre, ornamental crabs such as *Malus hupehensis* and 'Jargonelle' pears are planted.

Above: Currant bushes flank a path between guelder roses (*Viburnum opulus*) at Snowshill Manor.

Opposite: At Beningbrough Hall old espalier pears lining the central path through the walled kitchen garden have been trained to make curving arches.

Flowers for Cutting

It has often been customary to grow flowers to cut for the house in the vicinity of the kitchen garden. This is where many old perennials survived during the years when they were banned from parkland and parterres, before they were once again invited to reappear before society in the newly fashionable herbaceous border.

Flowers for arrangements in the public rooms in National Trust houses are chosen according to themes agreed with the Historic Buildings Representative and the Gardens Adviser. At Hardwick, Mr Allen grows flowers for cutting in two long borders flanking the herb garden. The choice is made by him and Mrs White, who arranges them in vases for the house. Colours are planned carefully so that the best use is made of the available growing space, and plants grown include:

'Iceberg' roses, sweet peas, dahlias, 'Madame Butterfly' antirrhinums, *Limonium sinuatum* (syn. *Statice sinuata*), *Eremurus stenophyllus* (syn. *E. bungei*), teasels, pyrethrums, *Zinnia* 'Persian Carpet' in mixed colours and *Z.* 'Chippendale Daisy', *Iris orientalis* (syn. *I. ochroleuca*), *Lychnis chalcedonica*, *Alstroemeria aurantiaca*, penstemons from seed, campanulas, lupins, taller ageratums, the National Collection of *Scabiosa caucasica*, both blue and white (some from Mrs Sylvia Parret who holds the National Collection of the whole genus *Scabiosa* at York), sweet Williams, delphiniums, gypsophila, *Cleome spinosa*, *Helenium hoopesii* (broad grey-green leaves, yellow daisies), *Chrysanthemum maximum* 'Everest', *Geum chiloense* 'Lady Stratheden', *Veronica virginica alba*, *Iris sibirica*, *Artemisia lactiflora* and lily of the valley 'Hardwick Hall' with cream edging to leaf. Beyond the hedge of sweet briar roses where vegetables used to be, more sweet Williams, chrysanthemums, gladiolus, sweet rocket, larkspur, and *Lavatera* 'Silver Cup'.

At Hardwick Hall old orchards have been replanted with original varieties of fruit.

At the end of the nineteenth century much of the flat area below the great hanging terraces to the east of POWIS CASTLE was still occupied by glasshouses which supplied hothouse plants and grapes. By the first years of this century all this was swept away; a new formal garden was made with dividing yew and holly hedges, leaving a double avenue of pyramid apples and pears and a cross-walk of grapevines grown over ornamental hoops, which could be glimpsed from points along the terraced walks. Since the Trust acquired the property, this area, while maintaining its symmetry, has been considerably developed.

The fruit trees, now more than 80 years old, are still carefully pruned to shape, those neglected over the war years retrimmed, and new trees planted to complete the pattern. Few, in fact, of these old types fruit freely, but their mature and often gnarled branches give the appearance of age, and interestingly more modern varieties such as 'Bramley's Seedling' do not respond willingly to this type of pruning. Among the original trees are 'Striped

Opposite: Vines, trained over arches, are underplanted with golden marjoram at Powis.

Below: Circles round fruit trees at Powis Castle are planted with grey grasses.

Beefing', raised at Lakenham in Norfolk in 1794, and 'Tower of Glamis', which originated in Scotland before 1800.

Around the base of each tree large circles 3 m (10 ft) across have been cut in the grass and planted with a strong ornamental ground cover, arranged in symmetrical pairs: the non-flowering grey-leaved *Stachys olympica* 'Silver Carpet', mauve-flowered *Lamium maculatum*, golden marjoram (*Origanum vulgare aureum*), and blue-flowered bugle (*Ajuga reptans*).

The soil in this lower garden is rich and moist and original plantings of Jackman's rue (*Ruta graveolens* 'Jackman's Blue') and forms of cotton lavender (*Santolina*) were lost each winter, but the Head Gardener, Mr Jimmie Hancock, continues to experiment with other greys and silvers in another formal walk where the June–July-flowering hybrid honeysuckle *Lonicera* × *americana* twines up high central poles. Here he still grows *Santolina chamaecyparissus*, which usually deteriorates and needs replacing every two or three years. In other squares surrounding the honeysuckle he plants a little feathery silver-leaved anthemis with yellow daisy-flowers (*Anthemis biebersteinii*), both the now-rare *Viola* 'Irish Molly', which has yellowy-brown flowers, and *V.* 'Limelight', with lemony-yellow blooms. In other beds he uses the black-leaved and variegated forms of ophiopogon (*Ophiopogon planiscapus* 'Nigrescens' and *O.p.* 'Variegatus'), and *Lamium* 'Silberteppich' (syn. 'Silver Carpet'). Each plant is massed separately in 3 m (10 ft) squares, and over a period will form a weed-suppressing carpet.

The hooped vines planted 2.5 m (8 ft) apart, with the highest part of the hoop at about 2.25 m (7 ft), have been extended by bamboos stretched horizontally to make a continuous pergola, cool and shady in summer, and an important feature breaking up the large expanse of flat lawn between the hedges and fruit avenues. The north-east end of the pergola leads to a painted seat set between wings of box, cut to a comfortable 1.5 m (5 ft) in height, and at the opposite south-west point the pergola carries the eye up steep yew-lined steps to the wilderness beyond. Most of the vines are the fruiting *Vitis vinifera* but at either end plants of the large-leaved *V. coignetiae* tend to overwhelm the ordinary grapes (which in fact seldom set fruit) and provide spectacular early-autumn red and orange tints. Round the base of each vine a 50 cm (18 in) square planting of the vivid young leaves of golden marjoram (*Origanum vulgare aureum*) contributes patches of colour in summer.

At FELBRIGG HALL the old kitchen garden has been completely replanted since the Trust acquired it in 1971. Along one south-facing wall, borders are interrupted by a handsome dovecote. In the western section herbs are grown in front of a large fig, which fruits regularly, while to the east the planting is more general to include shrub roses and grapevines. The latter, symmetrically planted in groups along the centre of the border, are trained decoratively on architectural frames. **Mr Ted Bullock**, the Head Gardener at Felbrigg, writes about the 'wigwams' which have been constructed as frames for the vines:

❧ These timber supports, called 'quadripods' were tanalized: they have been in the ground ten years, and they still look good and do not appear to be deteriorating. The posts were originally purchased from a local timber merchant as 2.7 m (9 ft) lengths, 38 × 38 mm (1½ in) sawn pressure-tanalized deal.

The vines grown on the quadripods are 'Muller-Thurgau', 'Brant', 'Seyve Villard', 'Morio Muskat', and 'Miller's Burgundy' (syn. 'Wrotham Pinot'). They are trained on the four stakes each of which is 1.95 m (6 ft 6 in) high. They meet so that the diameter of the space at their bases is about 1.5 m (5 ft) across. The vines are wound round the stakes as they grow. Pruning is done in January. This involves cutting back laterals to two buds on the knuckles or 'stubs'. If the sub-lateral shoots are not pinched out during the summer, the vines become a tangled mass of growth. The vines are mulched with well-rotted compost in the autumn and the compound fertilizer, Vitax Q4, is applied in the spring. Mildew is often a problem, especially in humid conditions, and Boots' yellow sulphur and Bordeaux Powder are used to control the disease.

The varieties at Felbrigg are all well known by growers and good nurseries, such as Scotts of Merriot and Reads of Loddon, Norfolk, should be able to supply them. The name of the vineyard I arranged to visit was R. S. Don at North Elmham in Norfolk. ❧

The recent history of the apple trees in the walled garden at Felbrigg – both the upkeep of the existing plants and the mixed success of some of the newer plantings – offers food for thought. Ted Bullock comments on what has been done recently and reflects on some of the difficulties that have been experienced here:

❧ Our original planting in February 1975 of 'Wellspur Delicious' grafted on semi-dwarfing stock MM106, to be trained as pyramids, was not successful. Over the years the trees did not produce sufficient growth to train into the shape required, although there was always an abundance of fruit spurs produced, followed by a heavy crop of apples. I would not advise, therefore, that this variety should be avoided in other gardens – I believe it would be a mistake to do so. The incorrect stock for our soil type may have been chosen, or perhaps there was a 'replant' problem. These young trees were planted on the site of an old apple orchard. Specific Apple Replant Disease, known as SARD, may therefore have been the major cause of problems. A great deal of research has taken place on SARD in the last few years. Interestingly the same 'Wellspur Delicious' bushes also proved a failure at GUNBY HALL in Lincolnshire, where they had been also placed in an old orchard.

A new planting was made in winter 1983. First the soil was thoroughly sterilized. These new trees, 'Norfolk Royal Russet' grafted on MM106, have responded well so far. The growth is most encouraging and this is now being trained so that the shapes of dwarf pyramids will be achieved.

Using methods rather similar to that of growing spindle-bush apple trees, practised by commercial growers, we have been training our trees, using twine and pegs. This is finicky but worth the effort. In August three or four of the new shoots on each two-year old plant are selected for tying down; the shoots chosen are well spaced about the main stem of the tree and are bent down to the horizontal, using twine or string. A loop – not a tie or a knot – is made about halfway along the shoot and tied to a tent peg in the soil, driven in at an angle to resist the upward pull of the shoots. This tying down does enable one to obtain the desired position of the shoots and encourages the growth of fruit buds.

A number of old neglected orchard trees in the same area were rejuvenated over a period of two or three years by the removal of large branches, which were riddled with canker. These trees were finally cut back to about half their original height.

Scab and mildew are a constant problem in old enclosed orchards and the trees are sprayed whenever possible to control these diseases. Since 1980 we have been planting older varieties of apples (and some pears) in the walled garden and these are listed below.

All our fruit trees, especially the wall-trained plums, peaches, apricots, cherries, apples and pears are pruned annually, with special attention to summer pruning – the vital finger-and-thumb pruning, not the often excessive use of secateurs and loppers. Sadly larger orchard trees have to fend for themselves as best they can. The lack of time and staff means that we cannot give the regular spraying programme which is desirable. Our young trees are given more attention, being sprayed against disease and given Vitax Q4 fertilizer, which is most beneficial for their growth. ✤

At Felbrigg Hall a part of the kitchen walled garden has been planted with specimens of thorn tree (*Crataegus*). Ted Bullock describes his experience:

✤ We obtained twenty species of thorn from Hilliers' Nurseries in January 1974 for planting in the walled garden. These were obtained as standard trees, some with rather large heads and tall spindly stems, which later caused a problem. Strong winds from the east are prevalent at Felbrigg and it was found that each tree needed to be supported with guy wires, four per each specimen, attached to posts driven into the ground at an angle. Although effective, the wires made mowing and upkeep impossible.

Replacements have since been obtained as half-standards with 1.5 m (5 ft) stems as a maximum height. A single stout stake is usually adequate support for a tree of this size.

Little pruning is necessary on these thorns, apart from removing crossing or rubbing branches, and any lower branches which obstruct machinery used for cutting the grass surrounding them. Suckers which arise from the rootstock are removed as early as possible while the growth is still soft.

When preparing planting positions a large circle or square of turf, at least 60 cm (2 ft) across, was lifted and the planting soil well prepared. The area surrounding the trunk of each tree should be kept clean and weed-free for at least four years; after that the turf may be allowed to close in. We did consider the use of tree spats to keep encroaching grass away, but because these are so unsightly we decided to use a residual chemical instead (simazine). After four years with grass allowed to grow up to the trunk we give an annual dressing of nitro-chalk in the spring. ✤

Apples at Felbrigg

Hubbard's Pearmain, Norfolk Beefing, Old English Pearmain, Striped Beefing and Winter Majetin were grafted at Felbrigg from budwood obtained from Wisley gardens in 1982. The rest were planted in 1980, and comprise: Ashmead's Kernel, Braddicks Nonpareil, Court Pendu Plat, D'Arcy Spice, Emneth Early, Golden Reinette, Nonpareil, Old French Crab, Pitmaston Pine, Wagener and Wyken Pippin.

Thorns at Felbrigg

Ted Bullock notes the particular interest of different species. The collection has been increased over the years. Perhaps the most beautiful of the thorns at Felbrigg is *Crataegus oxyacantha* 'Gireoudii', which is a spectacular sight in early summer, clothed with young pink and white foliage. It grows in the south section of the walled garden.

× *Crataemespilus grandiflora* (a bi-generic hybrid from *Crataegus* × *Mespilus*) of natural origin from France. Thought to be from *Crataegus oxyacantha*, the common hawthorn, and the medlar *Mespilus germanica*, this sterile hybrid has a broad head and large yellowish-brown fruits, and good autumn colour.
+ *Crataegomespilus dardari* 'Jules d'Asnières', a graft hybrid.
Crataegus dsungarica (a spiny tree with purplish-black fruits), *CC. altaica*, *arkansana*, *arnoldiana*, *azarolus* (the Azarole – very choice tree, white flowers and edible orange fruits), *coccinioides*, *crus-galli* (the Cockspur thorn) *durobrivensis*, *holmesiana* (oblong red fruits), *laciniata*, *macracantha* (largest spined of all crataegus), *maximowiczii*, *mexicana*, *monogyna* 'Stricta' (with almost fastigiate growth), *nitida* (quite distinct spreading habit), *orientalis* (fruits large orange-red), *oxyacantha rosea*, *phaenopyrum* (known as the Washington thorn), *pinnatifida*, *prunifolia* (lovely tree – rounded head), *punctata*, *stipulacea*, *succulenta*, *submollis* and *tomentosa*.

The three species, *CC. crus-galli*, *monogyna* and *oxyacantha* are all used as stock on which the other trees have been grafted, although it is not certain which for individual trees. The Royal Horticultural Society's *Dictionary of Gardening* suggests that most species, and particularly the American ones, will be grafted on *Crataegus monogyna*.

AT LYTES CARY in Somerset a large square orchard has grass kept to about 10 cm (4 in) under fruit trees, with tightly mown grass paths on cross-diagonals. In the centre four thickets of rugosa roses, both white and pink in single flower-form to ensure fruiting, surround a sundial. At the four corners of the orchard an arbour or archway of weeping ash has been constructed on four 2 m (6 ft) posts with cross bars to which the young ash shoots are tied. In flower beds round the base of each ash shrubs such as the guelder rose (*Viburnum opulus*) and lilacs have been planted. In the open area medlars (*Mespilus germanica*) and the crab *Malus* 'John Downie' are notable. To the south and marking the garden boundary a row of willows, to match the local osier (*Salix viminalis*) still grown for commercial use in Somerset fields, carries the eye into the landscape and gives wind protection.

Near the house, in the first lawn enclosure, two old apple trees reduce formality, and remind one that the house will have been surrounded by orchards in the seventeenth century. Two recently planted mulberries are beginning to take hold. In the second rectangular compartment, hedged round with yew, single specimens of the strawberry tree (*Arbutus unedo*) have been planted in the four corners of the lawn.

At TINTINHULL HOUSE, also in Somerset, a rectangular kitchen garden is at a lower level than the rest of the garden. Here a cross path leading to a typical Somerset cider orchard is lined with giant catmint (*Nepeta gigantea*). From the Fountain Garden to the south, where silvery-foliaged and white-flowered plants are grown formally, the eye is carried between a pair of crabs (*Malus* 'John Downie'), and two newly planted pears (*Pyrus communis* 'Beech Hill'), along the central gravel path to a gate and orchard beyond. An avenue of standard apples carries the view further. Many of the fruit trees are old, and two large trees of 'Morgan's Sweet' have grown to 12 m (40 ft); in 1980 the Trust replaced and filled in some gaps with specimens of 'Tydeman's Early Worcester' and 'Ellison's Orange'. The grass in the avenue vista is cut six times a year, probably every four weeks during the growing season, and the soil round the young trees is kept clean with the contact herbicide paraquat. The orchard is not intended for commercial fruit; rather it acts as a link between the house and formal 'compartmental' gardens in the foreground, and the Somerset farmland beyond.

Crossing the main path in the kitchen garden, a paved way runs between espalier pear trees, with a foreground planting of pink roses and blue-flowered *Caryopteris × clandonensis*. The pears are traditional at Tintinhull but new plants had to be obtained in 1981. Fortunately three-tiered specimens of 'Doyenné du Comice', 'Pitmaston Duchess', and 'Williams' Bon Chrétien' were available from a Devon nursery.

Vegetables are grown in straight rows in traditional fashion at Tintinhull, but round the outer edge of the rectangular garden shrub roses and other plants add interest: they include ordinary fennel (*Foeniculum vulgare*) for cooking, lovage, the biennial *Angelica archangelica* with ornamental leaves and attractive sulphur-yellow flower umbels, and the red-stemmed Swiss chard. The giant fennel from southern Europe, *Ferula communis* and *F. tingitana*, have still to produce their 2.25 m (7 ft) stems bearing yellow cow-parsley-like flowers, but the feathery mounds of foliage are ornamental in themselves. Statuesque artichokes, forms of *Cynara scolymus* with silvery leaves, mark the corners of the rose beds by the pear espalier walk. Plants such as the biennial woad (*Isatis tinctoria*), a now rare British native, the double-flowered soapwort or Bouncing Bet (*Saponaria officinalis* 'Roseo Plena'), sweet Cicely (*Myrrhis odorata*) and Bowles' grey-leaved mint keep the utilitarian theme in mind. Sweet peas are trained over tripods and dahlias, with pale pink flowers especially chosen for the drawing-room, which is open to visitors, are grown through a rectangular support of pig-netting. The ground is well dug, and plenty of farmyard manure incorporated before the plants are put in at the end of May. Recently some of the groups of dahlias in the main Tintinhull borders have been left in the ground over winter with considerable success. The crowns are covered with a loose packing of bracken, weighted down with old compost and the stakes used for herbaceous supports during the summer, as soon as the foliage has been cut down after the first frosts.

At UPTON HOUSE a south-sloping kitchen garden makes the optimum use of the sun's rays. The soil heats up earlier in the year, producing crops several weeks ahead of a garden which is flat, and, of course, the growing season is also prolonged at the end of the summer. At TRENGWAINTON, too, beds sloping west, raised against walls at an angle of 45 degrees were especially constructed in 1820 for early veget-

Espalier fruit where usually two or three tiers of branches stretch horizontally along tight wires, are grown formally against walls or, as often in the past, mark out free-standing divisions in walled fruit and vegetable gardens. Plants are placed 3–4 m (10–13 ft) apart and correct and regular pruning is essential. The plants are usually first trained by the nursery from which they are obtained; the espalier needing several years of exact selection and tying in of the best placed shoots to make the desired framework, and the elimination and pinching back of the remainder. Fruiting spurs will then develop along the horizontal stems. After the shape has been established and the plants are in their permanent growing site with branches trained along stiff wires, regular pruning for producing fruit is then carried out. While free-growing bushes or trees are generally pruned only in winter, the espalier is summer-pruned to maintain the shape, and to remove extra live foliage which reduces the vigour of the plant. In mid-August, once the base of new shoots begins to ripen, they can each be cut back to 10–13 cm (4–5 in) above the place where the new growth began. In winter, further cutting back is necessary, thinning out fruiting spurs to discourage over-cropping.

Opposite: In the orchard at Lytes Cary rugosa roses surround a stone sundial.

At Tintinhull House a path down the centre of the vegetable garden is lined with catmint. Beyond is a typical Somerset cider orchard.

able cropping. There is only 30–38 cm (12–15 in) of soil lying over drainage rubble, and into it well-rotted manure is dug during the winter months. The gardeners work down the slope. **Mr Peter Horder**, the Head Gardener, writes that:

❧ They use a long-handled Cornish fork and shovel to ease the strain on the back. The soil is turned uphill and any soil replacement is at the bottom as required. These sloping beds in the lower walled garden are still cultivated annually with vegetable crops as originally intended and provide great interest to visitors. The crops include: shallots, onions, spring onions, lettuce, radish, dwarf peas and beans and marrows. Some watering is necessary from time to time and generally we find that in dry seasons plants bolt more quickly on the slope than on a flat site. However, the exposure to the sun's rays does ensure that crops mature significantly earlier. ❧

IV
INFORMAL PLANTING

Where no wall or hedge gives a clear demarcation, and where woodland or open countryside can be seen, the outer fringes of the garden – whether woodland, shrubbery or meadow – should appear to be informally planted, the garden blending gradually into the landscape beyond. In fact this sort of 'natural' gardening needs planning and programming as carefully as the more formally defined themes nearer the house. But because clear-cut patterns and geometrical rules cannot be followed in this apparent imitation of nature, the gardener has to rely more on observation and experience of plant behaviour and requirements, as well as developing a sound sense of scale.

Whether the area in question is the transitional zone between the garden and the surrounding countryside or simply an area within the garden where rules are apparently relaxed and an element of 'wilderness' is allowed to prevail to create some sense of mystery, the principle is that planting should not look artificial or contrived. Exotics, which always look more appropriate when seen against the man-made structure of the house, should seem at home in their new environment placed side by side with British natives. Single plants should not call attention to themselves, but should rather harmonize with their neighbours. In spite of Robinson's strictures, plants are often distributed on a rather *ad hoc* basis, shrubberies added to with surplus bushes, coloured foliage turning trees into 'eye-catchers' where the prevailing effects should be quiet and green. Misplaced rockeries and pools that do not lie in the lowest hollows are similar lapses. At ground level plants need to make curving, interweaving shapes, bulbs to grow in drifts as they would naturalize in their own habitat, and even wild-flower meadows to be entirely successful should be confined to local flora.

This apparently more casual atmosphere is not necessarily more labour-saving than are expressly formal designs.

Woodland

Many woodland gardens began as a collection of plants; there was little deliberate interpretation of a 'style'. As plants arrived from overseas in rapidly increasing numbers, gardeners, without conscious thought about the aesthetics or 'rules' for their arrangement, evolved their own methods of cultivation. The primary concern had to be the well-being of the plant, and the quality and condition of the individual specimen was at first far more important than any contribution it could make to an overall garden design. What at first tended to be a plantsman's collection, arranged as an exotic wilderness entirely for the benefit of the individual plant, later developed into a much more definite and self-conscious desire to create woodland scenes which unfolded for the spectator as a series of static pictures.

As a form of garden craft the planted woodland lies closer to natural laws than any other, any attempt to use geometrical or even symmetrical planting schemes immediately destroying its whole spirit. Each plant chosen for the site should not only suit the conditions and general aspect from a practical point of view but should definitely seem to become part of an idealized 'paradise'. Perhaps like the 'wild' gardening recommended by William Robinson during the last quarter of the nineteenth century, it is the most difficult stylistic form of gardening. There is a constant need to balance almost ecological qualities with a coherent overall design, which firmly establishes that it is a garden and not a wilderness. The planting and layout should resemble nature, but should be firmly under man's control. In more domestic garden styles plants (even trees) are manipulated and contained; the essence of woodland planting is their apparent freedom.

As trees and shrubs came in, especially from North America, in the middle of the eighteenth century, several landowners found it possible to incorporate collections of these exotics inside their parkland. At BENINGBROUGH HALL and FELBRIGG HALL American gardens were established where trees such as *Quercus rubra*, the black walnut (*Juglans nigra*), acers, catalpa and tulip trees (*Liriodendron tulipifera*) and acid-loving shrubs such as kalmia, deciduous rhododendrons, vacciniums and magnolias were planted in groves. Interestingly, Holford's first planting in the arboretum at Westonbirt (1829) was in seventeenth-century style, with great blocks of trees divided by alleys in quite formal and related patterns. As the trees developed, each specimen needed space to realize its full potential, and gradually their shapes and habits took over the design. Paths and rides were diverted and curved to reveal a tree or group where tree and shrub association was particularly successful and natural open planting of low-growing foliage and flowering trees such as maples succeeded thick planting of dark conifers. Today the mature arboretum, owing much to the Victorian passion for collecting, shows woodland gardening as an art form, grassy sunlit glades alternating with shady groves, and many shrubs thriving under the natural canopies made by overhanging branches.

By the end of the nineteenth century woodland gardening became closely linked and almost synonymous with great plantings of rhododendrons introduced in quantity from the Himalayas. Sir Joseph Hooker (1817–1911), at first working in Glasgow but later Director at Kew, in succession to his father, also took part in major plant-hunting expeditions. From Sikkim *Rhododendron arboreum* and many of its hybrids were planted in Trust gardens such as BODNANT, KILLERTON, LANHYDROCK, NYMANS, PLAS NEWYDD, TRENGWAINTON and WAKEHURST PLACE.

KILLERTON, in fact, was already developing in the 1770s, when Sir Thomas Acland with the help of his Agent John Veitch, who later founded the great nursery of that name, laid out the pleasure ground and planted some of the trees which later provided shelter and shade for further exotic introductions. Veitch's nursery, later transferred to Exeter a few miles away and with a branch in London, sent out plant-hunters all over the world, and became a source of plants for the whole country. Conifers and trees from America and the Far East grew from the seed collected, and the south slopes at Killerton provided the ideal situation for the groves of *R. arboreum*. Today many of these have grown into huge bushes, the true species usually tall and growing to reveal erect trunks. At BODNANT the Second Lord Aberconway, whose grandfather had started by planting newly introduced conifers and other trees in the glen, developed the whole garden into a great terraced landscape, partly formal in concept, but retaining the steep-sided gullies ideal for rhododendron cultivation. After 1905 many new hybrids were introduced here, where the acid soil, humid atmosphere and high rainfall, combined with the dappled shade of overhead tree canopies, provided suitable conditions. Bodnant, in fact, does not

Above: At Rowallane rhododendrons grow in the half-shade of tall pines. These exotics need informal treatment where grass is kept at different lengths and paths follow the contours of the plant shapes.

Page 193: Hidcote is well known for its garden compartments; in woodland beyond the more formal areas planting patterns are more relaxed. Curving paths lead past massed shrubs which smother weed growth.

Opposite: In the severe winter of 1981/82 many rhododendrons died at Bodnant. Fortunately being shallow-rooted they can be transplanted even when large and used to fill gaps.

Giant lilies (*Cardiocrinum giganteum*) from West China need deep soil. At Sheffield Park they grow in the rich compost made from fallen leaves.

have very mild winters, but the site and the tree planting in the glen help to create favourable pockets of microclimate for tender plants. The average lowest temperature each winter at Bodnant is −10°C (14°F) and in 1981–82 temperatures fell to −14°C (8°F) combining with a Force 8 gale to produce a considerable chill factor. Thousands of rhododendrons died (Mr Martin Puddle, the Head Gardener says it could be as many as 10,000), including 80 per cent of the large-leaved varieties.

As the woodland garden developed beyond the idea of being just a collection of trees (strictly an arboretum or pinetum), it was realized that favoured coastal strips in the west and south-west, with a high rainfall, had microclimates where the more tender plants would thrive. Shelter belts to provide protection against salt-laden winds were planted. The acid but often poor soil could be improved and extra topsoil imported. For the shelter belts it was found that the Monterey pine (*Pinus radiata*) and Monterey cypress (*Cupressus macrocarpa*) grew quickly and survived the worst gales. Some of these coastal gardens, among which GLENDURGAN, OVERBECKS, TRELISSICK and TRENGWAINTON belong today to the Trust, are notable for their rare 'plantsmen's' collections (see Appendix).

The grand-style rhododendron gardens still exist today. Among National Trust properties perhaps PLAS NEWYDD now has the most favourable conditions. Inevitably, rhododendrons tend to become the specialist's obsession, and their culture, breeding and nomenclature highly skilled and technical. For these reasons this book will not describe the garden landscapes which are entirely dominated by the genus. Instead rhododendrons will be mentioned when, as so often, they are part of a rather broader scheme. Although they require many of the same climatic and soil conditions as do a great number of exotics which can be cultivated in our temperate climate, yet they do not permit the three layers of plant growth which seem to be such an important and satisfying feature of woodland gardening: their dense evergreen canopy does not allow other plants to thrive beneath them.

In 1881 William Robinson published *The Wild Garden*. In this book, written when the Victorian bedding craze was at its height, he advised growing hardy plants, both native and exotic, in conditions where they would thrive. What seems commonsense to us was revolutionary to the Victorians.

The site for each plant would provide as nearly as possible the conditions of a plant's native habitat. In

the outer garden fringes, in woodland and by streams, native and hardy plants from northern and temperate areas of the world might be naturalized together. To quote Robinson in the use of the hardy exotics: 'What it does mean is best explained by the winter aconite flowering under a grove of native trees in February; by the Snowflake growing abundantly in meadows by the Thames side . . . and by the Apennine anemone staining an English wood blue before the blooming of our blue bells.' Lilies, bluebells, foxgloves, irises, windflowers, columbines, rock-roses, violets, cranesbills, countless pea-flowers, mountain avens, brambles, cinquefoils, evening primroses, clematis, honeysuckle, Michaelmas daisy, wood-hyacinths, daffodils, bindweeds, forget-me-nots, omphalodes, primroses, day-lilies, asphodels and St Bruno's lily were some that he recommended. In his natural woodland native wood anemones (*Anemone nemorosa*), lily of the valley (*Convallaria majalis*), Lent lily (*Narcissus pseudonarcissus*), snowdrops (*Galanthus nivalis*), Solomon's seal (forms and hybrids of polygonatum), woodruff (*Galium odoratum*) and sweet violet (*Viola odorata*) would spread happily in drifts between hardy exotic woodlanders, which proved equally adaptable in suitable conditions. Small cyclamen species from Europe would contribute flowers and leaves through most of the months, and members of the *Boraginaceae* such as the blue-flowered *Brunnera macrophylla*, omphalodes, and coarse-leaved *Trachystemon orientale* would flourish beside the native forget-me-not (*Myosotis alpestris*).

At the time Robinson was writing many of the woodland gardens administered by the Trust today were being planted. A whole new garden 'style' was being established, a style which allowed for Robinsonian principles to be adopted. These hardy plants made the ideal 'cover' below tiers of deciduous shrub and tree canopies, and filled pockets of bare earth between rhododendron and other evergreen exotics. Since Robinson's time many new plants have been introduced from abroad and new cultivars of those he knew have much extended the choice.

The smaller perennials, bulbs (or even shrubs) that thrive at ground level below the skirts of taller, mainly deciduous, trees and shrubs make woodland planting seem natural. These plants can be native: snowdrops, wood anemones, primroses, bluebells, foxgloves and ferns, besides other woodlanders which we may consider weeds, such as rose bay willow herb, and dog's mercury, thrive at the lower edge of a wood, germinating and spreading rapidly from dispersed seed. The use of native vegetation clearly encourages the illusion that planting is natu-

Top: Bluebells flowering in the woods at Winkworth Arboretum.

Above: In winter aconites, mahonia and hellebores flower in an area of the garden at Polesden Lacey. In summer a large *Parrotia persica* casts deep shade over the beds.

ral, and emphasizes the woodland and 'wild' character of a site, but there are plenty of introduced small hardy plants which play their part.

Golden aconites (*Eranthis hyemalis*) spread under the bole of some large deciduous forest tree, and marbled-leaved cyclamen, among which *Cyclamen coum*, *C. repandum* or *C. hederifolium* are in leaf or flower most months of the year. Little anemones from Europe (including *Anemone blanda* and *A. apennina*), erythroniums, blue-eyed Mary (*Omphalodes verna*) from southern Europe and *O. cappadocica* from Turkey thrive in cool shade. In moist shade astilbes and hostas contribute both interesting foliage and flowers, and symphytum species and cultivars will carpet the ground to suppress weeds. One of the most invasive small shrubs, *Gaultheria shallon* with leathery evergreen leaves and pinkish-white flowers, flourishes where an overhead canopy is quite dense, and will colonize in moist lime-free soil. At CRAGSIDE it has become dominant over vast areas of the pleasure grounds. Many of these plants if given a cool root run are not fussy about soil type; in woods fallen leaves are a natural humus-making mulch which they find hospitable. In the alkaline soil at HIDCOTE both *Symphytum* 'Hidcote Pink' and *S.* 'Hidcote Blue' have effectively colonized shady beds by the stream. At POLESDEN LACEY aconites, colchicums and scillas underplant winter- and spring-flowering shrubs, to make an attractive area in a garden which remains open to visitors the whole year.

Many newly introduced trees and shrubs, including the rhododendron, were found to need not so much protection from extreme cold but shelter from dehydrating sunshine and cold winds. These plants, in order to develop their potential, required an aspect as nearly as possible like that of their native habitat. The woodland garden evolved to provide these 'natural' sites, where plants in beautiful associations with each other could thrive. Often the most suitable gardens were those where existing woodland already made adequate shelter belts round the most exposed part of a property, and where in reasonably mature groves, clearings could be made, with access paths following easy natural contours. Overhead branches of deciduous trees provided just the right amount of frost protection and summer shading. It was far more difficult to start in an open virgin site, where even establishing perimeter shelter belts could take years, and newly planted specimen trees needed firm staking as well as a summer mulch to prevent the soil drying out.

In a smaller garden the existence of a single large tree may be enough to create some of the same effects as extended woodland, at least providing some overhead shelter, although if shallow-rooting it may not be possible to plant near the bole. The roots of birch are very near the surface, taking all the moisture, while beech trees have such a dense overhead canopy and root system that few plants will thrive near or under them. Deciduous oaks are more benign but slow-growing, taking at least 30 years to influence the character of the planting site, while evergreen oaks, especially *Quercus ilex*, have such dense foliage that no rain showers can penetrate. At TINTINHULL HOUSE two large *Quercus ilex* shade camellias and azaleas growing in neutral soil, but even in winter the ground never becomes sufficiently saturated for the plants to do well. Unfortunately local tap-water is alkaline. Even a few large spreading shrubs provide the shade at ground level which allows this type of planting. Just as in other forms of gardening the whole scale is not so important as adjusting relative size of planting areas.

A wood or shrubbery does not necessitate a vast acreage, and many Trust gardens, perhaps better known for sunny borders or formal parterres, reflect the Victorian love of shrubberies, and have developed these in the Robinsonian sense with attractive lower layers of smaller herbaceous perennials and bulbs.

In the woodland at SHUGBOROUGH winding walks surround island beds on the edges of which suitable low-upkeep perennials such as *Geranium endressii*, which flowers all through the summer, spring-flowering *Brunnera macrophylla*, the lady's mantle (*Alchemilla mollis*) and great drifts of hostas cover the ground and much reduce hand-weeding. Through their low foliage clumps of lilies emerge to extend flowering interest. Between the shrub beds and around specimen cedars and beech, daffodils are naturalized to make a yellow carpet in spring, while in denser shade bluebells thrive to flower in May.

In many ways it may be the pattern of gardening which is most adaptable to a much more restricted space. In the 1930s at the annual Chelsea Flower Show Percy Cane first introduced the idea of a woodland glade incorporated into a suburban setting. Quite obviously man-made, with well-trimmed grass verges, selected plant areas were broken up with groups of birch and dogwood under which smaller plants rather than grass made a carpet. Planting appeared as informal as possible, but its success depended on keeping the scale in balance, and a willingness to replant and replace when essential framework plants grew too large. Winding grass paths linked each area and with the tree canopies above gave the garden a unity of design which seemed restful and satisfying. Each garden would appear to have been carved out of existing woodland, with as many natural features and contours as possible. A great woodland garden such as KNIGHTSHAYES COURT can today be a model for such quite small-scale planting. A modern Scandinavian garden is of this type, an area surrounded by enfolding woodland, with almost nothing except a sculpture or garden seat to emphasize its reclamation from the wild. Woodland streams with 'natural' waterfalls might run through such a property or be artificially constructed, extending the range of suitable plants. Obviously in a small garden it is not possible to imitate the natural habitat of Himalayan plants; in this sort of gardening the use of plants of appropriate scale and type is all-important.

For many amateurs the best lessons are learned from visiting large Trust gardens and then adapting a small part of one to the home site. Bedding out and traditional herbaceous borders call for a high degree of technical expertise, but there are limits to each plan and pattern. Successful woodland gardening, because there are no rules of design, depends on sympathetic interpretation of each site's possibilities and an awareness of appropriate plant association which can most easily be gained by observation in good gardens, which set a standard not only of how to plant but how best to maintain the planting over a period of years. While most perennial plants achieve their full potential in a few seasons at the most, trees and shrubs, which dictate neighbouring planting, and ultimately affect the site's characteristics, take many years to reach their maturity.

The fortunate owner acquires land which already is partly wooded. If this has been neglected, indigenous brambles, dog's mercury, bluebells, elder and sycamore seedlings may well have invaded. Many native British trees do not like shade and their seedlings do not germinate for natural regeneration where man has interfered, but seedlings of sycamore (*Acer pseudoplatanus*, probably introduced by the Romans) and the common elder (*Sambucus nigra*) will germinate in almost any conditions. The first task is to clear old wood and undesirable undergrowth, using machinery and modern chemicals if necessary. Then, before planting, thin back lower tree branches to let in light and air.

At DUNHAM MASSEY during years of comparative

neglect preceding the gift of the property to the Trust, good woodland had become infested with brambles and scrub. Each year, as time and labour permits, more stretches of wood are cleared and ground-smothering shrubs added to discourage any future weed germination; later clumps of perennial plants will be included when all trace of weed regeneration is at an end. It is easy to use selective chemicals round the base of woody plants; difficult to eradicate perennial weed or brambles which appear among clumps of herbaceous plants. If the area is large enough, plan at the outset to have open glades planted with grass to contrast with thicker planting, but it is useless to attempt to make grass grow under shade trees. It is important to remember that taking out a mature tree permanently changes the site's character, and any replacement needs a lifetime to grow. As at Knightshayes, it is important to ensure adequate replacements of mature trees many years before they are likely to fail. By so doing the essential woodland characteristics are maintained. If all the forest trees had to be felled at one time the next layer of canopy would be totally exposed to wind and sun.

The 'garden in the wood' at Knightshayes has been made since the Second World War by Sir John and Lady Amory. Now administered and owned by the National Trust, to whom Sir John left the house and gardens, the plantings of magnolias and other exotics which took place within the last 30 or 40 years have matured. At the same time the garden continues to grow in botanical richness, as new plants are introduced from modern plant-hunting expeditions. No garden stands still, fixed in time in a particular historical context, least of all Knightshayes, which expresses the vision of the Amorys and will continue to change and to be enriched as plants of quality become available. Gardening on this scale, as much as in a more modest-sized garden, requires a constant awareness of the growth potential of each tree or shrub, and the disciplined organization to ensure that each specimen can be allowed space to develop naturally. At times trees and smaller plants have to be removed to give space to neighbouring plant growth; the Head Gardener, Mr Michael Hickson, in common with the Trust as a whole, thinks and plans not only for a year ahead but for a far-distant future.

Knightshayes remains, perhaps, the best example of post-war woodland planting in any Trust garden. On a south-sloping site, in acid soil, large trees (mostly planted in the nineteenth century) were judiciously thinned (never easy, because of letting in wind) and successive layers of smaller deciduous trees and conifers, shrubs, carpeting plants and bulbs have been used to create one of the most beautiful and botanically interesting gardens in Britain. Wide grass paths follow open glades, and curl round the natural contours, while steeper ancillary ways follow steps cut between thick planting. Any quite small woodland garden could follow a similar pattern, although few sites offer such favourable aspect and soil conditions as this in East Devon. The planting at Knightshayes demonstrates how many good plants tolerate and welcome light shade; and how effectively overhead canopies prevent the worst frost damage. Young shrubs suffer particular damage from untimely frosts in late spring and early autumn. In spring the young shoots are vulnerable, and in autumn, especially after a good growing summer, lax vegetative growth has not had a chance to ripen and harden. Our island climate isolates Britain from the low winter temperatures and hot summers of mid-Europe, but its unpredictable quality is confusing to plants which are used to the extremes of a long period of cold, followed by a growing season of predictable length. So many gardeners want a garden site in an open situation where planting has to be limited to sun-lovers. In the Knightshayes wood vast roses, species clematis and honeysuckle clamber through shrubs and trees to reach the light, their roots in cool shade, in conditions approximating to their native habitats. The south-sloping site allowing free frost drainage and the rich lime-free soil together provide enviable conditions.

In one of the glades at Knightshayes an island bed, almost elliptical in outline, is planted with groups of shrubs, perennials, bulbs and grasses. The eastern and western corners of the ellipse (approximately 25 by 15 yards at the widest part) are overhung respectively with a fine specimen *Rhus potaninii* and an old Austrian pine (*Pinus nigra*). In autumn the elegant pinnate leaves of the rhus, introduced from Western China by E. H. Wilson in 1902 when collecting for Veitch, colour a rich red. To the south-west a tall golden Atlantic cedar (*Cedrus atlantica* 'Aurea') casts shade and a more fastigiate *Ginkgo biloba* grows on the south-eastern edge of the bed. Along the south a thicket of *Philadelphus coronarius* dates from earlier in this century when it marked the line of a path leading through the wood to the village church. The white flowers still fill the wood with fragrance in late June.

Pterostyrax hispida makes a light foliage canopy

towards the centre of the bed and contributes racemes of scented white flowers in early summer, flowers which hang on as attractive fruits during winter. Its leaves colour well in autumn. Michael Hickson considers this one of the best small ornamental trees, happy to grow in most soils (except perhaps in very shallow chalk) and conditions, and particularly suitable for a small garden. Another Wilson introduction, *Sorbus megalocarpa* with brownish-purple twigs, makes a loose spreading bush above clumps of hostas, and two birch seedlings (unnamed) have grown to substantial proportions.

At Knightshayes Court Lenten hellebores, forms of *Helleborus orientalis*, are massed under a flowering magnolia. The essence of woodland gardens lies in making plants appear to grow as naturally as they would in their native habitats.

Where the soil is driest near to the Austrian pine, the Montpelier broom (*Cytisus monspessulanus*) seeds itself. At Knightshayes the broom is almost evergreen and bears its clusters of yellow pea-flowers in April and May. *Hedera helix* 'Conglomerata' grows to a dense hummock edging the path near by, and also does well in the dry soil, where Spanish bluebells (*Hyacinthoides hispanica*) have naturalized. Along the front groups of purple-leaved and golden variegated sage (*Salvia officinalis* 'Purpurascens' and *S.o.* 'Icterina') give bulk, but need renewing from cuttings quite frequently, as they become woody and unshapely. Bushes of *Hypericum* 'Rowallane', a garden hybrid, thrive in this sheltered site, and produce their wide yellow saucers in late summer. This shrub is not reliably hardy in many gardens, often getting cut back in a severe winter. The rare *H. bellum* is also in the bed; smaller and denser in habit, its more cupped flowers are a deep yellow. At the back some new philadelphus plants, grown from seed introduced from Asia in the last few years, have been planted in groups.

Groups of hostas include *Hosta sieboldiana*, with perhaps the largest and most imposing leaves of the genus, grey to glaucous in colour, but with short stumpy flower-heads of pale lilac. *H. fortunei hyacinthina* is very similar, its grey-green leaves, edged with a paler grey line, and its flowers held on taller stems. There are also drifts of the green-leaved *H. fortunei*. These hostas can be left undisturbed for five or seven years. Growing tightly together, they prevent germination of annual weeds. At the back tall euphorbias, a form from Margery Fish called *Euphorbia characias wulfenii* 'Lambrook Gold', has yellowish-green flower-bracts carried above narrow grey-green leaves. Although very ready to seed prolifically, seed which often produces interesting variants, cuttings need to be taken regularly to perpetuate this particularly good strain. Running through the bed are pockets of self-seeding *Euphorbia dulcis*; growing to only 30 cm (12 in), this has leaves which colour vividly in late summer. The rampant spreading feathery *E. cyparissias* is controlled to make carpets under the spreading shrubs.

In 1976, the year of the drought, many meconopsis died away completely, but a new stock is being built up. Monocarpic and self-hybridizing in the wild and in gardens, the seed is precious and is unfortunately tempting to visitors. Here mostly forms of *Meconopsis betonicifolia*, *MM. grandis* and *regia* (the latter hybridized with *M. napaulensis*) are grown for the rosettes of handsome hairy toothed leaves which become a feature in the bed. They normally take two to three years to flower: seeds taken in summer are grown as seedlings to be planted out the following spring. These young seedlings are always planted in rich moisture-retaining compost. Foxgloves, originally from Sutton's Excelsior strain, now unobtainable, have been rogued so that only white and cream-flowering forms are grown. This type of digitalis differs from the ordinary native *Digitalis purpurea* by flowering all round the stem, instead of only on the side facing the light, and the tubular florets are held horizontally to reveal the markings.

Three different grasses complete the planting scheme. The Lyme grass *Elymus arenarius* is graceful, if invasive, with arching blue-grey broad leaves with wheat-like flower-spikes in summer. The golden sedge (*Carex elata* 'Aureau'), known as Bowles' golden sedge, and Bowles' golden grass (*Milium effusum aureum*) make eye-catching clumps throughout the bed, the latter being allowed to seed at will, to increase the casual atmosphere.

Cost of upkeep and general maintenance is low considering the area involved, but skilled hand-weeding is necessary, while the use of a hoe is forbidden, so that 'natural' seeding of the more desirable species is encouraged. The edges next to the grass path are cut with a strimmer using a nylon cord rather than tough saw-edged blades. In this nutrient-rich soil feeding and mulches seem not to be necessary.

Lower down in the wood at Knightshayes conditions for small woodland and alpine plants are improved by raising the beds with peat blocks which will give an easy acid root run. To be successful these must never be allowed to dry out, and need a shady situation and high rainfall, high atmospheric humidity or frequent watering. When watering by can or hose ensure that the water is sufficiently 'acid'; rainwater is ideal, but tap-water in a limy area would be harmful.

Woodland gardening can be a whole ecological world, closely related to 'meadow' gardening where native wild flowers are encouraged to spread and seed, and planting can be only of indigenous trees and shrubs. Great garden writers such as Gertrude Jekyll stress the importance of letting the outer rougher garden fade imperceptibly into countryside beyond the garden boundary, by merging foreign trees and shrubs with native plantings. In her own Surrey garden she prevented any abrupt transition between garden and landscape beyond by free planting of juniper, holly and birch, where the more formal garden ended. Most foreign woodland plants, particularly those from Asia, need the deep acid soil which allows them to take up traces of iron in the soil, and fortunately many thickly wooded areas in Britain have at least a top acid layer, which makes growing them possible. Lime-loving plants usually grow quite happily in these conditions and soil can easily be 'improved' for them. It is possible to bring in acid soil and make special beds for shallow-rooted acid-dependent plants, but this is seldom possible on a large scale. Nor indeed is it entirely desirable. In a region where the soil is clearly calcareous with corresponding native shrubs and flowers, it is rarely satisfactory to come across a garden, or a bed in a garden, where the planting is 'unnatural'. At BARRINGTON COURT azaleas grown in specially prepared soil fill central beds in the lily garden. Slightly raised to minimize leaching of alkaline garden soil, the beds are surrounded by a stone kerb. The massed planting, of deciduous early-flowering scented *Rhododendron luteum*, works well, its flower colouring of orange-yellow and scarlet autumn foliage matching the predominantly 'hot' colouring used in this garden compartment. In a sheltered woodland corner at Barrington a similar scheme would look absurd against neighbouring trees and shrubs suited to the alkaline conditions.

DUNSTER CASTLE on the northern coast of Somerset has a specially favoured climate, and recently many evergreen shrubs which would be considered marginally hardy in most gardens have been planted in the steeply sloping woodland and in beds surrounding the keep above. Three gardeners, under Mr Michael Marshall, look after 17 acres designed for relatively low upkeep. Shrubs such as *Choisya ternata*, *Senecio* 'Sunshine' and various hypericums (including *Hypericum calycinum* which is trimmed each spring with a weed-eater) are massed to give a splendid effect of contrasting textures in green and grey in the upper wood. The apple-green leaves of *Griselinia littoralis*, which will grow tall in this favoured garden, catch the light at the bottom of the slope. Rising on the rock, the castle is massive, and ephemeral flowers and 'colour' seem almost an irrelevance. Trust policy in the last few years continues a programme of gradual clearance of common cherry laurel (*Prunus laurocerasus*) to make space for what will be a unique woodland of strawberry trees (*Arbutus unedo*). The slopes are too steep for roots to be extracted without danger of banks collapsing, so each laurel stump is painted with glyphosate and trichlopyr as it is cut back. So far 300 new arbutus have already been planted in the hanging woods. Many other good evergreens such as azara, *Bupleurum fruticosum* and *Prunus laurocerasus* 'Zabeliana', are also in large groups, under which, in separate areas, ground-cover plants are beginning to grow densely together, covering the bare earth. Among these *Rubus tricolor*, with burnished trailing stems and glossy heart-shaped leaves, spreads quickly where the ground is almost bare rock. This tough colonizer was put in almost without roots, each hole made with a crowbar. In another place *Leucothoe fontanesiana*, with graceful arching stems, contrasts with the upright-growing bushes of an uncommon privet, *Ligustrum quihoui*, which has panicles of white flowers in summer. In fact, although flower colour is not the primary consideration, groups of philadelphus, libertia and, lower down the slope, in the damp Mill Garden, small brightly flowering azaleas, do contribute extra interest. The brown peeling stems of neillias and stephanandra arch above the invasive dead-nettle, *Lamiastrum galeobdolon*, which here has adequate space, but is seldom recommended for a small garden. Many other tender plants are grouped in the wood, and are grown as specimens near the castle walls.

Many gardens which become woodland in character as trees grow through the years initially had a period style. A seventeenth-century 'wilderness' might have been planned with shady walks which radiated from a lawn or central focus; over the centuries while the original design was neglected, the site might become a 'natural' wood. Sometimes even a formal garden can, over the years, develop a new character of its own. Trees and shrubs, especially evergreens, mature and create woodland where none was intended. In Italy, too, many of the great Renaissance villas, once in open sites surrounded by green alleys of cypress, clipped ilex and box have by the twentieth century developed a haunting woodland character, as trees have grown mature and spreading canopies filter the strong Italian sunlight.

Something of a similar atmosphere is evoked at ICKWORTH. The classically proportioned rotunda with its curving wings is today framed by great cedars planted in the early nineteenth century, just after the house was built, and evergreen trees and shrubs, originally chosen for their Mediterranean flavour, have turned open lawns to the south into shady walks. Instead of the tender aromatic myrtles and cistus of Italian woods, hollies, phillyreas and box are hardy in the cold but dry East Anglian climate. What was once a formal layout is now more sylvan, just as in Italy time and plant growth has often disguised and softened the clear-cut edges of an original design.

To the early planting of cedars of Lebanon (*Cedrus libani*) which described a sweeping curve to the north of the house, Atlantic cedars (*C. atlantica*) were later added, and in the 1880s a collection of wellingtonias (*Sequoiadendron giganteum*) were planted and still thrive. To the south of the house more evergreen trees and appropriate shrubs were massed to give a distinguished setting to the classical rotunda and curving wings of the house. *Quercus ilex*, phillyreas, ligustrum, ilex and box weave a pattern of textured green, some planted informally in groups, others lining paths or edging green alleys. Against the house walls a specimen Lawson cypress (*Cupressus lawsoniana*) and *Phillyrea latifolia* have grown large, but planting today continues in the same theme. *Ilex latifolia*, *Osmanthus decorus* (until recently still *Phillyrea decora*), *Ligustrum japonicum* 'Macrophyllum' and *L. quihoui* and Portugal laurel (*Prunus lusitanica*) are underplanted with large-leaved ivy, both *Hedera colchica* and its arborescent form, the Alexandrian laurel (*Danaë racemosa*) from southern Europe which thrives in dry shade, and with hellebores and ferns.

When the Trust took over the garden in 1956 it found that many of the originally planted evergreen trees needed severe pruning and this has now been carried out, at the same time as continuing to plant in the same theme.

Mr Jan Michalak, the Head Gardener, has played a part in the recent restoration of the garden. He comments that in the first years the dense planting to the south of the house needed to be partly cleared and large areas were put down to lawn. Eventually the big *Quercus ilex* had to be severely cut back, and it has taken eight years or so for these trees to make enough regrowth to once more assume their graceful proportions. At the same time shrubberies have been replanted to make dense masses of textured green foliage and to separate different garden areas, adding elements of surprise and mystery to a tour of the garden. The collection of box now includes many varieties and is being continually augmented: Ickworth now holds the National Collection for the NCCPG (see Appendix). Between two old yew trees, privet and box bushes are typical of planting at Ickworth. In the bed a pendulous privet (*Ligustrum sinense* 'Pendulum') dominates surrounding box bushes, although *Buxus sempervirens* 'Latifolia Maculata', with large leaves splashed with gold, is eye-catching among more sombre greens. *B.s.* 'Handsworthensis' has green leaves with a pronounced 'blue' tone, and *B. microphylla* 'Curly Locks' is a dwarf spreading bush with small rolled leaves which become distinctly bronze in winter.

In Loudon's 'Gardenesque' style, the Victorian shrubbery, partly evolved as a means of displaying a collection of trees and shrubs. Specimen conifers, newly introduced in the middle of the nineteenth century, and shrubs such as aucuba, arriving from Japan in 1861, augmented the 'evergreen' possibilities, and were planted in contoured island beds where winding paths and boskage disguised the sometimes quite modest proportions of a villa or suburban garden. Today many of these trees and shrubs have grown large, and although the areas are not 'woods', the site offers the conditions that the smaller woodland plants enjoy. One tree in a garden can create woodland conditions for the plants beneath it.

At PECKOVER HOUSE the Victorian shrubbery includes aucuba, hollies with green and variegated leaves, a large *Hydrangea sargentiana*, a thriving monkey puzzle (*Araucaria araucana*), the redwood (*Sequoia sempervirens*), planting of the prostrate *Viburnum davidii*, and a massed ground-cover edging of bergenias. At NYMANS the edges of the drive are shaded by tall trees, but the light canopy allows good shrubbery-type planting below. In front of tall holly hedges plants are tightly packed

Above: In the main garden at Nymans informal woodland planting is held together by a strong design of walls, hedges and pathways. Planting is in three layers; overhead trees, medium-size shrubs and, below, perennials and bulbs which thrive in half-shade.

Opposite: At Ickworth evergreen oaks (*Quercus ilex*) have grown tall over the years to create woodland conditions in a garden once Italianate in style. Now the heads of ilex are trimmed back and hedges clipped again to make formal green rides.

together to prevent weed germination, and deciduous shrubs such as deutzia, philadelphus and shrub roses spread over good flowering herbaceous perennials which need little attention through the seasons. *Deutzia longifolia* 'Veitchii' has rich lilac clustered flowers in July. Peonies, crambe, catmint, *Trachystemon orientale* with large coarse leaves, alchemilla and hostas all flower freely in spite of the shade. Through the holly hedge and twining over arches of clipped holly a vigorous small-flowered white rose, probably 'Madame d'Arblay', reaches up to the light.

Four gardens in the south-west owned by the National Trust have very favourable microclimatic conditions: high rainfall, mild winter temperatures and prolonged daylight. COLETON FISHACRE, GLENDURGAN, OVERBECKS and TRENGWAINTON provide the conditions most suitable for experimenting with the sort of semi-tropical plants which thrive on Tresco, not far away in the Scillies. At Trengwainton proteas and leucadendrons, plants which need a relatively mild climate, moving air and a soil almost devoid of nutrients, have been planted. Near the walled garden in deep shade a group of olearias succeeds. *Olearia ilicifolia*, *O. paniculata*, the rarer *O. arborescens* and grey-leaved *O.* × *mollis* all produce copious white daisy-flowers even in this sunless position. This Australasian genus, the daisy bush or tree daisy, is temperamental, but it is now thought that they prefer a soil low in phosphorus. Many of them are tender and at Trengwainton there is a further selection in the walled 'bays'.

At Glendurgan in south Cornwall exotic trees and shrubs are undercarpeted with wild flowers. On the steep banks in the valley grass is cut late to allow seeding.

In the Trengwainton woodland, originally of beech, ash and sycamore, further wind shelter has been given by Monterey pines and Monterey cypresses, and a recently planted stand of Leyland cypress to the south-west in the path of the prevailing wind. In the wood nothofagus species will grow quickly to give overhead canopies. *Eucryphia cordifolia*, its hybrid with *E. lucida*, and *E. moorei*, with evergreen pinnate leaves, are all outstanding. The tender *Lomatia ferruginea* and *Weinmannia trichosperma*, tree ferns (*Dicksonia antarctica*) and the walking fern (*Woodwardia radicans*), which roots at its tops, grow in sheltered pockets. Large-leaved rhododendrons such as *RR. grande*, *falconeri* and *sinogrande* grow with many of the late-flowering smaller species. *R.* 'Rose Vallon' (a *neriiflorum* form) has leaves with violet-purple undersides and scarlet flower-trusses. *R. griersonianum* produces its scarlet bell-shaped flowers in June. Under the trees clumps of hydrangeas flower prolifically in August, and both the blue and white-flowered forms of willow gentian (*Gentiana asclepiadea*) have naturalized all through the woodland. Along the streamside primula, astilbe and rodgersia and many other moisture-loving plants grow in natural drifts.

In the much more open site at GLENDURGAN snowdrops, Lent lilies (*Narcissus pseudonarcissus*) aquilegias and bluebells grow on the steep banks which edge the valley leading down to the harbour. Snowdrops grow in the shade where groves of trees are planted. On other banks St John's wort (*Hypericum calycinum*) makes a weed-suppressing carpet. At TRELISSICK the lavender-coloured wood anemone (*Anemone nemorosa* 'Allenii') is naturalized in grass.

In the clean atmosphere and humidity of many of

the woodland gardens of the south-west, and in the high-rainfall areas such as Northern Ireland, lichen growth on tree trunks and branches is a problem; rhododendrons and azaleas are particularly prone. The deciduous azaleas can be sprayed in winter with tar-oil, and trunks of magnolias and even larger trees also respond to this treatment. Evergreen forms have to have branches cut back to make them break below an affected area. Mr Peter Horder, the Head Gardener at Trengwainton finds that if plants are cut back early in the season new shoots have time to harden off before the winter. The rough-barked forms of rhododendrons are more ready to put out new shoots, but those which have smooth bark will seldom 'break' again. After trimming back the plants are given a slow-acting fertilizer such as Enmag, as well as Vitax Q4 as soon as growth begins. Healthy well-fed plants are much less likely to get disease. At Trengwainton Arbrex is still used on all cut stumps, although it is now believed that nature quickly seals and heals a 'raw' wound. This sort of 'pruning' is also essential in old woodland gardens, and Mr Mike Snowden, the Head Gardener at ROWALLANE in Northern Ireland, has found that many rhododendrons can be cut back to improve their shapes if half a bush is done at a time, rather than a drastic overall cut, which puts a lot of strain on the plant in its efforts to make new growth.

Meadows

Besides encouraging his readers to grow many flowers both native and foreign 'naturally' in rough grass which was not mown until after leaves died down in spring, William Robinson advocated meadow gardening, where only the true wild flora would be seen. Today as our native flora is increasingly threatened by farmers' sprays (or the predatory collector) its preservation is as necessary as a new style of more 'natural' gardening is attractive. Butterflies and other wildlife also benefit, maintenance programmes are less intensive and expensive, and visitors appreciate the chance to compare the appearance of the wild member of a genus or a pure species with the highly bred garden cultivar. In early English gardens up to the end of the seventeenth century, wild flowers were encouraged to grow under orchard trees to make 'flowery meades', but the idea of wild or natural gardening was not accepted again until the time of William Robinson and Gertrude Jekyll. While gardening fashions changed through almost two centuries, wild flowers still continued to flourish, in woods, ditches and hedgerows, and it was only recently that so many became almost extinct. Naturalists say that 95 per cent of the flowery English meadows have disappeared in the last 40 years and many that survive are now protected in National Trust open space properties.

In 1881 William Robinson wrote, 'Not to mow is almost a necessity in the wild garden: considering that there is frequently in large gardens much more mown surface than is necessary . . . surely it is enough to have a portion of lawn as smooth as a carpet at all times without shaving off the long and pleasant grass of the other parts of the grounds . . . mowing this grass once a fortnight . . . is a costly mistake . . . we want shaven carpets of grass here and there, but . . . who would nor rather see the waving grass with countless flowers than a close surface without a blossom.'

Partly because of the need for economy, but also to preserve scarce wild and naturalized flowers, the Trust has always taken this advice in appropriate places. In many Trust gardens, as in those privately owned, there are good reasons for establishing or retaining some sort of wild-flower meadow. Today when mowing and edging machines of every type are available for grass cutting, and selective herbicides and fertilizers make lawn management simple (if expensive), gardens can become too manicured. Most gardens do benefit visually from some smooth tightly cut conventional lawn, but even this can look better when a neighbouring area of longer grass-blades presents a pleasant textural contrast. The lawn area can be extended to grass paths which make a firm crisp line beside or around a section where the mowing programme is quite different. From a designer's point of view the rougher section can make as satisfactory a contrast as more colourful flower beds, and the two areas are linked together firmly by the horizontal ground pattern of mown paths. Both Robinson and Jekyll still preserved formality and shaven lawns near the house in the 'inner' garden, but they saw the value of a gradual transition, enhanced by changing height and texture, and hence appearance and colour, from this part to the outer garden edges where orchard trees or even countryside merged with garden plants. If this rougher grass could be encouraged to display a colourful range of flowering plants and grasses, so much the better.

Another reason for gardening in rough grass is to save maintenance costs. Instead of the weekly cut through summer months (usually about 29 times in the whole year, depending on weather conditions), cutting is done much less frequently. It is true that when it is done more work is involved if grass has to be carted off. But it is much less necessary to have a fixed timetable; a few days or even weeks one way or the other allows more relaxed gardening and other essential tasks to be completed. Even gathering and sowing seed to increase a range of plants does not have to be done as an exacting programme. At both SIZERGH CASTLE and SHEFFIELD PARK, flowers and grasses are only those which arrive 'naturally', their seeds carried by wind or insects (ants are said to transport primrose seed, while many of the daisy-flowered *Compositae* blow in).

A third and compelling reason for establishing a 'meadow' is in order to preserve the dwindling pasture population of flora and wildlife which modern farm sprays tend to eradicate or destroy. The National Trust, by encouraging this sort of gardening, plays its part in preserving the heritage of native flora, and in general provides an education in ecological gardening, which is much appreciated by the millions of visitors, including parties of schoolchildren.

Obviously the wild flowers or exotic bulbs which can also find a place here will vary with the type and pH of the soil. The native flora of chalk soils is different from that of deep clay or strongly acid peaty loam. It is possible to have a 'meadow' in woodland, in shade or sun, on north-facing or south-facing slopes. In moist boggy soil the flowers which thrive are different from those found to do their best in well-drained ground.

In poor soil, especially on chalk or limestone, undisturbed pasture can easily be encouraged to grow native local and other flowers, but establishing attractive 'meadows' where there is nutrient-rich soil is much more difficult. Fortunately where an area has been closely cut as lawn for many years there is usually a low level of fertility and when grass is initially allowed to grow to hay length wild flowers appear without being introduced. Natural colonization will take place over a period of years, but herbs and grasses can be introduced by seed. Small quantities of the seed is mixed with a seed compost and sown in autumn or spring in small pockets. Vetches and clovers are easily established in this way. Seeds can be taken from buttercups (*Ranunculus bulbosus*), ox-eye daisies (*Leucanthemum vulgare*), cowslips (*Primula veris*), fritillaries (*Fritillaria meleagris*) and meadow cranesbill (*Geranium pratense*) growing in some local waste ground, and either sown straight into the meadow or, best of all, raised to be planted out later. If an old pasture is being ploughed up locally it may be possible to obtain a few turves which will contain seed and seedlings of the flora.

If nettles and docks grow luxuriantly in a rough area this is usually an indication of nutrient-rich soils. For a few years the area should be mown tightly and all grass clippings removed. The larger weeds can be sprayed with herbicides. After a time even the most vigorous of the grasses will have been weakened and the 'meadow' programme can begin, and new plants introduced. If feasible the whole area can be ploughed up and reseeded with a fescue/bent mixture to which can be added small amounts of white and red clover seed, and other herbs. Most orchids spread by wind-blown seed, and should never be dug up in the wild.

As well as herbaceous plants, bulbs and tuberous plants will grow strongly in grass which is cut tightly towards the end of the season, or when the leaves have died down. Aconites (*Eranthis hyemalis*) and crocus species, especially *Crocus tommasinianus* and *C. chrysanthus*, flower early and are often grown in lawn which is tightly mown later, as leaves wither quickly, but they will also succeed in the longer meadow grass. The golden aconites prefer light shade from the canopy of a deciduous tree, and like snowdrops multiply most freely in a damp site. *Crocus vernus* grows in many coloured forms at LACOCK ABBEY. Narcissus species and especially the native *Narcissus pseudonarcissus* thrive in acid loam and filter through the woods at STOURHEAD. More showy daffodils can be planted in drifts of different colours. In the orchard at SISSINGHURST CASTLE clumps of daffodils mingle with red Darwin tulips, the tulip flowers becoming smaller and more pleasing in these rigorous conditions. Moisture is very important for daffodils and they prefer heavy to light soil. At ASCOTT bulbs of anemones, crocuses, fritillaries (*Fritillaria meleagris*), scillas and tulips are planted in the south-sloping banks, while on the level lawn, under and between trees, there are drifts of daffodils alone. At ACORN BANK a steep escarpment falling to the river valley is covered in spring with assorted narcissi, particularly the valuable fragrant late white *Narcissus poeticus recurvus*. Inside the garden among the orchard trees are wild native tulip (*Tulipa sylvestris*) and wood anemone (*Anemone nemorosa* and its double form 'Vestal'). The soil at Acorn Bank is an alkaline clay. On the sloping lawns at ARLINGTON COURT, Japanese primulas thrive naturalized in grass, and the wild primrose, violet and wood anemone continue to spread. In one corner of the lawn at TRELISSICK there is a carpet of pale lavender-blue *Anemone nemorosa* 'Alleni'. *Fritillaria meleagris*, and summer snowflake (*Leucoium aestivum*) which spread through Thames-side Oxfordshire meadows, will naturalize in damp sites. In a very dry site, where beech trees take much of the moisture, martagon lilies grow in rough grass at FARNBOROUGH HALL where there is also a mass of the yellow daisy *Doronicum pardalianches*. At BLICKLING HALL and WALLINGTON the yellow *Lilium pyrenaicum* is naturalized under trees. Dog's tooth violets (*Erythronium dens-canis*) will grow in the thinner turf in partial shade, but are likely to be swamped in more luxuriant grass. Camassia species and white-flowered star of Bethlehem (*Ornithogalum umbellatum*) do not like too strong competitors, but spread where grass is cut soon after they flower. In June the native bluebell (*Hyacinthoides non-scriptus*) makes dense carpets of blue in the woods at WINKWORTH ARBORETUM.

Colchicum autumnale and *C. speciosum*, autumn crocus (*Crocus speciosus*) and even the small gold-flowered *Sternbergia lutea* will survive in grass; for the latter, turf is kept as short as possible during the summer, to allow bulbs the maximum sun during the dormant period. Colchicums and autumn crocus usually start to appear for flowering at the end of August and grass-cutting programmes must be adjusted so that no more mowing is done until early November, just before daffodil spikes for the following spring start to shoot. These bulbs can be moved when in leaf early in the summer.

In a relatively large garden, it may be possible to 'stagger' mowing regimes to encourage different types of wild flowers. Snowdrops (*Galanthus nivalis*) and primroses (*Primula vulgaris*) will thrive in grass in which they are planted if it is given a first cut in June. This may coincide with cutting the leaves of naturalized daffodils, a task which should be left until six weeks after they have flowered, probably sometime in June. At CLANDON PARK narcissus and cowslips (*Primula veris*) grow happily together, the latter setting and scattering seed at just about the moment when daffodil leaves have faded sufficiently to allow them to be cut down. In another meadow area a mowing regime can be begun in spring, then left for a six-week period in the middle of summer. Grasses and quick-growing 'flowerers' will give a display even in that short period. The third section will not be cut until orchids have seeded in August or September. Whichever system is adopted, all grass-clippings should be removed, for composting if short, or for hay later.

Mr Malcolm Hutcheson, the Head Gardener at SIZERGH CASTLE in Cumbria, is a knowledgeable botanist and has made a meadow for local flora on a bank to the east of the castle. He writes:

✤ The meadow garden at Sizergh Castle is a south-facing embankment, which in spring is covered with the local wild daffodil (*Narcissus pseudonarcissus*). The area is then allowed to grow naturally through the summer months and the flowers of the various native plants give a profusion of colour.

After the daffodils sweet violets (*Viola odorata*), wood anemone (*Anemone nemorosa*), cowslips

(*Primula veris*), early purple orchids (*Orchis mascula*), a few green-winged orchids (*O. morio*) and double-flowered cardamine (*Cardamine pratensis* 'Flore Pleno') begin to appear. Among a yellow carpet of dandelions the tiny adder's tongue fern (*Ophioglossum vulgatum*) can be seen. As these plants fade they are replaced by the meadow and wood cranesbill (*Geranium pratense* and *G. sylvaticum*), moon or ox-eye daisies (*Leucanthemum vulgare*), bugle (*Ajuga reptans*), bird's-foot trefoil (*Lotus corniculatus*), fox and cubs (*Hieracium aurantiacum*), a few twayblade (*Listera ovata*) and numerous greater butterfly orchids (*Platanthera chlorantha*).

The soil of the bank is shallow as it overlays local limestone. It does not contain much humus and is starved, thus discouraging the taller 'rank' grasses. As a consequence, a range of the finer grasses prevails in the summer months, their nodding flower-heads and arching leaves adding much to the attraction of the meadow. Timothy (*Phleum pratense*), quaking and sweet vernal grasses (*Briza media* and *Anthoxanthum odoratum*), Yorkshire fog (*Holcus lanatus*) and wild oats (*Avena fatua*) are in evidence.

Among the final show are hardheads (*Centaurea nigra*), betony (*Betonica officinalis*) and the green and red fruits of lords and ladies (*Arum maculatum*) growing under the canopies of trees.

Maintenance of the area is relatively simple, as the first cut is not done until late August or early September, according to the season. By delaying cutting until this time of year most of the plants have seeded naturally, which is particularly important for the daffodils and various orchids. A wet season may give a longer show of colour, even if some of the grasses are flattened by the rain.

Cutting is done by rotary mower and all the cut 'hay' is removed and used for making compost. The whole area is then cut once or twice during the remainder of the growing season to produce a short turf to withstand the winter and to allow the bulbs to give a good show the following spring and summer.

The 'starved' soil, which is neither strongly acid nor alkaline, accounts for such a wide range of plants appearing on the site. No seed from a commercial or other source has been introduced. It is particularly pleasing to note that after some fifteen years of the same treatment some of the orchids and rarer flora are increasing.

Opposite: The meadow at Sizergh Castle.

Page 209: The steep bank under the wall at Sizergh is a mass of ox-eye daisies (*Leucanthemum vulgare*) in June. Opposite: The meadow at Sizergh Castle.

Left: *Gentiana sino-ornata* from China thrives in the deep acid soil at Sheffield Park.

In 1976–77 it was decided to develop a rough area at SHEFFIELD PARK which lies to the east of the third lake. In one section, on the site of an old cricket pitch (where Australian teams played in the 1800s), a meadow of wild flowers, of interest to botanists and the conservationists, has been encouraged to develop. Each year Mr Archie Skinner, the Head Gardener, ensures that all the wild flowers are allowed to seed and disperse before the grass is cut. By 1983 the Surrey Botanical Recording Society carrying out their annual survey found 169 different species. Rare orchids include *Dáctylorhiza fuchsii*, its stout stem rising from spotted leaves to bear lilac or whitish flower-heads. Butterflies also have greatly benefited from this meadow area.

At ROWALLANE in Northern Ireland a paddock is being treated as a meadow for wild flowers. Mown paths round the edge and a swathe through the centre define the shapes of the meadow area where cuts of the long grass are timed to allow seeding. Here the soil is also lime-free. Plants such as lady's bedstraw (*Galium verum*) and marsh bedstraw (*G. palustre*) mingle with knapweed or hardheads (*Centaurea nigra*), moon-pennies or ox-eye daisies (*Leucanthemum vulgare*). Vetches which do not need calcareous soil are also found here.

Orchis mascula flowers in late spring, and the cowslip and oxlip hybrid (*Primula veris* × *elatior*) has made a colony. The grass is cut in August when seeding is complete and then cut regularly until winter.

Bulbs at Wimpole

As in many large estate gardens, extensive plantings of daffodils can be found in the pleasure grounds at WIMPOLE HALL. Here nearly all the bulbs were first forced for house decoration, but were then planted out each year. Describing the culture as 'nothing out of the ordinary', Mr Malcolm Davy, the Head Gardener, attests that the display gets better every year:

From November onwards, grass cutting ceases. The bulbs continue to grow throughout the winter, flower in spring, and are then allowed to dry off completely until the end of July. At that point the area is finally cut as hay, dried, carted off and burnt. The bulb area is then cut every 14 days or so with a ride-on rotary mower, and cuttings are left on the surface.

By this particular method of culture we not only get a spectacular show of daffs, but also a marvellous collection of wild flowers, including cowslips, celandines, primroses, bluebells, blue and white violets, snowdrops, twayblades, forget-me-nots and lesser purple, early purple and bee orchids.

Narcissi at Wimpole include:

'Actaea'
'Bath's Flame'
'Beersheba'
'Carlton'
'Cheerfulness'
'Cragford'
'Fortune'
'Geranium'
'Golden Harvest'
'John Evelyn'
'King Alfred'
'Mary Copeland'
'Mount Hood'
'Mrs Barclay'
'Mrs E. H. Krelage'
'Mrs R. O. Backhouse'
'Red Rascal'
'Rembrandt'
'Sempre Avanti'

Natural Planting and Low Maintenance

William Robinson's theories on wild or 'natural' planting discussed under woodland gardens always sound invitingly labour-saving and practical. In fact this is not always so. Plants grown together in the ways he recommends seldom develop at the same rate, and the most vigorous tend to dominate the planting scheme after a few years. The skill in this sort of gardening lies not only in being able to visualize the ultimate 'picture' in an artistic sense, in some cases not to be realized for many years, but also in placing plants together which will grow in the same conditions *and* will enhance each other, and most importantly not need constant re-shuffling and careful hand-weeding where soil is bare between plants or groups of plants. Many gardens besides those belonging to the Trust show his influence but there are degrees of so-called 'natural' planting between the careful placing of suitable hardy plants in beds in light woodland and on the outer fringe of the garden, true meadow gardening and gardening at a low level of maintenance, where random seeding of desirable plants is encouraged, and grass is not kept as smooth and weed-free as a bowling alley.

To many gardeners the sight of dandelions growing in pavement or even colonizing a meadow brings to mind the dread of wind-blown seed. In some seasons if conditions of sun and rain have been just right the summer before and, if the previous autumn was warm and sunny, there is suddenly an explosion of germinating seedlings: alchemilla, brunnera, campanula, violas and biennial foxgloves and evening primrose to name but a few. Brambles, elders and milk-thistle benefit from the same conditions and become a pest, needing careful removal by hand, or judicious use of sprays (or a glove specially impregnated with a contact herbicide).

Many old gardens, in fact, become overrun not with traditional weeds but with plants which, originally planted as part of the design, have become weeds, as they are unwanted in particular places. The Welsh poppy (*Meconopsis cambrica*), the Byzantine gladiolus (*Gladiolus byzantinus*), *Allium siculum* (now more correctly *Nectaroscordum siculum*), tall verbascum, biennial evening primrose (*Oenothera biennis*) and *Alchemilla mollis* are all good garden plants but if allowed to seed freely will, in time, spoil planting schemes. This is particularly so if colour planning is strict in a garden.

At the same time the gardener in the very dry garden like the American Garden at FELBRIGG HALL, where old trees take much of the moisture, will envy the natural effects gained in a favoured garden with damp acid soil, such as TRENGWAINTON, where the willow-gentian, both blue *Gentiana asclepiadea* and its white form *G.a. alba*, make groups between exotic rhododendron or olearia bushes, and the walking fern (*Woodwardia radicans*) is vigorous in between specimen tree ferns (*Dicksonia antarctica*). At Trengwainton primulas seed along the stream but if the giant cow parsley (*Heracleum mantegazzianum*) was allowed to seed here it would quickly overrun and destroy other smaller plants. Yet it is statuesque and beautiful along the lake at BLICKLING HALL and on the orchard edge at HARDWICK HALL.

Low-upkeep gardening becomes a delicate balance between nature literally taking over the garden and a degree of disorder which is acceptable but will not become a danger to existing and desirable design effects, or to good ornamental plants. At GLENDURGAN snowdrops, Lent lilies (*Narcissus pseudonarcissus*) aquilegias and bluebells grow on the steep banks which edge the valley leading down to the harbour. On other banks in the garden St John's wort (*Hypericum calycinum*) makes a weed-suppressing carpet. Yet bluebells can quickly spread, their seed carried by birds, to neighbouring flower beds where they multiply. Bluebells have become a weed problem in the new stream planting at DUNHAM MASSEY.

In the last forty or fifty years the use of ground-covering plants has been recommended for reducing the high cost and burden of routine garden maintenance. There is still, however, considerable confusion in the mind of the amateur about how to use them, as well as about the necessary time-scale which enables these plants to grow together and become effective weed-smotherers. By visiting National Trust gardens and by hearing the behind-the-scenes story from the gardeners themselves, it is possible to assess how this sort of planting works.

The flower beds at HIDCOTE already planted in the first thirty years of this century made use of the same principles. Hardy perennials were densely packed together so that there was no space for weeds to develop. Today we usually consider ground-cover plants as those with strong foliage, in different textures and shades of green (and other colours); these plants are chosen for their density of habit

At Trengwainton wood anemones and primroses grow under the boles of trees.

rather than for their flower colour or seasonable performance. Ground-cover plants are those which over a period will grow together shading the soil beneath to discourage the germination of unwanted plant seedlings. The best ground-cover plants are those which have attractive foliage which is itself an asset. (Grass, of course, cut at different levels is a ground-cover, and its maintenance is far from being labour-free.) Other plants which quickly grow together such as St John's wort, most forms of comfrey (*Symphytum*), lamiums, brunnera, forget-me-not and forms of knotweed (*Reynoutria*) can be as invasive as ground-elder or creeping buttercup.

Ivy will flourish in deep shade, and other 'natural' climbers such as *Hydrangea petiolaris* and forms of parthenocissus will quickly spread on the horizontal. Ground-cover works in layers. Shrubs act as weed-suppressants under the canopies of trees; low growing woody or creeping herbaceous plants and bulbs cover the soil at ground level. Gardening economically means a constant balance between using plants which grow together and keep at bay the unwanted intruder and the problems these plants then create by themselves being so vigorous.

At KNIGHTSHAYES COURT, in the woodland garden made since 1945, foxgloves of the *Digitalis* 'Excelsior' strain are encouraged to seed through the beds to give interest after the predominantly spring-flowering plants are finished. The Head Gardener, Mr Michael Hickson, always 'rogues' out those with flowers of pink or mauve before their seed ripens, while encouraging the white forms to multiply. In many Trust gardens like KILLERTON, cyclamen, both autumn-flowering *Cyclamen hederifolium* and spring-flowering *C. coum* and *C. repandum* appear in drifts under trees and shrubs, their marbled leaves contributing colour at different seasons. At TINTINHULL blue scillas, *Anemone blanda* from south-east Europe and the Apennine anemone (*A. apennina*) spread in well-mulched soil; flowering to make a carpet of blue in early spring, they convey a feeling of maturity to the garden. These are all plants which can reasonably be controlled. More dangerously the Welsh poppy (*Meconopsis cambrica*) has been encouraged to seed in selected beds; elsewhere the biennial tall evening primrose (*Oenothera biennis*) flowers at evening and dusk through the last three months of summer, and the little yellow fumitory (*Corydalis lutea*) lurks in corners of steps. All these plants which cover the ground and control germination of 'true' weed seeds can become a nuisance.

At KNIGHTSHAYES forms of erythronium, omphalodes, Pacific Coast Hybrid Iris and acid-loving *Maianthemum bifolium* make an effective under-carpet to the taller shrubs. The latter and erythroniums from different parts of the world are also a feature at STAGSHAW, the woodland garden at Ambleside overlooking Windermere, where beds are less formally arranged and these plants seem to spread at will. Plants grown in this way need less attention than when grown in more formal borders. As William Robinson says in *The Wild Garden*, 'No disagreeable effects result from decay. The raggedness of the old mixed border after the first flush of spring was intolerable . . . when lilies are sparsely dotted through masses of shrubs, their flowers are admired more than if they were in isolated showy masses; when they pass out of bloom they are unnoticed amidst the vegetation, and not eyesores, as when in rigid unrelieved tufts in borders.' In fact many of these plants help each other: their foliage not only acts in time as a self-perpetuating natural mulch, but often protects the emergent shoots of some later-flowering plant. The almost evergreen and decorative leaves of spring-flowering hellebores provide the perfect cool yet frost-free cover for young lily shoots which flower in mid- or late summer.

Many plants such as the statuesque giant cow parsley (*Heracleum mantegazzianum*) would be too coarse for a flower bed, but find a place in a rough orchard or on the edge of woodland where they will seed freely in rough grass, as at ROWALLANE. Some foreign introductions such as winter heliotrope (*Petasites fragrans*) spreads and overwhelms choicer border plants, but a colony along a stream bank controls grass and needs little attention.

This sort of gardening calls for an understanding and awareness of the needs of both native and foreign plants, which, in turn, dictates their appropriate use in the informal garden. In planning ahead more consideration is given to plant associations which could occur naturally than to a prescribed colour theme or definite seasonal effect. On a sunny bank brooms, cistus and ceanothus will make satisfactory companion plants; in woodland American and Asiatic shrubs thrive together in deep loamy soil; by streams or pond-side moisture-loving plants from all over the northern and temperate zones of the world, often with strong architectural foliage, look good together. Primulas such as *Primula pulverulenta*, *P. japonica* and *P. florindae* (the latter thriving even in alkaline soils) flower and seed to become naturalized in the right conditions. At TRENGWAINTON they colonize as space permits, almost becoming garden weeds, but useful when transplanted in establishing new garden extensions.

At MONTACUTE HOUSE groups of decoratively foliaged hostas are used under shrub roses. Planted about 30 cm (12 in) apart hostas grow together within a few years, and the more vigorous large-leaved forms such as *Hosta sieboldiana* become impenetrable to weeds. On the west front at Montacute the very vigorous bramble *Rubus tricolor* spreads under the canopy of tall shrubs. Its attractive burnished leaves have silvery undersides, and it can be invasive if put in the wrong place. In a shady very dry corner at TINTINHULL under a pair of *Quercus ilex* a mass of the less common periwinkle, *Vinca difformis*, grows thickly, allowing hellebores, martagon lilies and even spring-flowering *Cyclamen repandum* to push through its foliage. It has very pale blue flowers which it bears in the winter, above pointed green leaves, on arching stems which root as they grow. Up the woodland drive at NYMANS strong-growing perennials such as alchemilla and herbaceous geraniums are massed to save hand-weeding. At BATEMAN's the creeping *Waldsteinia ternata* grows tightly under a yew hedge and controls the emergence of weeds, although it needs sun to flower itself. At

Above: Pink and white flowered *Cyclamen hederifolium* are naturalized under trees at Saltram, their leaves making a tight ground cover from September until May.

Opposite: At Glendurgan late-flowering pink rhododendrons and a tree fern look exotic above wild flowers and grass where yellow primulas naturalize in the rough grass.

HIDCOTE stream banks are covered with *Symphytum grandiflorum* 'Hidcote Blue'. At GREYS COURT the bright blue-flowering *Lithospermum purpureo-caeruleum* (now more correctly called *Buglossoides purpurocaerulea*) grows under a complete canopy of wisteria. This plant certainly suppresses weeds, but can itself become an invasive problem and needs cutting back. At CHARLECOTE PARK the little wild garden in light woodland is carpeted with lamiums, lungworts, herbaceous geraniums and other dwarf plants and bulbs to give a pleasantly informal air, and is very labour-saving. At DUNSTER CASTLE evergreen shrubs cover the ground under tall trees. Banks of *Hypericum calycinum* and *Senecio* 'Sunshine' make weed-free cover on steep slopes where weeding is difficult. In another area the vigorous *Rubus tricolor* spreads under new planting of arbutus groves.

Above: At Hidcote Manor the plants in the formal garden in front of the cedar are tightly packed to prevent weeds.

Today it is almost possible to say that gardening in formal patterns is no more labour-intensive than the constant shuffling and re-arrangements of plants in so-called Robinsonian or 'naturalistic' garden areas. By the judicious use of chemicals and plastic sheeting, a knot or maze of a hedging plant set among gravel, or even gravels in different colours, as at LITTLE MORETON HALL or MOSELEY OLD HALL, needs little attention except for an annual clipping and annual application of a simazine-based weed-suppressant which prevents germination of annual weeds. Even summer bedding needs little attention, except for occasional dead-heading, once the tightly packed flowers have grown together. Much of the work involved is in their production towards the end of the winter, and the adequate preparation of the beds and planting, a task usually completed at the time of the autumn planting of winter- and spring-flowering plants.

Gertrude Jekyll followed Robinson in encouraging another sort of labour-saving gardening. She loved to grow what she called 'free-growing' roses, letting them find their way up into old orchard trees or a shabby holly. With small-flowered species clematis and honeysuckle to extend the flowering season, pruning and tying in once a year is all the attention necessary. She planted her favourite white roses, 'The Garland' and 'Aimée Vibert', to grow as cascading fountains where the bloom would hang downwards for all to see, rather than flower-heads opening at the top of a pergola. Today at KNIGHTSHAYES, LYTES CARY, NYMANS, SIZERGH CASTLE and TRERICE, roses such as *R. filipes* and its giant form 'Kiftsgate', 'Bobbie James', 'Francis E. Lester', 'Rambling Rector' and many others give these natural effects, and are as beautiful as any fruit blossom early in the season. These bushes should be planted a few feet from the base of their 'host' and mulched thickly in the spring. At first young shoots are guided upwards into the branches of the tree, but after a season new shoots push up farther to the light and trail downwards to flower with little further help. Pruning consists of removing old wood. Some of these roses can be used as ground cover, growing horizontally, or even pegged down to make a weed-smothering mass of foliage. Some roses such as *Rosa* 'Paulii' and its pink-flowered form *R.* 'Paulii Rosea' actually grow naturally in this way.

V
PRACTICAL MAINTENANCE

Practically all gardeners welcome the idea of reducing the many hours spent doing repetitive tasks such as mowing grass and edging lawns, cutting hedges, brushing stonework, raking up leaves in autumn, composting garden materials for feeding and mulching flower beds, and even eliminating perennial weeds by soil sterilization. The National Trust have exactly the same problems of upkeep as the private owner, but because the Trust is a large organization each Head Gardener, Gardener in Charge or Gardening Tenant receives advice and guidance not only on policy and planting but also on the technical aspects of gardening. The right choice of a machine to do a specific job entails a decision about the level of maintenance desired. The right choice of ornamental plants will also determine how much time is spent dealing with weeds, the unwanted invaders which spoil a garden scheme.

Labour-saving gardening and the understanding of the use of good ground-cover planting, which with mulches will suppress annual weed germination, is synonymous today with good gardening techniques. Borders beside lawns are edged with brick or stone, tanalized wood or steel strip is used to make neat grass edges, soil is sterilized to control perennial weeds and prevent replant disease, and chemicals instead of labour-intensive digging are used to combat weed infestations.

At the end of this chapter is an account of how one of the Trust's gardeners who works single-handed manages the garden.

Lawn and Turf Care

The smooth or textured appearance of grass areas is an intrinsic part of a garden's design. In gardens where a manicured look is an essential part of formality, cylinder machines do weekly (or more frequent) cuts, and grass mowings are picked up. Immaculate edges are necessary to tightly mown lawns, and attending to these is time-consuming. In many Trust gardens beds and borders are firmly outlined with stone or brick set just below the level of the surrounding lawn, allowing plants to spill over the edges without making mowing difficult, and eliminating the need for maintaining firm vertical grass edges.

In less formal areas of the garden, however, grass cut at different levels is very visually satisfying, contrasts of colour and texture making a firm pattern. Varying heights can be used to define different areas: in the wilder woodland-type garden, where

Above: At Barrington Court an elaborately patterned brick path leads past seventeenth-century ox-pens to a modern pergola. Basket weave patterns surround a central strip laid in conventional stretcher bond. Today with modern chemicals weed germination in brick paths is easily prevented.

Page 217: At West Green House an hexagonal greenhouse is decorative as well as functional. Behind it July flowering species roses clamber through the old fruit trees.

grass can be kept longer, more closely mown strips will define a pathway and direct the feet. Longer grass can be cut perhaps only 13 or 14 times during a growing season if a length of about 10 cm (4 in) is satisfactory; the average is about 29 times for a smooth lawn. At ROWALLANE lawn areas, except for those directly round the house, are not kept tightly mown. Instead, paths which wind through woodland and more open glades are cut weekly; under the specimen trees the grass is allowed to grow longer and give an informal atmosphere. At ANGLESEY ABBEY the formal avenues are further emphasized by grass at varying levels. At ARLINGTON COURT spring bulbs and small plants such as primroses, claytonias and violets grow naturalized in the grass, and mowing is delayed.

The care of the well-kept lawn which is an essential feature of a typical English garden is one of the most time-consuming tasks of garden maintenance, and mowing alone can be responsible for about 60 per cent of the cost of lawn upkeep. **Mr James Marshall**, one of the National Trust's Gardens Advisers, analyses the interrelationship of mowing frequency, height of cut, grass varieties and overall appearance, and summarizes other factors in the maintenance of a good-looking and healthy lawn:

✣ Mowing heights and frequencies

A long-term trial on intensive turf culture by Reading University has come up with some interesting conclusions – confirming, for instance, that regular mowing is better than irregular mowing for intensively managed turf. Very close mowing, 10 mm (½ in) and less, can be damaging to the grass root systems and has to be counterbalanced with irrigation and generous amounts of nutrients. Higher cutting, i.e. 15 mm (¾ in), creates a sward that is both more resistant to drought and better looking in the winter months. The longer grass needs less frequent cutting, and the sward proves to be perfectly acceptable when compared with close mowing done at monthly intervals. A major cost reduction is possible by opting for the slightly longer grass.

For all lawns except bowling and golf greens, clippings need be removed only during periods of excessive growth – spring and early summer – so as to help recycle nutrients, provided that mowing is done frequently and kept at 15 mm (¾ in).

Frequency of cut is now being considered an important characteristic when breeding new turf cultivars. A choice of grass mixtures including small bent grasses (*Agrostis*), creeping red fescues and smooth-stalked meadow grass can reduce the frequency of mowing. However, where the sward has to withstand appreciable wear, new sports turf cultivars of perennial rye grass need to be considered.

It is also a question of style. Zones of different lengths of grass can help to differentiate between formal areas, pleasure grounds and wild gardens. The close-mown turf of the manicured lawn, 10–15 mm (½–¾ in), is obviously the most expensive and labour-intensive, requiring regular cuts with a cylinder mower with the clippings boxed at the appropriate time.

Medium-mown turf, 35–100 mm (1¼–4 in) high, in shrubberies, pleasure grounds and wild gardens, needs regular cuts with cylinder or rotary mowers, perhaps using a flail mower for the higher cut. It is possible to economize with 'medium' turf, but a balance has to be achieved between using the manoeuvrable triple-cylinder mowers at frequent intervals and rotary/flail mowers less frequently, but leaving more grass clippings lying on the surface.

Long grass meadows are more than simply the result of allowing grass to grow long. It is important to stress the time necessary to establish a meadow field from a relatively high-nutrient turf sward. To encourage a varied flora but not the competitive and vigorous grass species, the soil needs a low nutrient level and high pH. Another critical factor is the method of cutting. If hay is required, reciprocating cutter-bar machines can be considered, but if hay is not a problem, flail mowing is the best alternative; even a forage harvester might be chosen for larger gardens.

Fertilizers and top dressings

Grass, like all living plants, needs basic nutrients – especially when the foliage is regularly cut off and collected rather than recycled. Fertilizers, however, are expensive, and it is pointless to apply nutrients that will only increase the frequency of mowing. Apart from fine sports areas, lawns need to be fed only in the following situations: in important and formal areas where the clippings are collected; where an area of wear-and-tear needs to be invigorated; after a period of drought; where a lawn is on very thin, hungry soils. Good results can be obtained from relatively small applications of slow-release compound fertilizers: 35–50 g per square metre (1–1½ oz per square yard). A suitable analysis is 11 per cent nitrogen, 9 per cent potash, 6 per cent phosphate, with the possible addition of 1 per cent magnesium or iron to improve colour and disease-resistance.

Top dressing is a very good way of improving the structure of the soil, and is beneficial after scarification and aeration of a lawn. Most top dressings are a mixture of loam, peat and sand, and a fertilizer can be added to promote growth. Apply at no more than 1 kg per square metre (2.2 lb per square yard).

Scarification (see also under Machinery, below) is best done in autumn, early winter or early spring. It should be necessary only in areas of high compaction and in prestige lawns where 'thatch' has built up. In small areas, hand raking with a wire rake can help to lift the procumbent grasses to meet the mower blades and thereby achieve a finer appearance.

Weed and pest control

Regular herbicide treatment is necessary only in formal areas and prestige lawns. Combining a herbicide with a granular fertilizer is a simple, although expensive, method of application.

Moss infestations are often attributed to poor drainage, but may also be caused by low nutrient, lack of adequate aeration, and too low a setting of mower blades. Chemical control is only a temporary solution: it is far better to improve cultivation techniques, including the avoidance of compaction, improving drainage, correcting over-acidity and avoiding close mowing.

Lawns with a high level of nutrient can be prone to diseases, but Red Thread Disease (*Corticium filiforme*) can be a problem in all areas of turf. Brownish, bleached patches appear typically in conditions of damp, mild, humid weather. In most cases it is not necessary to apply fungicides, as the disease goes away after a change in the weather.

Moles are an increasing problem in fine-textured lawns: the most successful means of control is trapping. Leatherjackets, the larvae of the crane-fly, can cause dead brown patches on lawn surfaces. Damage in spring is usually most severe following a wet autumn and mild spring.

Earthworms, on the other hand, need to be encouraged, certainly not controlled, as they are excellent aerators of the soil. ❧

At Standen the lawn is cut in traditional cross stripes. This sort of effect can only be achieved with a cylinder mower.

Mr Marshall gives a more detailed survey of the range of machinery for mowing and other aspects of lawn maintenance in the section on 'Machinery and Equipment', below. Mr Robert Ludman offers the pragmatic approach from the viewpoint of the man operating the machinery in his account of caring for the lawns at STANDEN in 'The Single-handed Gardener'.

Mr Ted Bullock, the Head Gardener at FELBRIGG HALL, has found that wooden edging on all the lawns make maintenance much easier. It prevents the crumbling edges and 'side-wall' growth of grass and weed, which is so difficult to extract when edging in a conventional way. The wooden planks, correctly put in place, give years of effortless lawn-edging, although the initial cost is high. Mr Bullock describes the method used at Felbrigg to fix the planks in position:

❧ The timber, pressure-tanalized deal, is cut in 3.7 m (12 ft) lengths, 10 cm (4 in) wide by 2 cm

(¾ in) thick. At Felbrigg the method employed to fix the planks is the following: the turf edge is cut and rolled back about 30–35 cm (12–14 in). A garden line is then stretched along the face of the soil, usually just inside the line of the turf edge, and a channel about 15 cm (6 in) deep is taken out. The board is inserted and three pegs are driven in on the *inside* (the lawn side, not the path side), to just below the top of the board. The pegs used at Felbrigg are also of tanalized timber, 5 × 5 × 30 cm (2 × 2 × 12 in) long, and sharply pointed. The board is drilled and then screwed into position.

The turf, when replaced, should ideally be just above the top of the board. We have experienced little sinkage of the turf by using the above method.

Some lawn edges are undulating and in order to obtain a good level finish against the boards, it is necessary to add a little soil to raise the level of the turf (if it is lower than the edge of the board), or, of course, to scrape away some earth if the turf level is too high.

On lawns with curves it is possible to achieve reasonable bending of the timber edging by soaking it thoroughly before use. If the curve is a very tight one this may be difficult, and it may be necessary to make some shallow saw cuts. Strong metal stakes are used to hold curved lengths in position temporarily, until the planks can be screwed securely against their pegs, and on curved lengths extra pegs are advisable to hold the edging more firmly.

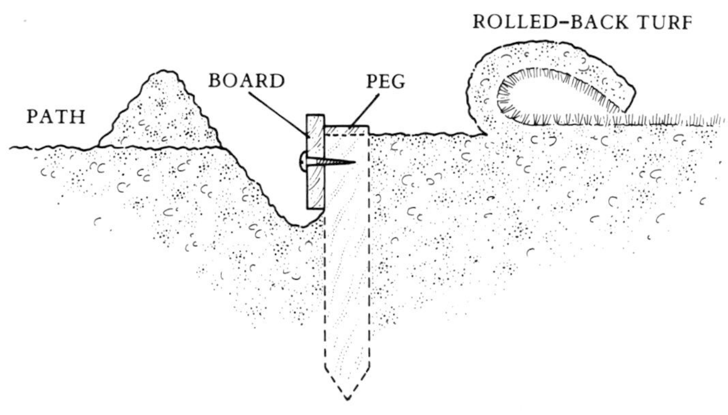

Machinery and Equipment

The reasons for using machinery in a garden are to maintain the garden as efficiently as possible, and to do menial work such as grass cutting, leaf sweeping and hedge cutting as speedily as possible. Many National Trust gardens could not be maintained to the required standard without the use of appropriate machinery and here **Mr James Marshall** appraises the range of types available for different functions.

Just how much to mechanize depends on the size and, perhaps more importantly, on the style of garden. A balance has to be achieved between under-equipping and using small machines which are under-powered on the one hand and over-equipping with lots of machines which are hardly used on the other. Hiring or even sharing specialist equipment such as turf scarifiers and slitters can avoid the latter danger, but poor maintenance is an obvious ill consequence of sharing.

TYPES OF MOWING MACHINERY

Cylinder mowers

The cutting action consists of revolving blades on a cylinder which bear on a fixed plate; a clean scissor-like cut therefore occurs. The number of blades on the cylinder determines the quality of cut.

Rotary mowers

The principle relies on a rotary disc on which are mounted several flexible blades, the grass being cut by a macerating action. Such mowers have become very popular because they are more versatile and need less maintenance and fewer blade adjustments. The hover types are especially useful for cutting banks and slopes. However, they do not make a fine cut and they tend to need more fuel to power the high-speed blades. Collecting grass is more difficult than with cylinder mowers, and swards cut continually by rotary mowers tend to develop more weeds and moss.

Reciprocating knife mowers

In this case a reciprocating knife is mounted on the front of a wheeled unit. Limited use, mainly for cutting long grass.

Flail mowers

Here a series of free-moving flail-type blades are mounted on a rotary cylinder. Too big for small gardens and in the main used only on long grass areas. Of recent introduction is a model with spring-loaded, quick-change knives, which depending on the type of knife fitted can be used to cut grass, scarify turf, or pick up leaves.

Brush cutters

These have a high-speed rotating disc to which are attached nylon cord flails, solid blades or even a circular saw. The nylon flails are perhaps the most useful for cutting grass fringes under trees and shrubs and fence lines. Their cutting rate is about four to five times as fast as hand scything. The electrical powered ones are not very robust, whereas the more useful two-stroke petrol-engined models are noisy and can be very fatiguing. There is now a front-mounted wheeled model which is far less fatiguing and much quieter.

POWER FOR MOWER UNITS

Electricity

Minimum maintenance required; free from starting troubles, but not as powerful as petrol engines. Maximum width of cutting unit being 35 cm (14 in). Only applicable to small gardens.

Petrol

Very reliable, long-lasting engines, but require routine maintenance. Over 12 HP, engines are less economical than the equivalent diesel engine.

Diesel

Less maintenance than petrol engines but more expensive in initial cost; water-cooled engines are far less noisy and smelly than air-cooled engines.

Equivalent water-cooled diesel engine uses about 40 per cent less fuel than a petrol engine.

Adequate manoeuvrability is essential in deciding the width of cut. For a series of small lawns and flower beds, 30–35 cm (12–14 in) should be used. For larger areas 45 cm (18 in), and for extensive areas of grass, triple-type cylinder mowers with widths up to 2.3 m (86 in) can be used. At Anglesey Abbey the width of cut is 3.4 m (11 ft).

There has been an upsurge of interest in combining the haulage capacity of a mini-tractor with a mid-mounted rotary mower. The advantages are obvious, but the main danger is to over-use an under-powered engine, and such a combination is less manoeuvrable and efficient for mowing than a front-mounted rotary mower.

TURF MAINTENANCE EQUIPMENT

Powered Scarifiers

The continual use of mowers and the passage of feet can compact the turf, thus reducing the penetration of water, nutrients and air, causing dead 'thatch' to build up round the grass roots. This dead organic material needs to be pulled out of the lawn and there is a range of powered scarifiers both for the large and small garden. The frequency of the operation depends on the type and size of the lawn and the priority of a fine surface.

Edge Trimmers

The rechargeable battery-powered trimmers are very economical and can edge a length of lawn five times as quickly as hand edging shears, but all powered trimmers need a firm edge to cut to.

OTHER EQUIPMENT

Mechanical Hedge Cutters

Both electrical and petrol-operated hedge cutters work on the principle of a reciprocating cutter bar. Twin-edged blades have become popular and are very useful for left-handed people. Depending on the size of the cutter bar, such machines can cut hedges at five to eight times the rate of hand shears.

Electrical cutters, operated from the mains and battery- or generator-powered, are relatively quiet, light and efficient. If a large number of hedges are to be cut, a portable generator would be a good investment. Petrol-engined cutters are much used, but their disadvantages are fumes, weight, and noise – making ear muffs desirable.

Chain Saws

Powered chain saws are now generally used and have done much to increase efficiency. When selecting a chain saw, due note must be taken of weight, engine performance, vibration and safety factors.

All saws are potentially dangerous and a very useful Code of Practice is published as a safety guide by the Forestry Safety Council, entitled 'The Chain Saw'.

Leaf Sweepers

The collection of fallen leaves in the autumn can be a major problem, and although there are a number of types of leaf sweepers on the market none is completely efficient. The main problem is that leaves can be very wet in the autumn.

The blower type works on the principle of a powerful directional fan which blows the leaves into heaps which can then be conveniently picked up.

The 'Hoover' type works on the principle of a great vacuum cleaner. These are available in a range of widths, engine units and bag sizes. Most are excellent when picking up leaves from hard paths and gravel drives, but are more limited on wet grass.

Trailed leaf sweepers consist of rotating nylon brushes which flick the leaves into a collecting bag. Over a large area the use of an independent engine to power the brushes is very worth while.

The flail type, a recent innovation, is very useful for large areas, and with the addition of a mulching screen the leaves are ground up and can be used as a shrub mulch.

It has been estimated that in ideal conditions either a 'Hoover' type or a trailed sweeper can do the work of ten people with brooms.

Fertilizer Distributors

Even spreading of fertilizers over large areas of grass is really only possible by some mechanical distributor. There are two main types available, and both are either hand-propelled or drawn behind a tractor.

The spinner type is the best. If possible always use a stainless steel hopper with a plastic spinner. The other type works on the principle of a revolving rubber belt, but however clean it is kept it tends to get clogged up, even when applying granular fertilizers.

Sprayers

Hand-pumped Knapsack Sprayers are a very simple and efficient means of applying chemicals; the main drawback is the quantity of water that needs to be carried.

The Controlled Droplet Applicator is a recent development by which the minimum active ingredient is applied, thus reducing the risk of drift and run-off. An added advantage is that the operator does not come into contact with the chemical and therefore only the minimum safety clothing is required. ✤

Soil Sterilization

Where perennial weeds have become a problem in an old bed or border, it is often advisable to sterilize the soil using dazomet (usually available as Basamid). Additionally, all danger of replant disease, especially prevalent among plants which are members of the *Rosaceae* family, is removed. At WIGHTWICK MANOR, for example, the problem was less of weed infestation than that of the presence of rose sickness in rose beds which had been in continuous use for roses for a period of 50 years: the technique is also proving successful in the rose garden at CLIVEDEN. **Mr Peter Cartlidge**, the Head Gardener at Wightwick, describes in detail the process carried out before the rose garden was replanted to a new design:

✤ Dazomet is a soil sterilent used as a pre-sowing or pre-planting treatment; it will control soil fungi, certain cyst-forming eelworms and free-living nematodes as well as weeds and the germination of weed seeds. It comes in a granular form which when subjected to moisture in the soil breaks down and releases the sterilizing gas methyl isothiocyanate.

It is a wise precaution to sterilize any ground prior to planting or replanting, whether it is for crops or ornamentals such as shrubs or herbaceous perennials. It is of paramount importance to do so before replanting old rose beds. The problem of soil sickness in rose beds where plants seem to lose their vigour is common; although the causes are not fully understood, it is partly caused by a build-up of root disease, rose root poisons and eelworm. Sterilizing the soil helps to prevent this condition recurring.

Dazomet can only be used when the soil temperature is over 7°C (44°F) and not likely to fall below 4°C (39°F) within the next four weeks. In most areas of the British Isles this will be between mid-April and late October. With a view to planting the new roses in late autumn or early winter, the ideal time to sterilize the bed would be late summer, possibly in September. When applying dazomet the soil must be evenly moist down to a depth of 20 cm (8 in); this can be done artificially during the few days before the treatment is begun.

We start the job by removing all the old roses and any obvious perennial weed. The soil is then cultivated to a depth of 20 cm (8 in) to give it a crumbly open structure which is then raked to make a level surface. The chemical is then incorporated into the soil and the bed sealed with heavy-gauge polythene.

Preparation for the sealing of the soil should be done before starting to incorporate the granules of dazomet. One successful method is to trench round the bed to a depth of 30 cm (12 in). The polythene sheeting can then be trapped in the trench into which soil is backfilled. This method will prevent the gas travelling out of the bed and damaging any surrounding cultivated areas. If the polythene is trapped or fastened along one side of the area before the chemical is applied it can be drawn quickly across the soil as the task is completed, and finally sealed along the other edges.

Having worked out the area to be treated, dazomet is applied at 1 kg per 26 square metres (1 lb per 14 square yards) on light soils, 1.5 kg per 26 square metres (1.6 lb per 14 square yards) on medium and heavy soils. It should be applied only on a dry windless day, and should be scattered evenly over the surface of the bed; a chemical spreader can be used. The next step is to work it into the top 20 cm (8 in) of the soil. This can be done with a rotovator on all but the smallest beds. A heavy roller is then used to create a surface 'pan' which helps to seal in the gas. Lastly the bed is sealed with the polythene which has already been prepared for immediate use.

Depending on the temperature, the bed is now left for between two and three weeks; the colder the weather the longer it takes for the chemical to do its work. When the polythene is removed, the soil is rotovated once again and this helps release the gas. The depth of cultivation should be slightly less than before; this ensures that no unsterilized soil is brought to the surface.

The bed is then left a further two weeks before a safety test is carried out to see if the soil is free from the gas and is ready for planting. Six random soil samples down to the depth of cultivation are taken, put into containers, sown with cress seed, and sealed with cling film. Another container is filled with broadly similar soil from an untreated bed, and also sown with cress seed. The samples are placed in a warm environment and if germination takes place in all six samples, at the same rate as in the 'control' container, then the soil is ready for planting. If seed in all or some of the samples fails to germinate, then the test must be repeated, after leaving the bed for a further few weeks.

It is important not to plant until the safety test proves satisfactory. The new rose bushes should be purchased from a reputable rose-grower and should be of strong disease-free stock.

Dazomet is a poison and should be treated accordingly. It should be stored in a safe place, and face masks and gloves worn when it is being handled. After handling it, clothing and boots should be washed off. ✤

The principles of the use of dazomet are broadly the same in the cleaning of the weed-infested herbaceous borders at ROWALLANE, which are being tackled in stages. The business of temporarily removing herbaceous plants and protecting trees and shrubs left *in situ* gives the Head Gardener **Mr Mike Snowden**'s account of the process a slightly different perspective:

✤ Over many years the walled garden planted with trees, shrubs, shrub roses and herbaceous plants became infested with perennial weed, particularly ground-elder and bindweed, which will have been brought in with leaf-mould and unclean compost. It is an impossible task to try and eradicate these kinds of weeds while keeping all the plants *in situ*, as the roots of the weeds become entangled with those of the ornamentals.

It was therefore necessary to take out all the herbaceous material. We decided to tackle a given area of the garden each year, over a four- or five-year period. This was done for a number of reasons, and partly because other more urgent work in the garden absorbed much of the time of

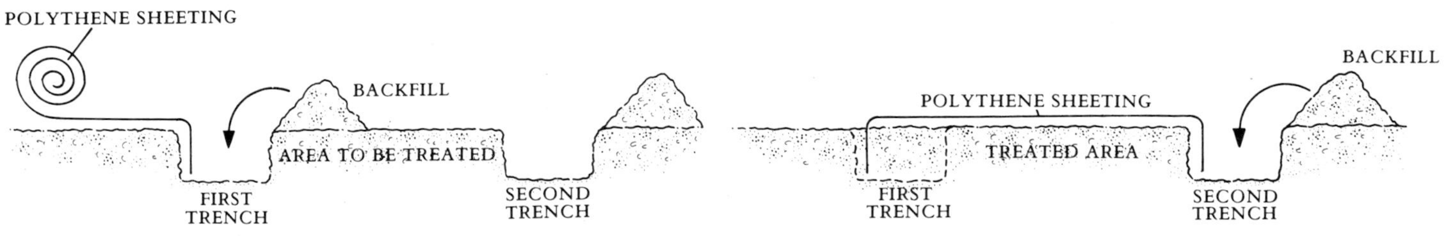

the staff. By doing the work of restoration in stages less nursery area for temporary storage of plants was needed. Finally, and perhaps most importantly, it is not possible to present a totally denuded garden to visitors, although, in fact, the majority show considerable interest in the work we do, and an explanation of 'work in progress' is posted on the property news of our notice board.

The method of cleaning involved lifting all herbaceous plants, spraying, cultivating and sterilizing the soil.

The clumps of perennials are labelled during the growing season. Once they are dormant, vigorous sections of each are lifted, divided and washed. Great care is taken to ensure all pieces of weed root are removed. The newly cleaned pieces are lined out and carefully labelled in the nursery beds. Bulbs are dug up as they begin to show. The parts of the plants not needed for the future replanting scheme are just left in the ground. It is possible to lift plants and to keep them in a clamp of leaf-mould until a spell of wet weather allows adequate time for washing and cleaning them.

In the beds the remaining plants and leaves are allowed to develop, until foliage is reasonably mature. They are then sprayed all over with

Below: The sterilization programme at Rowallane. Shrubs which remain in the bed during the treatment programme have their roots protected by vertically sunk sheets of polythene. Bottom: The borders in the walled garden when covered with airtight polythene.

glyphosate, using a hooded sprayer to prevent 'drift' and possible damage to adjacent shrubs and lawn areas. An explanation to visitors is essential at this time. One of the visitors this year could not understand why we had such localized frost damage. Ground-elder is very resilient and almost always reappears and needs a second application of the spray. As the leaves wither there is a temptation to remove the unsightly foliage. This must be resisted as glyphosate is a translocated herbicide, and to ensure full penetration throughout the system of the plant, leaves must remain until the plant is totally dead. Then all the surface debris is removed and burnt.

The bed is now trench-dug; all roots are removed and also burnt. At this stage as digging progresses a vertical wall of polythene is placed around trees or shrubs that remain in the bed and are part of the permanent planting scheme. The polythene should be at least 30 cm (12 in) in depth and should be round the outer rim of the shrub's canopy so that none of the small fibrous roots will be affected by the chemical which is to sterilize the soil. Care must be taken not to damage the roots, particularly with grafted plants, as this will result in suckers later. Compost is also dug in at this stage.

The next move is the application of dazomet, a soil sterilant. This is in the form of fine granules which when incorporated in the soil will break down with moisture to release gases, which circulate through the soil structure killing pests, soil fungi etc. The soil temperature must be high and the gas must be trapped within the soil. To ensure this we work the granules into the top 15 cm (6 in) of soil, leaving the soil loose in structure but with a level surface.

The granules are added to a stretch of soil a few feet at a time, and a film of polythene is rolled out over the soil almost at once, trapping the gases. The polythene is held tight against the soil surface, and is secured along the edges with planks or heavy fencing posts, which are also laid at intervals along the surface to prevent the wind getting under the sheet and lifting it. A good wide overlap is made when a sheet has to be joined, in order to ensure a continuous airtight film. This work is done in the opposite direction to the earlier digging programme to prevent the soil becoming higher at one end, which would happen if always worked in the same rotation. At the points where trees and shrubs are still in their places in the bed the sheet is cut and folded back to the vertical polythene wall which protects the root system, and firmly secured. The surface round the plants is left exposed so no gas can be trapped in the soil.

After the whole bed has been treated and covered it is left for four or five weeks. No harm results from leaving it longer, so the film of polythene can be removed when the weather is dry or the work programme permits of a return to the job. After the sheet is removed the bed is left exposed for several days to allow the gases to escape. The surface is then lightly forked through to make sure all the gas has gone. A further week is allowed before replanting. Plants from the nursery area are again examined for any residual weed roots in their soil.

Under the permanent trees and shrubs some perennial weed will reappear; this is treated once again with glyphosate.

The whole operation has been very successful with us. The first border was completed three years ago, and is now well established and relatively weed-free. One weed we have found a problem with is creeping sow-thistle. Not because of its resistance, but because at the recommended rate of application of glyphosate, the foliage is burnt off before translocation into the root system has taken place completely. Recently we have found that spot treatment at a lower rate of dilution delays burning off and appears successful.

Right: Mr Mike Snowden working in the walled garden at Rowallane.

Opposite: At Sheffield Park planting is luxuriant. Gunnera and Chusan palm (*Trachycarpus fortunei*) look tender and semi-tropical.

A light nylon mesh net protects emergent buds and shoots on a wall at Sissinghurst.

Winter Protection

Mr Ted Bullock describes some of the tactics used at FELBRIGG HALL to protect plants against damage in winter:

❧ Cuttings of tender plants

Cuttings of tender plants are taken in August and September. Any plants which are prone to possible damage in a severe winter are included. In the relatively severe climate of Norfolk, these include bays, *Carpenteria californica*, cistus, ceanothus, hebe, myrtles, rosemary, thymes, lemon-scented verbena, pineapple sage (*Salvia rutilans*) and others. These are rooted in a mixture of ½ peat and sand in the greenhouse or frame over winter. This is a precaution taken every year to guard against losses which may be difficult to replace next season.

Protection of shrubs in winter

Protection of some of the tender shrubs and plants is done before Christmas, using hessian and straw mats. This particularly applies to ceanothus, myrtles, bays and *Carpenteria californica*. We find that the old mats, made up of old wire netting (rabbit or chicken wire) joined together, with a good thick layer of straw or bracken in the middle – like a sandwich – are particularly effective against the freezing winds. ❧

At KNIGHTSHAYES COURT Mr Michael Hickson uses a similar standard protection for young plants. Knightshayes has a much milder climate than Felbrigg, and a higher rainfall. In winter lowest ground-temperatures experienced are −10°C (14°F) but the important chill factor can reach as low as −21°C (−1°F), easily freezing the sap in young rhododendrons or tender woody plants. Wire rabbit netting is laid on the ground; a half-section is filled with straw laid out in vertical strips as in thatching, to ensure that rain will run downwards once it is fixed in an upright position, then it is doubled over like a sandwich. Wire or tarred string is threaded through the mesh to bind it. Stiff strands of wire are used to stiffen the completed 'mat' and it is fitted round a plant, fixed to the inside of a tripod of stakes, and then tied securely to the stakes, leaving some movement for air between the plant and the mat. At the top a further wigwam can be erected, Indian-style, and bound together, using fronds of Christmas trees or other conifers. For smaller plants Michael Hickson makes a wigwam in the same fashion, but at ground level.

Compost

Mr Graham Kendall, the Head Gardener at MONTACUTE HOUSE, describes his method of making compost:

Most National Trust gardens have been cultivated for a very long time, and Montacute has been a garden for three and a half centuries. As soils inevitably become leached and tired, nutrients have to be added either by using proprietary fertilizers or by the application of manures and composts, which have the additional benefit of improving soil structure.

We do use proprietary fertilizers because they are quick and easy to apply. We also prepare our own compost, which we use mainly as a mulch. Time, however, prohibits too scientific an approach to the preparation of our heap, and lack of availability of plant material limits its quality. The bulk of our material consists of grass cuttings through the growing season and fallen leaves gathered in the autumn. We acquire these in large enough quantities to swamp other ingredients, which include fibrous rooted weeds – hopefully with some soil still attached – and bonfire ash. The latter, while containing potash, is of more dubious benefit and is composted as a convenient method of disposal.

A limited range of ingredients can still produce a very useful compost. Grass cuttings are rich in nitrogen, phosphate and potassium as well as other nutrients. Leaf litter, especially beech leaves, which are plentiful here, has virtually no nutrient value, except for calcium which is retained in the leaf skeleton. This skeleton adds fibre to the heap, which forms humus. Humus is a black jellied material which coats individual soil particles. On light soils it will hold the particles together and retain water. On heavy soils it reduces stickiness and makes soil more friable.

Our heap is started in early spring, on forked-over earth. It is contained in a bay constructed of corrugated iron sheets. We use compost left over from the previous year as an activator. As we are constantly adding to it, we do not cover the heap, although it would be beneficial to do so through the winter to keep heat in and prevent the leaching of nutrients.

The more often a heap can be turned the better, especially when using large amounts of grass clippings which tend to stick in one soggy mass. A more open structure allows air into the heap, encouraging the right organisms for decomposition. Moisture is also necessary and, because of the amount of grass used, our heap seldom dries out. We make our heap wide and low and this increases the surface area for absorbing rainfall. Lime is often added to a heap to prevent acidity, but as the garden at Montacute stands on limy soil we have not found this necessary. The compost from the first year is ready to use in the spring of the second, and is put on as soon as the soil is warm enough to accept the mulch.

At Sissinghurst a mulch protects the tender shoots of *Eremurus robustus* which emerge before the danger of frosts is past.

A Single-handed Gardener

At STANDEN, one gardener looks after the 12-acre garden single-handed. Created at the turn of the century in Robinsonian style, the informal garden is remarkable for the high standard of upkeep attained by **Mr Robert Ludman**.

It is possible that there has been some kind of garden at this site since the building in the 1450s of Hollybush Farmhouse, the cottage with a Horsham tile roof which faces on to Goose Green. A map of 1776 shows the outlines of the garden to be very similar to those of today, but it seems to have been a totally informal family garden.

When the Beales asked Philip Webb to design the large house which was built in 1890, they had already engaged a London landscape gardener named G. B. Simpson to design the garden. The orientation of the house, the terraces, steps and summer-house show Webb's influence, and the rest is Simpson – later modified by Mrs Margaret Beale. As well as having a family who needed to play and grow up in the garden, Mrs Beale was – as were many people in those days – interested in collecting the wealth of plants being introduced from the east, together with some from America. Much of the mature planting today dates from her time.

The Trust acquired Standen in 1973, and Mr Ludman describes both the alterations that have been made at Standen since that date and the day-to-day running of the garden:

Views of the garden at Standen where the single-handed gardener looks after twelve acres.

Restoration and alterations made under the National Trust

The Trust had already taken over the property the year before I was transferred from Trelissick in Cornwall to try and manage the garden on my own – with a small amount of help from my wife Frances. In that time many large firs had been removed from the garden as they were deemed to be out of scale with the house. Also a start had been made on reducing shrubs which had grown too tall. The old kitchen garden was turned into a car park and an area for tenants' and staff cars.

In Cornwall I had been fortunate to have worked under one of the old-style Head Gardeners, Jack Lilly, whose main principle was 'Keep the toes shiny and you don't notice the dirty heels.' This meant keeping the paths and lawns as good as possible. They both badly needed attention when I came to Standen.

Paths

There was a simple solution to the paths – gravel. By spreading quarter-inch shingle on all the paths, the badly deteriorated hoggin was transformed and in most cases levelled. To keep weed-free, all that is necessary is to spray simazine over the lot in February or March. Timing is important, as the ground must not be too dry or too waterlogged: run-off on to adjoining grass edges or borders may do damage. I find that I can guarantee two weeks of fine weather despite the presence of giant depressions in the Atlantic simply by doing the simazine spraying. One of the good things about a gravel path is the effect a raking over has: it brings freshness to the whole garden. We used to say 'A good rake livens the gravel.' It does. I find it takes about an hour and a half to do all the paths and the terrace. Any odd patches of weeds which emerge later in the year are quickly destroyed with a simazine/paraquat mixture.

Lawns

Lawn and grass care is of course a major horticultural subject and practice. Fortunately we do not have time here to be too fastidious about the 'state of the sward'. For the last ten years my main concern has been to improve the appearance rather than become over-zealous about thatch and moss. Thus true lawn connoisseurs would find plenty to criticize here. On the other hand, the grass is pleasantly spongy to walk on and the appearance is deceptive.

To feed the lawns I spread (for years by hand) a sprinkling of the slow-release fertilizer Enmag in early March. This contains the three main necessities for growth, nitrogen, phosphorus and potassium, as well as that most important little extra magnesium. I think it is a useful tip to vegetable and shrub gardeners alike that magnesium in the form of commercial Epsom salts enhances the vigour of all green plants. It is a main

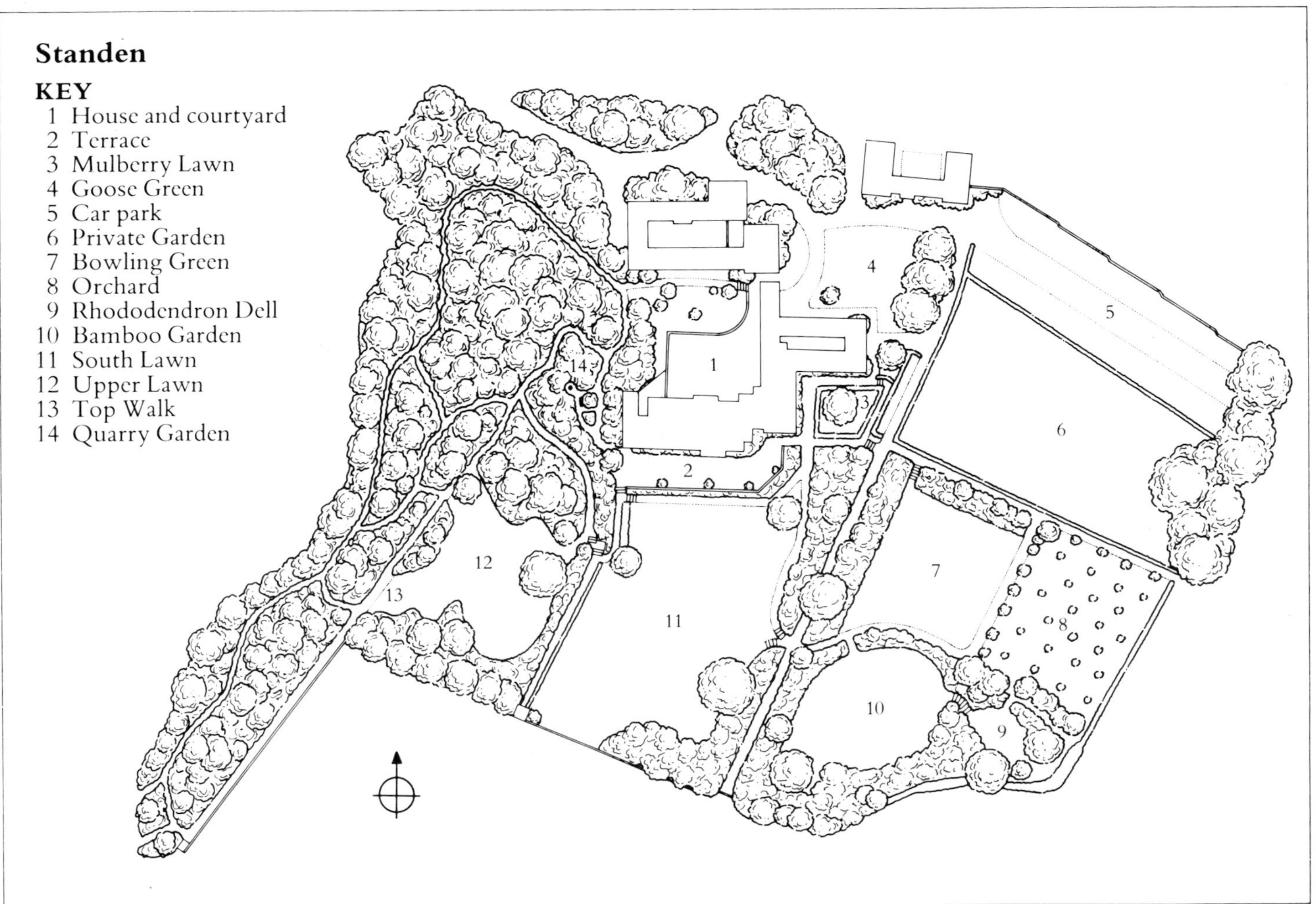

constituent of chlorophyll. Enmag is especially good as it does not scorch the grass if there is no rain to wash it in. I have found scorch a problem with many other feeds, or even organic-based ones. Unfortunately, Enmag is expensive. I use three 25 kilo bags (about 165 lb) on the south lawn and two each on Goose Green and the Old Tennis Court. About every other year, depending on the weather and the need to improve the appearance, the grass gets an additional autumn feed. This ensures a sudden spell of warm, wet weather in October and some frantic mowing to keep pace. I do not recommend autumn fertilizer unless 'The Queen is coming to tea.'

Spiking is definitely a good thing. I spike with a half-core motorized machine after the season's last mowing, which always seems to be in the second week of November. Surprisingly, it is never earlier or later. The cones drawn out by the tines are left to weather down during the winter. You will need survival rations if you only have a fork.

The lawns are usually cut twice a week during the strong growing season of May, June and July. I set the machine very high by most people's standards, as this does seem to prevent the moss getting too invasive. A useful time-saving tip is to take the back-plate off the mower when cutting the lawns if they are dry. This is called 'flight-mowing', because one can fly over the lawns without stopping to empty the grass box all the time, since only excessive grass trimmings are thrown into it. The rest remain to provide a drought-preventing mulch. Some would say this helps to build up thatch – we are not Wimbledon.

In order to be in keeping with the period of the house, there are stripes on the lawn. In 1902 Ransome patented the first petrol-driven cylinder mower, and as a 'modern' family, the Beales would have had one. Thus there would have been the stripes which a cylinder mower leaves. Stripes are also very effective eyewash. To mow straight I put a mark on either side of the grass-box a short distance in from the cutting edge. These are used to aim at a point ahead. I do not think rotary mowers are a substitute for cylinders, except for cutting banks. In fact cylinder mowers are much better for wet grass. This is with the proviso that one keeps on top and does not let the grass get too long. For the week after coming back from a holiday a rotary is essential.

Excessive weed growth in lawns is dealt with by selective weedkiller; creeping buttercups by the old-fashioned but excellent 'daisy-puller', which is the only thing that works.

Restoration and changes of the garden above the lawn

This part was in better shape than the lower garden, and the main change has been altering the shape of the sloping lawn and planting more summer-flowering shrubs and spring bulbs. The vigour of most plants has been improved by simply raking or blowing, by wind or machine, all the autumn leaves into the various beds. I don't think it is necessary to compost the leaves except perhaps for planting purposes. I certainly don't have time here. I should say, however, that there is no better way to treat rhododendrons than to put a decent mulch of composted beech/ash leaves on top of their roots. However, using leaves for mulch is a science all of its own, as some leaves can make an alkaline compost and should be avoided for ericaceous plants. Talking of leaves, the leathery leaves of the London planes on Goose Green are a menace if used on borders: they are inclined to blow around everywhere except where they should be for a whole year. They take ages to calm down and rot. Also holly and holm oak leaves have the irritating habit of falling throughout early and mid-summer. I should not like a holly hedge in a 'tidy' part of the garden.

We removed a hundred trees from the shelter belt at the top of the garden with the great help of the two woodmen from Outwood, one of the Trust's country properties near here. The wood was sold to Sweden. The end plantation was a mess of dead and under-thinned trees and was almost completely cleared. We have planted instead sweet chestnuts, which grow well on our basically very poor sandy soil.

It should be said here that over-staking of trees should be avoided. When I stake a tree, I try and leave some of the trunk free to sway in the wind so that the tree realizes that it has to stand on its own two feet. As a general rule only standard trees with a large head need to be staked properly. Now that most plants are container-grown, they come with their own anchors.

We have tried to create a small 'meadow' garden in the grass at the bottom of the sloping lawn by first 'icing' it with a layer of chalk and then throwing seeds in and planting wild flowers and bulbs. Unfortunately the badgers that live over the brow of the hill love bulbs of any sort, so we have, in effect, unwrapped the menu of a four-star hotel

for them. In fact, badgers have always been a problem here, especially when they decide to rotovate the lawns in their search for worms and roots. We are completely nonplussed. There is no way to deter them (we've tried). There is no way we could shoot them – lumbering tanks that they are. So we have all learnt to like them; after all, it is not them or us yet.

Restoration and change in the garden below the lane

This part of the garden was fairly derelict when we came to Standen, especially as the orchard area was full of old apple trees, wild raspberries and brambles which, triffid-like, extended through the whole area. A daunting sight, but one which was fairly easy to change by a few (I mean few) days' scything with a Turk scythe. The only really hard work was digging out the old apple tree roots (or motts), having taken down the tops. If you want the dreaded Honey Fungus in your rhododendrons, leave a few apple stumps to rot. The only panacea to the fungus I have found is to discover the root cause (sic) and then if it is not possible to remove it, pour on plenty of granular nitrochalk. This, I think, sates the appetite of the armillaria and eventually leads to a surfeit. Having cleared the area of rubbish, the remaining weeds – docks, sprouting brambles, shooting raspberries etc – were simply cut each week by the tractor rotary mower (used for other rough grass areas). At the end of the year grass had re-established itself without seeding and only the docks remained, eventually to go after another year of cutting. The apples were kindly given by another Head Gardener, Mr Snowden, who had spent some time grafting old varieties on to the right stock.

The yew hedge was straightened as much as possible and stepped. For two years I used hand shears and it took two days to cut. Now I can go over it in a day with a petrol-engined shearer, but it is noisy and hard work. One tip when using loud machinery is always to wear ear-defenders. I find even such jobs as tractor mowing much less tiring without the continual buzz.

The Bamboo Garden has not altered much, except for the wooden steps which replaced some disintegrating concrete ones. However, there has been a large problem recently as two of the bamboo species have flowered. When this happens the shoots die and look very unsightly. Sometimes the whole plant dies and cutting down and digging up is the only course. I have found that the best way to cut a mass of bamboos is with a motor saw. We have interplanted the continually flowering bamboo with an alternative species, *Arundinaria murielae*.

The weed in the borders round the old tennis court was initially eliminated by putting dichlobenil on the beds. This is a very effective weedkiller among shrubs, but has a fairly persistent smell. Here, as elsewhere in the garden, the soil between shrubs has been well covered with ground-cover plants.

Ground-cover plants are a huge subject but here I shall confine myself to four different ones. First place must go to the true geraniums which are excellent weed-suppressors and also give the garden a natural feel with their wild type of flowers; *Geranium endressii* is especially good and long-flowering. Second place goes to the rose of Sharon (*Hypericum calycinum*). It is excellent for all purposes and totally weedproof. Third is the woodrush and sedge which can be seen under the rocks along the drive. Weeds such as nettles, goosegrass and bindweed which come through this can be knocked out with a mild selective lawn weedkiller. The fourth is the most easily managed – grass. I often think this is overlooked as a ground-cover, but with some cutting it usually remains relatively weed-free.

General Comments

I am often asked how one person can manage to maintain 12 acres of garden. It is done largely by working with the weather and giving nature a helping hand only where needed. Thus the herbaceous border is usually an area of low-maintenance requirement as, once it has been planted and fed, all that is needed is occasional dead-heading and a good clear and clean in the autumn. The same applies to the Quarry Garden which, apart from occasional attention, is cleaned through really well in November when the ferns are brown. In fact my busiest time is October to Christmas. In January and February I am fortunate in having some warm and most rewarding work in 'clearing through' Hollybush Wood. This is the 15 acres adjoining the garden. It used to be the site of the ancient Wealden Iron Industry. All that can now be seen of this are the large holes dug for marl (clay that was spread on the sandy fields) and ore.

The rest of the year is spent on the usual routine maintenance of mowing, spraying, pruning and raking. I am lucky in that my wife enjoys cutting the grass edges, as this is a long-winded job. It gives her a good chance to chat to the visitors with the shears to lean on. New plants are usually bought in, preferably from local nurseries such as Perryhill, though there is time for a small amount of propagation of easy subjects such as buddlejas which can be struck in July.

In conclusion the best advice I can give on how to look after a fairly large garden is: 'Keep on top'. This might mean some extra effort when needed, but can save a lot of extra work later on. I was very fortunate and privileged to have been trained to learn to love the glorified labour of gardening by one of the unsung heroes of National Trust gardening: that other ex-stalwart of Trelissick Gardens – Mike Roskilly. ✿

National Collections in National Trust Gardens

Over a thousand different kinds of cultivated plant are lost each year from Britain's gardens: plants may be destroyed by disease or simply go out of fashion and disappear, and those that are slow or difficult to propagate are often dropped by the nursery trade. The National Council for the Conservation of Plants and Gardens was formed from the Royal Horticultural Society in 1978, and since then has built up over 250 National Collections of cultivated plants that would otherwise be in danger of disappearing from gardens. **Mr Anthony Lord**, one of the National Trust's Gardens Advisers, writes of the role of the Trust in maintaining National Collections for the NCCPG:

Gardens of the National Trust come to hold National Collections not by chance, nor by the whim of their latter-day staff, but through the recognition of groups of plants, usually already in the gardens, which are particularly suited to their traditions and character.

The character of historic gardens derives largely from the plants they contain. To conserve gardens it is therefore necessary to conserve the character of the planting. This may have evolved over many centuries, by association with one or a number of families who added the plants they liked over successive generations. The Trust's gardens now comprise a plant collection of extraordinary richness and scope which must surely constitute the largest such collection in single ownership.

The choice of plants was often determined by either fashion or function: the border planting at Packwood in Warwickshire is of hardy herbaceous perennials which were fashionable from Victorian times until the last war, but which have since markedly lost their popularity; flowers for cutting were required in most houses and the choice of plants for the border and cut-flower garden was clearly influenced by the plants' suitability for this function; fruit and vegetables had to provide crops under local conditions to suit local tastes and the choice of varieties differed widely around the country accordingly. Even now, when fashions have changed and the functions required of the plants are different, the Trust must continue such traditions of planting, irrespective of modern taste.

Accordingly, the fruit trees planted at Nunnington in Yorkshire are of varieties long popular in the area but seldom available from nurseries. In Cornwall, quite different varieties of orchard fruit were preferred and the Trust continues to use these for its Cornish gardens, although most are not grown by nurseries and have to be propagated specially.

The particular enthusiasms of individuals, whether for a range of plants or for a particular genus, are still apparent in many gardens. At Antony House in Cornwall, the nearly 500 day-lilies collected by the late Lady Cynthia Carew Pole remain an integral part of the garden and are an historically interesting group of a genus which continues to be much changed by the plant breeder. (This is now a part of the National Collection of *Hemerocallis*). Other enthusiasts subscribed to plant-hunting expeditions and the introductions of, for instance, Harold Comber from Chile or Frank Kingdon-Ward from the eastern Himalayas, still contribute significantly to the character of planting at Nymans and Trengwainton respectively. This tradition continues and plants raised from seed collected recently by Roy Lancaster in China give interest to Nymans and numerous other Trust gardens.

Specialized gardens such as the pinetum, fernery or rock garden, each housed their own particular range of plants, each of which contained many representatives, almost collections, of certain genera.

Thus the gardens of the National Trust have come to hold a great wealth and diversity of plants chosen over the centuries to suit all tastes and conditions. A study of the contents of each garden will reveal trends in the planting: occasionally we find that a garden might contain large numbers of a particular sort, family or genus of plants which may be regarded as a collection. Enriching the content of such groups of plants to make more comprehensive collections is one means of sharpening the individuality of our gardens. These groups are not necessarily botanical: for instance, there are collections of autumn colour plants at Sheffield Park, dwarf conifers at Sizergh and Shakespearian plants at Charlecote. When a garden has sufficient area, resources and staff to house and maintain a collection of all the representatives of a certain botanical group of plants, and when this group is appropriate historically and aesthetically to the garden, the National Trust can consider proposing it as a National Collection.

Opposite: Beningbrough Hall.

The Trust houses some two dozen collections at present, but each year more are designated as such by the NCCPG. It is important that the Trust should only undertake such collections where they can be adequately housed without altering the character of the garden. Not even the largest of our gardens could accommodate the 4,000 fuchsias believed to exist in Britain without their significantly changing the character of the garden. The estimated 30,000 extant cultivars of *Hemerocallis* would be even more overwhelming. The Trust's paramount objective must remain the conservation of its properties, including gardens. Rare garden plant conservation is a worthwhile secondary objective and is supported wherever it helps fulfil this primary role.

Collecting tree genera is often difficult; many sorts of, for instance, oak or lime are available and a large number would dominate the character of even our largest garden. Whitebeams (*Sorbus* section *Aria*) are smaller and more manageable. These were favourites of Dr Wilfrid Fox, the founder of Winkworth Aboretum, where they are held with the smaller *Sorbus* section *Micromeles* as a National Collection. Dr Fox is commemorated by the fine whitebeam bearing his name which grows at Winkworth.

At Mottisfont, a vast London plane, in fact two trees fused together, is the largest tree and therefore the biggest living object in the country. What better place to house a National Collection of planes (*Platanus*), which appreciate being near to the water of the 'font' or fountain which gives the place its name? Also at Mottisfont is one of the largest and most impressive of the Trust's National Collections, of old roses dating from before 1900. These were assembled by the Trust's former Gardens Adviser, Mr Graham Stuart Thomas, and are mainly French in origin. They provide a spectacular and sweetly scented display in the walled garden through late June and early July.

Another tree genus, of which the Indian bean tree (*Catalpa bignonioides*) is the best known, is collected at Cliveden. Here, too, is the National Collection of lilies of the valley, with unassuming and pretty flowers, exquisitely perfumed, pink or white, single or double, and leaves of plain green or striped with gold. Wood anemones are another charming group collected here, useful in the woodland garden or among herbaceous planting where they can provide a useful spring display before other plants have leafed. They, too, can have single or double flowers, in many shades of pink, mauve, blue, white, yellow or green.

Bodnant boasts four National Collections, all of them of genera particularly suited to the character of the garden. Of the tree genera, magnolias start the season with their mostly spring blooms of white or pink. These are followed by forms of *Embothrium*, the dazzling scarlet Chilean Fire Bush, in May and June, the season continuing through to autumn with eucryphias. The fourth Bodnant collection is of the scarlet-flowered *Rhododendron forrestii* and its close allies, excellent low-growing plants flowering mostly in April and May.

Also strictly rhododendrons, the collection of Ghent azaleas at Sheffield Park provides scent and colour in May and June and includes a number of historic nineteenth-century varieties.

Box has always grown in the garden at Ickworth. Although always neat and attractive, both for hedging and for understorey planting in shrubberies and woodlands, the usefulness of this worthy shrub is often overlooked. Ickworth's National Collection contains most of the forms and species in cultivation in this country.

Elder, like box, is remarkable for its tolerance of dry shade and the collection of *Sambucus* at Wallington contains forms of the common elder (*S. nigra*) of much more garden interest than the plain green form, with leaves variegated, gold, purple or finely divided, as well as numerous other species.

When the garden at Erddig was restored, its many shady brick walls needed some planting to soften their hard appearance. A National Collection of ivies filled this role admirably; the plants are allowed to grow both up the wall and over the adjoining ground to prove their merit as ground cover.

At Hidcote the collection of peony species and primary hybrids (first generation offspring of a cross between two species) bridges the gap between shrubs and herbaceous plants. Since the days of its creator, Lawrence Johnston, the garden has contained many of these, both tree peonies and herbaceous ones, and the Trust hopes to plant yet more. Although the species are mainly single and fleeting in flower, they have a charm and beauty which the larger, double hybrids lack.

The planting of the terrace borders at Upton derives largely from the first half of this century. Throughout this time, aster borders were a feature of many gardens and were championed by many leading gardeners including Gertrude Jekyll. The Michaelmas daisies (*Aster novi-belgii* and *A. novae-angliae* forms) which made up the bulk of the planting in these, have become prone to mildew in recent decades and most are no longer good garden plants; most need staking, a job for which few gardeners can find time today. Small-flowered asters such as *A. cordifolius* and *A. ericoides* cultivars and hybrids and also the cultivars and hybrids of *AA. amellus* and *thomsonii* do not suffer from these disadvantages and have been unjustly neglected recently. The Aster Border at Upton houses the National Collection of these and includes a number of excellent varieties, many of which had been lost from British gardens and had to be re-introduced from Europe.

Scabiosa caucasica is another plant which has lost popularity recently and many varieties have disappeared. The remainder have found a home as a National Collection in the cut-flower border at Hardwick Hall, where they are perfectly suited to both the alkaline soil and the traditions of the house.

Not all herbaceous plants are fully hardy and it is such rather tender plants that can most easily be lost from cultivation. Many of the more tender *Crocosmia* hybrids (montbretias) bred in France and Britain late in the last century and early in this century, are extinct but the survivors, along with the species and more recent hybrids, are grown as a National Collection at Lanhydrock in Cornwall.

Upton House has a collection of Asters. Clumps of arching pampas grass are planted at regular intervals along the border.

The disappearance of many penstemons may be attributed to their inability to survive cold winters and ten years ago it seemed that only a handful of large-flowered hybrids remained. The assembling of some four dozen *P. gloxinioides* and *P. campanulatus* hybrids to form a National Collection at Rowallane demonstrates that an excellent range of these still exists; the plants themselves bear witness to their continuing value for dazzling late summer display.

Felbrigg Hall is renowned for its plantings of *Colchicum lusitanum* (*C. tenorii* of horticulture) and the success of this and other meadow saffrons in the garden have led to the establishment of a National Collection there.

At Sizergh Castle, the impressive rock garden, which dates from 1926, is particularly suited to the growing of ferns and contains good collections of a number of genera. Of these, four are particularly suited to conditions in the garden and have been designated National Collections. Osmundas, including the native royal fern, enjoy the damp conditions alongside the stream which runs through the garden, while *Cystopteris* thrive in damp crevices, particularly beside waterfalls. Aspleniums, including forms of the native hart's tongue, appreciate the alkaline soil of the garden, while *Dryopteris* species and forms thrive where conditions are akin to their native woodland.

Of cultivated plants in Britain, the species are generally well conserved by botanic gardens, and most are secure in their natural habitats around the world, but gardeners must conserve garden varieties if they are to survive. By doing this and by supporting the National Collections' scheme of the NCCPG, the National Trust helps to preserve the richness of our garden flora and to make our gardens more interesting and attractive for us all.

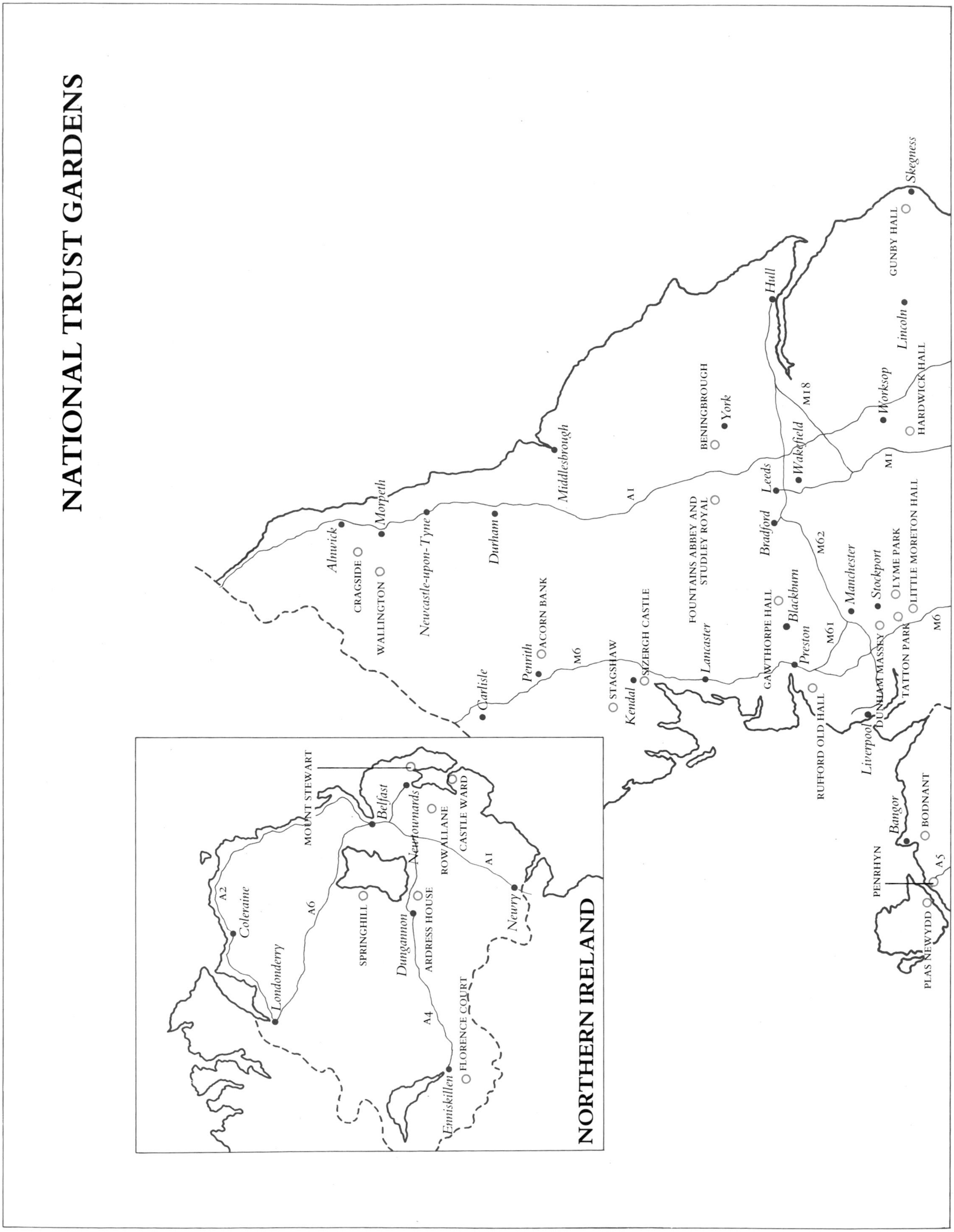
NATIONAL TRUST GARDENS
NORTHERN IRELAND
Skegness
GUNBY HALL
Hull
Lincoln
HARDWICK HALL
Worksop
M18
BENINGBROUGH
York
Wakefield
Middlesbrough
M1
A1
Leeds
FOUNTAINS ABBEY AND
STUDLEY ROYAL
Bradford
M62
Manchester
Stockport
LYME PARK
LITTLE MORETON HALL
Alnwick
Morpeth
Newcastle-upon-Tyne
Durham
CRAGSIDE
WALLINGTON
ACORN BANK
SIZERGH CASTLE
GAWTHORPE HALL
Blackburn
M61
M6
Penrith
STAGSHAW
Lancaster
Preston
DUNHAM MASSEY
TATTON PARK
Carlisle
Kendal
RUFFORD OLD HALL
Liverpool
BODNANT
Bangor
PENRHYN
A5
PLAS NEWYDD
MOUNT STEWART
Belfast
Newtownards
CASTLE WARD
ROWALLANE
A1
Newry
A2
Coleraine
A6
SPRINGHILL
ARDRESS HOUSE
Dungannon
Londonderry
A4
FLORENCE COURT
Enniskillen

Wrexham
ERDDIG
Llangollen
CHIRK CASTLE
A5
M6
Stoke on Trent
Stafford
SHUGBOROUGH
Derby
Nottingham
BELTON HOUSE
Cromer
FELBRIGG HALL
BLICKLING HALL
King's Lynn
Norwich
Shrewsbury
MOSELEY OLD HALL
A1
Wisbech
PECKOVER
Peterborough
Swaffham
OXBURGH
Welshpool
POWIS CASTLE
BENTHALL HALL
Telford
Wolverhampton
Bridgnorth
DUDMASTON
WIGHTWICK MANOR
Birmingham
Coventry
M1
PACKWOOD HOUSE
A40
A11
Northampton
Stratford-upon-Avon
CHARLECOTE PARK
CANONS ASHBY
HANBURY HALL
Worcester
HIDCOTE MANOR
FARNBOROUGH HALL
Banbury
Cambridge
ANGLESEY ABBEY
Bury St Edmunds
ICKWORTH
M5
UPTON HOUSE
SNOWSHILL MANOR
M11
Cheltenham
WESTBURY COURT
Gloucester
A40
Oxford
Aylesbury
High Wycombe
BUSCOT PARK
Faringdon
M4
Swindon
ASHDOWN HOUSE
BASILDON PARK
Reading
CLEVEDON COURT
Bristol
DYRHAM PARK
LACOCK ABBEY
Cardiff
Bath
THE COURTS
Trowbridge
THE VYNE
Basingstoke
Croydon
Guildford
Maidstone
Canterbury
A2
Dover
A20
M5
Tunbridge Wells
Crawley
SISSINGHURST CASTLE
Folkestone
ARLINGTON COURT
Barnstaple
DUNSTER CASTLE
STOURHEAD
Salisbury
A30
LYTES CARY
MOTTISFONT ABBEY
Romsey
Rye
LAMB HOUSE
BARRINGTON COURT
TINTINHULL
KNIGHTSHAYES
Ilminster
Yeovil
MONTACUTE
Southampton
FOR INSET SEE OVERLEAF
Chichester
Brighton
Hastings
KILLERTON
Wimborne Minster
Okehampton
Exeter
KINGSTON LACY
Portsmouth
CASTLE DROGO
A30
COTEHELE
Bodmin
LANHYDROCK
Plymouth
ANTONY HOUSE
SALTRAM
COLETON FISHACRE
Dartmouth
Truro
TRELISSICK
OVERBECKS
Salcombe
TRENGWAINTON
Penzance
GLENDURGAN
Miles 0 25 50 75
Km. 0 50 100

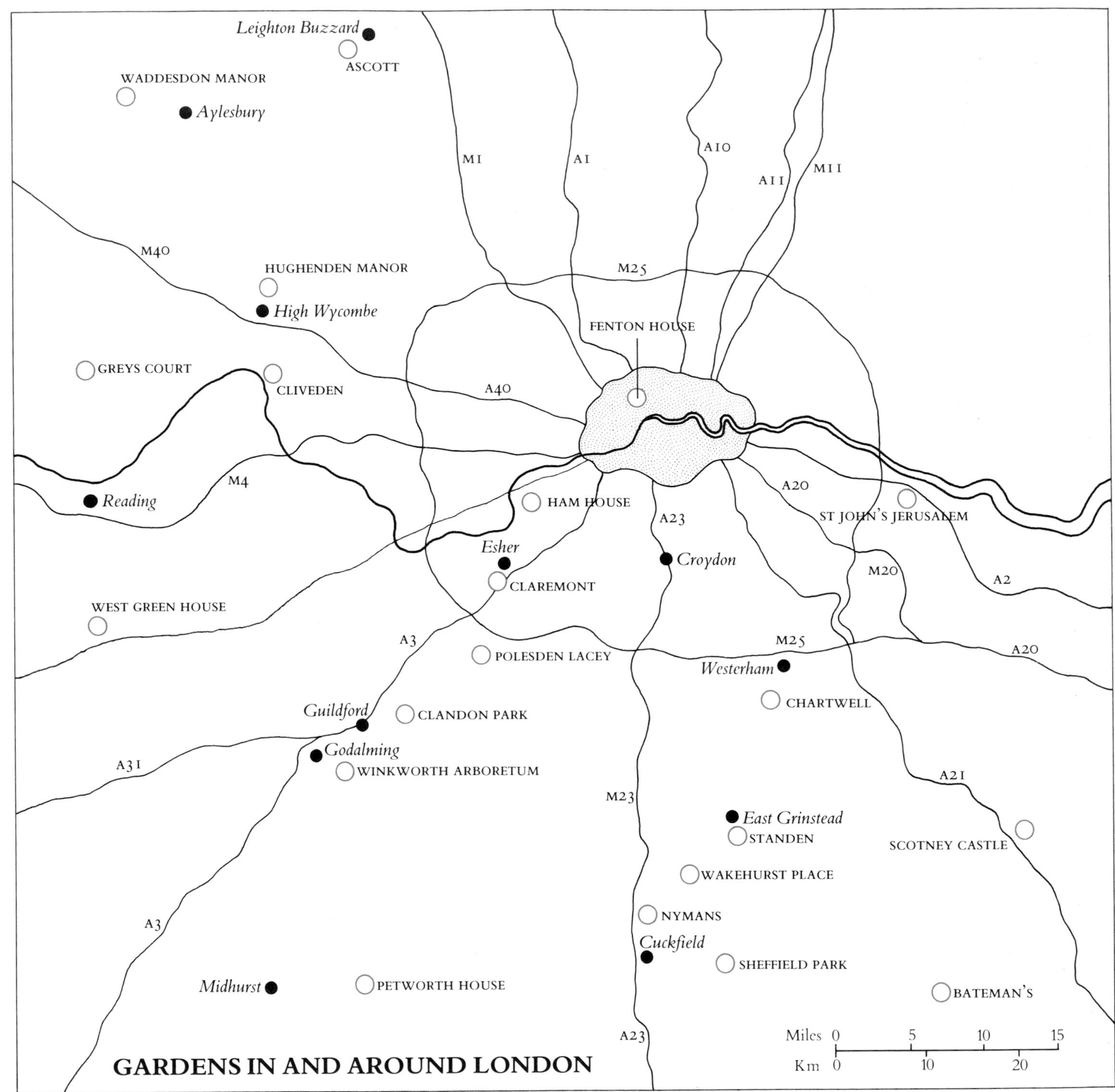
Leighton Buzzard
ASCOTT
WADDESDON MANOR
Aylesbury
M1
A1
A10
A11
M11
M40
HUGHENDEN MANOR
High Wycombe
M25
FENTON HOUSE
GREYS COURT
CLIVEDEN
A40
M4
Reading
HAM HOUSE
A20
ST JOHN'S JERUSALEM
A23
Esher
Croydon
CLAREMONT
M20
A2
WEST GREEN HOUSE
A3
M25
POLESDEN LACEY
A20
Westerham
CHARTWELL
Guildford
CLANDON PARK
Godalming
A31
WINKWORTH ARBORETUM
A21
M23
East Grinstead
STANDEN
SCOTNEY CASTLE
WAKEHURST PLACE
A3
NYMANS
Cuckfield
SHEFFIELD PARK
Midhurst
PETWORTH HOUSE
BATEMAN'S
A23
Miles 0 5 10 15
Km 0 10 20
GARDENS IN AND AROUND LONDON

Features in Trust Gardens

NOTE The chart indicates National Trust gardens where subjects discussed in the book may be seen: it is not a comprehensive listing of every type of feature in these gardens.

	Landscape	Hedging	Avenue	Pleaching/Pergolas etc	Topiary	Knot Garden	Maze	Formal Parterre	Ornaments	Container Planting	Borders	Rose Garden	Herb Garden	Formal Water	Informal Water	Stream Garden	Fernery	Rockery/Quarry Garden	Wall Planting	Orchard/Kitchen Garden	Woodland	Meadow	Naturalized Bulbs	Single-handed Gardener	Plantsman's Garden
Acorn Bank Cumbria		■	■									■	■						■	■			■		
Anglesey Abbey Cambridgeshire		■	■	■					■		■				■								■		
Antony Cornwall	■	■	■		■				■						■										
Ardress Co Armagh											■	■													
Arlington Court Devon				■					■						■			■			■		■		
Ascott Buckinghamshire		■	■		■			■	■									■					■		
Ashdown Warwickshire			■					■																	
Barrington Court Somerset		■	■	■	■			■	■		■	■		■					■				■		
Basildon Park Berkshire								■				■													
Bateman's East Sussex		■		■					■					■	■	■			■						
Belton House Lincolnshire	■	■	■					■				■													
Beningbrough North Yorkshire								■	■	■	■								■	■			■		
Benthall Hall Shropshire		■																	■						■
Blickling Hall Norfolk		■	■	■	■				■		■	■			■						■				
Bodnant Gwynedd	■	■		■					■		■	■		■		■					■				
Buscot Park Oxfordshire		■	■						■					■	■				■	■	■		■		
Canons Ashby Northamptonshire					■			■																	
Castle Drogo Devon		■		■	■						■	■							■		■		■	■	
Castle Ward Co Down	■											■		■	■				■		■				■
Charlecote Park Warwickshire	■	■	■						■						■				■		■		■		
Chartwell Kent		■									■	■			■								■		
Chirk Castle Clwyd		■			■							■											■		
Clandon Park Surrey		■		■				■	■														■		
Claremont Surrey	■														■						■				
Clevedon Court Avon								■											■				■	■	■
Cliveden Buckinghamshire								■	■		■	■			■						■				
Coleton Fishacre Devon																■			■		■				■
Cotehele Cornwall											■	■			■	■			■		■				■
Cragside Northumberland															■			■			■				
Dudmaston Shropshire									■		■	■											■		
Dunham Massey Gtr. Manchester	■		■					■							■	■					■				
Dunster Castle Somerset											■					■			■		■				■
Dyrham Park Avon	■														■								■		
Erddig Clwyd		■	■	■				■	■					■					■	■			■		

Features in Trust Gardens
(continued)

	Landscape	Hedging	Avenue	Pleaching/Pergolas etc	Topiary	Knot Garden	Maze	Formal Parterre	Ornaments	Container Planting	Borders	Rose Garden	Herb Garden	Formal Water	Informal Water	Stream Garden	Fernery	Rockery/Quarry Garden	Wall Planting	Orchard/Kitchen Garden	Woodland	Meadow	Naturalized Bulbs	Single-handed Gardener	Plantsman's Garden
Farnborough Hall Warwickshire	■										■	■			■										
Felbrigg Hall Norfolk	■	■									■		■						■	■			■		
Fenton House London								■											■						
Florence Court Co Fermanagh	■														■						■		■		
Fountains Abbey & Studley Royal North Yorkshire	■														■										
Gawthorpe Hall Lancashire								■																	
Glendurgan Cornwall							■								■	■			■		■		■	■	■
Greys Court Oxfordshire				■		■	■												■	■			■		
Gunby Hall Lincolnshire													■	MOAT					■	■			■		
Ham House Surrey						■		■	■												■				
Hanbury Hall Hereford & Worcester	■														■								■		
Hardwick Hall Derbyshire		■							■	■	■	■	■						■	■			■		
Hidcote Manor Gloucestershire		■	■	■	■			■		■	■	■		■		■			■		■		■		
Holt: The Courts Wiltshire		■									■			■	■										
Hughenden Manor Buckinghamshire								■				■													
Ickworth Suffolk	■	■						■	■					■					■		■		■		
Killerton Devon	■		■								■							■	■	■	■		■		■
Kingston Lacy Dorset	■	■	■		■			■									■								
Knightshayes Devon	■	■			■			■	■	■	■			■	■				■		■		■		■
Lacock Abbey Wiltshire																							■		
Lamb House East Sussex								■			■	■													
Lanhydrock Cornwall	■	■	■		■			■	■	■	■	■				■			■		■	■	■		■
Little Moreton Hall Cheshire					■			■																	
Lyme Park Cheshire								■			■	■	■		■								■		
Lytes Cary Somerset		■	■	■	■						■	■							■	■			■		
Montacute Somerset	■	■	■		■				■		■			■											
Moseley Old Hall Staffordshire			■	■				■											■	■					
Mottisfont Abbey Hampshire	■	■		■		■					■	■			■								■		
Mount Stewart Co Down	■	■	■	■				■	■	■				■	■				■		■		■		■
Nymans West Sussex	■	■		■	■			■	■		■	■						■	■				■		■
Overbecks Museum Devon											■													■	■
Oxburgh Hall Norfolk								■						MOAT									■		
Packwood Warwickshire		■	■		■						■			■					■						

Features in Trust Gardens
(continued)

	Landscape	Hedging	Avenue	Pleaching/Pergolas etc	Topiary	Knot Garden	Maze	Formal Parterre	Ornaments	Container Planting	Borders	Rose Garden	Herb Garden	Formal Water	Informal Water	Stream Garden	Fernery	Rockery/Quarry Garden	Wall Planting	Orchard/Kitchen Garden	Woodland	Meadow	Naturalized Bulbs	Single-handed Gardener	Plantsman's Garden
Peckover House Cambridgeshire					■						■												■	■	
Penrhyn Castle Gwynedd			■					■						■			■		■		■		■		■
Petworth West Sussex	■									■					■								■		
Plas Newydd Gwynedd	■														■						■				■
Polesden Lacey Surrey	■	■	■	■	■							■						■	■		■		■		
Powis Castle Powys	■	■			■			■	■	■		■			■				■		■		■		■
Rowallane Co Down	■										■							■	■		■	■	■		■
Rufford Old Hall Lancashire											■	■													
St John's Jerusalem Kent											■								■	■					
Saltram Devon	■		■		■				■	■											■				
Scotney Castle Kent	■										■		■					■			■		■		
Sheffield Park East Sussex	■		■												■	■					■	■			■
Shugborough Staffordshire	■				■					■		■			■						■		■		
Sissinghurst Castle Kent		■	■	■	■			■	■	■	■	■	■	■	■				■				■		■
Sizergh Castle Cumbria	■		■								■			■	■			■	■			■	■		■
Snowshill Manor Gloucestershire		■			■						■			■					■					■	
Springhill Co Londonderry			■										■							■			■		
Stagshaw Cumbria																■					■			■	■
Standen West Sussex											■							■		■	■		■	■	
Stourhead Wiltshire	■		■						■						■						■		■		
Tatton Park Cheshire	■	■	■		■		■		■	■	■	■		■	■						■		■		■
Tintinhull Somerset		■	■		■			■	■	■	■	■		■					■	■					■
Trelissick Cornwall	■														■				■		■		■		■
Trengwainton Cornwall		■														■			■	■	■		■		■
Upton Warwickshire		■									■			■	■	■			■	■			■		
The Vyne Hampshire		■	■												■									■	■
Waddesdon Manor Buckinghamshire	■	■			■			■	■	■		■									■		■		
Wakehurst Place West Sussex	■							■			■				■				■		■		■		■
Wallington Northumberland	■								■		■				■	■			■	■			■		
Westbury Court Gloucestershire		■		■		■		■					■	■					■	■					
West Green House Hampshire		■	■	■	■			■	■	■	■				■					■			■		
Wightwick Manor Staffordshire		■			■						■	■											■	■	
Winkworth Arboretum Surrey	■																				■				■

Index

Figures in bold face refer to photographs; figures in italics refer to planting plans and diagrams

Photographic Credits

KEY: b = bottom c = centre l = left r = right t = top

Brian Batsford: 30
Geoff Dann: 67, 91bl and br
Mark Fiennes: 63tr, 126, 146t
Jerald Harpur: 13t, 20, 24, 78, 80, 97, 107, 108, 110–11, 114, 115, 153, 164, 190, 196, 198b
W. A. Lord: 56, 230, 240
John Malins: 180
Tania Midgley: 13b, 14, 23, 40t, 41, 59b, 65b, 95, 105, 112, 113, 120, 149, 158, 177
National Trust:
- John Bethell: 11, 128, 161, 184–5, 193, 195
- BKS Services, 51b
- Michael Brown: 227
- Graham Challifour: 144
- Nancy Cowen: 205
- Peter Craig: 2 (frontis.), 62t, 77b
- Nigel Forster: 6, 39b, 65t, 150, 216
- R. Hillgrove: 46, 206
- Angelo Hornak: 129
- Horst Kolo: 91t, 182
- J. Kot: 16
- P. Lacey: 136
- Raymond Lea: 22
- Tymn Lintell: 154
- Nick Meers: 40b
- Tania Midgley: 135
- Alan North: 160b
- Sheila Orme: 79
- C. M. Radclilffe: 42, 215
- Smith of Coventry: 37
- Tim Stephens: 27
- Richard Surman: 50, 83, 133, 65, 183
- R. Thrift: 207, 210
- Martin Trelawny: 148
- Charlie Waite: 102b
- Michael Warren: 31, 51b, 73, 75, 124, 125, 140, 146b, 178
- J. Whitaker: 152, 160t
- Andy Williams: 25, 198t
- Mike Williams: 226

Cressida Pemberton-Piggott: 17, 28, 31, 32, 33, 39t and c, 44, 59t, 60t and b, 61, 62b, 63tl and bl, 66t, 68t and b, 70, 71, 77t, 85, 102t, 116, 123, 131, 134, 143, 157, 163, 186, 187, 192, 201, 217, 218, 220, 234, 236
Photos Horticultural: 1 (half-title), 38, 47b, 66b, 76, 141, 167, 168, 169, 204
Martin Puddle: 138, 197
John Sales: 19t and b, 47t, 48, 53t and b, 54, 57t and b, 88
Pamela Toler: 34, 35, 63cl and br
P. Schwerdt: 228, 229
Mike Snowden: 225t and b

635.9 H68B
Hobhouse, Penelope.
A book of gardening : a
practical guide / by

SV 162084

RAMSEY COUNTY PUBLIC LIBRARY
Shoreview, MN 55126